To Peter
with love and best wishes,

Julie
(Julie M. Lloyd).

Something Exciting,
Something Inviting

Something Exciting, Something Inviting

The Story of Darlington Operatic Society

JULIA M. LLOYD

The Pentland Press
Edinburgh – Cambridge – Durham – USA

First published in 1995 by
The Pentland Press Ltd
1 Hutton Close,
South Church
Bishop Auckland
Durham

ISBN 1-85821-303-7

Typeset by Carnegie Publishing, 18 Maynard St, Preston
Printed and bound in Great Britain by Bookcraft (Bath) Ltd

To my dear Ginny and Martin – and to John, who got me into all this in the first place – this book is dedicated, with my love

Detective Inspector Purbright: 'Have you ever come
across something called amateur operatics?'
Detective Inspector Bradley: 'Ah, now there's an
exotic aberration for you.'

Plaster Sinners by Colin Watson

Author's note: Some readers may think that the title
'Something Exciting, Something Inviting' comes
from the opening song in Stephen Sondheim's
'A Funny Thing Happened on the Way to the
Forum'. So did I. It doesn't.

Contents

List of Illustrations

Acknowledgements

I have been given a great deal of assistance in preparing this book by a number of people and I give my most grateful thanks to the following:

My ex-colleagues and friends, the assistants at the Edward Pease Public Library: the two Catherines (Copeland and Williamson), Margaret (Tiny) White, Gillan Wilson and Kimberley Bennett, of the Reference and Local Studies sections, for rooting out information for me.

Clive, Reg and Tommy, the library caretakers, for staggering up and down to the basement with bound volumes of newspapers for me.

The members, past and present, of Darlington Operatic Society for photographs, information and anecdotes, and for being so ready to inform on others!

Marjorie Hall for the loan of Jos. Hall's memoirs and Elsie Campbell for making me aware of their existence and borrowing them for me.

Patrick O'Meara, of Chelmsford, for not throwing away some pre-war programmes he found in a local sale, but sending them to me – they filled in a lot of gaps.

Alison Laidler, of the Darlington Memorial Hospital secretarial staff, for obtaining and typing the Henry Pease pep-talk quoted at the beginning of this book.

Judi Kent for offering an alternative title: 'Is Adrenalin Brown?', which I loved, but dared not use!

Glenys Powell, a much-treasured 'lady-who-does' for beavering away at my housework so that I had more time to write.

My daughter, Ginny, for constant encouragement, not to say goading.

Jill Cole and Daniel Russell of The Pentland Press for their constant help and advice.

Last, but by no means least, Martin R. Jones for going through the drafts with a fine tooth comb, refining the text (where I would let him!), and acquainting me with modern punctuation.

To the Young People and Others in the Employment of Henry Pease and Company

The evils resulting from the attendance of theatres are so great and so well known that it is with much concern we learn that a licence has again been granted for opening a theatre in Darlington.

Contrary to known wishes of those who are year by year bestowing their time and means in promoting every effort that has for its object your temporal moral and religious elevation. We know, full well, how great a temptation is this, unkindly thrown in your way. We know that too often our evening classes are neglected and the theatre preferred, at whatever the sacrifice, even to pawning the Sunday dress, and so becoming unable to attend a place of worship, and we know how ruinous both to character and health this dissipation has proved to many around us.

While then we would in no way wish to forego any reasonable or beneficial amusement, we beg you when tempted to go into a theatre to ask yourselves the following questions:

Shall I hear or see anything that can do me any good?

Shall I hear that which is consistent with the Bible and with what I have heard from Christian teachers?

Have I money to spare for such a purpose, after paying for needful clothes, providing for home comforts, and future wants?

Above all, what does conscience say?

We have no object in these remarks but your true comfort and happiness.

We ask you then as you value the confidence of your employers, your character, your claim to the title of Christians – never go within the doors of a theatre.

Henry Pease and Company
Darlington Mills
2 November 1859

xviii

Chapter I

1912–1944

In 1995 Darlington Operatic Society celebrates its Golden Jubilee after fifty years of entertaining the public and simultaneously raising money for charity. This book tells the story of the fluctuating fortunes of a provincial amateur company and the ways in which it has survived, often in the face of adversity, trying to stage shows as 'professionally' as possible while making enough money from them to fulfil its charitable intentions. The story of the society is inextricably linked with that of a theatre which narrowly escaped demolition and went on to be described as the most successful provincial theatre in the country. Despite all the ups and downs there has been a good deal of fun along the way!

Darlington Operatic Society as we know it today began in 1945, but for its real roots one has to look much farther back than that.

A society combining music and theatre had already begun in 1912 and called itself the Darlington Dramatic and Operatic Society. A meeting had been held – 'a largely attended and enthusiastic meeting' according to the *Northern Echo* [1] – and a society was duly formed with a Mr Burdekin as Chairman of a temporary committee, the other members being Mr Kelso, Miss Jordan, Miss Ormston, Mr E. Cox-Walker, Mr Fitten, Miss Toole, and Miss A. Eglin. Mr W. G. Chandler was appointed Honorary Secretary for the time being, and another meeting was arranged for 1 October.

The Society was certainly eager to get under way, for it gave its first performance three weeks later, on 23 October, at Feethams Hall. The group wisely did not embark upon any 'operatic' activity at such an early stage but gave three sketches: *The Lady Interviewer, Mere Man* and *The Boots at the Sun* – 'Boots' not being footwear but a bootboy. These were preceded by a selection by a ladies' orchestra and interspersed with songs and a monologue.

The critic in the *Northern Echo* of 24 October 1912 confessed to adopting a 'tolerant' frame of mind before attending this offering, although '. . . cheerfully prepared to allow for many little imperfections, but without resorting in the least to fulsome flattery, it can conscientiously be said that seldom was this tolerant frame of mind necessary.' Apart from the ladies' orchestra, twenty-one people appeared in this first performance.

The Society's second production was given on Friday 13 December 1912, again at Feethams Hall. It took the form of a variety performance which included comedy playlets and songs, a 'special concertina solo' by Mrs P. A. Smith, and, 'time permitting', a recitation by Miss Emilienne Terry: '. . . for the first time on any stage an Original Monologue by Bertram Damer, *The Song of the Nightingale* suggested (only) by *Monsieur Beaucaire.*' (Mr Damer was the Producer of the entertainment and, incidentally, Miss Terry's husband.) It is noted on the front of the programme* that 'Club performances will be held at frequent intervals throughout the season at this or some other Hall. Likewise at Richmond. Also arrangements have been made for a series of performances at the New Hippodrome, Darlington.'

The Society was obviously fully confident in its ability to attract audiences. This confidence was justified by the reviews of the performance in the *Darlington & Stockton Times*, the *North Star*, and the *Northern Echo*, all of 14 December 1912. While each gave praise to the enthusiasm and ability of the performers, the *Northern Echo* had reservations about the quality of the 'scenic effects' and would have preferred less 'clowning' in one of the farces. (Oh – and there *was* time for the world première of the recitation!) Following this the Society continued to give performances in aid of charities. Its first offering at the New Hippodrome was a matinée, *Our Flat* – a 'farcical comedy' by a Mrs Musgrave – on Saturday 26 April 1913. The show was hailed by the local newspapers as an 'unqualified success', despite the performers' tendency to overact!

In addition to the Darlington Dramatic and Operatic Society there were other acting groups in the town. The Medley Amateur Dramatic Club and a group under the leadership of Mrs Paget Steavenson were also performing plays and some musical entertainment in aid of various charities.

Alongside these there appeared, in June 1913, a Darlington Operatic Society which was affiliated to the National Association of Amateur Dramatic Companies (NAADC),† a body which raised money for charity as well as acting as a central body for amateur societies.

Founded in 1899, the NAADC and its affiliated societies had, by 1914, raised £60,000 for charity (around £1,000,000 in today's money) which was quite an achievement considering that there was no such thing as a 'Telethon' in those days!

The Darlington Operatic Society was inaugurated to produce operettas

---

* Memoirs of Jos Hall – see Appendix 1

† This body changed it name to NAODA (National Amateur Operatic and Dramatic Association). Then the word 'Amateur' was dropped and it is now NODA.

(as opposed to plays and musical entertainments of a more diverse kind). One of the driving forces behind its formation was Mr George A. Williams, a local music shop owner, whose shop still exists in Blackwellgate in Darlington. According to Mr Williams (when he was interviewed some years later on the subject)* there had been 'no amateur operatics in Darlington' up to this time and 'all the local prophets forecast disaster'.

This society made its first public appearance in February 1914 when it presented *HMS Pinafore* by W. S. Gilbert and Arthur Sullivan, under the direction of Mr Shelford Walsh and Mr J. Dobson Clyde of the Royal Stock Company. Mr W. Deans-Foster, formerly of Lloyds Bank in Darlington, teamed up with Mr Williams (who was Musical Director) and got financial backing for the venture. The production took place at the Theatre Royal (later the Regal and then the ABC Cinema) in North Road, Darlington.

This entirely amateur production played to 'well-filled houses for the week of its run and was received with great enthusiasm', according to the review in the *Darlington & Stockton Times* which declared the piece an 'unqualified success'.[2] Indeed the production cleared about £38, which was quite a good profit for those days. The leading roles were played by Miss Elsie Johnson (who apparently sang and acted well as Josephine), with Mr Edward Fleming (newly arrived from Gateshead) playing opposite her as Ralph Rackstraw and Mr Tom Adamson as Captain Corcoran. Miss Lily Toole seems to have been the only defector from the Darlington Dramatic and Operatic Society and was said to have played the part of Little Buttercup admirably.

Sadly, after this first venture the First World War intervened. Though the small dramatic groups carried on manfully, it was impossible for the Darlington Operatic Society to present full musical shows, despite having had a membership roll of sixty at the time of that first performance.

In 1920, however, the Darlington Operatic Society regrouped to present its second show, Gilbert & Sullivan's *Trial by Jury*, on 29 and 30 April 1920 at St James's schoolroom, Albert Hill, and it was so popular that the run was extended for a further two nights. Mr Williams was Musical Director once more, with Mr William McIntyre as Producer, the performance being in aid of St James's Church funds. The Gilbert & Sullivan piece formed the second half of the entertainment: the first half was a comedy playlet. The review in the *Northern Echo* for 30 April was ecstatic about *Trial by Jury*. It did not mention the playlet.

The vicar of St James's Church, the Revd T. C. Gobat, told the *Northern*

---

* Reminiscences printed in the *Darlington & Stockton Times*, 6 March 1937.

Echo that behind the production of the show '. . . lies an endeavour to raise the tone of operatic and dramatic culture in Darlington and to encourage a respect for the stage apart from its aspect as a paying commercial venture.'

Joseph Hall,* who had hitherto confined his theatrical activities to smaller local acting groups, had by now also joined the Darlington Operatic Society. He had played the Judge in *Trial by Jury* and continued with the Society until 1926. This is most fortunate as he assiduously kept press cuttings about the Society's productions. No other similar collection appears to exist.

After this first regrouping following the war, the Society began to get into its stride with more Gilbert & Sullivan works, producing *The Pirates of Penzance* at the end of 1920. 'Capital performance by amateurs,'[3] said the *North Star*, though the critic in the *Darlington & Stockton Times* remarked of Frederic that his acting suffered '. . . the stiffness of pose that seems to be inseparable from tenor singers – the tenors in England who can really act may be counted on the fingers!'[4] The five-night performance at the Temperance Institute in Gladstone Street resulted in a donation of £70 towards the Darlington Memorial Hospital.

A year later the Society was back in full force, with a chorus of nearly sixty once more, to perform *The Gondoliers* at the New Hippodrome Theatre for the week commencing 5 December 1921. This change of venue was prompted by the popularity of the previous show. The hall had been packed to capacity and people had had to be turned away. Bookings for *The Gondoliers* were 'tremendous'[5] and the audiences were not disappointed, 'demanding double and treble repetitions of many of the numbers'.[6] Messrs Williams and McIntyre were keeping up to the standard of their earlier successes, though the *North Star* remarked that the orchestra sometimes drowned out the singers.[7] The *Northern Echo* was fulsome in its praise.[8]

Prices were: Box for four, £1 5s. 0d.; Dress Circle and Fauteuils,† 4s. 3d.; Grand Circle & Orchestra Stalls, 3s. 6d.; Pit Stalls, 2s. 4d.; and Gallery, 1s. 3d., and it seems that the audiences got their money's worth.

At this stage the three shows already produced had been so successful that £200 had been donated to charity. The people running the Society hesitated to continue without a change to the business side of the arrangements because they were now dealing with quite large sums of money. Accordingly, a meeting was convened on 26 February 1922 'for the

* see Appendix 1.
† Fauteuils were middle seats in the stalls and dress circle. Orchestra stalls were front stalls. Pit stalls were rear stalls.

purpose of considering the formation and founding of an amateur operatic society in Darlington', for previous shows had been arranged without a formal society being in existence. The leading lights at the meeting, who became part of the Committee, were Messrs William Heslop, William B. McIntyre, Sidney Spoor, Fred Chamberlin, William Blakey, George A. Williams, Thomas Gibson and Fred Leeming. There was some concern expressed about a formal system because, having looked into other societies' arrangements, the Committee had found that several unsatisfactory conditions had arisen such as petty jealousies arising from selection of principal actors in the cast, and other (unspecified) effects which often resulted in breaking up the harmony and good feeling. It could also result in the formation of cliques. They agreed, therefore, that the Committee should always be composed of non-active *(sic)* members of the society. It was unanimously agreed that ladies were not eligible for election! The meeting also decided that the society was to be known as 'The Darlington Amateurs' though this name did not last for very long and it seems odd that it was ever changed in the first place – a case of new brooms sweeping clean, perhaps? Mr Heslop was elected Chairman, Mr Leeming Secretary, and Mr Blakey Treasurer. Lord Barnard was asked if he would become the first President (which he did) and thirteen other local dignitaries were asked to give their support as Vice-Presidents. The Society also appointed an Honorary Solicitor – Mr J. F. Latimer – whose name can still be seen on the firm's plate at Latimer Hinks in Priestgate.

Subscriptions were 5*s.* for gentlemen and 2*s.* 6*d.* for ladies, and the Committee, as a group, agreed to be guarantors to a sum of £50. They also decided that the next show was to be *Patience*. Advertisements were placed for applicants to become members of the Society, and the Committee forged ahead, even going so far as to have the Society become patrons of another society – Bishop Auckland – at a cost of two guineas!

At a committee meeting in October some small refinements were introduced: it was agreed that principals would receive a coloured photo each (presumably of themselves), and refreshments during the performance would be provided up to a value of £20. It was at this meeting that the name of the company changed. The word 'Amateur' was dropped and the group would be known once more as 'The Darlington Operatic Society'.

At the end of that year (1922) the production of *Patience* took place at the New Hippodrome. Prices of admission ranged from four in a private box at 25*s.* (now about £100) through Dress Circle Fauteuils at 4*s.* 3*d.*, to the Gallery at 1*s.* 3*d.* The list of Vice-Presidents contained such illustrious names as The Right Hon. Lord Southampton, DL; The Right Hon. Lord

Gainford, PC; Sir Henry Havelock-Allen, DL; Sir Arthur Francis Pease, Bt; Sir Vincent L. Raven, KBE; Sir Thomas Putnam; The Right Hon. H. Pike Pease, MP, PC; and Sir Charles W. Starmer. All this support must have been highly gratifying to the Committee who had given much thought and time to the Society (not to mention the £50 guarantee!)

Fred Burgin, Choirmaster at Bondgate Methodist Church, attended the performance of *Patience* on 6 December with Lord and Lady Barnard and, like them, was full of praise. His only criticism was that the twenty-five-minute interval was too long. 'I felt quite sure,' he wrote in a tongue-in-cheek letter the following day to Joseph Hall, 'struck as I was by the high respectability of the audience, that a hymn might have been sung during the wait and a collection could have been made by men in squeaky boots, and it would not have been out of joint with the class assembled. In case you wish to take a hymn tonight,' he added, 'I suggest *We Love This Place*.' There was no bar in the theatre in those days (even if there had been, Mr Burgin, as a Methodist, would not have patronized it), so the waiting time may well have seemed long to other patrons also!

The show received almost unreserved acclamation from the press, and left the Society with an impressive balance of over £112, of which £100 was distributed to local charities. Greenbank Hospital received £70, The Queen's Nurses Association £10, the North Eastern Railway Cottage Homes £10, the Masonic Benevolent Fund £5, and the Commercial Travellers' Benevolent Fund £5.

In January 1923 the committee of Darlington Operatic Society invited the Darlington Light Opera Company (which turns up later in the story) to send their Chairman, Secretary and two members to a joint meeting. At the joint meeting a small amount of sparring took place. Since Darlington Operatic Society had only produced shows by Gilbert & Sullivan they asked about the plans of Darlington Light Opera Company. The Light Opera Company said that they had no minute which said they would not produce Gilbert & Sullivan! The Operatic Society said it might produce two shows that season, to which the Light Opera Company replied that it might also wish to give two productions. After this, however, the two societies settled down to amicable co-existence. For instance, the Operatic Society agreed to postpone its production of *Merrie England* to December 1924 so as not to clash with the Light Opera Company's production of a show in April. There was an unwritten but understood agreement that members would belong to one society only.

In the mean time, *The Mikado* was presented by Darlington Operatic Society in December 1923. By now the list of Vice-Presidents had grown to eighteen and a further innovation was introduced: that on certain nights, four to be exact, the show would be presented under the patronage of local organizations; The Darlington Motor Club took the Tuesday performance, President and Hunt night was Wednesday, the LNER* had Thursday and the Mayor and Corporation took Friday. The show was very popular. Mr Burgin addressed another complimentary letter to Joseph Hall following his attendance at the production. He remarked, in conclusion to his appreciative comments: 'This testimonial is quite voluntary, no gratuity having been offered to me – up to now!' It is easy to see where his sons, the late Herbert and Raymond,† acquired their love of theatre and their sense of humour!

After this production the funds amounted to £67 3s. 3d., plus the previous year's surplus of £12 3s. 6d.

December 1924 saw the Society moving away from the Gilbert & Sullivan tradition when a highly successful production of Edward German's *Merrie England* was performed with more than seventy members taking part. (Mr McIntyre boldly wrote to Edward German asking him to conduct the orchestra at one of the performances and offering him hospitality and expenses. The composer did not avail himself of the opportunity, though he did write a very kind letter, a facsimile of which was printed in the programme when Darlington Operatic Society gave *Merrie England* again in 1970.) The Treasurer and four other committee members met with Signor Pepi, the manager of the New Hippodrome, and got him to agree to split the profits 60%/40% in favour of the Society while guaranteeing him £150 and not more than £175, though Signor Pepi had asked for £200 – his finances were not too healthy at this point. This was quite a reasonable agreement for the Society (the seat prices had remained the same as they were in 1922); moreover, for the sum of one guinea, Patrons could have four prime seats in the Dress Circle or Fauteuils *and* have their names in the programme, a scheme which brought in extra revenue.

After this production it was announced to the press that £465 had been given to charity by the Society in five years. The *Northern Echo* and the *Northern Despatch* later said, however, that after the return of £104 9s. 8d. Entertainment Tax paid on *Merrie England* the total paid to charities, inclusive of that sum, came to £574 9s. 8d., so someone's arithmetic left something to be desired! No matter: what is certain is that, owing to the return of this tax, the Society was able to distribute £164 9s. 8d. to charity, purely from the profits of *Merrie England*.

In 1925 Councillor S. A. Sadler took over as President and the Society

* London and North Eastern Railway
† Raymond died some time ago, but Herbert died at the age of 85 in 1995.

was re-affiliated to NODA. Dr Arthur Kitson FRCO* was established as Musical Director and *A Country Girl,* the musical comedy by Lionel Monckton, was presented in December of that year. It was produced by Mr McIntyre and broke the record for takings. These amounted to £20 1s. 0d. more than for *Merrie England* despite the fact that the seat price in the pit stalls had been reduced from 2s. 4d. to 2s. A little extra was made by some 'Lady Attendants' who sold tickets to the public inviting them to guess the weight of the two live pigs used in the production! This show must have cost more to put on, however, because the net profit was disappointing – only £38 18s. 0d. The *Newcastle Journal,* the *Northern Echo* and the *Northern Despatch* critics loved *A Country Girl.* The *Darlington & Stockton Times* detested it – though, to be fair, the criticism was levelled at the frailty of the play itself as much as at the players for their lack of 'briskness'.[9] Fortunately, the audiences must have liked it or the piece could not have taken so much money.

A Country Girl introduced a new singer to Darlington audiences: Miss Lily Thompson (later to become Mrs Lily York). She was a remarkably pretty girl and her voice was praised by all the press critics.† She was to star in five productions before the birth of her elder daughter, and was a tremendous asset to the company.

One or two names which are still familiar in Darlington appeared in the cast lists of the 1920s: Ernest Wilde, who owned a flourishing gents' tailoring business in Bondgate, Darlington, appeared in several shows, and the name of Graham Tennant appears in the cast list for *The Gondoliers* of 1921.

Graham was ten years old at the time and his father had been cast as Luiz but became ill and was unable to take part. Graham played the part of a page and fell in love with the very pretty twenty-one-year-old Miss Mary Little who played Casilda. Forty years later Graham was giving a talk on theatre to the Coniscliffe Road Methodist Church Ladies' Guild and mentioned this fact. There was a rustle in the back row of his audience and a delightful lady stood up and said that she was the lady in question – they had never set eyes on each other since that show. (Mary Little was indirectly responsible for the entry of one of the later singers of the Operatic Society onto the scene. The mother of Nancy Bertram was a singer herself and was a great fan of Mary Little, and this is what first aroused the young Nancy's interest so that she was to be in the Society for many years and sang leading roles.) Graham Tennant went on to

---

* Fellow of the Royal College of Organists.
† She sang in the concerts given by Cockerton Townswomen's Guild in the late 1940s and early 1950s and her voice still had a remarkable sweetness and purity.

work in radio shows and plays for over fifty years – notably playing the small and unintelligible child, Horace, in a radio show which starred Harry Hemsley in the 1940s. Another 'child' (Winnie) always had to interpret, and the words 'What did Horace say, Winnie?' became a well-known and enduring catchphrase.* Graham also worked in television.

He appeared with the late Kenneth Horne in a programme called *Trader Horne* alongside Ann Croft who was the wife of David Croft, the scriptwriter whose work included the 1970s television series *Dad's Army* and other situation comedies. Graham also played Defence Counsel in the television dramatization of *The Trial of Mary Ann Cotton* (a North-East murderess of the late nineteenth century) though he has remarked 'I can't have been that good – because she was still hanged!'†

In 1926, Alderman Sir Charles W. Starmer JP was installed as President (remaining so until his death) and the Society reverted to producing Gilbert & Sullivan operas, with a production of *Iolanthe*. Lily Thompson took the part of Phyllis, with Tom Adamson as Strephon, and Ernest Wilde played Lord Tolloller. Miss Thompson was described by the *Northern Echo*

Iolanthe 1926. Lily Thompson

as a 'fine singer and a born actress' and as the 'heart and soul of the production',[10] though all the players received high praise. The chorus had a special mention, and so did the orchestra, which must have pleased Dr Kitson. Perhaps the increased advertising helped the success of the show; as well as being advertised in the press there had been a streamer in the Market Place and tickets had been on sale from October.

Whatever the reason, ticket receipts for the week's performances of

---

* It was even quoted in episodes of the television series *The Good Life* (by John Esmonde and Bob Larbey) in 1975, and *The Beiderbecke Affair* (by Alan Plater) in 1985.
† Sadly, Graham died suddenly on 30 April 1993, aged eighty-two.

Iolanthe were £588 19*s*. 4*d*., while the total receipts (including Patrons' donations) reached £653 11*s*. 10*d*. Of this, £165 16*s*. 8*d*. was clear profit, which was good news for the charities amongst whom it was distributed as follows: Darlington Hospital – £100, Darlington Queen's Nurses – £20, the YMCA – £10, the Blind Association – £10, and the Ragged School – £5 16*s*. 8*d*.

Just before the production of *Iolanthe* the Committee felt that it was time that a Sub-committee of ladies was formed – but only to cater for the special supper during the week of the show. Their expenses were not to exceed £10! Taking inflation into account this would be in excess of £300 today and therefore a lavish allowance.

In 1927 the Society presented *Ruddigore*, by which time Boots the Chemist's had taken an interest and provided the greasepaint. Both the Producer and Musical Director were being given honoraria of £15 each; only Dr Kitson had been favoured in this way the previous year – he had been given ten guineas.

Jos. Hall was not in the show. There was, said the Committee, 'no part quite suitable for him in it', but they made sympathetic noises and hoped he would 'still place his valuable services at the disposal of the Society'.

Lady Starmer, President 1945–79

Princess Ida followed in 1928, and then *Yeomen of the Guard* in 1929. By this time Sir Charles Starmer had married and his new wife Lady Cecily (née Willink – daughter of the Dean of Norwich) became interested in the Society: her photograph appeared in the programme of *Yeomen of the Guard*. *The Gondoliers* was presented (for the second time) in 1930, when the price of the programme – sixpence (about £2.50 by today's valuation) – was printed on its cover for the first time. The list of Vice-Presidents was scrapped and a new list was arranged, requiring from each Vice-President a donation of one guinea to help towards production costs. Lady Starmer provided the refreshments for Sunday rehearsals. In the programme for *The Gondoliers* there appears a name which today's Society members all know well – for

Mr T. A. Walton Wedge is still with us. He was one of the three Honorary Secretaries, then Patrons' Secretary, and was the Society's Honorary Auditor for many years.

The Society was still in reasonable shape financially, though there had been a hiccup in early 1929; they had been unable to reclaim Entertainment Tax because the Financial Secretary, Mr Heslop, had not given the requisite fourteen days' notice prior to the date of *Princess Ida*; there was apparently some confusion over who was responsible for applying for this refund. Mr Heslop resigned but was persuaded to withdraw his resignation. This incident, however, led to the production of a document dated 24 June 1929 outlining the exact duties of each committee officer.* By now, though, costs were rising steeply. The cost of producing *Yeomen of the Guard* was about £180 – for *The Gondoliers* it was £275 and the Society felt the first stirrings of financial embarrassment.

In 1931 major changes occurred. At the committee meeting of 20 January Mr Heslop announced that he was to resign for business reasons and it was decided that the Committee be elected each year. No progress had been made on the next production (though *The Vagabond King* by Rudolf Friml had been mooted) and Mr McIntyre had declined to continue as producer. There seems to have been a good deal of unrest in the Committee generally, though Mr McIntyre withdrew his resignation at the meeting of 7 May and the Committee expressed its 'satisfaction and loyalty'. By the July meeting the show was definitely decided upon. It was to be *The Vagabond King* and its budget was £80 more than for *The Gondoliers*. The role of Vice-Presidents was now redefined. Instead of being solely philanthropic figures they could also pay two guineas and be given in return four of the choicest seats – the Patrons would continue as before, paying one guinea for four seats or 10s. 6d. for two, and having their names printed in the programme. At this meeting it was also agreed that a special meeting should be arranged for Sir Charles Starmer to talk to members and to enable the Committee to assess the strength of the Society. (Mr Heslop reappeared at this point to serve in a lesser capacity as Chairman of the Sub-committee for Patrons. The reason for his wishing for lesser involvement became clear in a committee minute of 14 October – congratulations were extended to him on being elected to the Mayoralty.)

The Vagabond King was duly presented in 1931 but the after-show news was not good. On 28 January 1932 the provisional statement showed the startling loss of £85 6s. 8d. on the show. The Society had problems. The

* see Appendix 2.

decision was made to write to Fox's (costume suppliers) and Samuel French Ltd. (the rights holders) to see if any discounts were possible. Fox's replied that they were prepared to give a discount on the next production. French's refused to consider any reduction. Desperate to gain funds, the Society asked D'Oyly Carte for permission to perform a concert of Gilbert & Sullivan songs. (The D'Oyly Carte Opera Company owned all the Gilbert & Sullivan rights and it seems likely that the Committee hoped that by doing bits and pieces, rather than a full show, the payment of royalties might be avoided or reduced.)

By the committee meeting on 24 February the Society was almost on its knees. William Dresser and Sons Ltd. (who printed the Society's programmes and eventually did so until the firm closed down at the end of 1966) had made a kind offer to give a 5% discount and three months' credit, for which the Committee was very grateful, but French's were about to issue writs so Mr Trevor Morris, now Chairman of the Society, asked for the cheque to be sent. D'Oyly Carte had refused permission for a concert and the deficit from *The Vagabond King* was even greater than expected: £92 3s. od. The Committee took two weeks out to think. On 6 March they convened again with money-making ideas. A Bridge Drive was suggested and also a Flitch Trial* in conjunction with Darlington Chamber of Trade. To this end a Flitch Committee was set up comprising Messrs Morris, G. A. Williams, Craig, Jameson and T. A. W. Wedge. The ladies arranged the Bridge Drive and other social activities.

By 13 September, when the Committee met after its summer break, the Flitch Trial had been held and had been a success, as had the other money-making activities, and the Society's deficit was reduced to £4. The question was: what to do now? Three possibilities were open to the Committee. Putting on a show would involve liabilities of around £400 – should they risk it? Should they suspend all operations for twelve months? Or should they pursue a middle course to keep the Society together without incurring large liabilities? They took the middle course, deciding to organize a Sunday evening concert.

Mr McIntyre proposed that the concert should consist of a combination of *Trial by Jury* and other vocal entertainment. The theatre would cost £6 6s. od. to hire and the Darlington Amateur Orchestra could play. The enthusiasm of members was on the wane, however, and by November the lack of attendance at rehearsals was a problem. Furthermore Mr McIntyre was moving to York and therefore resigned. On 20 November

---

* A light-hearted 'trial' at which a flitch (a side of bacon) is awarded to any couple proving conjugal harmony for a year and a day.

a meeting was held at Mr G. A. Williams' house when it was decided that a better idea might be to hire the Cooperative Hall in Priestgate (which they could have for £3 per night with a 5% discount for three nights or more) and to perform *HMS Pinafore* and *Trial by Jury* with a budget of £115. The budget was based on tickets being sold for each night as follows: 200 at 2*s*. 6*d*., 300 at 1*s*. 6*d*. and 200 at 1*s*. This would leave a reasonable profit margin (less tax) if all the tickets were sold.

Sadly, though, the show was not a sell-out and thus the Society made what turned out to be its last appearance as an independent group: a four-night run of *Trial by Jury* and *HMS Pinafore* from 30 January to 2 February 1933, produced by Geoffrey Johnson (who had been in the Society since its inception) and with Dr Kitson, of course, as Musical Director. The profit from the show amounted to only £7 17*s*. 10*d*. This was not enough to provide any charitable donations, let alone solid financial back-up, so at this point Darlington Operatic Society was barely ticking over.

Another light opera group had been formed in 1922, and, like Darlington Operatic Society, it was affiliated to the NAADC. They began by calling themselves 'Amateurs of Darlington' and amassed their own following of Patrons; they did not have a President though The Very Reverend The Dean of Durham, Bishop Welldon, was the leading Patron. They avoided Gilbert & Sullivan and gave their first production in 1923 in the Temperance Institute: it was *Dogs of Devon*, 'an opera of comedy and romance' set in the time of the Spanish Armada, and it had a cast of forty-eight and a twenty-eight-strong orchestra. The music was by W. H. Bullock, the lyrics were by R. Bell and Harold Ellis, and it was produced for the company by Mr W. S. Waldie (who had been with Mrs Paget Steavenson's amateur theatrical group in the early days), under the Musical Directorship of Mr T. Henderson. The leading man was Robert Farrage, LRAM.* (His name had cropped up, late in the previous year, in the minutes of the Darlington Operatic Society, when he had been accepted as an active member. Though he had not stayed with the company for long at that time, he was to become very much involved again later on.) In the chorus there also appeared a Mr T. W. Oxley who was the grandfather of Ann Oxley, a present-day member of Darlington Operatic Society.

After this first show the group changed its name to 'The Darlington Light Opera Company'† and Robert Farrage joined the Committee and

---

* Licentiate of the Royal Academy of Music.
† This is the name on the theatre programmes but the press sometimes referred to it as 'The Darlington Light Opera Group'.

continued to play leading roles. They gave one show each year, presenting *Highwayman Love, Dorothy* (with live foxhounds provided by Lord Southampton), *San Toy, The Rebel Maid, Miss Hook of Holland, The Runaway Girl, The Quaker Girl* and, in 1931,

Robert Farrage

My Lady Molly, all produced by Avalon Collard. By this time the company had had a succession of Presidents and, like Darlington Operatic Society, a supporting number of Vice-Presidents, of whom Sir Charles Starmer was one. Robert Farrage was Hon. Musical Director for *My Lady Molly* and the Hon. Stage Manager was George Welford, later Headmaster of Eastbourne School, Darlington. The Hon. Dance Producer was Miss Gladys ('Timmie') Mutimer who, much later in life, as Timmie Morrison, wrote a history of the Darlington New Hippodrome Theatre (now Darlington Civic Theatre).* Miss Evelyn Berry, who became a stalwart of the post-war Darlington Operatic Society, was also in the company.

(As far as the necessary furnishings were concerned no credits were given in the programmes by Darlington Operatic Society for scenery and it is most likely that it was provided by the theatre. They normally hired their costumes from B. J. Simmons & Co. Ltd. of London, as did the Darlington Light Opera Company. From 1927 onwards the Darlington Light Opera Company was getting its scenery from various hire firms in the North – it seems to have been built by local people before then. By 1931 Mr J. Waters, a local chemist, not to be outdone by Boots the Chemist's generosity towards Darlington Operatic Society, was donating greasepaint to the Light Opera Company. Darlington Operatic Society's costumes for *The Vagabond King* in the same year were, for once, from Chas H. Fox, London instead of B. J. Simmons.)

The Darlington Light Opera Company's next production, in 1932, was *The Geisha* written by Sidney Jones, Henry Greenbank and Owen Hall.

---

* *A Theatre for the People* by Timmie Morrison. Proscenium Publications Ltd. 1983.

The President of the company was by now Charles U. Peat, MC, MP. The show's Producer was Graham Roberts and the Musical Director was Mr W. H. Pearson, who had been Hon. Accompanist for *My Lady Molly*. For *The Geisha* the company was more diverse in its hire of costumes and wigs, of scenery, and of 'ladies' gowns'. Though the costumes and wigs came from B. J. Simmons & Co. Ltd. once more, the scenery now came from C. E. Grantham & Sons of Leatherhead and the gowns from Modes, of Berners Street, London. So, although we have no minutes of The Darlington Light Opera Company to serve as a guide, it seems to have been thriving at this point. Miss Mutimer again produced the dances and George Welford had now taken to the boards to play the part of The Marquis Iman.

In March 1933, however – six weeks after Darlington Operatic Society presented *its* last show – the Darlington Light Opera Company did likewise and presented *Our Miss Gibbs* by Monckton, Caryll, Ross and Greenbank. This time George Welford produced the show and Mr Pearson was once more Musical Director.

The reason for this winding down was that it was becoming clear by now that the town was unable to support two major operatic societies. It was decided that a joint meeting of the two societies should be held because of the acute economic situation. The *Darlington & Stockton Times* reported that each group had formed a committee to enter into discussions.[11] The paper pointed out some of the problems involved in fusing the two societies. It would, for one thing, bring together over eighty acting members – no easy task, therefore, for any casting committee. Also, although Darlington Operatic Society had given over £1,200 to charity in its fourteen years of existence it was now in debt to the tune of £45 – the Light Opera Company was at least solvent. The *Northern Despatch* commented, on 5 October, that the individual characteristics and the friendly rivalry would be lost but that nevertheless the advantages would outweigh the disadvantages. While there was not enough financial support for two societies, the *Northern Despatch* writer felt that one might flourish. It would also provide a really good chorus of mixed voices, it said, and 'amateur societies do not principally exist to bring honour and glory to a host of little stars who twinkle in their own firmaments for the satisfaction of themselves and a few admirers' – an oddly acid remark.

The joint meeting of the two societies took place on 3 October 1933, the intention being to pool resources rather than to amalgamate. The representatives were Messrs Morris, Johnson, Renshaw, Adamson, Wilde (standing in for Mr Williams) and Dixon for Darlington Operatic Society and Messrs Berry, Griffiths, Jowers, Pearson, Welford, Wood and Stevenson for the Light Opera Company.

They proceeded briskly about their business, forming a joint committee of which Mr Trevor Morris was to be President, Mr Berry Chairman, Mr Griffiths Treasurer, Mr Timms Finance Secretary, Mr Jowers Stage Manager, and Mr Dixon General Secretary. They decided that the next show would be a costume show but not Gilbert & Sullivan. Rehearsals would be on Thursdays and the subscription would be 3s. 6d. per year. A further meeting was held on 18 October when the show was chosen. *The Arcadians, Tom Jones, The Duchess of Dantzic,* and *Chinese Honeymoon* were all considered, and finally *The Arcadians* ('A Fantastic Musical Comedy in 3 Acts by Lionel Monckton') was chosen to be presented at the New Hippodrome for the week beginning 5 March 1934, as a joint venture by the two societies under the Musical Directorship of Dr Kitson. It was decided that a professional producer would be too expensive, so George Welford was to produce the show. The other contender would have been Geoffrey E. Johnson who had been a producer for Darlington Operatic Society during his twenty years' service to it, but the *Darlington & Stockton Times* reported that Mr Johnson was heartily in favour of a merger between the two societies and, 'to preserve harmony during the initial stages of the amalgamation',[12] withdrew his nomination. Rehearsals began at Reid Street School.

The enthusiasm generated by this joint venture could not combat rising costs, however, and the minutes of the committee meeting of 14 January 1934 record the continuing problem of finance. There was a balance in the coffers, but standing at 8s. 8d. it was not going to gladden the heart of any accountant. It was decided that a reserve fund was essential and it seemed that the best course would be to ask members for an additional sixpence per week to form such a fund. The Committee mulled this over until the General Meeting on 6 June 1934.

In the mean time *The Arcadians* had been performed by an 'augmented Orchestra and Company of 70 voices' and had been very highly praised by the press. 'The experiment of Darlington's two leading amateur societies pooling their resources after a long period of adversity has been eminently successful. Indeed we hope the happy partnership will continue,' said the *Darlington & Stockton Times.*[13] The seat prices had ranged from 4s. 3d. down to 1s. with 19 Vice-Presidents and 146 Patrons. Boots the Chemist's and Mr Waters had both donated greasepaint and 31 advertisers had paid to appear in the programme. A Mr H. Coleman had even provided a horse! Despite all this, *The Arcadians* had resulted in a loss of £31 which was only offset by the Patrons' subscriptions and the efforts of a Financial Assistance Committee which had been formed. At 15 June 1934 the balance in hand was still 8s. 8d.

So, at that meeting on 15 June, the die was cast. The two societies would now amalgamate and become the Darlington Operatic Company. The date of the next show would be November or December 1935 – '. . . it being felt that the usual month for productions – March – was not altogether suitable for this purpose, owing to Lent and the fact that many people had other financial calls to meet at that period.'[14]

There were no further meetings until 3 October 1934 and then the talk was all of financial problems. The most important things agreed were that a show would still be put on in late 1935 and that each member would give the Society sixpence per week. Morale was at a very low ebb by this stage, however, and the 1935 show never materialized. Mr Berry resigned from the Committee for health reasons and at the meeting of 1 November 1934, at which only nine committee members and fourteen active members were present, it was decided that activities be postponed. The Committee rallied briefly for a meeting on 9 October 1935, only to decide that meetings be 'postponed *sine die*'. Mr Morris and Mr Jones said they would reconvene a meeting 'when it seemed appropriate', but after this there were no more official minutes of the Society. There can be little doubt that at the root of the Darlington Operatic Society's troubles lay the fact that it had given too much money away and not built up suitable financial backing. For example, a show would cost about £400 to put on, and in January 1931 the Society gave £148 to charity. This is equivalent to the present-day Society donating £15,000 per show!

There were further stirrings, however, in 1937. The *Northern Despatch* reported in March of that year that 'a new amateur operatic society is to be formed *(sic)* – the Darlington Operatic Company',[15] and the paper appealed to the public to support it. An organizing committee had been formed with George A. Williams (as Chairman) and ten others (including Geoffrey E. Johnson, Robert Farrage and Ernest Wilde) but caution was undoubtedly their watchword. The *Northern Despatch*'s report, while stating that the society needed members who were interested in dancing, elocution or backstage work as well as music, stressed that these members should be willing to take their share of responsibility and 'do their bit in making the company pay its way'. 'Only if the committee are assured of this assistance,' the article went on, 'can they go forward with the ambitious policy they have in mind. It is their intention to break away from the hoary tradition of amateurs in presenting out-of-date musical plays. The choice of the first production is as yet undecided, but one thing is certain, and that is that it will be made from good-class modern musical comedy or popular light opera.' The paper then made an appeal for members, saying that such shows would require a large number of principals and a considerable chorus. The Musical Director was to be Robert Farrage, and this show marked the beginning of his long association with the Society. Lady Cecily Starmer, who had begun to take such a great interest in the company on her marriage, and who was now a widow since Sir Charles had died in June 1933, was to be the Society's President, and when the show was staged it was supported by 27 other named Patrons.

On 10 March the *Northern Despatch* recorded an 'encouraging response' to the appeal for members and supporters. Dangling a mouthwatering carrot the paper said that this encouraging response was '. . . proof that the town is ready for a revival of the richly-costumed, gay-melodied musical show performed by the town's own artists.' At least 77 people could not resist the carrot for that was the size of the cast which performed H. Fraser-Simpson and Harry Graham's *The Maid of the Mountains* at the New Hippodrome in the week beginning 29 November 1937. Despite the *Northern Despatch*'s comment the chosen show was not *that* modern – it was first performed in London in 1917. Sheridan Morley, in his book *Spread a Little Happiness*, [16] says that it had been '. . . cobbled together from an old stage plot by Frederick Lonsdale, which had already been rejected by most of the managements in town.' Nevertheless, Morley reports, it had certainly been 'good box office' in 1917 and had shown a profit of £200,000 from its run of over 1,300 performances.

Some of the people who were to become post-war stalwarts of the Operatic Society appeared in *The Maid of the Mountains*: Robert (Bob) White, James Fraser Murray and his wife Connie, Marjorie Farrage, Nancy Bertram, and Eileen Young, who is still a member of Darlington Operatic Society (and whose rendering of *Nobody Loves a Fairy When She's Forty* is surely un-surpassable!)

Eileen Young

Since no committee minutes are available we do not know whether or not *The Maid of the Mountains* made any money but the *Darlington & Stockton Times* was optimistic about the future of the society: 'As the first production of the new Darlington Operatic Company draws to a close there seems to be a general feeling abroad in the town which might be put into the words "Well, they've done it after all".

Frankly, the reports which have been going around in the last few weeks regarding the prospects of *The Maid of the Mountains* have not all been reassuring. There have been significant hints that it could never succeed with a cast so young in years, with such an outworn choice of play, with such alleged evidence of apathy on the part of the local playgoers.'[17] The paper went on to declare the performance 'excellent' and to say that the company had '. . . shown that amateur operatics are not dead in Darlington.' The *Northern Despatch* agreed and remarked 'It really looks as though amateur operatics have come back to Darlington to stay.'

Despite this optimism, information about the Society now becomes sketchy. We do know that in November 1938 it presented *Tom Jones* by Sir Edward German, produced by Arthur Ridley, with a cast of 71 players, and that the show was supported by 95 named Patrons. The chorus included Kenneth Richardson, who became another great linchpin of the post-war Society and remained with it, as an acting member, until his sudden and untimely death in 1982; also appearing in the chorus was John Reed who was to make such a great name for himself performing roles in Gilbert & Sullivan operettas with the D'Oyly Carte Opera Company, though he did not receive a special mention in the reviews. (They did, however, praise the colourful production and fine singing, while not being particularly enthusiastic about the content of the show itself.)

We also know that *The Student Prince* went into rehearsal but the prospect of war was now looming over Europe. By the time the Darlington Operatic Company would have presented *The Student Prince* at the end of 1939, Britain had been plunged into the Second World War and the Society was, to all intents and purposes, one of its early casualties.

Chapter 2

1945–1949

The end of the Second World War was to bring a resurgence of the Society in grand style. It is not known precisely what prompted this revival but the *Northern Despatch* of 4 May 1945 reported that a meeting had been held at Bondgate Hall the previous night, with about 80 people present, under the chairmanship of James Hewitt. At this meeting it was unanimously decided to form the Darlington Operatic & Choral Society under the Musical Directorship of Robert Farrage. Tom Bourn, a NODA councillor, who was to serve the Society for six years, becoming Hon. Treasurer, was elected Business Manager.* Mr C. J. Turner (formerly of the Darlington Light Opera Company) was to be the Treasurer, and Walter Hamilton the Secretary. Also on the Committee was James Fraser Murray, for whom the Society remained an absorbing interest up to the end of his life and whose family was gradually drawn in, forming a far-reaching network of loyal members. His brother, J. C. Murray, was on the list of Vice-Presidents for the first show of the re-formed Society. Since the meeting coincided more or less with VE Day, it was decided that a production of Edward German's *Merrie England* should be given at the New Hippodrome Theatre for the week beginning 29 October 1945, as this show 'would best meet the sentiments of the times'.[1] Having settled on this they lost no time in putting the wheels in motion. A committee of 'voice selectors' was chosen there and then to hold the first audition the following Thursday (10 May) at Bondgate Memorial Hall and it was announced that practices would be on subsequent Thursdays, as they still are. (The Mayor, Councillor J. Blumer, was equally quick off the mark and also full of faith: he had already sent a letter asking if the Society would consider giving the proceeds of this first production to King George's Fund for Sailors, on behalf of which he had recently launched an appeal.)

The Society was properly constituted with a committee of eight (which included two ladies, Miss Minerva Davison and Miss B. Nelson) and a rule book. It also had an official Hon. Patrons' Secretary, Isabel Farrage

---

* He was to be made a Life Member of the Society in 1950 (when he was also elected President of NODA), and Honorary Vice-President in 1954, a signal honour which is conferred for life and which thus lasted until his death, early in 1962.

(wife of Robert Farrage) who served the Society in that capacity for fourteen years. Lady Cecily Starmer agreed to be President again. There were 25 Vice-Presidents, each of whom paid a subscription of two guineas (£2 2s. 0d.) and received four of the best seats, and 62 Patrons who paid half that amount and received two of the best seats. Their names were printed in the tiny programme which measured four inches by two-and-a-half, had a single-sheet insert, and cost sixpence.

Members could have priority booking of ten tickets and, after these had been allocated, Dressers (Stationers) Ltd. of High Row would sell to the public.

The show was produced by Dorothy Forster from Tyneside, who had a cast of 81 to deal with, and the Stage Manager for this first production was Fred Thompson who was to play a major part in the Society in various capacities for many years. The hardworking accompanist was Mrs Edith Kershaw, who also served the Society with hardly a break until her death in 1962.

The costumes were supplied by B. J. Simmons & Co. Ltd. of London, and the scenery by Scenic Display Services Ltd. of Bradford, whose original quotation of £45 plus carriage was considered too high by the Committee. Scenic Display Services then offered a cheaper set of scenery for £27, but the Committee finally decided that it would push the boat out and went for the more expensive set.

The seat prices were set: Fauteuils 6s.; Dress Circle & Orchestra Stalls 5s.; Back Stalls 2s. 9d.; and Gallery 1s. 6d. A Mr Perry was given £4 4s. 0d. to supply the make-up. The leading parts would be taken by Nancy Bertram,* Rita Hamilton, Audrey Walker, Jack Lyall, Minerva Davison and W. Roy Heylings.

The Committee was well satisfied with its arrangements. The only ripple occurred at the committee meeting of 31 August 1945 over the proposed 'Britannia tableau'† opening to the show. The question was deferred until another meeting since there was a 'wide divergence of opinion' – in other words there was a considerable altercation, albeit genteel. Euphemisms such as this occur many, many times in committee minutes over the years. The term 'full discussion' can usually be interpreted as the flying of fur and feathers!

By 2 October 1945 the Committee was expressing its 'extreme satisfaction' at the financial situation. The cost of the advertisement printing had been £17 and programme printing about £30. Royalties had been

---

* Nancy had appeared with the pre-war Society in *The Maid of the Mountains* in 1937.
† Despite enquiries no one now seems to remember the Britannia tableau, though it was obviously a controversial subject at the time.

settled with Chappell & Co., the rights holders, to the tune of 10% of the gross takings with a minimum of £10. The band cost £51 18s. 0d. (with a small fee for the amateurs among them – Musicians' Union rules seem to have been very flexible then). Robert Farrage was given an honorarium of £25 and Mrs Kershaw £5 5s. 0d., and the Committee (possibly mindful of Mr Heslop's lapse in the 1930s) remembered to claim back the Entertainment Tax.

So, after all this, how did the show go?

According to Eileen Young, who was in the chorus, it went very well (and she greatly admired Dorothy Forster, the Producer). The press agreed. Indeed, the *Darlington & Stockton Times* waxed lyrical: 'The Darlington production has brought a much-needed sparkle into the somewhat sombre atmosphere created by the war, and signalled, let us hope, the end of the winter of our discontent at wartime restrictions.'[2] * The *Northern Echo* and the *Northern Despatch*, as well as the *Darlington & Stockton Times*, paid tribute to Nancy Bertram for her performance as Bessie Throckmorton. Rita Hamilton (Jill-All-Alone) and Audrey Walker (The May Queen) received similar mention. The comic talents of Jack Lyall and Charles Clifford were also singled out for praise, as was Minerva Davison (Queen Elizabeth I) – despite her 'uncertain progress on the state barge', which must have been a producer's nightmare! The *Darlington & Stockton Times* concluded by saying, 'It has been a memorable show and the gratifying measure of support by the public will no doubt inspire the society to greater achievements.'

This was gratifying for the Committee of this first post-war venture – 'very highly gratifying' said the minutes of 12 November 1945 – because the income from *Merrie England* amounted to £1,283 18s. 9d. and the expenses were £1,095 18s. 2d., giving a profit of £188 0s. 7d.

The Committee was much encouraged by this for, just over a week after the end of *Merrie England*, it decided that the Society would perform its next show in the spring of 1946. It was decided to perform *Katinka*, an involved romance full of intrigue and spiced with comedy, by Rudolph Friml. There was a practical rather than a purely aesthetic reason for this: the end of the war had seen the resurgence of many societies and there was therefore a rush on costumes for many shows! The Society was able to hire the costumes for *Katinka* from F. A. Smith Ltd. of Manchester for 15s. 6d. each, the scenery was £55 from Scenic Display Ltd. and NODA would hire out the vocal scores for one shilling per copy per month. (Some

---

* It was a shame that the review did not appear until the day of the show's final performance, since the *Darlington & Stockton Times* has always been a Saturday paper only.

things do improve – the Society is now able to borrow vocal scores from Durham County Library for nothing!) The hire of the theatre for a week cost £200 plus 40% of any takings over £600, and McDonald & Young, the rights holders, were asking 10% of the gross takings with a minimum of six guineas per performance.

So rehearsals commenced, auditions were held for principals, and the show was cast. It would run for a week from 29 April 1946. Nancy Bertram played the leading role but this time Fred Thompson, who had been Stage Manager for *Merrie England*, was producing the show. The Society's aim *was* to make money for charity, after all, and professional producers cost quite a lot of money. Fred Thompson was ready, willing, and confident that he was able; he had the right background, having been a member, since 1919, of operatic societies in towns as far afield as Stockport, Blackheath, Wolverhampton and West Bromwich, and he was well known for his championing of live theatre. As a young man he had been offered a chance to play with the then-famous Arcadians* but turned it down because he 'didn't want that precarious sort of life'. He and his wife, Doris, had appeared in many shows in Stockport before coming to Darlington in 1934 to set up Fred's leather merchant's business. Indeed it had been as a result of their shared interest and participation in amateur theatricals that they met and were married. Fred had already produced *Katinka* twice before, and what is more his services would be free. Things went swimmingly until the middle of March when the member cast as Thaddeus T. Hopper announced that he would be unable to attend two weeks of the rehearsals. Fred Thompson was disenchanted by this but, nothing daunted, told the Committee that he had not been fully satisfied with the member's performance anyway and undertook to play the part himself, as well as producing. The crisis was averted.

Jim Fraser Murray had designed a souvenir programme four times the size of that for *Merrie England*, complete with photographs of all the performers and some of the Committee, and partly financed by advertising space for local businesses. He had 3,000 of these printed, to be sold for a shilling each.

By the committee meeting of 14 April, 3,627 of the 4,194 tickets had been sold – the Darlington public were keeping the faith – and the estimated profit was £130, out of which Robert Farrage, the Musical Director, was given £25. Fred Thompson was given an honorarium of £40 but handed it straight back, a gesture received at the Annual General

---

* The Arcadians seem to be one of those elusive groups of whom a number of people have vaguely heard, but of whom no details are apparently now known.

Meeting at the end of May with 'grateful acclamation'. He had earned it, however, judging by the reviews of *Katinka* in the local papers. The *Northern Echo*, which had given the show publicity a week before it opened (stressing the fact that a large amount of money was donated to charity), gave it an excellent write-up remarking that it '. . . reached a standard that is not common even to the best amateur societies.'[3] The *Darlington & Stockton Times* went further and said that '. . . the standard of the production was so high that one might be forgiven for assuming it to be a professional performance.'[4] The *Northern Despatch* commented that it had been '. . . warmly acclaimed by a full house.'[5] Not bad for a first night. The principals, the comedy element and the chorus all received their share of praise and not a jarring note was heard, so the Society was in buoyant mood when it met for its first Annual General Meeting on 30 May 1946, knowing that the balance in its General Account was £374 8s. 9d. After considerable deliberation alterations were agreed upon to the part of the Constitution concerning the election of officers and committee. Henceforward the Committee would consist of a President *(ex-officio)*, and twelve members elected at the Annual General Meeting. Of these twelve, four should retire annually but be eligible for re-election. During the first three years, the four to retire would be chosen according to the number of votes they received at the initial election. Seven members of the Committee would form a quorum. Once the Committee was elected the Annual General Meeting would then appoint from among these a Secretary and a Treasurer (to hold office for one year but to be eligible for re-election). The Committee itself would elect annually from among its members a Chairman, a Vice-Chairman (who would be Chairman the following year), an Hon. Assistant Secretary, and an Hon. Assistant Treasurer. The Committee would be empowered to fill any vacancy which might occur but that member would only stay in office until the next Annual General Meeting when the vacancy would be filled, for the remainder of the original period of office, by the member receiving the next highest number of votes after the four elected in the ballot to fill the automatic vacancies.

The officers were all duly elected, with two ladies among them, and Messrs Hamilton and Turner were unanimously elected to continue as Secretary and Treasurer.

It was announced that the New Hippodrome had been booked for the last week in March 1947 for the next show – whatever it might be.

At the following committee meeting of 4 June 1946 elections for the various jobs were held and resulted in Jim Fraser Murray becoming Vice-Chairman, N. W. Thompson Assistant Secretary and Librarian, and A. E. Angus Assistant Treasurer. Publicity was to be managed by Jim

Fraser Murray and Neville Dodd – who brought into the Society his wife, Irene, and later his daughter, Shirley. Shirley, in particular, proved to be a considerable asset, playing to great effect in many shows, particularly in comedy parts. (It says much for the credibility of her performances that one elderly person who saw her play an exceedingly myopic Nesta in *La Belle Hélène* in 1989 was overheard to express genuine concern about her poor eyesight!)

A social sub-committee was also formed, to arrange Society events to raise more money. The distribution of money to charity consisted of small amounts to a number of causes – £25 to twelve of them and £5 5*s. od.* to two others. Whatever was left went to the Memorial Hospital.

All was peace and harmony – until the next meeting on 20 June when there was not just 'lengthy deliberation' but 'very lengthy deliberation' about what the next show was to be. It was 'thoroughly discussed from many angles'. The contenders were *The Vagabond King, Bitter Sweet, Gipsy Love,* and *Goodnight Vienna.* These were reduced to the last two, then Robert Farrage threw in *The Desert Song* which stirred things up a good deal. Robert Farrage also 'stressed frequently' the advantages of having a resident producer. *Goodnight Vienna* by Posford and Maschwitz was finally chosen and Fred Thompson was asked to produce it. Maybe he had a grievance or he did not care for the choice of show because he declined (though this may be doing him an injustice because he may also have been thinking about the possibility of election to the local council and the amount of time this would involve). He further declined to be Stage Manager. The Committee consequently began to look for professional producers. Six were approached, including Charles Simon, an actor/director who ran an acting company in the town until 1951 when he went to London, but his fee was £150 and even over the years one can hear the sharp intake of breath in the committee-room! His name was not mentioned again as a potential candidate and none of the other five who were approached found it practicable, so there was much consternation. However, at the meeting of 4 July, Fred Thompson was finally wooed and won, and agreed to be Producer '. . . on condition that he had the full support and cooperation of the Committee and the Society.' He then '. . . proceeded to outline his intended procedure and requested that a copy of the latest Script and Band Score be obtained for him . . .' – he was undoubtedly a force to be reckoned with.

The personnel at the New Hippodrome had been a trifle miffed that they were being dealt with on the footing of 'tradesmen' and Mr E. J. Hinge, the Managing Director, intimated that it would not go amiss if he were made an Honorary Vice-President of the Society. The Society was always keen to foster a good relationship between itself and the theatre so this was done, and in 1948 his name appeared in the programme in this capacity, remaining there until 1957. Mr Hinge had many theatrical interests and had, among other things, a scenery-hire business at New-castle-upon-Tyne. The Society hired scenery from him for three of its shows, which strengthened the link.

Goodnight Vienna – the first performance by an amateur society of the new, up-to-date version – went into rehearsal on 12 September 1946 and opened on 24 March 1947 with Nancy Bertram once more in the leading role. This time her leading man was Eric Thornton, a newcomer to the Society. This was his first appearance in a musical play, though he had done dramatic work in the town. He was another member of the Society to go on to make a professional career in acting. He went to London to appear in Gilbert & Sullivan shows and from there went to settle in Australia, first touring in Gilbert & Sullivan from 1956 to 1958 and then going on to make even more of a name for himself in other musicals there.* Oddly enough, the *Darlington & Stockton Times* review of *Goodnight Vienna* remarked that his ability as an actor fell rather short of his ability as a singer!

Appearing in the chorus in his second show with the post-war Society was John Reed, a producer and dancing-instructor for Darlington Educa-tion Committee. By the autumn show of 1947 he was playing one of the lesser parts and in the spring of 1948 he played the comedy lead, Alex-ander, in *The New Moon*. He played more comedy roles with the Society until 1951 when he was hired by the D'Oyly Carte company as understudy to Peter Pratt. He took over Pratt's entire repertoire of comedy roles in 1959 and became justly famous in the many years he spent with the company, earning the sobriquet 'The Great Savoyard'. He was awarded the OBE in 1977.

A representative of the rising generation in the Murray family also made her Operatic Society début in *Goodnight Vienna*. Greta Murray, daughter of J. C. Murray (one of the first Vice-Presidents) and niece of both Jim Fraser Murray and Eileen Young (Jim's half-sister), was a dancer in the show and has been involved in some capacity with every show since then, as a Committee member, a behind-the-scenes worker, frequent performer, Chairman (twice), and, most recently, as Secretary.

How many people saw *Goodnight Vienna* over the week of its run is not known but the *Northern Echo* and the *Darlington & Stockton Times* both stated that on the first night there was a capacity audience. The reviews were

---

* See *Brisbane Courier Mail* 17 October 1958.

full of praise and obviously it was good news for the charities which would benefit.

It is recorded in the minutes of the Annual General Meeting of 8 May 1947 that so far over £1,000 had been given or promised to local charities. The Society was certainly on a financial high after its first three shows and it was decided that the cost of the installation of a telephone for the Hon. Secretary should also be met. The job of Secretary has always been an onerous one for he or she must make all the arrangements for the shows: book scenery and costumes, negotiate with the rights holders and so on, as well as coordinate the whole operation.

It was also felt that, since business was booming, a Ticket Secretary should be appointed to deal with bookings. Jim Willans, a local headmaster and new member of the Committee, got the job. The Ticket Secretary dealt with priority bookings for Members, Vice-Presidents and Patrons, and then some of the local shops like Bainbridge Barkers and Murrays the Bakers would offer booking facilities to the public for a week before any remaining tickets reverted to the theatre box office. Jim Willans also spread his wings a little and managed to get shops at Piercebridge, Barnard Castle and Staindrop to participate. Members were not allowed to book more than four seats for the last night out of their priority booking; this was soon amended to the effect that they were '. . . not to be encouraged but not declined.'[6]

Jim Willans

The next show was to be *The Duchess of Dantzic* by Caryll and Hamilton, to be produced by Fred Thompson and presented for the week beginning 24 November 1947. Demand was so great for tickets by 21 October that the Ticket Secretary was worrying that there was going to be a shortage and wondered if it would be possible to give a Saturday matinée performance. The question was 'discussed at some length' and matinée performances have been a vexed question from that day to this! Difficulties abound: for example, many members must take time off work, and there is always doubt as to whether the ticket receipts will cover the extra costs. In 1984, John Lloyd, the Ticket Secretary, pressed hard for a matinée performance of *The Gondoliers*, on Saturday 19 May, because the tickets were selling so well. The Committee decided to humour him. What he had forgotten – and, to be fair, so had everyone else – was that it was Cup Final day and the audience only numbered around one hundred. Since then that performance has been nicknamed The John Lloyd Memorial Matinée – because he has never been allowed to forget it! There was, in the event, no matinée for The *Duchess of Dantzic*.

The job of Ticket Secretary was, even then, an unenviable one. In the 1940s Patrons received a circular and returned it with their seat-requirements. Their tickets were then allocated by balloting. After this the members were next in line of priority but they had to turn up and queue for tickets on one of two designated nights. They also had to pay on the spot and the Ticket Secretary gave the money straight to the Treasurer and was given a receipt. After this the Ticket Secretary allocated seats for organizations who had asked for blocks of seats, and gave out complimentary tickets to the press, to shopkeepers who had agreed to act as outlets for tickets, to the caretaker of the school used for rehearsals, and to a few others. Next, the remainder would be sold by the said outlets and last of all by the theatre. It is a very different proposition in the 1990s. Since the Society is a registered charity it feels duty-bound to raise as much money as possible. If the theatre sells tickets for an Operatic Society show it naturally charges a percentage of the ticket-price for the service, so it is practical for the Society itself to handle ticket sales as far as possible. Therefore, the Ticket Secretary deals with all the tickets, with the exception of one side-block in the stalls which is allocated to the theatre for each night but the last. Around 1,500 envelopes are addressed and furnished with a booking-form and a self-addressed envelope by the Ticket Secretary, and sent out about two months before a show. Customers are asked to return the form with their requirements filled in, and with a cheque enclosed in payment. Since booking must be done with priority given to Vice-Presidents (who give a donation of £2), then to Patrons (who give a donation of £1), then to block bookings and Members, before all other advance bookings, very little allocating of seats can be done until the majority of the forms are returned. This makes for frantic activity during the whole of the booking period with hundreds of booking-forms being returned, and with telephone calls for as much as sixteen hours per day. The Ticket Secretary banks all the money, balances the ticket accounts ready for the Treasurer (not as easy as it sounds), and allocates and sends out all the tickets. And deals with all the complaints!

Jim Willans doubtless received complaints, too. Since the idea of a matinée was rejected, the shortage of seats forced him to transfer to the

Orchestra Stalls some of the Fauteuils bookings. Undoubtedly some of the customers concerned would have taken this as though Jim was insulting them personally, but that is part of the lot of a Ticket Secretary!

While rehearsals for *The Duchess of Dantzic* were taking place, discussion was going on in the Committee about future shows and attracting new members. It was felt by some that it might be advantageous to present a choral work in spring and a spectacular show in the autumn. Others favoured two spectacular shows. So an Extraordinary General Meeting was held on 5 November 1947 to discuss this. The choice of the anniversary of the Gunpowder Plot seems uncannily appropriate in retrospect, for the subject turned out to be quite a hot potato. There was 'much discussion', and 'many proposals and counter-proposals', and argument continued for over an hour, but it seems that in the end the general feeling was that it would be better to leave choral works alone so as not to seem to be in competition with societies who performed nothing else but choral works.

In the background to all this another, apparently insignificant, event was taking place. With only about two or three weeks to go before the opening of the show, no Dancing Mistress had yet been found for the current production. Then Miss Joy Beadell, an Associate of the Royal Academy of Dancing with Advanced Honours, and owner of a local dancing school, agreed to undertake the task. This lady had trained for the theatre in music and ballet under a number of famous teachers, and in drama at the Guildhall School of Music and Drama. She had first appeared in the West End at the age of twelve in the Garrick Theatre and after further training appeared there again playing child leads in the well-known Tod Slaughter melodramas. She gained further experience in concert party shows, cabaret at a number of London's famous hotels and restaurants, and seasons of pantomime in which she appeared as a principal dancer for Howard and Wyndham. This was followed by variety, two films with Maurice Chevalier and Jack Buchanan, and another with Cicely Courtneidge and Mary Lawson. She then appeared at the Lyceum in *Paganini* with Evelyn Laye, Richard Tauber and Esmé Percy. On the outbreak of war she volunteered for ENSA* and went to France with the very first concert party, touring with Will Fyffe and Albert Whelan (the comedians), and Jasper Maskelyne, who was the magician grandson of John Nevil Maskelyne, one of the greatest magicians of all time. Joy came north during the war to perform at the old Empire Theatre at Middlesbrough, and it was there that she met Dr John Bishop who was doing voluntary work. Not long after they met they were married, and when

* Entertainments National Service Association.

the war ended they came to live in Darlington. From this first appearance as an urgently-required Dancing Mistress onwards, Joy Beadell came to mean a great deal to the Operatic Society and its members and produced many, many shows, doing all the choreography as well.

1947 also seems to have been a good year for introducing members who have stayed with the society 'till death us do part'. Jim Willans and his wife, Marjorie, did just that, as did Kenneth Richardson. He had been in the chorus before the war, but now he was to play Napoleon in *The Duchess of Dantzic* and many more leading roles of all kinds right up until his death in February 1982. After his death his mother, knowing how much the Society meant to him, made provision in her will for the Society to institute The Kenneth Richardson Memorial Trust, which allows grants to be given for members, particularly young people, to have special training. Cecil Grieveson also joined in 1947 and is still with the Society and appearing on stage nearly fifty years on.

With all these assets *The Duchess of Dantzic* did well. It played, on the first night, to what the *Northern Echo* called a 'crowded audience'.[7] The *Darlington & Stockton Times* devoted a whole column to its review.[8] Irene Ross, who played the part of the eponymous heroine, was much praised – 'magnificent' said the *Darlington & Stockton Times* – but it was her first and last performance for the Society. According to Eileen Young, she was a very nice person who had a beautiful voice. She worked in Duke Street, in charge of a Home for Fallen Women, and then became a professional singer. Unfortunately she died young.

Joy Beadell's début as Dancing Mistress also received mention. 'It was a pleasure,' said the *Darlington & Stockton Times*, 'to find that for once an amateur society had cut away the usual stereotyped kind of dance inter-lude and launched into something different.' Kenneth Richardson was also selected for special praise. His performance as Napoleon Bonaparte was, according to the *Northern Despatch*, '. . . a piece of skilful and intelligent acting . . . Although probably not so well known to the Society's followers, he has, in a short time, become one of the town's most prominent amateur actors and his characterization in this production is one of his best. He commanded attention whenever on stage and his diction and mannerisms were excellent.'[9] John Reed emerged from the chorus to play the comedy role of Papillon (a pedlar who later becomes the Court Dressmaker), and received enormous praise, as did Eric Thornton.

The *Northern Despatch* also expressed the hope that the show would be a financial success and although no accounts are available it seems that the box office receipts were at least as good as those for *Goodnight Vienna*. Certainly, by the time *The New Moon* was performed in the spring of 1948, £1,600 had been donated to local charities. The number of Vice-

Presidents and Patrons, particularly Patrons, was rising rapidly: *Katinka* had attracted 36 Vice-Presidents and 59 Patrons, *The Duchess of Dantzic* had 55 Vice-Presidents and 67 Patrons, but for *The New Moon* there were 70 Vice-Presidents and 121 Patrons and naturally this showed in the charitable donations. After *Katinka* just over £1,000 had been given – after the end of *The New Moon* eighteen months later this amount had more than doubled.

There were apparently special reasons why Sigmund Romberg's romantic piece was chosen as the spring 1948 show and an Extraordinary Meeting was held on 12 December 1947 to tell the members why. Unfortunately the minutes of this meeting do not share the reasons with us! Certainly a lot more men would be needed to join the Society for such a show; there was still a superabundance of ladies. Indeed there was discussion about methods of reducing the number of ladies. 'Several suggestions were made,' said the minutes of the meeting – fortunately culling was not one of them!

There had been a personality clash between Fred Thompson and Jim Fraser Murray during the production of *The Duchess of Dantzic* but this was not the reason why Fred was not about to produce *The New Moon* – it was because he had become Councillor Fred Thompson, Independent Member for Pierremont Ward, in 1947, and would now have civic duties to perform. He was cajoled into stage-managing the show instead but later resigned from this job, for reasons unknown. Arthur Ridley, a retired inspector from Martin's Bank, who hailed from Chester-le-Street and who had produced shows in that area (as well as the Darlington society's last pre-war production), was booked to produce it. He also agreed to stage-manage it, with the help of Tom Bourn and Neville Dodd, and charged £70 plus expenses, a relatively small amount compared with the hire price of the costumes which was nearly £200 (though admittedly this was for 252 costumes). There were so many ladies in the cast that the producer had indicated

Fred Thompson

that all of them could not be on stage for all of the scenes; they had to be divided into groups so as to fit them all in – not easy for the producer. So many ladies made a lot of work for the wardrobe-mistress (Mrs Alan Hanson) and there had to be a dresser in each dressing-room.

Whatever the reasons for choosing to perform *The New Moon* there is no doubt that the choice paid off. Two weeks before opening night Jim Willans told the Committee that the receipts from ticket sales already exceeded the final figure for the last show and it was therefore decided to do a matinée. The manager of Doggarts shop, where Kenneth Richardson worked, was prevailed upon to release him for this.

It was pleasing that so many extra people were able to see this show as it proved to be the best yet for some of the cast as well as the public, despite the grumble from the critic of the *Darlington & Stockton Times* who described the piece as '. . . a composition whose libretto was rather indifferent and whose music, though popular, had a quality that was decidedly commercial . . . Artificial scripts have resulted in quite a number of composers of musical comedies failing to create works of permanent value. This is even more obvious when one compares the form of entertainment with the "musicals" of Strauss, Lehár, Kalman and Monckton whose librettos usually contained substance superior to those of their "successors". However, within the limits of the music and script, the show was a success.'[10] (Oddly enough, however, in terms of musicals performed these days, Romberg seems to have stood the test of time better than Monckton and, in particular, Kalman.) Having said this the critic paid tribute to the performers, praising their fine singing and polished acting. The *Northern Echo* pronounced it 'well up to the standard of many professional companies'[11] while the *Northern Despatch* thought that the acting by all the principals was on an even higher level than in the previous shows, that the singing was rich in tone and quality, and that the impression was given of first-rate teamwork – 'in every way a distinguished piece of work'.[12]

These reviews were most pleasing in view of some of the difficulties experienced by the Society with this particular show. The scenery, for instance, had not arrived until the day before opening night, and, according to Eileen Young, was then set the wrong way round. Consequently it was around 8 p.m. when the final dress rehearsal began and around 4 a.m. when it finished. Then, after a day working in their normal jobs, the cast had to return and perform at night. Richard Sampson, who stage-managed for the Society for many years, confirms that this sort of thing used to happen, and in doing so highlights the particular problems of the days when the Society produced shows for one week only. The Society had its own stage-crew and, since time used to be so short, they would start work at around 10 p.m. on the Saturday evening. They would help to 'get out' the previous week's show before unloading the sets for their own production and installing all the extra lighting gear which was necessary – the theatre, at that time, had the bare minimum of equipment. They usually had to labour through the night if the show was a complicated one, not being helped by the customary failure of scenic contractors to supply proper plans or to mark out all the 'flats'.* Lighting rehearsal was usually scheduled to start at 10 a.m. on Sunday, but was often delayed until after lunch, when the dress rehearsal was due to start. Lighting tended to be a very cursory affair, therefore, to be sorted out as they went along. The dress rehearsal usually took at least six hours, so it was not surprising that by late Sunday evening the stage crew was completely exhausted.

At one particular dress rehearsal things had become particularly fraught by this stage. When the time came to drop the last curtain, which, at that time, was operated from the fly gallery, the Stage Manager giving warning and curtain cues by means of lights, it was only natural that the flymen were rather slow to respond. The orchestra thus had to hold on to their final chord much too long for the Musical Director's liking, so he protested loudly to the Stage Manager that he should get the thing down as his trumpeter could not hold onto his top E-flat indefinitely. The exasperated Stage Manager suggested that the trumpeter should be inflated from the other end to sustain his note. The curtain came down right on cue on the Monday night . . .

The New Moon is the show which stands out in Nancy Bertram's memory as being her favourite. Nancy had rejoined the Society in 1945, almost, it might be said, on the rebound. A member of the choir at Bondgate Chapel, and trained in singing by Robert Farrage, she used to go to Leeds, to Madame Styles Allen, for a lesson each week. She wanted to go to London for further training but was prevented when her mother became ill. As the next-best thing, Robert Farrage encouraged her to join the newly-formed Operatic & Choral Society, purely for enjoyment and as an outlet for her singing. Her elder sister, Doris Leslie (who used a family name instead of her real surname to avoid confusion), joined in 1948 and both sisters played leads, as well as playing lesser roles and being in the chorus.† *The New Moon* was Nancy's favourite show despite the uncomfortable memory of being required to sing *Lover Come Back* melodiously and look beautiful while sitting, supposedly on board ship, on a highly

* A flat is a large section of scenery mounted on a frame.
† Doris Leslie died in 1981.

uncomfortable barrel and of being unable to supply to her 'father' his lines when he had forgotten them. Fortunately he was endowed with a gift for improvisation! (Eileen Young did not have much *chance* for improvisation when the gates of the 'stockade' were supposed to open to allow her and the rest of the chorus to rush in. When the gates opened the remainder of the potential crowd had not made it in time and she was the only one there – a teeming crowd of one does not look convincing no matter how accomplished the actor!)

At the Annual General Meeting on 13 May 1948 the Chairman and the Secretary congratulated the members of the Society on their year's work and commented on the fact that bookings reached a record level for *The New Moon*. The Society's name had indeed got around: a party from an operatic society in Wales had come to see *The Duchess of Dantzic*. The Society's membership now numbered a healthy 100 and it was announced to them that the next show would be *Gipsy Love*. This, however, was not to be, because a number of members did not wish to perform it and wrote a letter to the Committee to say so, also asking that the whole Society should be called together to discuss the matter. 'Very long discussion' ensued and the Committee finally called an Extraordinary Meeting of the Society, at which *Gipsy Love* was vetoed by a large majority and was supplanted by Friml and Harburg's *Rose Marie*, which promptly went into rehearsal. It had already been decided that potential new members would have to audition in front of the whole Committee, but suddenly there appeared five new *male* applicants, just before the summer holiday season – and *Rose Marie* was a show needing a full force of Royal Canadian Mounted Police! Desperate times call for desperate measures: it was agreed at the meeting of 28 June that these five could be accepted without the whole Committee vetting them, lest they slip through the net.

Rose Marie, produced, like *The New Moon*, by Arthur Ridley, ran from 22 to 27 November under the company's changed name – now simply 'Darlington Operatic Society'. The change had not involved 'full discussion'; it had simply passed through as a one-line minute, an almost imperceptible *fait accompli*.

This time the red-haired Doris Leslie played the leading role and Nancy Bertram was in the chorus. The leading man was George Goodyear, a leading tenor in Saint Mary's Church choir and choirmaster of Heighington Parish Church choir, who had joined the Society in 1946. He was tall, dark and handsome and had a beautiful voice. He was very popular with the public and sang many leading roles over the next sixteen years, whenever his business commitments permitted. His was another untimely death, in 1979, when only middle-aged.

Vivienne Farrage, daughter of Robert and Isabel Farrage, emerged from the dancers to play Wanda, the half-caste squaw. Her elder sister, Marjorie, had been in the pre-war society and, in 1939, at the age of twenty, had won the title of 'Miss Britain' in the the *Daily Sketch* and the *Chicago Tribune*'s search for Britain's best under-25 voice. She made head-line news in the *Chicago Tribune* when she 'thrilled a throng of 100,000 people at Soldier's Field, Chicago, with her beautiful voice' and received 'thunderous applause'.[13] Her accompaniment was provided by a symphony orchestra directed by Henry Weber. She made a broadcast on American nationwide radio and appeared as guest star at a concert at Grant Park, Chicago. It was a far cry from her work as a clerk at Barclays Bank: she referred to herself in an interview as 'a Cinderella in Chicago'. This was only the beginning for Marjorie for she became a very successful opera singer, taking the stage-name Ingrid Hageman, and appearing at Glyndebourne and other top venues in this country and abroad. (Robert and Isabel Farrage's great-niece, Clare Rutter, is also an opera-singer and actress.)

Kenneth Richardson appeared as a second lead in *Rose Marie* and John Reed and Joy Beadell took on the comedy roles of Hard Boiled Herman and Lady Jane. Bernard Sanderson appears in the list of chorus members and is still working hard with the Society today. He married Greta Murray – they celebrated their fortieth wedding anniversary in 1992 – and they produced a family of three sons – Stephen, Peter and Nicholas – all of whom have given service to the Society. (Nicholas works backstage at the theatre and had constantly and resolutely refused to appear on stage until forced to do so when members of the stage staff were required to appear in costume during a visit by no less a body than the Royal Shakespeare Company in 1993!)

Rose Marie was described by the press as being 'an outstanding success'.[14] It was a very well-known show, having run for 850 performances in the West End from 1925 onwards, and having been performed there again in 1942. The *Darlington & Stockton Times* had feared that '. . . unless it was staged in the "approved manner" the audience who, for the most part, had already full appreciation of its high qualities, would possibly react adversely to the performances.' The reviewer went on, however, to say that '. . . such a situation did not arise. On the contrary the production was an outstanding success and added greatly to the laurels already won by this society, which can count itself fortunate in the talent it possesses.'[15]

Doris Leslie, Vivienne Farrage, and George Goodyear received particular praise and John Reed and Joy Beadell were hailed by the *Darlington & Stockton Times* as a comedy team which '. . . ranks with the best seen in any amateur – or perhaps professional – performance.' 'John

Reed,' said the *Northern Despatch*, 'seems to excel in comedy parts.'[16] There, indeed, was a prophet!

(This particular part of the show's success may have cleared up a little dissatisfaction in the Society at Joy Beadell's having been allowed to audition for the part she played. It was felt by some that, as Dancing Mistress, she had had a head-start on any other contenders. This provoked the ruling which still stands: that members can and should apply for more than one part and, in the event of there being no suitable applicant for a particular part, that part is thrown open to all members of the Society.)

The large chorus and the dancers were also complimented on their management of the complicated staging. The press was fortunately not present on the evening on which the major hiccup occurred. There was a scene where the chorus men became 'artillerymen', and loaded and fired three guns on the stage. They had been very well drilled, and all went well until one evening when somebody walking behind the set tripped over a tangle of wires and noticed that he had pulled out a number of plugs from a plugboard, so he dutifully bent down and plugged them in again. Came the great moment and the 'battery sergeant' ordered, 'Number One gun fire!' and the maroon* went off inside Number Two gun. Undaunted, he ordered, 'Number Two gun fire!' and off went Number Three gun, which really brought the house down. It was fairly disconcerting for the cast, too, as Cecil Grieveson, who was in the chorus, will testify!

There were letters of appreciation from two members of the public, one of whom was interested in joining the Society as a non-acting member. Tom C. Gilchrist was his name and he had been a manager with the National Provincial Bank. On his retirement in 1949 he returned to Darlington to live – to the town, in fact, where he had been a boarder at the Queen Elizabeth Grammar School (now the Sixth-Form College) over fifty years earlier. He was to serve the Society in an administrative capacity with great efficiency. He had had plenty of practice, having been Hon. Treasurer and Business Manager of both Stockton Stage Society and Hexham Amateur Stage Society. Having become Hon. Treasurer of Darlington Operatic Society in 1951, he remained so until 1959. He moved to Surrey in 1963 but retained the distinction of being an Honorary Vice-President – a special honour conferred upon him in 1962 – until his death in August 1967.

Despite the success of *Rose Marie*, cracks were beginning to show on the hitherto smooth patina of the Society in the shape of niggling little matters.

---

* A maroon is an explosive flare.

Perhaps in a way the Society was a victim of its own success, as little dissatisfactions began to appear: some members felt that the tone of the Society was lowering and that some people were not attending rehearsals as regularly as they should. Others wanted auditions to be held by an independent board and also felt that members should re-audition from time to time (or possibly from show to show – this is not clear from the minutes). There had been a grumble or two about honoraria, too, but this was soon scotched by a decision to pay the same honoraria but to call them professional fees.

The theatre rental had become something of a problem. Since the tax payable on the shows had been reduced, the theatre was now taking a higher rent, in accordance with the agreement that its percentage be taken from a net receipts figure. It was resolved, therefore, to try to have a new contract drawn up; the shows, because they had to look as professional as possible in order to maintain the current high standard, were costing such a large amount to put on that the Society would be dependent on the return of the Entertainment Tax to give charitable donations. Happily, agreement was reached quite amicably over this. It was agreed by the theatre that the rental should be the customary £200 guarantee plus 35% instead of 40% of all net profit over £600. For its part, the Society agreed to let the theatre manager have a small block of seats for each show for his regular patrons.

This having been satisfactorily resolved, the Society proceeded with rehearsals for quite an ambitious production – *The Lisbon Story* by Davies and Purcell – in November 1949. This would be *The Lisbon Story*'s first presentation in the North-East, having been newly released for amateurs, and an outstanding production was required since there was to be no spring show. (There is no indication in the minutes why this should be but expense seems to be the most likely reason.) Fred Thompson was again to be the producer at a fee of £80 and naturally he was very keen indeed that it should be a huge success. As he pointed out at the Annual General Meeting on 19 May, the Society was financially stable and was showing all-round improvement, and he and the Committee wanted to keep things that way. To this end an addition was made to the Society's rule book: that only the vote of two-thirds of the full Committee could elect a musical director, a dancing mistress and a producer, and choose a show. At the same time one word was added to what is now Rule 15 so that it read: 'The Committee, by a majority of two-thirds, may remove from the list of members the name of any *unsatisfactory** member without assigning any reason for their decision.'

---

* My italics.

The following month there came the auditions meeting. Such was the anxiety of the Committee to get the casting right that it took four hours to allocate five parts – those of the principal ladies. Nancy Bertram was given the leading role of Gay, with her sister Doris as her secretary Panache, Vivienne Farrage as Lisette (the *ingénue*), Doreen Robinson as Carmelita, and Eileen Young as Lola (the maid). It was decided to leave the male castings until two nights later. Two nights later, after two and a half hours, only two minor parts were cast. A week later they tried again. After nearly two hours and further discussion the cast list was almost complete but they were not out of the wood yet. George Goodyear had auditioned for the part of David, one of the two leading male roles, but did not get it, instead being offered a lesser role, and Kenneth Richardson was given David. Some unrest must have ensued. The committee meeting of 7 July shows a reversal in the casting of the two roles, which was accepted by Kenneth Richardson but not, apparently, by George Goodyear, for a committee minute of a week later shows him '. . . not suitably disposed to take the part of David.' The summer break came and went with no David. Then, at the meeting of 9 September, the Chairman reported the audition of a young man called Philip Greenwood to join the Society. He made a very favourable impression and was invited to audition for David four days later. He did so and was accepted – in more ways than one, for he eventually married Nancy Bertram. A collective sigh of relief must surely have gone through the Committee that the part was cast, at least until Jim Willans and Alan Hanson had to withdraw from the show and the first person who was approached to sing the famous solo *Pedro the Fisherman* was unable to do so. All was eventually settled satisfactorily, however. Kenneth Richardson was moved yet again – this time into the role of Stephen Gorelle – and David Ormerod was offered Jim Willans's part as Sargon. Possibly the Committee was beginning to feel insecure because it was agreed by a majority of six to one that there should be understudies for the parts of Gay, Von Schreiner and Panache – and understudies were, and are, a rare luxury! The vexed question of a matinée was next introduced in mid-October but by this time the Committee probably felt that it ought not to tempt providence and the idea was abandoned, particularly as the tickets for the evening performances were not going especially well and opening night was close at hand: indeed, it had been agreed to put large adverts in the newspapers. There were difficulties over the supply of costumes for Gay – a further headache for the Committee, which was already engaged in deliberations over whether to present a show in spring 1950 and if so, what it should be.

All in all it was an anxious time for everyone concerned and amidst all the difficulties the Society must have looked forward to the show with considerable trepidation. Nancy Bertram certainly did (though she was somewhat comforted by the fact that the costume problem had been resolved and that she had some beautiful gowns to wear) because of the ultimate fate of her character. The plot concerns Gay, a star of the theatre but working for the French Underground Movement, and Gay is shot dead on stage! Nancy was never quite able to convince herself that the gun would *really* only fire blanks and, moreover, it is not easy to fall gracefully through the curtains when 'shot'. Nevertheless Nancy's were surely not the only fingers to be crossed for a show so fraught with difficulties.

Everyone awaited the press reports. The *Northern Echo* said 'To think of giving one of the first amateur performances of a West End success is ambitious. To put on that show if it is a big one is in some measure brave. To make it succeed is an achievement of which amateurs can be proud. Yet this is what Darlington Operatic Society is doing with *The Lisbon Story* at the New Hippodrome this week.'[17] The review went on to praise '. . . spectacular choral and dancing features, charming singing of gay and light music and some moments of striking drama . . . Joy Beadell gives a polished lustre to the dancing and [these things] have combined to make this the biggest show the company has attempted and they have brought off a grand feat of colour and gaiety.' The *Northern Despatch* also regarded it as 'memorable'.[18] The *Darlington & Stockton Times* was more critical, guessing accurately that there was anxiety both in the wings and in the orchestra pit, and remarked that the show had both triumphs and weaknesses, the men receiving more praise in the review than the ladies. (At one point, Cecil Grieveson remembers, there was a horrible hiatus when George Llewellyn, who played Gonzales the fruit seller, missed his cue and the small chorus of men on stage were left high and dry when the orchestra ran out of music. However, Doreen Robinson – as Carmelita – bravely struck up a note, the band followed and everything caught up!) Still, since *The Lisbon Story* had only enjoyed 'modest success'[19] in its London debut in 1943 the Society cannot have been too downhearted with the reviews. Box office receipts were down by £100, though – it was true then, as now, that potential audiences are suspicious of shows which are unfamiliar – and the Committee, though generally pleased with the first five years since the Society's revival, knew that its resources would have to be very carefully managed so as to achieve maximum box office receipts with minimum expenditure. The process was to be more complicated than any juggling act, and many hard lessons would be learned!

Chapter 3

1950–1954

1949 had closed with discussion on future shows and 1950 opened with further discussion. The Committee would have to think very carefully when making its selections.

We do not know what was said about *The Lisbon Story* at the Annual General Meeting in spring 1950 as the full minutes have disappeared, but the accounts show only £200 profit compared with £342 for *Rose Marie*. It seems that the Committee had suspected that this might be the case – the royalties, for instance, were double those of *Rose Marie* – for it had seemed a good idea, in the discussions in late 1949, that the spring show for 1950 should be Sigmund Romberg's *The Desert Song*, a tried and tested favourite, first performed professionally in 1927. Who, then, was to produce it? By early December there had been five contenders and five prices: Miss M. Griffiths (sixty guineas plus rail fares from London plus board and lodging), Mr and Mrs Handel (one hundred and ten guineas plus rail fares from London), Mr B. Cameron (£126 plus rail fares from Stoke), Fred Thompson (£80), and a Mr Cullam (£50).

The competition was speedily reduced to the last two and Fred Thompson left the room while voting took place. Voting still left the matter undecided, which did not please Fred, who promptly distanced himself from the proceedings by withdrawing his application. This caused some consternation among certain of the Committee – not only was he the second line of defence if Mr Cullam proved unsuitable but he had produced the earlier shows very successfully. Five days later the Committee met again. It was proposed and seconded that the minute accepting Fred Thompson's withdrawal be rescinded and that he be asked to reconsider his decision. This proposal being carried he offered his services as producer for *The Desert Song*. This was proposed and seconded. Six of the nine members present voted in favour. Eight votes were necessary. There was 'lengthy discussion'. Finally the dissenters agreed to a majority decision being carried. Fred Thompson was back in the saddle – booted and spurred! His Musical Director would be Robert Farrage and his Choreographer Joy Beadell.

At this point the five members of a ticket-booking sub-committee, having co-opted Tom Gilchrist, evolved a new system of ticket-booking.

This, even when read out loud with one's finger following each word, still proves incomprehensible and one wonders how they ever managed to operate it effectively! They did, however, introduce a proper ticket order form which was a major advance. They were not short on ambition either – they aimed to have a sell-out on advance bookings alone!

Twenty days before the opening of *The Desert Song* the final two parts were cast. They were cutting it rather fine, but they had been hard-pressed to find a suitable General Birabeau and a Sid El Kar. Mark Kay, however, had been pressed into the 'baddie' role again (he had played the evil Karl von Schreiner in *The Lisbon Story*), and Ken Smith (Chief Cashier at the Midland Bank, Darlington Choral Society member, and tenor singer with the All Squares Octet) had been found and pressed into service as Sid El Kar. Casting had not been the only problem. Another very delicate matter had arisen: one of the lady members of the chorus had had all her teeth removed. Consequently it was the lot of the unfortunate Chairman, Neville Dodd, to speak to her and suggest that she should drop out of the show – clearly a task requiring the utmost diplomacy!

The Desert Song, however, certainly had teeth enough to make a deep impression on the newspaper critics; indeed the *Darlington & Stockton Times* described it as a 'triumph'[1] after initial misgivings that this production might be received with diffidence by the public since it had already been presented on stage professionally twice in the town (and there was a film version).

The Desert Song 1950
Eileen Young, John Reed.

George Goodyear's Red Shadow and Doris Leslie's Margot received rave reviews and John Reed and Eileen Young in the two comedy roles of Benny and Susan were lavishly praised. Since the latter pair's especially-mentioned duet, *It*, had appeared before the interval no one could accuse the reviewer of having his or her judgement sweetened by the application

The Desert Song 1950. *Centre front*: Greta Murray. Immediately behind is Doris Leslie with Nancy on Doris's left. *See page ix for full list.*

of alcohol, even though the theatre had received a liquor licence at last (in February 1950).

A dancer named Vera Simpson who played Azuri also came in for a lot of praise. She had been in the ranks of the dancers for the previous four shows and it is a shame that this brilliant solo performance was her swan-song – her name does not appear in any more cast lists.

The show for autumn 1950 was problematical and storm clouds were already on the horizon for the spring 1951 show, had the Committee but known it. Still – 'sufficient unto the day is the evil thereof'.

Six shows had been considered for autumn 1950 and *Wild Violets*, by Robert Stolz and Desmond Carter, decided upon. Curiously, Fred Thompson opted out, proposing that Arthur Ridley be asked to produce it and this proposal was carried unanimously. After considerable difficulty and much effort by Norman Thompson, the Secretary, the performing rights for *Wild Violets* were secured and the fees for performing the show would be 12½% of the total receipts excluding Entertainment Tax.

From the minutes of the committee meeting on 4 June, the reason emerges for Fred Thompson's earlier proposal that Mr Ridley be asked to produce *Wild Violets*. Fred had other fish to fry. 1951 would be

Festival of Britain year and he had been asked to produce a special show in the spring of that year – to open on 9 April. Hence the storm clouds, for the Operatic Society's show's opening date had been 'pencilled in' as 23 April and the intention for the Festival of Britain show was that it would be a combined effort, the cast being chosen from the five societies in the district. Jim Willans was cross. No prior reference had been made to the Society about this piece of timing. Tom Bourn was not pleased either. He pointed out that as approximately twelve people from each society would be required, the remaining members would be unfairly treated: they would not take part in a show, in some instances for as long as two years, if the usual show were cancelled. The general feeling was that the production of a combined effort at the time stated would be detrimental to all the societies in general, and to Darlington Operatic Society in particular, and that none of the societies who were to be involved had had any say in the matter. Mr Hinge, of the New Hippodrome, who had allowed the Town Effort Committee's booking to go through without a word, was not too popular either – and he was to be told so!

It was decided that a small representative committee – the Chairman, the Secretary and Jim Willans – should meet the Town Effort Committee 'to discuss the matter fully' (ominous phrase!) and try to have the timing altered. They lost. The Society's proposed spring 1951 show was cancelled. Fred Thompson only ever produced one more show for the Society though he remained on the Committee until 1959.

In the mean time the current show must go on. The minutes of some of the meetings around this time are missing which leaves an aggravating gap, but there was a change of Stage Manager for *Wild Violets*. Jim Fraser Murray took on the task assisted by a newcomer, Richard Sampson, who was to become a very loyal and hardworking member of the Society, doing stage management or properties for many years – he did not profess to be an actor. He had come to the town to work for a company at Aycliffe and had sought out the Society since this sort of thing was an interest of his. It was he, incidentally, who constructed the Society's first 'fog machine'. This consisted of a large drum containing boiling water, with a lowering device in which was placed a block of solid carbon dioxide – 'dry ice'. The block would be lowered slowly into the water, releasing mist, and a vacuum-cleaner motor blew it out onto the stage to give 'atmosphere'. The night on which it went wrong they certainly got atmosphere! The lowering device failed and the whole block of dry ice fell into the water, releasing such vast quantities of mist that it became a pea-souper fog, enveloping both orchestra and cast and causing the loading bay doors (leading into the back lane behind the theatre) to have to be opened to disperse it!

Apart from sundry chunterings from Norman Thompson about the enormous difficulty in obtaining props (a kitchen plate-rack and a refrigerator were his particular bugbears!) *Wild Violets* appeared to be progressing well. Nancy Bertram and George Goodyear were playing the leading roles, Robert (Bob) White and Vera Dickinson were the secondary leads and there were a number of satisfying smaller roles being taken by Kenneth Richardson, Teresa Howell, Ken Smith, Vivienne Farrage, Greta Murray, Mary Johnson and Alan Hanson; George Cummings, Fred Eddy and Elsie Chapman took the minor parts. In addition, Shirley Dodd appeared in her first show playing the cameo role of the young Greta opposite Alwyn Robinson, as well as being in the chorus.

There were opening night problems (the *Darlington & Stockton Times* called it a '. . . first night triumph of improvisation over misfortune.'[2]) For instance, not all of the costumes had arrived at the theatre even when the show began. The public did not appear to notice any shortcomings although the Committee was disgruntled about the quality of the scenery and some of the props. (Vera Dickinson recalled playing a romantic scene on a settee with Bob White when the settee suddenly fell off its castors.)* The critics all enjoyed it, though, and agreed that in this show Vera Dickinson should be singled out for special praise for her portrayal of Augusta, the innkeeper's wife. (The plate-throwing scene had considerably impressed the *Darlington & Stockton Times* critic – though Vera did not, in fact, manage to smash *all* the plates purchased. One crateful remained intact and the Committee thriftily sold it to Bondgate Methodist Church.) Alan Hanson, as the Grandfather, may not have been quite so delighted when one reviewer described him as being 'deliciously crustacean'[3] – it makes him sound like dressed crab!

For all that, the show played to good houses and the box office receipts were almost the same as for *The Desert Song*, but the scenery and especially the costumes had cost considerably more, leaving little profit. Nevertheless the Society had managed to distribute £3,400 among local charities between 1945 and February 1951.

Of course, there was no Society show in spring 1951 but, out of the cast of 65 which performed Noël Coward's *Bitter Sweet* for the opening of Darlington's Festival of Britain celebrations, 26 players were from Darlington Operatic Society. Fred Thompson was, of course, directing it,

* It is sad to have to report that Vera Dickinson died suddenly in March 1995 when this book was in the process of publication.

Wild Violets 1950. *Left to right*: Kenneth Richardson,
George Goodyear, Ken Smith, Vera Dickinson.

Robert Farrage was Musical Director, Joy Beadell was Dancing Mistress
and played the part of Manon, her husband John Bishop was Stage
Manager, and Edith Kershaw was one of the accompanists. Thus the
Society was well represented, though there was a small faction which did
not approve and would have no part of it, principally because of the way
in which it had been arranged.

Much praise was accorded by the press to Eunice Taylor, who played
the lead. She was a concert performer rather than an actress but she
obviously achieved a highly successful transition to stage work. Other
individual performers received praise too (the *Green Carnation* number had
gone down particularly well) but the feeling gained from the reviews is
that although each individual performed well the whole thing did not
quite gel as a piece of teamwork. The *Darlington & Stockton Times* described
it as 'above the average'[4] – praise, but restrained praise.

The Darlington Operatic Society Committee, meanwhile, was getting
down to organizing a show for autumn 1951. Rudolf Friml's *The Vagabond
King* had been chosen – perhaps it would have more impact this time than
it had had twenty years previously – and Arthur Ridley was to produce
again. To tide them over the lack of a spring show they kept the pot
boiling by circulating a letter to the Vice-Presidents, Patrons and members
to the effect that although there was to be no spring show their continued
support would be appreciated. This move was decided upon at the

committee meeting in January 1951 and then all is silence. No more minutes exist until the Annual General Meeting on 19 April.

At this meeting there were stirrings of discontent among some members – they felt that *The Vagabond King* was a 'dull' show and thought that something lighter would be better. *Sunny*, by Hammerstein and Kern, was suggested as an alternative. The Committee would have none of this. The Chairman ominously quoted Rule 16: 'The selection of Operas . . . shall be in the hands of the Committee.' Jim Willans pointed out 'the excellencies of *The Vagabond King*' and the Secretary enumerated the various commitments already incurred for its production. *The Vagabond King* it would be. (Jim Fraser Murray was extremely disappointed not to be voted back onto the Committee at this meeting but his disappointment was not to last long – Tom Bourn resigned a week later and Jim was co-opted to replace him.)

The Vagabond King did not have an easy passage. Once more there were casting difficulties among the men – for the parts of Tristan and Noël. It looks as though each of the two candidates wanted to play the part *not* allotted to him but after personal visits to the parties concerned by the Chairman and Vice-Chairman they agreed to do as they were asked – four weeks before opening night.

This time Nancy Bertram and Doris Leslie would both have principal parts: Katherine de Vaucelles and Huguette du Hamel respectively.

This turned out to be Nancy's most taxing show. Two weeks before the opening night Doris lost her voice and was unable to sing a note. Confident that Doris's voice would return in time her sister said that *she* could always sing the role of Huguette through a microphone off stage and Doris could mime, since the two characters were never on the stage together. Nancy admits that when she said this she never thought for a moment that that was exactly what she would have to do in the end!

It was undoubtedly Nancy's finest hour! The sisters' voices were sufficiently alike to make the effect convincing and Doris mimed so well that, according to the *Darlington & Stockton Times*, '. . . the first night's audience had fiercely contested arguments in whispers in various parts of the house as to who was singing.'[5]

Doris had other problems, too. It was her turn to be 'killed' in full view of the audience, The 'dying' part was not a problem – the problem was that the four characters who bore her body from the stage were an *ad hoc* bunch recruited from the non-acting portion of the Committee, owing to the shortage of men. However it is to her eternal credit that she never flinched when they almost dropped her, and these non-thespians – Neville Dodd, Jim Fraser Murray, Jim Willans and Frank Walker – also had their own moment of glory. These hitches received more press coverage than

The Vagabond King 1951. *Left to right*: Barbara Hopps, George Goodyear, Alan Hanson, Doris Leslie, Philip Greenwood, Kenneth Richardson.

did the virtues or otherwise of the show itself. Nevertheless it seems to have made a generally good impression. It is as well that the press were not present on a night later in the week when the dashing hero leapt upon the table to give the stirring speech to the 'rabble' which leads into the '. . . *and to hell with Burgundy!*' number. Unfortunately the 'rabble' actually on stage consisted solely of the diminutive Eileen Young. 'Where *is* everybody?' hissed the hero. 'I'll go and get them!' announced Eileen, in ringing tones. She knew very well where they would be; they were in the backstage bar upstairs and had missed their cue. No one knows how the hero filled in the time-lapse, alone on the stage!

The Committee must have hoped fervently for an easier passage for the next show. It had to be one with more box office appeal than *The Vagabond King*, which, had it not been for the reclaimable Entertainment Tax, would have lost a very great deal of money. As was customary the Society had claimed exemption on the grounds of giving 20% of the gross takings to charity, and thus had to donate £393 of of its back-up funds to meet with this requirement – the misgivings of those dissenting members who had prophesied that the show itself would be of lesser interest to the general public had proved to be justified. Now the choices before the Committee were *Floradora*, *The Student Prince*, *The Girl Friend*, *The Mikado* and *The Gondoliers*. Fred Thompson had once produced *Floradora* and did not consider it suitable. Neville Dodd agreed with him. When the vote was taken so did everyone else. *The Gondoliers* was out because another society (not named but probably Bondgate Gilbert & Sullivan Society) was about to produce it. Opinions were divided over the other three. *The Student Prince* was difficult because of the shortage of men in the Society and *The Mikado* was difficult because Bondgate produced Gilbert & Sullivan shows exclusively. No scores or libretti were available for *The Girl Friend* and there was very little chorus work. So they voted. The result was three votes for *The Girl Friend*, four for *The Student Prince*, and six for *The Mikado*. None of these measured up to the requisite number of votes required by the rules so Frank Murray (one of Greta's two brothers) proposed that *The Student Prince* by Sigmund Romberg be given in the spring and *The Mikado* in the autumn and this was agreed.

Peter Miller was employed to produce *The Student Prince*. He had a 100 per cent theatrical background and lived and breathed theatre, having begun his career when a small child in pantomime, continuing as a dancer when he was a little older, going on to spend five years in repertory touring in musical comedy, and then being in West End shows and films. He was a colourful character, as many members of Darlington Operatic Society can testify, and was an advocate of the application of alcohol as a lubricant both to the vocal cords and the mind's ingenuity. Indeed, Bill Jones, who joined the Society in 1952 and was, until 1992 when he left to live in South Africa, one of the Society's most valuable assets, remembers being sent out to buy jugs of beer for Peter Miller (during preparation for a later show) even after the Committee had banned alcohol at rehearsals. H. R. (Sam) Herdman, who joined at the same time as Bill, remembers this lubrication process too.

Apart from one or two minor hiccups (a 'doubtful' tenor and a slightly sluggish dancer, and the resignation of Fred Thompson from the part of Ruder) rehearsals proceeded more or less without incident. Dr Bishop said that he would take on the part of Ruder subject to his not being called upon to sing, but in the event Fred Eddy, who was in the chorus, took on the role. The problem of obtaining furniture for the stage, notably a gilt suite, was solved by borrowing it from Fred Robinsons, a local firm.

Jim Willans reported at the committee meeting of 19 April 1952 that although the first night was thinly booked there were no dress circle seats left for the rest of the week. It was certainly much more popular with the public than *The Vagabond King*, for many of the songs would be familiar to them even though the film version did not appear until 1954. Vice-Presidents and Patrons subscribing numbered 249 as opposed to 204 for *The Vagabond King*, and for some reason a rash of local 'names' gave their support: the Marquess of Zetland; Lord Bolton; Lord and Lady Beveridge;

Sir William Chaytor; Sir Thomas Dugdale, MP; Sir Fergus Graham, MP and Lady Graham; Sir Frederick Milbank; Sir Richard Pease; Colonel Sir Leonard Ropner, MP; and Lt. Colonel M.J.B. Burnett, DSO were involved, as well as the Mayor and Mayoress of Darlington, Councillor and Mrs H. Sansom.

Bookings had picked up by the first night. The *Northern Echo* reported that what had been advertised as a 'spectacular musical'[6] had played to a full house on the first night and that advertising it as such had been fully justified. George Goodyear and Doris Leslie had played the leading roles of the Prince and Kathie (Nancy Bertram was in the chorus this time), and Kenneth Richardson was referred to, along with them, as being 'in excellent voice'. The *Darlington & Stockton Times* also picked out Ken Smith and Barbara Hopps (Captain Tarnitz and Princess Margaret) as being a most successful team of which the Society could be proud. Vera Dickinson (Duchess Anastasia), Philip Greenwood (Detlef), and Sid Plews (as a 'servant's servant') were all highlighted by the *Northern Echo*. The latter two also received special mention in the *Darlington & Stockton Times*, which also remarked that it was a pity there was not a better acting role for Philip Greenwood. It is sad that after appearing in the autumn show (*The Mikado*) he was not in any more productions.

Peter Miller's production was generally well-received, though two of the newspapers particularly mentioned his lighting of the piece. They seemed puzzled by it – the *Northern Despatch* said that it was 'ingenious and varied though sometimes there seemed to be little reason for it'[7] and the *Northern Echo* called it 'irrational but never dull'.[8] The Society itself was happy enough with his production, anyway, because he was asked to produce three more shows later on – not the next one, though, for *The Mikado* was to be produced by Arthur Ridley.

At the Annual General Meeting on 29 May the Chairman, Alan Hanson, told the 70 members present that, although two excellent productions had been given, and despite the optimism over the ticket sales, the financial results had been disappointing. *The Student Prince* had been expensive and had failed to compensate for *The Vagabond King* because it, too, had lost money. Indeed the drop in income was caused by 1,400 fewer seats sold over the last two productions – a fall of over £300. The Society had been obliged to dip into its General Account in order to donate enough to charities to be able to reclaim the Entertainment Tax. Fred Thompson said that more social events should be organized to make money so that the charities might not suffer and, as usual, members were urged to make a real, personal effort to sell tickets – for there were some who never sold a ticket at all. There was talk of introducing a rule that each member should sell a minimum number of tickets to qualify for

The Mikado 1952
Left to right: Ena Hart, Hilda Whitman, Vivienne Farrage.

membership, but this was never implemented. Norman Thompson, the Secretary, endorsed what had been said and reiterated the other old chestnut: the appeal to members to try to induce more men to join the Society. As for *The Mikado*, there had apparently been an undercurrent of unease about the show but Norman Thompson speedily quoshed the objections of the few dissidents by pointing out that there had been excellent attendance at the first rehearsal.

A major problem arose, however, only three weeks before *The Mikado*'s opening night. The actor playing Nanki Poo, the male lead, dropped out of the cast. This was a tremendous setback at such a stage in rehearsals and it was not easy to fill the gap. According to the committee minutes George Goodyear could not accept the part and Philip Greenwood would not.[9] So, for the first time, the Society had to get in someone from outside the membership: Ron Brown of Heddon-on-the-Wall. Did this pay off? Well, the show certainly made a profit. While there had been a loss of over £61 on *The Student Prince*, *The Mikado* showed a profit of just over £320! Part of the reason for this must surely have been that, while people liked Gilbert & Sullivan and were used to the music and the format, in Darlington it had only

Sam Herdman –
Elected President, 1989

been performed at small venues. The fact that it was to be performed in a proper theatre with the attendant advantages of full lighting, space for a full set of scenery, and upholstered seating, must surely have made it a great crowd-puller. Indeed, the *Darlington & Stockton Times* said in its review that by doing this particular Gilbert & Sullivan show the Society was 'half way to success already'.[10] The press loved the show. They used the words 'splendid'[11] and 'exhilarating'.[12] Kenneth Richardson, in particular, was singled out for his performance as Koko – 'a little gem',[13] said the *Northern Despatch*. (Kenneth loved playing this part and it showed – he played it again when the Society repeated the show in 1981.) The *Northern Echo* said, 'His lively performance and clever pantomime are in the Henry Lytton and Martin Green tradition but bear the imprint also of an alert and original personality.'[14] A member of the Society, for whom this was his first show, also received particular praise. He was Sam Herdman and he played the part of Pooh-Bah with enormous relish. The Herdman sneer which accompanied the words 'I was *born* sneering' was most impressive, as those who saw this production (or the one in 1981 when he played the part again) can testify! Sam Herdman has the longest continuous service record with the Committee. He came from Sunderland and, after performing in two more shows, was elected to the Committee in 1954. He is still on it! He has done every job on the Committee except Secretary and Ticket Secretary and has been Chairman five times. He has been

Treasurer since 1977, and was appointed Honorary Vice-President in 1985. By the end of 1994 he had been in seventy productions, on many occasions in a principal role!

Another newcomer to the Society, having arrived in time to be in the chorus for *The Student Prince*, was Hilda Whitman and she had now stepped into the limelight to play the leading role of Yum-Yum. An Austrian by birth, Hilda came to Darlington when her husband's job brought him to Aycliffe and she played several principal parts for the Society before they returned to Austria. In its review of the show, the *Darlington & Stockton Times* described her as an 'outstanding singer' and remarked that '. . . it would do the Society credit to find her a prominent role in another production.'[15] Teresa Howell was also very highly commended for her portrayal of Katisha. (A new little dancer, Irene Skippon, also appeared as a member of the chorus. Little did she know that she would appear in quite a number of shows, let alone return many years later – after doing her dancing training and setting up her own school of dance – to do choreography for the Society, along with her daughter, Joanne Hand, starting with the 1993 production of *Oliver!*)

Though Kenneth, Sam and Hilda had received special praise for their roles the press was full of plaudits for the whole cast. Since two of the reviews came out the day after the first night, it is easy to see that anyone hesitating over buying tickets could certainly be influenced by the reviews in good time. So the Society's first post-war Gilbert & Sullivan show was an enormous success and made a lot of money. It is therefore not surprising that, having already settled on *Magyar Melody* by Posford and Maschwitz to follow *The Mikado*, the Committee would put its collective shirt on another Gilbert & Sullivan show, *The Gondoliers*, for autumn 1953, with Arthur Ridley to produce it since he had had such a signal success with *The Mikado* (and he was £20 cheaper than Peter Miller!)

In the mean time it was necessary to concentrate on *Magyar Melody*, the entire production of which was to be undertaken by Peter Miller (though some misgivings had been expressed that there was to be no extra dancing instruction). The Darlington production had received the blessing of both composer and librettist who wrote a letter of good wishes to the Society. *Magyar Melody* would be denied three strong members of the Society: John Reed and Eric Thornton had now joined the D'Oyly Carte company and Teresa Howell had obtained a scholarship for singing which gave her professional training, also with D'Oyly Carte. They would be missed; though the Society now had 132 members, some had a habit of picking and choosing which shows they would be in, rather than giving constant support. The Committee was clearly rather perturbed about this because it came up in the minutes of the Annual General Meeting on 23 January

1953. The Secretary made particular reference to the fact that the members themselves had voted to do two shows per year rather than one, and that some team spirit was needed even though the Society was doing quite well now. It had managed to invest £150 in National Savings and £300 in War Stock, and had donated £25 to the NODA Building Fund. Nevertheless, there was to be no resting on laurels, and sources of improvement were constantly sought. Tom Gilchrist said that he would like the souvenir programme to be made more interesting to the public – but did not say how. This nettled Frank Walker, the Publicity Manager, whose ruffled feathers had to be smoothed by the rest of the Committee. He said he would always be pleased to have any suggestions that would improve the programme and at the same time be economical. The programme format remained the same! This was all buried in the background, however, along with the fact that one of the stage crew nearly came to blows with Peter Miller at one point and was only restrained by Peter Miller's 'minder'!

Magyar Melody opened on 4 May 1953 and got good reviews. It was a long show – three hours – with a cast of seventy. The *Darlington & Stockton Times*, at least, was more impressed by the cast's performance than by the content of the show itself. Hilda Whitman, the leading lady, met with very high approval and the comedy partnership of Vera Dickinson, Frank Robson and Sam Herdman was seized on by all three local papers as being outstanding. In general, though, the show *looked* beautiful – which counts for quite a lot. There was not much in the way of hiccups, either, except for one night when Kenneth Richardson, as a *maître d'hôtel*, was supposed to bring bread rolls to Hilda Whitman and Vera Dickinson – and no rolls had been provided. Kenneth was not much help. He simply whispered, 'There's no rolls, girls!' and left them to ad-lib their way out of it. However, the costumes, the scenery, and the lighting (Peter Miller's speciality), together with excellent chorus work made it into a visual delight. The effect had cost the Society dear, though: £24 was the total cost to stage each member of the cast and this, added to the fact that the Vice-Presidents and Patrons were forty fewer than for *The Mikado*, was alarming to the Committee. The final loss on *Magyar Melody* was £111 15s. 10d. They had a 'lengthy discussion' and finally agreed that the Society should perform only one major costume show each year, in the autumn; this resolution would be conveyed to the members at the next rehearsal.

It must have been with mixed feelings that the Committee, after the meeting of 15 July, broke for its summer recess. The financial fortunes of the Society seemed to see-saw from show to show.

As the Chairman was to say in his remarks much later, at the Annual General Meeting in March 1954, increasing difficulties were facing amateur operatic societies. There were the rising costs of wardrobe, orchestra, theatre rental, production fees and stage lighting, to say nothing of the competition from the growth in ownership of television sets. There was also the problem of price-rises in general and the increasing popularity of hire-purchase schemes, which, by allowing people to pay for expensive items over long periods of time, encouraged them to buy more. Hence the general public did not have the spare money they had had a few years previously for the support of amateur theatre. This problem created great difficulty for the Committee over the choice of shows. To play expensive modern shows with big box office receipts in the Darlington theatre was out of the question but at the same time the prestige of the Society must be kept up. A lot had been lost on *Magyar Melody* and this had had to be offset from the General Account – a big drain on capital. This was not good, especially at a time when the Society was about to buy a new President's Chair for NODA for its new headquarters. The Society had very close connections with NODA, for Jim Fraser Murray was its Regional Representative. Looking back at those minutes of the pre-recess meeting of July 1953 there is already a clutching-at-straws feeling about the third-from-last item which suggested that prizes should be given to the best three ticket-sellers and their names should be published in the next programme. (Even if prizes were given, no such list of names appears in the *Gondoliers* programme.) The last item on the agenda was the one show to be performed in 1954, and three possibilities were listed: *Chu Chin Chow, Bless the Bride*, and *Annie Get Your Gun*. These must all have fallen by the wayside, however, because the minutes of the second meeting after the break (22 October) refer to the question of who is going to produce *The Dancing Years*, by Ivor Novello, in autumn 1954!

The Gondoliers, meanwhile, was drawing near and Kenneth Richardson (Duke of Plaza Toro), Alice Howes (his Duchess), Hilda Whitman (Casilda), Sam Herdman (Don Alhambra), Ken Fraser (Luiz), George Llewellyn (Marco), Nancy Bertram (Gianetta), Barbara Hopps (Tessa), and Harry May (Guiseppe) were all rehearsing their leading roles – well, most of them were. Harry May did not turn up to Thursday rehearsals and this caused some consternation among the Committee. Four weeks before the show it was decided that it was impossible to continue without a full complement of principals so Bob White, who had played Hans in *Wild Violets*, was asked to play Harry May's part.

After such a loss on the last show, and in view of the fact that there was to be only one show in 1954, everyone was eager for a massive success. From the point of view of the press and the public it was just that, and Barbara Hopps, playing her first leading role, was clearly outstanding. The comedy, as always, was delivered with a sure touch by Kenneth

Richardson and Sam Herdman. The singing and the whole 'feel' of the production were praised, though the *Darlington & Stockton Times* was critical of the diction of many of the players and most disparaging about Kenneth Richardson's wig, which 'made him look at times rather like a decrepit cocker spaniel'![16] (Could it, one wonders, have been that same critic who described Alan Hanson as 'deliciously crustacean' in *Wild Violets*?) The *Northern Despatch*, on the other hand, praised the whole show, making especial reference to the 'clear diction'(!)[17] and the *Northern Echo* remarked on how much the cast seemed to be enjoying themselves.

The Gondoliers 1953. *Left to right*: Bob White, George Llewellyn.

The number of Vice-Presidents and Patrons had risen again to 235 but still the profit was not going to be very large, which was worrying. The Treasurer pointed out, at the next meeting of the Committee, that if Entertainment Tax was to be reclaimed on the understanding that a fixed amount would be given to local charities then the General Account would have to be broached again in order to make up that amount. In the event it was decided to reclaim the tax and pay over to the charities 20% of the gross receipts less tax. Fred Thompson mentioned that it might be possible to get a donation from the Mayor's Fund to enable the Society to produce the next show and it was hoped that a producer could be obtained for not more than 120 guineas for a six-week period including the run of the show. (It seems a lot more money than Peter Miller charged – 90 guineas – for *The Dancing Years*, but he only attended for four weeks.) Fred Thompson and Tom Gilchrist, who agreed with him, were erring a little on the pessimistic side, for despite the financial fluctuations from show to show the General Account still contained over £1,800 and the Society was financially sound. Perhaps, though, they had looked over the minutes from pre-war days and noted how little solid financial back-up the Society had had at that time. Help was at hand, however, from an unexpected quarter. On Sunday 8 November, the eve of the opening of *The Gondoliers*, the Committee was informed that E. J. Hinge had approached the Society to inquire about the views of the Committee as to the possibility of performing, in February 1954, a pantomime – *Cinderella* – which he had written and wanted to produce. A sub-committee consisting of the Secretary, Treasurer and Minute Secretary was appointed to look into the matter. They reported to the Committee on 14 November that Mr Hinge was prepared to let the Society have the theatre on the usual terms, he would give the Society 10% of the net receipts and pay all expenses, and '. . . should anything unforeseen happen so that the Society were unable to carry out their obligations they would be free from all liability.'[18] It was unanimously decided to agree to this and the contract was duly signed, the cast to be viewed by Mr Hinge in the last week of November. It was a good cast, too. Vivienne Farrage was to be Cinderella with Vera Dickinson and Eileen Young as her Ugly Sisters. Young Meg Leeming (daughter of Winifred Leeming of the Boylan-Leeming School of Dancing) was to be Dandini. (She had joined the Society for *Magyar Melody* at the same time as Ken Bodden and Wade Cobban, both of whom brought their own special talents to help the Company along.) Nancy Bertram was to be Prince Charming and Bob White, Buttons; with Sid Plews as the Baron and Sam Herdman as his Baroness. Shirley Dodd would be the Fairy, and Cecil Grieveson and Carl Knight would be the Broker's Men. Robert Farrage would be in charge of the music and Joy Beadell would choreograph as well as being the principal dancer. Bernard Sanderson and Fred Boddy completed the main cast list as Flunkeys and there would be a chorus of eighteen singers (including Doris Leslie), and fourteen dancers (including Irene Skippon). Unfortunately, Sam did not get to appear in the pantomime. He was compelled to withdraw owing to 'unforeseen circumstances'[19] and Fred Thompson took over the part of the Baroness.

The Society's first attempt at a pantomime was a great success – Mr Hinge had undoubtedly delivered the goods as far as material was concerned. Everyone threw themselves into the spirit of sparkle and fun and it all looked and sounded superb. Nancy Bertram says that it was enormous fun to do. She had not been able to resist auditioning for Prince Charming as pantomime was something she had always wanted to do and a principal-boy role was something she had always yearned to try. Besides, other people had said she had the legs for it! She particularly remembers the beautiful costumes: they were all that pantomime costumes should be, and the one that she had for the ball was sumptuous – black velvet with sequins.

The *Darlington & Stockton Times* was moved to remark that '. . . one was led to hope for further ventures of this kind.'[20] Everyone in a named part received individual attention from this critic, whose only adverse comments were that care needed to be taken with the timing of some of the 'business'* and that not enough was seen of the Broker's Men. The large amount of comedy and 'specialities' were much enjoyed. Vera Dickinson and Eileen Young had 'abandoned themselves to the grotesque', which was well-received, though they had had one or two sticky moments such as when Eileen's two false front teeth fell out on stage, reducing them to helpless laughter. Fred Thompson had been a riotous Baroness ('immense', the *Darlington & Stockton Times* called him, little knowing that he had unexpectedly gone to pieces on stage and had had to be pushed around and fed his lines by Eileen and Vera!), and Sid Plews had been a tremendous foil for him – 'a dear little wisp of a man'. The Baroness's skirt bustle, once untied, moved offstage under its own power, which brought the house down. What is more, what better finishing touch was needed than a team of four black and white ponies to draw the spangled and light-bedecked coach?

Anyway, everyone had fun and it brought in £94 5*s*. 6*d*. as the Society's share of the profit, thus providing a bit more money for the kitty. The Mayor's Fund had also supplied £60 to help with the next show so this would take care of the producer's fee. At the April committee meeting (after 'full discussion') it was decided that War Stock should be sold and the money invested in the Darlington Building Society. Once this was done the Committee was happy with the financial condition of the Society and turned its attention to other matters – like the possibility of another pantomime or a revue early in 1955 when there was again to be only one major show during the year. The Secretary was instructed to contact Mr Hinge to look into the matter.

In the mean time, John Denis, a producer from London, had been approached and had said he would be able to produce *The Dancing Years* for £150; that is £126 plus his rail fare and accomodation. It was settled that this show should be performed for the week beginning 22 November – the rehearsals would begin in good time, on 18 February. Auditions for principals (and, incidentally, for the Society's full complement of female members) were held on 17 May. The dancers auditioned on 16 June and though Joy Beadell, as Dancing Mistress for the show, would be there, it was up to the Committee to make the final decisions. They were certainly being very painstaking in every case.

All this having been accomplished the members had their last fling before the summer holidays in the form of one of Lady Starmer's famous

---

* 'Business', in theatrical terms, is movement or action by actors.

Social Evenings. She was always most hospitable to the Society and did everything in the 'grand manner': those who witnessed her when she got rather older, proceeding in regal style along the centre of Coniscliffe Road in her car, waving and greeting people as she passed, have never forgotten it. Lady Starmer made a point of acknowledging everyone, whether they were 'somebody' or 'nobody'. To her, everyone was 'somebody' and it was simply a part of her great charm. The garden parties and social evenings which she put on for the Operatic Society were always something special and the members always organized some entertainment including sketches and songs.

The Committee returned, refreshed, to its duties in September. Everything was on-line for *The Dancing Years*. Scenery was ordered from Scenic Displays Ltd. of Bradford, Homburgs of Leeds were supplying costumes and wigs, and the loan of stage furniture had been organized from members of the Society – though Mr Farrage's offer of a standard lamp was 'subject to confirmation by Mrs Farrage'![21]

John Denis had asked to have Sunday rehearsals but the Committee thought not – it could not expect (the relevant minute said) the members to agree to more than one Sunday rehearsal on top of the Sunday of the dress rehearsal. (Things are very different now. Sunday is the big rehearsal day once the floorwork* begins.)

Things then began to take a downward turn. There were problems looming over the proposed pantomime, written and produced by Mr Hinge, as in 1954, and due to be performed by the Society in February 1955. Reading between the lines it looks as though Mr Hinge wanted to reduce the Society's percentage of the box office receipts from the 10% which had been offered and accepted the last time. The Committee agreed to cancel the pantomime rather than have the percentage cut – and that was that.

When the Committee convened for a special meeting on 29 September 1954 it was to discuss and decide, if possible, on the shows for 1955. Mr Hinge had been obdurate: the resident manager of the theatre, Dudley J. Edmonds, had orally informed the Assistant Secretary that Mr Hinge '. . . did not intend to engage the Society in pantomime that season.' So the Committee turned its attention to the shortlist of shows which had been proposed for 1955. Kalman's *Maritza*, and *Zip Goes A Million* (a show based on a book by G. B. McCutcheon called *Brewster's Millions*) were the favourites, so the Committee decided to perform *Maritza* towards the end

---

* Floorwork is the setting by the Producer of all the placings and action.

The Dancing Years 1954
Kenneth Richardson

The Dancing Years 1954
Kenneth Bodden

of March, if arrangements for the theatre could be made, and *Zip Goes A Million* in November.

Three weeks later the picture had changed. Mr Hinge's resolve had softened and he was willing to discuss a pantomime once more.

A 'gang of four' – Messrs Bell, N. W. Thompson, Gilchrist and F. Thompson – went along to parley. They returned to the Committee with all their requirements met: full company to be employed, 10% of the net receipts to the Society, and Mr Hinge to pay all other expenses – the same contract, in fact, as for the previous year. The pantomime was to be *Aladdin* and a piece advertising it was quickly inserted into the *Dancing Years* programme, along with that for *Zip Goes A Million* (the latter being billed as 'a musical extravagance').

What happened next is a mystery. During the week's run of *The Dancing Years* an emergency committee meeting was held and the one-line account of the proceedings is stark: 'It was decided to rescind the minute' (of the last meeting, around a week previously) 'booking *Zip Goes A Million*'. The minute is not dated, there is no further mention of this show in any minutes and the Society has never performed it.

In the mean time, what of *The Dancing Years*? Well, it had a cast of 64, 74 Vice-Presidents (including an impressive selection of 'names') donated their two guineas, and 209 Patrons donated their one guinea. The show had a London producer who was fresh to the Society, and it had the capable Robert Farrage as Musical Director. The leading roles were in good hands: Hilda Whitman (as Maria) and Kenneth Richardson (as Rudi Kleber). Meg Leeming played the part of Grete and gallantly fought an attack of laryngitis to appear on the first night but she was replaced by Joy Beadell (who, to her eternal credit, learned the whole part in one day) for the Tuesday, Wednesday and Thursday. Meg returned for the final two nights. Ken Bodden (who had proved to be an accomplished character actor) played Prince Charles Metterling. The show got excellent reviews – the *Northern Echo* described it as 'outstanding'.[22] The *Northern Despatch*'s only criticism was that it was too long (nearly four hours) but had given it a huge promotional spread the week before its opening. The *Darlington & Stockton Times* almost went overboard about it. Meg Leeming, said the critic, had, despite her illness, given an almost flawless performance and Kenneth Richardson showed '. . . acting qualities of the highest order, playing with confidence and consummate skill.' Hilda Whitman had added credibility because she was Austrian-born, and she excelled both in her singing and acting, while Ken Bodden's portrayal was '. . . an accomplished characterization. It was a virtually faultless interpretation of a role which could have been spoilt by careless handling.' Of Marjorie Willans (Jim Willans's wife), in one of her rare appearances with the Society, it was said that she '. . . presented an uncommonly good portrait of the matronly Cacille Kurt . . .' – a minor role – and that she was '. . . gifted with a voice of infinite range and clarity of which we would like to have heard more.'[23] The paper then went on to comment on the large number of costume changes and on the excellent chorus and dancing work. John Denis '. . . undoubtedly inspired the players with his enthusiasm and competence . . .' and had worked hard '. . . to secure perfection.' It was a review that amateurs would kill for if it had appeared the morning after a first night instead of on the morning of the last performance! This timing would, however, have made no difference in this case, because, for the first time in the Society's history, all bookable seats had been sold a fortnight before the show opened. Capacity audiences meant that more than 6,000 people saw it – but still it lost money: approximately the amount of the reclaimable Entertainment Tax – £189.

It must have been a heavy-hearted Committee which met on 16 December for its final meeting of 1954. It was generally agreed that the Society could take on big shows similar to *The Dancing Years* only very occasionally, as it had proved that even capacity bookings could not cover the expense. The one bright spot was that there had been such a large number of Vice-Presidents and Patrons that their donations (which went into a separate account) would help to offset the loss and reduce it to between £68 and £70.

Life, however, must go on, despite such disappointments. After all, the Society had now branched out in two ways, having employed two London producers and having ventured into pantomime. The meeting – and the Society's first decade – ended on a forward-looking note, with a provisional cast agreed for the forthcoming pantomime, *Aladdin*, and the decision that the show for November 1955 would be *The Quaker Girl* (music by Lionel Monckton).

Joy Beadell, President 1981–1988

Chapter 4

1955–1959

1955 began quite well: the casting of the parts for *Aladdin* does not appear to have been troublesome. Nancy Bertram was not taking part this time and Meg Leeming was playing Aladdin, with Vivienne Farrage as the principal girl (Princess Baldroubador). Vera Dickinson and Eileen Young were taking comic roles again, as Widow Twankey and Wishee Washee respectively, and Sam Herdman was to appear as the Grand Vizier. Bob White and Carl Knight were to be Hoh Heh and Long Nek, the policemen, and William Clark the evil Abanazar. A male voice choir which had proved a great success in *Cinderella* was to be used again and special ballet scenes were being arranged by Joy Beadell.

The Entertainment Tax refund from *The Dancing Years* had enabled the Society to distribute £190 among the usual thirteen charities – in small amounts, it is true, but sufficient to show the Society's continued interest.

The receipts from the pantomime went a long way towards replacing this amount – it made a net profit of over £136, so it obviously sold well; this despite what the *Darlington & Stockton Times* referred to as the 'arctic temperature'[1] of the theatre building. Goosepimples notwithstanding, the players made a good job of a show which, although apparently not outstanding in the matter of its script, nevertheless stayed close to the traditional story and did not rely too much on gimmickry – the *Northern Despatch* headline read 'A panto in the true tradition'.[2] Meg Leeming was clearly outstanding in her role but the comedy was a highlight, despite the part of the Dame being taken by a woman rather than a man. Eileen Young was labouring under considerable difficulty, having injured her arm (now encased in plaster) yet her comedic talents were undiminished. Sam Herdman sang extremely well and his Grand Vizier received universal praise despite the *Darlington & Stockton Times*'s reference to 'the apparent incongruity of such a rank in the Chinese hierarchy'. Still, as the review observed, his rendering of the anachronistic song *The Road to Mandalay* won tremendous applause – and '. . . if China was to be credited with a spurious Grand Vizier there was no reason why that Vizier should not sing such a song!'

The reviews were somewhat critical of the technical aspects of the show's staging and the backstage staff did indeed have a few difficulties.

Richard Sampson recalls the occurrence of one problem, whose magnitude unfortunately accumulated as the week went on. Every entrance of the Genie (Robert Kirton) – dressed solely in a pair of very tight trousers of a brilliant green hue surmounted by his magnificently hairy chest – was heralded by both the rubbing of the lamp by Aladdin and by a magnesium flash ignited by the electrician from a special plugboard. Early in the week the flashes were not very spectacular and produced a lot of smoke, as the crew were using some very old flash powder, so, to produce a satisfactory effect, more and more powder was used each night. Everybody concerned was working during the day so nobody had time to go and buy fresh powder from the photographer's. On the last day of the show, however, the Secretary, Norman Thompson, found time to buy some but omitted to mention it to the Stage Manager or the crew. At the matinée the usual extra-large charge of powder was put into the flashbox and, on the cue, there was an enormous flash which lit up the theatre, followed by the smell of burning hair and the entrance of the Genie, beating his smouldering chest. It may or may not be coincidence but the name of Robert Kirton does not appear in any more cast lists! *Aladdin* was a success financially, though. The Society's 10% of the net receipts amounted to over £87, which, with nearly £50 in donations from the Vice-Presidents and Patrons, enabled the Society to make nearly £137 on it.

The fact that it had been a good year was stressed by the Chairman, J. G. Bell, at the Annual General Meeting in March. The Society, he said, was the envy of practically all other societies as it had gone from strength to strength, having given about £4,700 to charities, besides having around £1,800 to its credit – a magnificent achievement in ten years. A little note of caution came up, however, on another matter. He referred to the need for tact in dealing with Society affairs and offered the quotation: 'A soft answer turneth away wrath. Harsh answers call for grievous words.' So there were obviously still undercurrents of unrest! It was good, however, that the Society had had, in general, a happy and successful year during his term of office, for J. G. Bell died less than a year later.

From this Annual General Meeting of 1955, Norman Thompson took over as Chairman and was confronted with a major problem within three weeks of his appointment. *The Quaker Girl* was already into singing rehearsals and a Mr Quinton Golder had been booked to produce it. Mr Golder then died suddenly during a rehearsal for *Oklahoma!* in Bangor, Belfast. So the hunt was on to find a producer, a local one if possible (an expensive London producer having been employed for *The Dancing Years*), who was not already committed. Crunch-time – as ever – revealed Fred

Thompson in readiness to oblige for £60 plus £20 expenses and the day was saved.

Norman Thompson, however, was still not going to get an easy ride for there were very serious problems on the horizon with the theatre. There had been some inkling of this – though no one took much notice of it at the time – in April 1955 when the Society's theatre contract for the November show had not yet arrived. The Committee was told that the Hippodrome orchestra were all on their notice and perhaps the delay in sending the contract was something to do with this. It did not seem highly significant and everything continued much as usual. After 'long discussion' the Committee decided to go back to performing two musicals a year, and two shows were accordingly mentioned for 1956: the Gilbert & Sullivan double bill *Trial By Jury* and *The Pirates of Penzance*, and Ivor Novello's *Perchance to Dream*. Robert Farrage asked for a £20 rise in his fee, which had been the same for several years, but did not get it – the Committee felt that if the fee went up to £50 the office of Musical Director might become 'competitive' and this was not desirable. Robert tried to get his fee increased from time to time – it became a familiar ritual – but though he was unsuccessful he was still content to be Musical Director. A month later he was in the position of having to find his own orchestra for *The Quaker Girl* as the theatre no longer had a permanent orchestra. This, had the Committee but known it, was the first stage in the downward slide of the Hippodrome, for Mr Hinge was already a sick man and his lease of the theatre was within a year or so of expiry. Since they did *not* know they forged ahead.

The D'Oyly Carte Opera Company was unable to confirm the performing rights for *Trial By Jury* and *The Pirates of Penzance* immediately, so the Committee abandoned the idea of Gilbert & Sullivan and booked *Perchance to Dream* as the spring show. Then they cast about for producers.

A month later Charles Ross, of Edinburgh, had been chosen. His track record was excellent. He had been in theatre for 55 years, having sung with the Carl Rosa Opera Company, stage-managed for George Edwardes (universally known as 'The Guv'nor') at Daly's in London, and produced dramas for Drury Lane and pantomimes for Howard & Wyndham, so at £125 plus rail fares and accomodation for five weeks' rehearsal he was expected to give good value for money. It was to be hoped so because *Perchance to Dream* would be an expensive show in other ways. It is set in three eras – Regency, Victorian and Modern. Twenty-five people would play 34 named parts, 43 chorus members would be appearing in various guises, and 23 dancing parts would represent the four seasons. The deal with Chas H. Fox, the London costumiers, was 250 costumes for £266 3s. od. ('curls and ringlets 3s. 6d. per extra set if required'). If there were less than 200 costumes ordered the cost would be 3*d.* per costume extra. (Just as a matter of interest here: at the committee meeting of 15 June 1955 there was a note about an increase in the scale of charges for the caretaker of Beaumont Street School where committee meetings and rehearsals took place – they went up by approximately threepence per hour, making the charge 3*s.* 2¾*d.* per hour plus preparation and cleaning time, which provides an interesting mathematical problem in comparing it with present-day prices.)

One of the problems of having to plan so far ahead is that one never knows how well the present show-in-rehearsal is going to do. From the point of view of the cast, though, *The Quaker Girl* looked promising, with a newcomer, Joyce Shipman, in the title role. Arthur Clarke and Kathleen Pipe played her strictly Puritan uncle and aunt, contrasting with the exotic Princess Mathilde (Audrey Hartley), Madame Blum the fashionable Parisienne (Hilda Whitman), and the dashing naval attaché Tony Chute (Kenneth Richardson) – to say nothing of the Parisian actress Diane (Joy Beadell wearing the last word in hats!)

The summer break thus arrived with everything on an even keel, even extending to the unusual safety-net of having understudies to the main roles. Indeed, all went well until October – three weeks before opening – when a Mr Hutton (an unknown quantity as he appears in no other cast list) resigned from the role of Prince Carlo. A Mr H. Foster was supposed to be his understudy but has vanished without trace from the cast, for after much talk of reshuffling parts it was decided that Arnold Grieve of the (by-now defunct) Barnard Castle society should be asked to play the part. Furthermore, since there was the usual man-shortage, it seemed a good idea if Jim Fraser Murray were to approach the ex-members not only of Barnard Castle but also of Darlington's Coniscliffe Road society (which had also folded) to see if they would like to join Darlington. Only Arnold Grieve was willing to oblige, but that, at least, meant that there was a Prince Carlo. Two other members dropped out of the cast but fortunately they were women! So *The Quaker Girl* took the stage and though the press felt that it was rather dated (the *Darlington & Stockton Times* also called the score 'undistinguished'[3] and the *Northern Despatch* thought it was 'lacking the character and inherent impact of previous productions'[4]) the overall view was encouraging. The principals – especially Hilda Whitman, who proved to have a great sense of fun in the interpretation of her part – were warmly praised. The few first night hiccups were confined to the chorus, though later in the week Hilda Whitman and Vera Dickinson had a spot of difficulty in the dress-shop scene when they both got their feet entangled in some wires on stage and needed a rather ungainly shuffle to get themselves free. Arnold Grieve proved to be a successful import and had 'a rich bass voice'[5], and Kenneth Richardson, as always, turned in a polished performance. The *Darlington & Stockton Times* said that he '. . . brought cheerful inanity and fresh gaiety to the part, which made the most of the well-worn humour.' 'Joyce Shipman,' said the paper, was a 'great success in her first lead, despite a little "hardness" in the middle register of her singing voice, which was probably attributable to nervousness.' She made Prudence an attractive figure, said the review, '. . . and we look forward to seeing her in future shows.' The *Northern Despatch* also thought she showed 'considerable promise'. The comedy was admirably carried off by Bob White, Sam Herdman ('wholehearted buffoonery') and Vera Dickinson, and scenery, costumes, lighting and dancing were of the usual high standard. Though the press voted it a success, it did lose money – although not much. The deficit amounted to only around £22 which was not too bad considering that the number of Vice-Presidents had dropped by ten since *The Dancing Years* (though the 'names' were still there) and the Patrons by about 25. Nevertheless, once the tax return had been settled and the books balanced, the resultant donations to charities brought the grand total distributed since 1945 to £5,000.

Now, of course, the Society had to remain in a high gear since two shows a year were to be presented henceforward and the spring show for 1957 had to be decided upon. At a committee meeting in mid-January *The Dubarry* was chosen for autumn. It had been a European import in 1932, with original music by Karl Milloeker arranged by Theo Makeben and adapted and augmented by Bernard Grun, and lyrics by Rowland Leigh and Eric Maschwitz. John Denis was invited to produce once more, with Robert Farrage (after his customary cash request – asked and refused) as Musical Director. The spring show for 1957 would be *The Belle of New York*, to be presented in March. It all sounds like confident planning, but the situation at the Hippodrome was obviously at the back of the Committee's minds; at the meeting of 12 January 1956 a note at the end records that '. . . the Secretary was asked to write to the Management Board of the Regal Cinema and make enquiries as to the prospects of booking their theatre for some future shows.'

At the Annual General Meeting Neville Dodd left the Committee and Kenneth Bodden, after serving a three-year 'apprenticeship' in the Society, joined it. Messrs Herdman, Walker, Willans and N. W. Thompson were all re-elected, and Norman Thompson, at the following week's meeting, handed over the Chairmanship to Frank Murray for 1956 and went back to being Secretary again. The costumes for *The Dubarry* were booked from Homburgs of Leeds, performing rights were agreed with Samuel French Ltd., and the Hippodrome was booked. A slight hiatus occurred when Charles Ross asked if his wife could take the first two weeks of rehearsals but reference to his contract soon took care of the matter! So, these things being out of the way, the rehearsals for *Perchance to Dream* were at their height. By the week before opening night, however, the Ticket Secretary was uneasy. The news had been voiced at a meeting early in the year that programme sales at the theatre were very much reduced. Now, said Jim Willans, the advance bookings were not very satisfactory. His fears were to some extent justified: while the number of Vice-Presidents had only reduced by three the number of Patrons was down by 45, so there would be a reduction of around 51 guineas in donations.

The show itself contained a number of faces which were quite new to the Society, though the *Northern Echo* in its review regarded the show as being 'carried on the able shoulders of its "veteran members"'[6] – and went on immediately to pinpoint Kenneth Richardson which must have afforded him mixed feelings! Hilda Whitman was his leading lady and, as always, acquitted herself well. Shirley Dodd, as the blunt, outspoken aristocrat, Lady Charlotte Fayre, excelled herself in the opinion of all the reviewers, which must have been particularly pleasing as the producer had had some doubts about her suitability for the part. She served as a pivot for the comedy, assisted by accomplished performances by Sam Herdman and Florence (Lorrie) Boddy. Greta Sanderson had excellent notices for her performances in the Melinda/Melanie/Melody parts, and appreciation of her charm, emotion and grace in those roles appeared in all three local papers. This must have been gratifying since this was her first chance to play a major role. The dancing, as ever, was warmly praised and generally the reviews were all good – apart from criticism of backstage noise. To be fair, the scene-changing must have been extremely difficult for Frank Murray and Richard Sampson (the Stage Managers) and their little band of helpers. The *Northern Echo* summed up the show as 'a vivid interpretation by Darlington amateurs', and the *Northern Despatch* opined that '. . . parts of the production are open to criticism but the general impression is a pleasing one.'[7] The *Darlington & Stockton Times* thought it was '. . . one of Darlington's best amateur shows.'[8]

At the time of the committee meeting of 17 May 1956, two weeks after the end of *Perchance to Dream*, however, the problems the Society faced were beginning to increase and gather momentum. First of all the Treasurer, Tom Gilchrist, reported that the Inland Revenue had written to him saying that the tax from *Perchance to Dream* would not be refunded, and mentioned that he was going to take it up with them again. This, as can be imagined, would be a heavy blow to the Society's finances. On top of this, the news had been received that the Hippodrome was closing down for the summer and the contract to perform *The Dubarry* there had been returned unsigned. There followed 'long discussion'. A summer closedown was a very serious matter for the Society. If the theatre was going to remain closed until the Society's production there would be no staff and the building would not be fit to sit in owing to dampness and dirt. Norman Thompson said that he would go to Newcastle to see Hinge Productions Ltd. and '. . . get a very definite understanding and adjustment of contract as the position of expense would be totally different with regard to staffing and heating.'[9] Two weeks later the Inland Revenue continued to be obdurate over the tax refund. The Committee was considering approaching the management of the Royal Astoria Theatre (the result of the conversion of an old cinema in High Northgate) for the production of *The Dubarry* since the Hippodrome situation was so uncertain. The latter question, at least, was resolved a week later. Though the Hippodrome had closed on 6 June, Hinge Productions Ltd. had assured Norman Thompson that the theatre would be in 'full swing' long before November so at least *The Dubarry* could go ahead in the customary location. The Committee could take its summer break with at least a crumb of comfort.

Any comfort taken was soon dispelled in October when the Chairman called a special meeting. He was very concerned about the general apathy leading to the poor demand for tickets for *The Dubarry*; the closure of the theatre, though supposedly temporary, was, naturally enough, having an adverse effect. The best solution the Committee could come up with was to ask Mr Barker of Bainbridge Barkers store in Skinnergate if tickets could be sold from there since the box office was not open. Mr Barker was quite amenable to this. Certain economies had to be made too. Robert Farrage was asked to be as economical as possible with his orchestra and the usual grant for liquid refreshments for the show would be dispensed with – though Murrays the Bakers (being 'family') would provide the refreshments for the dress rehearsal. A friend of Frank Murray was willing to bring the hired stage furniture from London and take it back again for £20, which was a great help. In addition the curator of Bowes Museum had allowed the photographs for the programme to be taken there, surrounded by furniture which had actually belonged to Madame Dubarry – this must have given the cast a certain lift. The production itself had had one major difficulty: Hilda Whitman, who was to play the leading role, had had to pull out owing to illness. Though she had gamely said that she would do the part if she could, she had to spend several weeks in hospital which prevented her from doing so. Curiously enough the remedy for this absence was already provided for. John Denis, the producer, was a superstitious man (as are so many in the world of theatre)

The Dubarry 1956
Left to right: Lorrie Boddy, Audrey Hartley.

and felt that there was a curse on this show. When it had been performed both in Vienna and in London by professional companies the original leading lady had, on each occasion, been unable to take the stage at the last minute and the understudies had to go on. He had therefore insisted that for the Darlington society's production there *must* be an understudy to the leading lady. He was so very determined over this that the Committee had decided to humour him – and now his insistence was justified. Audrey Hartley, who had received very good reviews for her appearance as Princess Mathilde in *The Quaker Girl*, therefore took on the role, while Veronica (Vicki) Tringham, who had joined the Society as a chorus member for *Perchance to Dream*, would take over Audrey's more minor role.

So *The Dubarry* finally took the stage. Despite the general public's comparative lack of interest, the Society's regular supporters had, in the main, stayed faithful. There were only 56 Vice-Presidents (as opposed to the 61 who had supported *Perchance to Dream*) but the number of Patrons had increased from 139 to 193, despite what the *Northern Echo* said about the show's lacking the '. . . popular appeal of many that the Society has given.'[10] The *Darlington & Stockton Times* declared it 'sumptuous'.[11] The *Northern Despatch* concurred, pronouncing it a great success despite the shortcomings of the piece itself, and commented on the first-class cast.

Indeed, as well as all the principals' receiving individual commendations, the many lesser character players also received plaudits. There was something for everyone in *The Dubarry* – quartets, octets and sextets – and as a result many people had a chance to shine. Lorrie Boddy, Bob White, Donald Clayton, Eileen Young, Shirley Dodd, Beryl Gregg, Ken Bodden and Sam Herdman all had a special mention. This was especially pleasing for Lorrie (as was the chance, as Madame Sauterelle, to wear the most glorious auburn wig ever seen by the Society!) The wife of Fred Boddy, she had been a dancer and chorus member since 1949, but this was only her second major role (she had played a comic 'wilting theatrical' in *Perchance to Dream*), and her singing teacher had helped to lower her range, putting her in very fine voice. The dancing had taken the eye of all the reviewers and especially that of the *Darlington & Stockton Times*, which particularly selected the ballet of the Court Cards. Peter Henderson (this was his first show) remembers that it was a spectacular sight. The Kings and Queens were magnificently costumed and in the finale to this wonderful build-up the last person brought onto the stage was The Queen of Hearts as represented by Madame Dubarry. She wore a beautiful, heart-decorated, white satin crinoline, to sing *I Give My Heart* to her leading man.

Though the Committee was naturally delighted with the reaction of the press, the production still lost money (approximately £250) and uncertainty still prevailed. Mr Hinge's lease on the theatre would expire on 30 March 1957 so they reluctantly decided not to perform a show that spring but to go ahead with one for the autumn – venue unknown. The show chosen was *No, No, Nanette*, a mid-1920s musical.

In the mean time, in the quest for funds, some of the Society's assets were reinvested and various social activities were arranged, such as a highly successful 'cabaret ball'. The Social Committee also opened a separate bank account.

By mid-February no venue for *No, No, Nanette* had yet been found. Bondgate Chapel hall was not available and Eastbourne School hall had been mooted. Fred Thompson, who was now Chairman again, suggested the possibility of booking the hall at the Girls' High School which had relocated from Cleveland Avenue to a new building at Hummersknott (now Hummersknott Comprehensive School) in 1955. On the question of a producer, Frank Murray proposed that Joy Beadell be asked, and this proposal was carried unanimously so *No, No, Nanette* was the first of many of the Society's productions to be performed under Joy's direction.

Happily for the Society the use of the High School hall was obtained for the week beginning 21 October at a cost of £5 for the dress rehearsal and £10 for each subsequent night, making £65 in all, with the proviso that the Society put protective coverings on all floors and the stage. Robert

Farrage managed to get together an amateur orchestra of five members (the size of the hall had to be taken into consideration as well as the cost) and the Secretary ordered the scenery from Scenic Display Ltd. for £40 plus carriage. Lady Starmer was kind enough to provide a number of props for the ever-scrounging stage crew and Homburgs of Leeds provided some of the costumes for the (fortunately) small cast.

Mavis Hudson, who had appeared as a dancer in the previous two shows, was cast in the title role, backed by a solid cast of regulars: Kenneth Richardson, Vera Dickinson, Shirley Dodd, Lorrie Boddy, John Brown and Vicki Tringham. Raymond Simmons (who had joined the Society for *The Dubarry*) and Elizabeth Bartram (a newcomer) completed the named character parts. There was a chorus of nine ladies and eight men, plus five dancers.

Everyone had a difficult time of it. 1957 was the year of the Asian-flu epidemic and this caused attendance at rehearsals to be very poor – hardly surprising, as the disease was particularly virulent. All the work of setting up the show had to be done from scratch at the weekend for the Monday opening; for instance all the floor-covering had to be laid and the seats numbered, which took up a lot of time. The players were not familiar with the stage or the acoustics – there was no such thing as a radio-microphone to be had then – and the lighting had to be organized without the facilities of a proper theatre set-up. The school was situated on the outskirts of the town, and this was reflected in the much-reduced atten-dance. Even though the hall was nowhere near the size of the Hippodrome auditorium there were a number of seats unfilled; this despite the fact of the Vice-Presidents and Patrons continuing their support. The *Darlington & Stockton Times* noted the empty seats and confirmed that the journey was 'discouraging for supporters'.[12] The reporter, obviously full of sym-pathy for the company, described all the arduous preparation for staging the show as 'a labour of love'. The press enjoyed it, however, and they praised the fortitude and abilities of the cast. The *Northern Despatch* was impressed by the vitality, freshness and crispness of their performances and much was made of the fact there were new faces among the leads. The *Northern Echo* referred to 'the warmth and sparkling freshness'[13] with which Mavis Hudson played her part, but everyone had a mention in the reviews – and Shirley Dodd was referred to as 'one of the Society's stalwarts'.[14] She must have had mixed feelings about *that*, considering her tender years! What is more, the show, due to the various economies, made almost as much money as *The Dubarry* lost: £240, plus £100 in donations, which must have been a real morale-booster for the anxious Committee. There had been a little morale-boosting going on behind the scenes, too – or perhaps it was a form of medication for the flu epidemic! One of the firm conditions of using the school was that no intoxicating liquor be brought in. However, it was not entirely surprising ('knowing some of the members', said the author's anonymous informant) that when clearing-up time came, a considerable pile of beer-crates had to be loaded up onto the open truck which had been borrowed to transport all the furniture loaned by Lady Starmer. When the truck stopped at the front door of her home, Danby Lodge, it was met by a horrified housekeeper, Dorothy, who was more than dismayed by the large pile of empties. The truck was hastily despatched out of the back gates, just as the Bishop was arriving to lunch through the front door!

Despite the fact that the Society was in funds once more a paramount problem remained unsolved: what of venues for future productions, now that the theatre had closed following the expiry of Mr Hinge's lease and the owners had decided to put it up for sale? The other theatres in the town, having struggled to keep their heads above water, were now going down for the third time. The Little Theatre in Kendrew Street and the Royal Astoria had more or less had their day. The High School hall was possible, but by no means ideal, partly because of its location; the Baths Hall (once in Gladstone Street, now demolished and the site turned into a car park) was a faint possibility but did not have much in the way of theatrical facilities: after all, its main function was, as its name suggests, a swimming pool. At the committee meeting of 20 November 1957, however, a ball was started rolling which turned, to everyone's surprise, into a snowball. A sub-committee consisting of the Chairman (Fred Thompson), the Secretary (Norman Thompson) and the Treasurer (Tom Gilchrist) was appointed to inspect and report on the condition of the Hippodrome, discuss with the owners the possibility of renting the theatre, obtain any further information, and report back a week later. This they duly did; they considered that it was fit to play in provided that a certain amount of cleaning was carried out and the building was heated for some time before a show. Fred Thompson said that the owners were willing to let the theatre to the Society subject to certain conditions – for instance, that the Watch Committee would grant the Society a licence. All other things being equal it seemed like a good idea to the Committee and worth some effort to be able to use their old familiar venue. They were told that they would be allowed access to the building from 30 March for cleaning so they asked Metcalfe's, a local decorator, to quote for the difficult work such as brushing down the walls and distempering.

An Extraordinary General Meeting was therefore held on 12 December 1957 when members, Vice-Presidents and Patrons could have the matter placed before them. A great many people attended. Fred Thompson then held forth. He told the assembled company the position and outlined why the Hippodrome was preferable to any other venue. He explained that the Society wanted the next show to be Benatzky and Stolz's *White Horse Inn*, which was big and spectacular, and that the members were keen to make every effort to put the building into fit enough shape to get a licence from the Watch Committee. He reminded them that the Society had built up an excellent reputation and that standards could only be maintained if it could have the Hippodrome not only for April 1958 but for all future shows. The Town Council had been advised to buy the place as a civic theatre, said Fred, and it was going for a song. If the Council *did* decide to buy it it would be available not just for Darlington Operatic Society but for concerts, shows, plays, Boy Scout Gang Shows and the Film Society, all of which should be encouraged in the town. He warned that seat prices might have to go up when the Society performed *White Horse Inn* and that the gallery (known now as the upper circle) might have to be closed, but asked everyone to rally round to try to support the Society. If the town missed the opportunity of buying the theatre at this stage the likelihood was that the people would never get another theatre in their lifetime. Having uttered his rallying-cry he sat back to await results, though he did tell the Committee, at its regular meeting a week later, that he did not think there was very much chance of the Town Council buying the Hippodrome because it knew nothing about running a theatre. It was agreed that he should write to the Council to offer that the Society would be prepared to take over the running of the theatre if the Council bought it.

By 12 January 1958 a letter had been received from the Borough Surveyor pointing out the repairs and so on which would have to be carried out before the Watch Committee would consider granting a licence. The Society gave an undertaking to carry them out. Fred spoke again about wanting the Corporation to buy the theatre and gave his idea of what the running expenses and the possible income from lettings would be. There followed a 'very full discussion' – which Fred said would be very useful when he presented his case – and, to be on the safe side, he, Norman Thompson and Tom Gilchrist formed a Civic Theatre Committee to deal with such matters ('as long,' a cautious amendment to the minutes said, 'as they remained members of the Society').

They were determined that, come hell or high water, the Society would present a spring show. *White Horse Inn* was now the definite choice and would run from 28 April to 3 May. Peter Miller had been engaged to produce it and it had already gone into rehearsal.

The Civic Theatre Committee met the Town Council at the theatre on 15 February 1958 and Fred explained the result of the deliberations to the Operatic Society Committee the same evening. Unfortunately those minutes do not record just what passed at that meeting, but the minutes of the Annual General Meeting on 26 February reveal that the Corporation had not yielded to persuasion either to buy *or* to lease the theatre. The Corporation's explanation of the lack of willingness even to take out a lease was '. . . because in its present condition it would be a disgrace to the town as a civic theatre.' They had then suggested that the Operatic Society lease it and said that they would give a farthing rate if it ran at a loss. That, Fred told the assembled company, was how matters stood and it was now up to the members to give all the support and assistance required. They agreed. The Committee did not let the grass grow under its feet. A letter was drafted to the owners offering to lease the building on a four-year term with option to renew or purchase, but always subject to the Corporation's helping the Society with up to £1,100. The owners replied that they were prepared to lease the theatre on a full-repairing lease at a rental of £450 per annum. The Society would pay rates and fire insurance and would have an option to buy for £8,000. The two sides agreed on these terms.

A quotation of £225 was received from Metcalfe's for the cleaning work required of them and this was quite reasonable for brushing down and washing the walls (including the dressing-rooms) and distempering the lavatories. It was arranged that the theatre should be heated from 17 March so that the Society could do a lot of the cleaning work, too, and Frank Murray, who was desperately keen for the venture to be a success, volunteered to take care of the heating. The theatre building was indeed in a filthy state. In addition to the work done by Metcalfe's, the Society members set upon it with a will in their spare time – as soon as the heating boiler had been inspected by the Royal Insurance inspector and duly lit. They cleared the stage of rubbish and scrubbed out the whole place. Horace Wilson,* who had just joined the Society, said that he remembered the big clean-up; the dressing-rooms in particular were in a terrible state and all the stone steps up to them had to be scrubbed. An enormous amount of time and elbow-grease was expended, and also, since the theatre had no paid staff now, members of the Society volunteered to be usherettes and so on when the time came.

The show was cast with relative ease, and 66 Society members were taking part – 66 members there were indeed, but the cast actually numbered 70. Peter Miller wanted four extra men to play the parts of Councillors to Bill Jones's Mayor so he simply went up to men on Darlington's High Row whom he thought looked right and more or less

---

* Horace, who was looking forward to seeing this book published, sadly died early in 1994.

hijacked them into rehearsals. If he were still around today, Peter Miller would surely have been much amused by the fact that one of them – Eric Roberts – actually ended up as Mayor of Darlington in 1990, though it was his one and only appearance on the stage! His step-daughter Karen Wright, however, is now a member of the Society.

Even while living in hope it seems very likely that many members of the Society were still wondering if *White Horse Inn* would prove to be its swan-song, but the ticket-sales, Jim Willans cautiously said, were about up to standard compared with previous shows, which was good news, and a team of volunteers was assembled to do the day-to-day cleaning as well as to staff the theatre for the week of the show. Intent on preserving the 'theatre experience', Jim got Marsh Dipaolo – a local retailer best known as an ice-cream man – to supply chocolates, ice-cream and cigarettes to be sold during the show's interval.

More storm clouds had gathered, however. Fred Thompson now reported that the owners of the Hippodrome had changed their minds and refused the Society's terms for leasing the theatre (no reason is given or even hinted at) and that since the Society's solicitor, Mr A. B. (Tony) Little, considered that the owners' own terms would be suicidal to the Society, he had written to the owners' solicitors informing them that the Society's terms were final.

Under this cloud *White Horse Inn* was performed. Jim Fraser Murray's faith was undiminished. Now the Society's Chairman, he wrote in the programme (which, incidentally, cost one shilling) a special message which he concluded by saying that if the theatre were unavailable in the future the Society would still band together and find some other hall to play in and he hoped that the public would continue to give support. He had also appealed to the public directly in a specially-written announcement sent out to the Patrons. This informed them of the leasing of the theatre to a Civic Theatre Group to be formed from Darlington Operatic Society and to be called 'Civic Theatre (Darlington) Ltd.' He urged them to become 'Founder Members of the Civic Theatre' by sending a donation of one guinea, and a Founder Members' club would be started. He also said that the theatre was now available for booking and that interested parties should contact Norman Thompson. A booking had, indeed, already been granted to the prestigious Band of the Royal Marines School of Music who would give a concert on Sunday 11 May. Of course the Darlington Operatic Society would give its usual twice-yearly productions. This looks like jumping the gun in view of the theatre owners' refusal of the Society's terms, but faith, they say, can move mountains.

The Vice-Presidents and Patrons did rally round. *White Horse Inn* produced almost a record number of donations in the history of the Society at that time. It was beaten only by *The Dancing Years* three and a half years earlier. The near-record donations must have been very encouraging for a committee which, however optimistic Jim Fraser Murray might be, was still living on a knife-edge. Public support was vital, especially with television becoming more and more popular.

The day after *White Horse Inn*'s opening night, however, there appeared in the *Northern Echo* the good news: 'Darlington's New Hippodrome . . . is now a Civic Theatre. After long negotiations the terms of a four-year lease have finally been arranged with the theatre owners and the Civic Theatre (Darlington) Ltd. has now been formed.'[15] Perhaps the owners had decided, on reflection, that this was the best deal they were going to get. The Town Council had promised a grant of £1,150 per year (which was, as forecast, equivalent to about a farthing on the town's rates) for the four years, with the first year's grant to be paid immediately.

No wonder the performers were in sparkling form. 'During the three-hour duration of the show,' said the *Northern Echo*, there was never a moment which dragged . . . [it] could only be described as spectacular [and it] deserved the frequent applause of a well-satisfied audience.'[15] The reviews in all three of the local papers were uniformly enthusiastic and all the principals were praised individually, especially Greta Sanderson for her portrayal of the comic, lisping, pigtailed Gretel, with John Brown as her partner Sigismund Smith. Kenneth Richardson and Vera Dickinson, as Leopold and Josepha, gave their usual polished performances while Sam Herdman, as the comic Lancashire manufacturer Grinkle, was described by the *Darlington & Stockton Times* as being 'robust'[16] and 'reminiscent, once or twice, of the comedian, Max Miller'; the *Northern Despatch* reviewer described him as looking 'as though he had just stepped off Blackpool pier after a meal of tripe and trotters'![17]

Peter Miller had seen the show when it was first produced at the London Coliseum where it really *was* spectacular. As well as a first-class cast and a large chorus its producer, Emile Chapel, had had the finest technicians in the country. The theatre was equipped with three revolving stages to move the scenery, the White Horse Inn was built right out into the auditorium, the steamer arrived on a lake of real water, and the swimmers went into the lake and really swam. In the storm scene, when it rained, the water came down in bucketfuls and the company was drenched. Peter Miller, of course, had none of these facilities at Darlington so he compensated by playing up the comedy while making the show as spectacular as he could. He seems to have succeeded in his aims. The *Northern Despatch* closed its review with the words: '. . . as the curtain fell the capacity audience erupted into spontaneous resounding applause. They had witnessed two treats – a first-class musical and the rebirth of a theatre.'

The Society was not slow to capitalize on this. During the run of *White Horse Inn* the Committee held a special meeting, actually at the theatre, simply to decide on the next show and its producer. It was brief and to the point: *Oklahoma!* – and Peter Miller.

In the mean time much organization of the theatre was going on. Articles of Association had been drawn up by the middle of May and a list of possible directors of a Civic Theatre Group was being compiled.

On 19 August 1958 the official (non-profit-making) company was incorporated and Darlington Civic Theatre Ltd. legally came into being. The Council of Management consisted of Fred Thompson (Chairman), Norman Thompson (Hon. Secretary), John Brown of Lloyd's Bank (Hon. Treasurer), Lady Starmer, Councillor Mrs Mary Lyonette, A. B. Little (the solicitor), E. W. Hammond, Councillor J. H. Park, Jim Fraser Murray, Wilfred Downing and Jim Willans. (Tom Gilchrist was on the original list but did not take up his place, which was then filled by Jim Willans.) The Management Sub-Committee consisted of the five members of Darlington Operatic Society who were on the Council of Management. Their work was all voluntary and work there was in plenty; but the main thing was that the theatre had been saved from the demolition to which it had been very close.*

The members of the Operatic Society continued to work on the theatre, getting vital structural work carried out throughout the building, but it was no oil-painting from the outside and only so much can be done with voluntary workers in their spare time. Thus, despite advertisement of the fact that it was available, very few people hired the theatre. It was primarily used for the Society's shows, with occasional wrestling matches and, now and again, a little theatre group. Though it seemed a terrible waste the theatre soldiered on somehow and the Society planned to perform what they were confident would be a money-spinner in spring 1959 – Franz Lehár's *The Merry Widow*. Peter Miller was unable to produce this so they went for another London producer – Edward Royce Jun. – and got him for a fee of £150 (plus rail fares) for five weeks, which was very reasonable considering his wide experience. Like so many producers he had been in theatre from childhood, being from a theatrical family. His father had produced shows in London and on Broadway and had, in fact, brought the original production of *The Merry Widow* from Vienna to Daly's Theatre in London. Edward Royce Jun., for his part, had produced shows in Australia and South Africa as well as in London. He

* See *A Theatre for the People* by Timmie Morrison.

had also done a great deal of work with amateur societies so seemed eminently suitable.

The under-usage of the theatre was a thorn in the Committee's side and they had been asked to plough some more money into it. Therefore, they decided to perform a pantomime in January 1959 as well as their usual two musicals. They asked Jack F. Hilton to come and discuss his own pantomimes with them in September – as well as writing them he also produced them.

Meanwhile, singing rehearsals for Rogers and Hammerstein's *Oklahoma!*, a musical play based on a book called *Green Grow the Lilacs* by Lynn Riggs, had been progressing and the floorwork began in October. There is hardly a mention of the casting in the minutes so it must have been accomplished with relative ease. The only cast member in some doubt was Terry Frame as Curly, the leading man. He had played Sutton the solicitor in *White Horse Inn* and was a flying officer with the RAF at Goosepool (now Teesside Airport). In the event all was well and he played the role.

Oklahoma! was an interesting show in that many of the principal roles were taken by people who had not played leads before. Joan Geeves was to play Laurey, and the Swift sisters, Carol and Susan, were playing Ado Annie and Aunt Eller. Susan had to age considerably to play Aunt Eller, as she was, in fact, not long out of Teachers' Training College. Who would have believed that she would play the part twice more for the Society – in 1976 and in 1991! (Sue says that the only difference between her first performance and her most recent was that the last time she didn't need make-up . . .) The 'anchormen' were Sam Herdman as Jud Fry, Kenneth Richardson as Ali Hakim, and Bill Jones as Will Parker. In all there was a cast of 68. There were some changes in jobs and a newcomer or two backstage, too. Bill Bishop, Joy Beadell's elder son, joined Michael Dickinson as call boy, and Lorrie Boddy, who had not been in a show for two years, was asked to come back to be Wardrobe Mistress along with Fred Thompson's wife Doris. Bernard Sanderson joined Norman Stairmand and Richard Sampson as Joint Stage Manager and there was a newcomer, George Todd, who joined the stage staff. George and his wife, Peggy, were both in drama groups in the town. Peggy acted, but George had worked backstage with Roxburgh-Kelso's acting group. He had learned a great deal about stage plotting and the like with them, and also with the group at Darlington Rolling Mills, where he worked. George and Peggy are still with the Society, though they have rarely appeared on stage. George has made one appearance, and only then when he was dragooned into it (as the Decorator who appears at the very end of *Hello Dolly!*) in 1985. (George says that he was doing props, and was told, 'You'll do,' when the producer realized that the part was vacant.) Peggy has made two appearances. She played Lady Devon in *Bitter Sweet* in 1974, but in 1968's *My Fair Lady* she was hastily drafted in when Margaret Teasdale, a front-line chorus member, was taken ill. Peggy is the first to admit that

she is not a singer – to hear her tell it she makes it sound as though her vocal prowess falls short even of Kermit the Frog – but she filled the gap and mimed. Peggy remembers with amusement that Frank Murray, who was Musical Director for that show, gave her a special thank-you – for not singing.

George and Peggy have served the Society ever since that show in 1958. Peggy was on the Ladies' Committee from its formation, in 1962, until 1980 and was its first Chairman. As for George . . . well, name it and George has done it: props, stage management, Chairman, Ticket Secretary, NODA Representative, and, from 1978 to 1979, Chairman of NODA (to say nothing of the fact that he kept most of the press reviews from 1960 onwards, thus saving a great deal of time and effort in the compila-

George and Peggy Todd (George as Chairman of NODA in 1978).

tion of this book). Now in his eighties he still goes to the shows as often as he can to do front-of-house duties and help with props! Back in 1958, though, he and the rest of the stage staff were to have an onerous job. Darlington Operatic Society's production of *Oklahoma!* was to run from 24 to 29 November, but Middlesbrough Operatic Society would not end their run of the show at the Middlesbrough Empire until the 22nd and they had the scenery. Norman Thompson received a letter from them saying that the Empire staff were not in the habit of striking scenery on Saturday nights (whereas the Darlington society always clears the theatre of all of its scenery, costumes and props immediately after the last performance – and a tough job it is, too) so Darlington could not have the scenery until the Sunday morning. This would make things very tight, for the 'get-in' of the scenery and the dress rehearsal would have to be squeezed into a much shorter time. However, they managed it.

It was comforting that the advance ticket bookings were going well nearly six weeks before the show. The theatre rental was £300 but, in the event, this was more than covered by the Vice-Presidents' and Patrons' donations, the numbers of both of which were well up on those for *White Horse Inn*. There had been nearly £200 surplus from that show and the Society's finances were in quite reasonable shape considering that so much money had been given to the theatre as well as to charities.

The reviews of *Oklahoma!* were also comforting. Peter Miller had boosted the standing of the Society with his two productions in the once-beleaguered theatre. Terry Frame had proved to be an ideal hero and Joan Geeves had made a pleasing Laurey (a rather thankless part at the best of times). Carol Swift's debut as Ado Annie was a triumph of 'strident gusto'[18] (the *Darlington & Stockton Times* reviewer feared for the safety of her vocal cords) and had been well-matched with Bill Jones's Will Parker. Sam Herdman's Jud ('sinister')[19] and Kenneth Richardson's Ali Hakim also received good reviews, though one might take issue with the *Darlington & Stockton Times* that the role of Jud is thankless – it has more meat in it than that of Laurey. The *Darlington & Stockton Times* also said that Susan Swift as Aunt Eller bore a 'striking resemblance to Eleanor Roosevelt'. One dare not ask how Sue feels about this! The *Northern Despatch* voted the show '100% fun'[20] and, to quote the last line of the show's title song, the general verdict of the press was '*Oklahoma!* O.K.' The choreography for the show was created by Peter Miller himself and was rehearsed by Joy Beadell, who also danced the Laurey role in the 'dream ballet' scene. It was one of the highlights of the production, so much so that the *Darlington & Stockton Times* reviewer mentioned each of the dancers by name. Peter Henderson had partnered Joy in the dream-sequence role of Curly with Ivan Stockdale as the dream-Jud, and the incarnations of Jud's picture postcard pin-ups were danced by Pauline Hardy, Greta Sanderson, Julia Thornton and Brenda Halliwell. Ann Thompson's little cameo dancing role as Aggie Pigtails was also spoken of as being outstanding. The opinions of the reviewers were echoed by the sizes of the audiences – all seats were booked throughout the week. The show showed a profit of nearly £450, so the Committee would be in a somewhat better frame of mind than it was at the beginning of the year.

Jack F. Hilton's pantomime *Dick Whittington* was to be given less than two months after the end of *Oklahoma!* so, with Christmas also intervening, there was no time to sit back and rest on one's laurels. The cast of the pantomime was composed mainly of members who had had a rest (if one can call chorus and backstage work a 'rest') during the last show or who had not been in that show at all. The exceptions were Susan and Carol Swift, who were playing Captain Bold and Fatima respectively. Eileen Young, who had been prompter for *Oklahoma!*, was Idle Jack, with Vera Dickinson as Lazy Larry. Meg Leeming was principal boy with Vicki Tringham as Alice Fitzwarren. Anne Henderson, who had joined the chorus for *Oklahoma!*, played the Cat, and Arthur Messenger, playing in his only show for the Society, was Mrs Whittington, the Dame. A new member, Glennis Beresford, played Zulika, and Bob White was Musical Director.

Jack Hilton himself took, as his fee, 5% of the gross box office receipts but even so the pantomime made a profit of over £150 which was ploughed back into the theatre. The papers accorded it qualified praise. Meg Leeming was, as usual, outstanding, and Anne Henderson gave an ingenious performance as the Cat. Eileen Young and Vera Dickinson provided plenty of laughs – 'with an adept and loving hand', said the *Darlington & Stockton Times*, '. . . [they] polished up even old panto jokes.'[21] The paper also highlighted the performance of Arthur Messenger as a 'lively and competent Dame', taking his cue from Eileen and Vera. Adela Iveson, another newcomer, possessed an excellent speaking voice and made an 'attractive and energetic Fairy Bowbell'. The Stage Managers (Messrs Stairmand, Sampson, Sanderson and Hathaway) even got a special mention for the final scene – a Highland glen – and the two accompanists, Edith Kershaw and Alan McDonald, were also singled out, along with Bob White. This was ultimately pleasing as there had been a number of slip-ups on the first night. Vera Dickinson remembered that she and Eileen Young had to sweep the stage with large sweeping-brushes during the song *Busy Doing Nothing* and the head came off one of the brooms and shot into the orchestra pit. Luckily this all added to the general hilarity which constantly swept through the audience. The *Northern Echo* and the *Northern Despatch* both recorded the fact that at the end of the first night the children in the audience 'broke into tumultuous cheering',[22] and the *Northern Despatch* concluded that the show was 'great for the young (of all ages!)'[23]

It was quickly 'off with the old and on with the new', for the next show was less than three months away. Auditions were held for *The Merry Widow* on 7 February and the whole thing was cast (apart from Anna Glavari, the female lead) that same day with a minimum of trouble – although after William Foster got the part of Danilo, which George Goodyear had wanted, and George got the smaller part of Cascada, George never spoke to William again! Kern and Hammerstein's *Showboat* was chosen for autumn and ten days later another pantomime – the John Denis production of *Jack and the Beanstalk* – was chosen for 1960. At that same meeting Vera Dickinson joined Lorrie Boddy as a wardrobe mistress and the Committee also recommended that the office of Ticket Secretary and Patrons Secretary should be combined: Norman Thompson took the job over for the ensuing period. At the meeting of 18 March, Bob White became Secretary with Bill Jones as his assistant, Jim Willans became Treasurer with Frank Murray as assistant, and Jim Fraser Murray became Librarian. Sam Herdman became Chairman for the first of several times, and Robert Farrage was to be Musical Director, as usual, for *The Merry Widow*.

There was a problem over the appointment of a Producer for *Showboat*. Edward Royce Jun. had been asked, but was unfortunately unable to help, and Peter Miller could only do it if the date of the show was postponed by a week. Frank Murray and Bill Jones proposed that this should be done, but since the vote was only carried by six to three it was further proposed that John Morton, a young local producer and musician, should be asked and, if he was unavailable, then steps would be taken to try to change the date of the show and get Peter Miller. That settled, Norman Thompson reported that he had received confirmation of the contract with Arthur Garside for a production of *The King and I* by Rogers and Hammerstein in the spring of 1960. (There had been no previous mention of this choice of show, unless it came up at the Annual General Meeting, from which no minutes survive.) Clearly they were both well ahead and well organized.

It was too good to last. Less than two weeks later Robert Farrage died suddenly. It was a blow to everyone. He had been associated with the Society for so long that he was like part of the furniture and had been Musical Director for 23 shows since the war. Fortunately Bob White was able to take over for the time being, and Frank Murray took over Bob's position as Secretary. An advertisement would have to be placed for a Musical Director for *Showboat*.

Tribute was paid to Robert Farrage in the programme for *The Merry Widow* while Bob White managed to carry off the musical directorship with great success – the *Northern Despatch* and especially the *Northern Echo* acknowledged this. Indeed, the whole show was an outstanding success, the *Darlington & Stockton Times* taking nearly two columns over its review. June Williams, making her debut with the Society, had performed in the title role with great charm and her rendering of *Vilia* was particularly warmly received, while William Foster made a suitably dashing Danilo. Ken Bodden's performance as the bumbling Njegus was also especially enjoyed, and the *Women, Women, Women* number was one of the comedy highlights, not least because of George Goodyear. He was by no means a gifted dancer and consequently never got the steps right, but while it drove the other dancers mad the audience loved it! The *Darlington & Stockton Times* summed the show up: 'At the end of this spirited and highly competent performance,' it said, 'I heard a number of the audience say that it was the best amateur show that had been seen in Darlington for years. Assessing this conservatively and with no special brief for the amateur theatre one can say quite firmly that Darlington Operatic Society's performance of *The Merry Widow* will long be remembered as a landmark in the Society's progress and a splendid contribution to the town's live entertainment.' [24]

By this time there was a little more live entertainment at the theatre, for a few more organizations had booked it for their productions. The programme for *The Merry Widow* lists the future attractions and bookings. Three local dancing schools had booked to perform dancing displays (Darlington School of Music and Dancing, Winifred Boylan's School of Dancing, and Joy Beadell's own School of Dancing). The Pilgrim Players were doing a play for four nights and some professionals were also coming: the Max Jaffa Trio, Ballet Rambert, and an opera quartet from Sadlers Wells. So at least a bit more revenue was coming in to keep the theatre going. There was good news for the Society, too: the number of Vice-Presidents and Patrons had crept up just a little from *Oklahoma!*, and even a little increase is better than none. In addition, the profit from *The Merry Widow* was approximately £250. There was something of an upset in the committee room over the appointment of a new Musical Director. Bob White, fresh from his triumph as Musical Director for *The Merry Widow*, was present at a special committee meeting convened on 6 May to discuss this subject. There was 'considerable discussion during which several viewpoints were expressed' and the majority vote was that the post should be advertised. At the normal monthly meeting exactly two weeks later the Secretary reported that he had received the resignation of Bob White, not only from the Committee, but from the Society. He had, on behalf of the Committee, tried to persuade Bob to reconsider but was told that the decision was final.

Harry Stanley was appointed Musical Director. He had had connections with the Society since its inception – not the post-war Society but the original one;* he and his wife Edith (née Williams) were the principal tenor and soprano singers when the Society was revived after the falling-off caused by the First World War. They went to Teesside in 1927 and Harry was a founder member of both Redcar Operatic Society (1928) and Middlesbrough Operatic Society (1934), being Musical Director and Producer for both. When he returned to Darlington in 1937 he became Choirmaster at Coniscliffe Road Methodist Church and formed an operatic society

---

* The *Darlington & Stockton Times* review of the 1914 production of *HMS Pinafore* (see Ch. 1 Ref. 2) records that '. . . owing to the indisposition of Mr Frank Dixon the important part of Mr Joseph Porter was undertaken at short notice by Mr Henry G. Stanley and under the circumstances he is to be congratulated on the excellence of his acting and singing.'

there in 1938 – the one which was so unfortunately disbanded in 1955. The Committee also decided to appoint a Deputy Musical Director. A week later Bob White was back in the fold, not only in his customary place on the Committee but also installed as Deputy Musical Director!

Someone else was retiring from the Committee, however – someone who would be sorely missed. Susan Robinson (née Swift) has described him as 'a lovely man'. On 20 May 1959 Tom Gilchrist attended his last committee meeting and said how much he had enjoyed his time with the Society. Sam Herdman (the Chairman) replied by saying how much the Committee was indebted to Tom for the excellent work he had done over the years. In appreciation he was made an Honorary Life Member of the Society, along with Isabel Farrage, widow of Robert and for so many years the Patrons Secretary. This honour is not bestowed lightly and not many people have been awarded it. Tribute was also paid to Norman Thompson for his sterling service over many years now that he had stood down as Secretary. Engraved cigarette boxes were given to both the gentlemen.

To bring the Committee up to full strength Richard Sampson, George Todd and Ken Bodden were co-opted. Frank Murray took over the job of Secretary.

They, together with the rest of the Committee, auditioned the encouraging number of prospective new members on 11 June 1959 – twelve of them, of whom ten were accepted. One in particular was a name to watch, for Mollie Jaques was a future leading lady. *Showboat* presented a large cast (72) for John Morton (who *had* fortunately been available to produce) to deal with. A talented young man from Darlington, John had begun his theatrical career acting with the local Repertory Company. He went to the Nottingham Playhouse, and then to various places around the country, before giving up acting to take up production in 1953. As well as directing provincial productions he also lectured in scenic design, lighting, acting and production, and had written a musical adaptation of Lewis Carroll's 'Alice' stories which he directed in America and South Africa. He went on to work with film director Anthony Asquith. John is also a musician, being one of the few British performers on the *Ondes Martenot.** He has written and performed film music as well as performing some of the music, on the *Ondes Martenot*, for the TV series *Flambards*.

Showboat was fraught with difficulties. There was still the perennial problem of insufficient men six weeks before the show – so much so that the members of the Committee were expressly asked to try and round up

* *Ondes Martenot* (Martenot waves): a hauntingly beautiful electric instrument invented by Maurice Martenot in 1928 and still hand-made, in Paris, today.

some men who would be useful to fill the numerous small parts which still remained to be cast. Also, despite telegrams and telephone calls to Scenic Display Co. Ltd., the stage plans had not yet arrived and when the scenery itself arrived the Stage Manager was not too pleased with it. Joan Geeves, who was to play Magnolia, was pregnant but Glennis Beresford was appointed understudy. Ticket bookings were going well, however; Wilfred Downing had spent £50 on publicity. By the time the Committee met on 21 October over £1,400 worth of tickets had been sold. The three and a half hour show went on and played to full houses. The reviewers received it with mixed feelings, the *Northern Despatch* being the most critical, saying that, technically speaking, it had several faults, not least the noise from backstage. The co-ordination of singers and orchestra also left something to be desired. It also felt that the show lacked movement and that the groupings were repetitive, though the *Darlington & Stockton Times* disagreed. The *Northern Echo* felt that it would have benefited from more rehearsal. The *Darlington & Stockton Times*, however, recognized that it was a very ambitious show from every point of view, let alone the scene-shifting aspect. *Showboat* posed more problems than any other musical which the Society had tackled and the limitations of the stage had added to the difficulties. Having said all this the press were unanimous in saying that it was an enjoyable show and that there were some memorable performances by individuals. Joan Geeves gave of her best as Magnolia, as did Sam Herdman as Joe, particularly in his rendering of *Ole Man River*. Carol Swift and Brian Thorpe's comedy was entertaining as Ellie and Frank and they made a good team (in more ways than one, for they later married). Kenneth Richardson as Captain Andy with Susan Swift as his wife Parthy Ann were also singled out for their performances. The dancing was regarded as being first class under the training of Joy Beadell and Greta Sanderson. (One of those dancers, incidentally, was Irene Skippon, who had become an Associate of the Royal Academy of Dancing the previous year.)

It had been an expensive show to do so the profit was not so very great – at approximately £170 it was £80 less than for *The Merry Widow* but the Society was able, that year, to donate a total of £300 to charity, which made a most satisfactory end to 1959.

The last five years had been a time of turbulence, what with the death of Robert Farrage and the consequent problems of the musical directorship, coupled with all the worry over the theatre. The great triumph, of course, had been the rescue of the theatre, though its long-term future was still uncertain. Despite all the difficulties, however, the Society had still managed to fulfil its aim of supporting charities; by the end of 1954 it had donated just over £4,500 – now, five years later, that figure had risen to around £7,000.

Chapter 5

1960–1964

The Society hoped to do well with its first production for 1960 – the pantomime. The original choice had been *Mother Goose* but in view of the great difficulties encountered in obtaining scenery for this, it was left to Frank Murray and Norman Thompson to choose something more suitable. They chose *Jack and the Beanstalk* by Jack F. Hilton with music by Thomas F. Robinson. John Denis came to produce it, Bob White was Musical Director, and Joy Beadell the Choreographer. John Morton designed the settings and lighting, and since the scenery was being built by a Mr J. Dodd (with the help of an Operatic Society working party) and would be *in situ*, the theatre rental of £130 would include the use of that scenery. Admission prices were to be 5s., 3s. 6d., 2s. 6d., and 1s. and if patrons wanted to book in advance prior to the opening of the box office bookings there would be a surcharge of sixpence per ticket (obtainable from Ken Bodden).

Alas, one of the audience's favourite faces would be missing from this pantomime, for Vera Dickinson had decided to call it a day and was working backstage doing make-up. She was much missed. She and Eileen Young had been a comedy team *par excellence* over the years and Vera had many happy memories. She remembered how Eileen Young had a strip torn off her by Robert Farrage for ad libbing during *Cinderella* (it was in the scene of trying on the slipper which would not fit – 'The corn isn't all in Egypt!' said Eileen). They had not been too popular with Mr Hinge at first, either. He did not like women playing the Ugly Sisters, parts normally allotted to men, even though the Dame was played by Fred Thompson. To be fair to Mr Hinge, once he had seen Eileen and Vera's double act he had offered them places in his own theatrical troupe, but it was out of the question for Vera, who had a three-year-old son by that time.

Jack and the Beanstalk had quite a large cast, with 46 chorus and dancers, two teams of children from Joy Beadell's Dancing School and an orchestra of fourteen. Meg Leeming was playing her customary role as principal boy with Greta Sanderson as the Princess and Eileen Young as the Dame. The Swift sisters were there again as Prince Robin (Susan) and Maudie Trot (Carol) with Adela Iveson as the fairy once more, Horace Wilson as the Giant, and Ivan Stockdale and David Todd (son of George and Peggy) as Daisy the Cow. Fiona Bishop, daughter of Joy Beadell, and Susanne Murray, daughter of John and Lona, Frank Murray's brother and sister-in-law, were among the children.

In addition to the cast, many other people were putting in considerable amounts of work. George Todd had asked if a working party could be organized to help with the many jobs which had to be done at the theatre before the pantomime could be put on, so these workers were also toiling away. The vexed question of musical directors for future productions had caused 'considerable discussion' at the last committee meeting of 1959. In the end they compromised. Harry Stanley would be invited to deal with *The King and I*, and Bob White would do the autumn show, which was to be *Brigadoon*. All unpleasantness thus circumvented, they were able to have, at least, a peaceful Christmas and New Year; they had even got as far as selecting a spring show for 1961 – Rodgers and Hammerstein's *South Pacific*. As always the pantomime was a great success – much more, it seems, with children than with adults. The singing seems to have been under par but the younger members of the audience did not find this of any consequence. They were too busy enjoying the comedy and spectacle. John Morton was, and is, a very gifted theatrical designer and his settings were all that could be wished. There were pop tunes for the children to sing along with, Eileen Young and the Cow made them laugh, and Horace Wilson scared them half to death, which was exactly the recipe for success in a child's eyes. The *Northern Despatch* critic, in fact, wrote the review from the point of view of the child who accompanied him or her – Kathy aged nine. The reviewer tactlessly remarked in the middle of the first half that someone was singing out of tune and was told 'Shush!'[1] In the reviewer's opinion the skeleton ballet, performed by Peter Henderson and Ivan Stockdale, was a bit garish, lit as it was with ultra-violet light. 'At this Kathy got positively angry,' says the critic, so he or she decided to obey orders and shut up! Kathy directed the writing of the rest of the review and said to mention especially Eileen Young whose Dame was the funniest thing she'd ever seen, and Herbert Burgin's Basil the Bailiff, which was the next funniest. She also said not to leave out King Merrythought (Denis Quinn) or the Cow because she had liked them a lot, too. 'Out of the mouths of babes and sucklings . . .'!

At the first committee meeting of 1960, on 20 January – four days after the last night of the pantomime – the Treasurer reported that it had grossed £1,147, so it seemed a good start to the new year. They swiftly organized all the appointments. Joy Beadell was to be Ballet Mistress for Arthur Garside's production of *The King and I*, and, having experienced immense difficulties in getting rehearsal pianists from time to time in the past, the Committee had secured no fewer than three – as well as the faithful Edith Kershaw there were Kathleen Coulson and June Chambers to assist her; they all received small fees for their work.

By 17 February all the principal parts had been cast (including under-studies!), and the King's children were chosen soon afterwards. Kenneth Richardson was the King. Lun Tha, the younger male lead, was Raymond Simmons, and playing opposite him, as Tuptim, was Dorothy Matthew, a pretty former High School girl who had just joined the Society and who had Ann Thompson as her understudy.* Mollie Jaques came from the chorus to play Lady Thiang, the King's head wife, and Jean Herdman (no relation to Sam) understudied her. Ken Bodden played The Krala-home (a court official) and was understudied by Denis Quinn, George Goodyear was Sir Edward Ramsey, and Wade Cobban was Captain Orton. There were many other new faces in the cast, however, besides Dorothy Matthew. Una Strong re-joined the Society to play Anna, the leading lady, having played a small role in *Perchance to Dream* four years earlier. Una was married to a local doctor and had had no formal tuition in singing – she was simply a 'natural'. She was very striking in appearance and, according to a member of the show's cast, was a superb Anna, though she had difficulty, at first, in coordinating actions and singing. David Todd also appeared, fresh from his triumph as half of the Cow in the panto-mime, as Phra Alack. Some of the new faces were smaller ones and reflected the 'family' aspect of the Society. Stephen and Peter Sanderson, Bernard and Greta's two boys, were among the Royal Princes, and so was Barry Grieveson, son of Cecil. Frank Murray's two sons, John (who was playing Anna's son Louis) and Philip were there, too. The Society now had the entire family involved as Roula, Frank's wife, also appeared in the chorus – as an Amazon, no less! Philip was another Society member who made a career in the professional theatre after attending the Guildhall School of Music and Drama. Using the name Philip Tsaras (Tsaras was Roula's Greek maiden name) he joined the Dougie Squires Dancers and then the Second Generation troupe of dancers, with whom he went to Hong Kong, before returning to the London stage to appear in musicals. Another new small face among the Royal Princesses was that of Michelle Newell. Her mother, Margot, had been in the three shows just before the war and Michelle was already showing the promise which she was amply to fulfil in later years, for she went on to make a career in theatre and television. After leaving the Central School of Speech and Drama in London, she appeared in *Cranford* and then as a young wife in *When the*

---

* Dorothy died, tragically early, in 1991.

Boat Comes In (in which, incidentally, she had to die – so she had the dubious pleasure of being able to watch her own funeral on TV). She has had to 'die' quite a lot on television. When she was recording *The Hunchback of Notre Dame*, playing Esmeralda, and had to 'hang' three times (until the scene was to the director's liking), the director wanted her to do it herself rather than use a stuntwoman. She drew the line at that, even though she quite likes 'dying' in the cause of art! One of her very demanding roles on TV was as all the eponymous heroines of the series *The Cleopatras* in which she had to age from eleven years old to sixty. Her 'death' in that programme also caused some uneasy moments as the asp they used was a live one! She was 'hanged' yet again in an episode on TV of *Under Suspicious Circumstances*. Michelle, now married and with a junior-school-age daughter, is still very busy in the theatre, having played all the female leads in *The L.A. Plays* on the London stage, as well as being co-director with Beatie Edney, daughter of actress Sylvia Sims, of a writers' company.

The King and I was a great show for bringing in the young. Even backstage the teenage Eoin Bishop had joined his elder brother Bill as a Lime Boy* and they were accompanied by Barry Todd (David's brother and George and Peggy's other son), who was of a similar age.

Rehearsals were well under way by the time the Annual General Meeting and the next monthly meeting were held on 9 and 16 March, though there was some consternation about irregular attendances at rehearsals. There was also some question about whether it was too much of a burden on the Society to present three shows a year. The Chairman wondered whether it might be a good idea to substitute a play for one of the musicals so as to give acting opportunities to people not able to be in the musicals, though this idea did not, in the end, bear fruit. The panto-mime, despite its popularity with the young and the apparently large gross takings, had, unfortunately, lost money – about £55 – but the Society had been able to give £1,000 to the theatre because of the success of the other two shows.

In the event the Committee finalized the decision to present a panto-mime plus two other shows for 1961. *The Wizard of Oz* had first been discussed but the efforts of Frank Murray to find out about the chances of presenting it had met with a dead end so it was decided that John Morton should be asked to write, produce, and design sets for a version of *The Sleeping Beauty*. As to future shows, Rodgers and Hammerstein's *South Pacific* seemed like a good choice for spring 1961 since the film had been released in 1958 and had proved to be a great hit with the public.

* A Lime Boy is a person who operates a spotlight.

The songs were therefore well known and it should be good box office. *Naughty Marietta*, Victor Herbert's show written in 1905, was a possibility for the autumn and the reintroduction of a Gilbert & Sullivan show, *Iolanthe*, might be viable for spring 1962 since there would have been a ten-year gap since *The Mikado*.

The next event was, of course, the performance of *The King and I*. It had been well advertised and W. Mutrie and Son Ltd. of Edinburgh – the only costumiers, incidentally, who were able to supply costumes for it (though Torbay Operatic Society kindly loaned pagoda hats and collars free of charge) – had sent some of the costumes early so that they could be displayed in the window of G. A. Williams' music shop for a week before the show, thus whetting the public's appetite. Whether or not this helped we do not know, but they flocked to see the show – and a profit of £300 was mentioned at the May committee meeting. The press enjoyed it, too. The only adverse criticism they could offer was that Kenneth Richardson's delivery of some of his lines was so quick as to render them less effective and that Una Strong burlesqued the soliloquy in which Anna rails at the King's tyranny (though, in fairness to her, this would be planned by the producer). Other than that it got rave reviews. They said it was 'spectacularly inventive, sentimental without being mawkish and undeniably a great hit',[2] that 'it will easily be one of the most successful and rewarding productions ever put on by Darlington Operatic Society – ingenious, novel, colourful and ambitious',[3] and that it was 'ingeniously inventive, without resorting to unnecessary, unscripted tomfooleries'.[4] They all agreed that Una Strong ('looking like the young Queen Victoria', said the *Northern Echo*) and Kenneth Richardson gave performances which were, that first small criticism apart, just as they should be. Tears were suspected in the audience in the deathbed scene. Mollie Jaques had made a tremendous impression in her first major role – she had given the part all the dignity and tragic resignation it required and also had a beautiful voice. The young lovers were suitably romantic and the ballet sequences devised by Joy Beadell were outstanding. Of course, though, it was the children who proved to be the showstoppers. 'Captivating' and 'adorable' were the words the reviewers used and John Murray and Michael Airey, the latter as the young Prince who would succeed his father the King, received special mention.

It was all too much, however, for little Peter Sanderson. He was only five years old and as the week went on the late nights caught up with him. He did not make himself popular with John Murray (who was, of course, his cousin) by yawning prodigiously during John's big moment in the show. Moreover, he finally excelled himself, at the end of the week, in a scene where the children all had to crouch down with their heads

Frank Murray

lowered. When the time came to get up there was no response from Peter. He had fallen sound asleep.

This show had done so well, even for the matinée, that the Committee decided at the meeting on 18 May that there should be a matinée performance of *Brigadoon* in the autumn.

The Sleeping Beauty, as was customary for pantomime, would have a matinée, too, when it was performed from 9 to 14 January 1961, and it was hoped that it would be cast as soon as possible after 30 June. A pleasing item of news was that Watts and Corry Ltd. of Manchester would be supplying new scenery for *South Pacific* – it is always nice to have something brand new for a production, be it scenery or costumes.

The penultimate committee meeting before the summer break saw the departure of one of the founder-members of the Society, for Norman Thompson was moving away from the district. Special tribute was paid to him, for he had worked extremely hard in the interests of the Society. His place on the Operatic Society Committee was taken by Jim Fraser Murray, and on the Civic Theatre Committee by Frank Murray. This would fulfil one of Frank's wishes, as he had been quite hurt not to have been elected when this committee was formed. The theatre situation was still unsatisfactory. In August the papers reported that the Council was seeking further information before deciding whether or not to buy it. Many people were supporting local councillors in thinking that it would be wrong to spend £8,000 on a building 'which might turn out to be a white elephant'.[5] In the last few years there had been a country-wide decline of public support for live theatre and the Council, though wanting to retain such entertainment, did not want something which would be a financial drain on the town. In spite of all the work by the Operatic Society the theatre was still looking quite shabby. The balance would seem to be coming down, at this point, in favour of heads ruling hearts.

The Society, meanwhile, proceeded with rehearsals for *Brigadoon* and was addressing the problem of finding someone to play the bagpipes for it.* This show was a major 'first' for Joy Beadell, for two reasons: she had been elected to the Committee, which had been a male stronghold for many years, and she was producing the show – her first major production for the Darlington society in the Civic Theatre.

During the rehearsals auditions were taking place for *Aurora* (John Morton's version of *The Sleeping Beauty*), and by 21 September all the parts were filled except for that of Bertram, a footman. Anna Saunders – who was playing Meg Brockie, the chief comic character, in *Brigadoon* – was to be Aurora with Kenneth Richardson as the bad fairy Aloysius Candlewick. Corin, the male lead, was to have been played by Bob Witcher, a regular army officer and professional singer, trained at the Royal Academy of Music, who had joined the Society to play Charlie Cameron in *Brigadoon*, but he dropped out and the part was played by Brian Thorpe. The comedy would be taken care of (alongside Kenneth Richardson) by Eileen Young as Alicia Canticle, the Good Fairy, and by Glennis Beresford, Vicki Tringham, Ray Simmons and (eventually) Colin Musgrave as Ladies-in-Waiting and Footmen. Members of West Hartlepool and Shildon Operatic Societies were helping out, some of the latter helping backstage, and George Todd and Norman Stairmand were busy building scenery. The Committee was even thinking as far ahead as *South Pacific*, as far as casting went, for they decided that Fiona Bishop, Joy's daughter, should play Ngana the little girl.

Tickets for *Brigadoon* were going well. This was the first show for which a discount on tickets was introduced for block bookings, though only for the first night and the matinée, and there were even block bookings from operatic societies as far away as Stoke-on-Trent and Kelty (near Lochore in Scotland). Did they enjoy it? Well the press certainly did, and according to the press the audience did, too. George Goodyear, as Tommy the

---

* They got someone: Cpl/Tec. D. G. Clark, of RAF Leeming.

leading man, gave his customary polished performance with Tony Trees as his comic companion Jeff. The latter's scenes with the irrepressible Anna Saunders were hailed as one of the highlights of the show.* Mollie Jaques was an endearing leading lady as Fiona McKeith, and Peter Henderson, in his first major role (as Harry Ritchie, the discontented villager who nearly causes tragedy), was described by the *Darlington & Stockton Times* as having 'outstanding dramatic ability'.[6] His dancing – along with that of Adela Iveson, Irene Skippon and Ann Thompson – was also singled out, but as always Joy Beadell's expertise had ensured that the dancing was particularly effective. The *Northern Despatch* was a little discontented with some of the singing and a lack of balance with the orchestra under the baton of Bob White. Since the *Darlington & Stockton Times* complimented them on 'commendable balance' and the *Northern Echo* made no special comment on this, opinions were divided down the middle. A new member of the Society, who had joined to be in the chorus for *Jack and the Beanstalk*, appeared in the cameo role of Jane Ashton, the American fiancée of the leading man. She was Betty Gargett (who would marry Gordon MacFall the following year) and was yet another Society member who went on to a career in the theatre, though on the administrative side. She appeared in several other shows but became assistant to the Director's secretary, Sylvia Tweddle, at the Darlington theatre in 1975, and then became secretary when Mrs Tweddle retired. She is still there and in familiar surroundings, for her office is the room in which her brother was born. The original shop which stood where the theatre box office is now was the Regent fish and chip shop, owned by J. C. Moody, her grandfather, and the family lived above the shop so she is at home in her work in more ways than one.

Brigadoon did well at the box office and made a profit of approximately £450 – Joy Beadell had good cause to be elated with her success. It was especially pleasing to the Society as they were uncertain as to how *Aurora* would be received, being a completely new work. They had inserted a booking form for tickets for it in the *Brigadoon* programme and they awaited the production eagerly.

John Morton had set the show to Tchaikovsky's music for *Swan Lake* and *The Sleeping Beauty*, and Colin Tarn was arranging and orchestrating it. At the dress rehearsal he was still writing down the music! Again, apart from one or two quibbles about some of the timing and lighting and a rather long first act, the press loved it. It was original, it was inventive, it

---

* Tony was in several shows with the Society and his was yet another early and tragic death, in January 1979.

was lively, and it had a good cast playing in gorgeous costumes and settings ('West End standard',[7] said the *Northern Despatch*). In short, it was fun* and both the *Darlington & Stockton Times* and the *Northern Despatch* regarded it as a 'triumph'.[8] Eileen Young and Kenneth Richardson had lived up to expectations – Eileen's part was especially written for her and disappointment was felt that Kenneth's bad fairy had to suffer defeat. The audiences participated fully and greatly enjoyed it but the takings were well down on those for *Brigadoon*. It lost £280, which was a great pity as it was supported by the attendance of several of John Morton's well-known friends from the theatre world. The actor Paul Massie and his wife were there, along with Peter Mardon the television personality and his wife, though sadly Anthony Asquith was unable to attend. In addition, Lady Crathorne brought her two sons to see it. Nevertheless it was good that those people who saw it had the opportunity of seeing an original show put on by local talent.

Problems had been experienced with the proposed staging of *Naughty Marietta* in the autumn of 1961, so this was now abandoned. In its place the Committee decided on Rodgers and Hammerstein's *Carousel*, to be produced, like *The King and I* and *South Pacific*, by Arthur Garside of London, with Wright and Forrest's *Kismet* to follow in the spring of 1962, produced by Joy Beadell. Ticket prices, however, would have to rise. The circle and front stalls would be 7s. 6d. with the back stalls at 6s. and the upper circle 2s. 6d. except for the final night when the circle and front stalls would be 10s. Most costs were rising (though Watts and Corry Ltd. were making the same scenery charge – £75 – for both *Carousel* and *Kismet*) and there was a slow but steady decrease in the number of Vice-Presidents and Patrons, thus reducing donations. There were also, at this time, yet more unsettling rumblings about the future of the theatre and the Committee wanted to have a meeting with the theatre committee about it. There was very little going on there save the Operatic Society's productions (though the rent was paid up to the end of the lease, which would be 5 May 1962).

South Pacific was fully cast except for the chorus ladies, but therein was a hornets' nest. It was rumoured that they would have to audition in bathing costumes, and this, as Brian Thorpe pointed out at the Annual General Meeting on 9 March 1961, 'caused a lot of mixed feelings within

---

* Sue Robinson (née Swift) remembers representing a statue, standing at one side of the stage with her back to the audience. One arm was bent at the elbow with hand extended, palm upwards, towards the side of the stage. One night one of the stage crew eased the side curtain across to mask her hand, placed a bread bun on her upturned palm and stealthily withdrew, allowing the curtain to return gently to its place . . .

the Company'! Brian had quite a lot to say at that particular meeting on the subject of auditions and aired a few grievances on behalf of a number of members. He felt; a) that the Committee should be fully conversant with the songs and story of each show before hearing auditions; b) that if members wished to audition for more than one part they should be allowed to do a full audition for each part rather than be offered one role on the strength of their audition for another; c) that though Ken Bodden was excellent at reading-in male parts, a suitable lady should be found to read in female parts; d) that parts should be filled by existing members of the Society through re-auditioning throughout the Society if those parts were not cast first time round; and e) that the little matter of the bathing costumes should be raised. The tone of the minutes gives the impression that the Committee was pole-axed by this flow of rhetoric – Jim Willans (the Chairman) replied, rather faintly one feels, that the Committee had been very interested in what he said and would bear it in mind. Brian was then elected to the Committee! It was as well that the rest of the meeting's business was already concluded. In the main this consisted of the Chairman and the Secretary remarking on what happy shows all the three previous productions had been and paying tribute to the members for their performances. It was irritating, though, that members were not buying their own vocal scores and were therefore sharing at rehearsals; also there were the perennial problems of members not selling tickets when they were not in a show and of former principals not helping out in the chorus when no longer principals. This would not help the cause of the preservation of the theatre now that it was in such dire straits. (At this meeting Tom Bourn, the Hon. Vice-President, was reported as absent because of illness and it was resolved that a letter of good wishes for his speedy and permanent recovery be sent to him. He was lucky to survive this, if only by less than a year. Looking back over the minutes for the early days of the Society it seemed to occur with disturbing frequency that get-well wishes would be reported as being sent to sufferers at one committee meeting and a minute's silence would be observed for them at the next!)

With the interests of the theatre in mind the Committee ensured that *South Pacific*, which ran from 1 to 6 May 1961, had stapled into its programme a slip directed at all theatre-lovers, eloquently exhorting them to help the Operatic Society in its aim of preserving live theatre in the town by supporting events which took place there and by getting in touch with the Town Council to press them to buy it as a civic theatre. To the extent of supporting the Operatic Society's next production a few of the public did take notice. Where the Vice-Presidents' and Patrons' numbers had decreased by 50 between *The King and I* and *South Pacific*, they rose

South Pacific 1961 – Chorus. *See page x for full list.*

by 26 for *Carousel* – not much, it is true, but half a loaf is better than no bread and at least the message was getting through to *some* members of the public. *South Pacific* was an enjoyable show despite its faults (the orchestra, under Bob White, was chided by the press for being too loud) and the leading lady, Meg Leeming as Nellie Forbush, was as outstanding in a straight musical as she had been in pantomime. She had first-class reviews in all the papers and Roula Murray – taking her first leading role, as Bloody Mary – ran her a close second. (This was interesting as Roula had had no voice-training and in fact only began to have singing lessons after this show.) George Goodyear and Horace Wilson also gave good performances as Emile de Becque and Luther Billis (the companion role to Bloody Mary). Irene Skippon was a charming Liat – the first time she had played a major role for the Society – and of course Fiona Bishop and Philip Murray as the two children were appealing to the audience. The show moved at a good pace and it was 'well-dressed, cleverly danced and superbly produced'[9] – but it was Meg Leeming's performance which gave it its 'lift'. There is no record in the minutes, however, of how financially successful *South Pacific* was, because other matters became paramount. Things were going fairly smoothly, the Committee thought, for Arthur Garside's production of *Carousel* with Bob White as Musical Director (they could not know that the show would cause a small but bitter storm in the press) and Frank Murray had been elected to the Board of Management of the Civic Theatre with several other committee members also up for appointment. Also the Society proposed to give the theatre a donation of £1,500, but by the committee meeting of 18 October 1961 things were looking grave on the theatre front.

Jim Willans reported that he felt unable to pay over the £1,500 the Society had promised to the theatre after what had been said at the Annual General Meeting of the Civic Theatre Group (though we do not know what this was), and it was decided that legal advice should be taken over the Society's position concerning the theatre. An emergency meeting of the Operatic Society Committee was to be held with the Chairman of the Civic Theatre along with any other members of the Civic Theatre who were members of the Operatic Society, on 22 October, to discuss terms.

There was a certain amount of acrimony at that meeting, which was chaired by Bernard Sanderson. The conditions under which the £1,500 donation would be made, now that legal advice had been taken, were laid before the assembled company. These were, in essence, a) that the Civic Theatre Ltd. should henceforward be composed exclusively of members of the Operatic Society or their nominees; b) that the Articles of Association should be altered to increase the number of Councillors on that body to at least twelve; c) that the terms of lease from the Council should be made known to the Operatic Society; and d) that the £1,500 should be handed over only when the first and third of these terms had been completed and the second agreed to; the £1,500 was to be refunded at the rate of £100 for each letting to the Operatic Society. What it boiled down to was whether Darlington Civic Theatre Ltd. should take up the option to buy the theatre for £8,000 and then sell it to the Darlington Corporation for £5,500. (The Operatic Society had already given the Civic Theatre £1,000 at its inauguration.) This was dependent on the Operatic Society providing the difference in the buying and selling prices. Moreover, the Operatic Society Committee was unhappy at the way the Civic Theatre Company had been run.

Fred Thompson (by now Alderman Fred Thompson) was nettled. He said that the purchase and sale going through was dependent on the money provided by the Operatic Society and that that money must be forthcoming within the next few days or the option to buy would be lost. The fixed date for the option was 4 November. Besides, it would take time to get a decision from the Civic Theatre Committee and it would take two or three months to alter the Articles of Association. Therefore a decision by the Operatic Society Committee would have to be made immediately. Heated discussion followed and finally Fred, after a recital of his woes at the situation, agreed to put the Operatic Society's terms to the Civic Theatre Committee. There seems to be no doubt from the tone of his capitulation that he knew in his heart that a merging of the two committees – the Operatic Society's and The Civic Theatre's – was the best thing possible for their mutual satisfaction. He certainly had the interests of preserving the theatre at heart. There also seems to be no doubt that he had found his chairmanship of the Civic Theatre to be onerous. He would recommend to his Committee on 25 October that the Operatic Society's terms should be accepted.

And so it was done. The Darlington Corporation paid £5,500 and the Civic Theatre Company paid the other £2,500 with money from Darlington Operatic Society.* This having been accomplished the theatre then belonged to the Darlington Corporation, and the Civic Theatre Company, now having no reason to exist, was wound up, but the theatre was saved and got its new name – the Civic Theatre, Darlington (though this was modified to Darlington Civic Theatre, which sounds less clumsy, in 1972).

Against the background of all these fireworks *Carousel* was performed and created its own storm. The press did not care for it and said so in no uncertain terms, and the public reacted angrily to their comments. The unfortunate *Northern Despatch* took all the flak, though the other two papers were just as scathing. It was not so much the performance of the show which displeased them (though they criticized the slowness of the American drawl adopted by the cast) but the show itself. The *Northern Echo* suggested that it would benefit from 'drastic cutting',[10] while the *Darlington & Stockton Times* said that it 'dragged in a painfully slow fashion right from the beginning',[11] but the public ire was roused by the *Northern Despatch*'s statement: '*Carousel*,' it said, 'dragged slowly through nine well-dressed scenes . . . When the curtain finally fell at 10 o'clock it gave a sense of relief rather than fulfilment after three hours of hard work from Darlington Operatic Society.'[12] Despite going on to say 'the amazing thing is that the company went on to do so well with such an unpromising work' and to praise many of the cast – Anna Saunders, Denis Quinn, Sam Herdman, Glennis Beresford, Muriel Lees and the troupe of children – the review provoked angry reactions from two correspondents to the paper, one of whom dismissed it as 'arrant nonsense' and the other said of the critic: 'How wrong he was!' The latter writer praised especially the dancing of Peter Henderson (the Carnival Boy) and Ann Thompson (Louise), agreeing with the *Darlington & Stockton Times*, which also had

* That £2,500, incidentally, was virtually the entire assets of the Society.

pleasant things to say about Glennis Beresford (Carrie Pipperidge), Muriel Lees (Nettie Fowler) and Denis Quinn (Mr Snow). The *Northern Echo* singled out Sam Herdman, too, for his portrayal of the 'baddie' – Jigger Craigin – describing him as looking like 'a villainous version of Bob Hope'. Sam was rapidly building up quite a store of startling descriptions in his reviews!

The dust from *Carousel* having died down, rehearsals began for *Kismet* – by which time show-selection was also in progress for autumn 1962 and for 1963. Kerker and Morton's *The Belle of New York* was definite for the autumn of 1962 and *Song of Norway* was a possibility for 1963. The members of the Society had now been informed, at an Extraordinary General Meeting on 30 November, of the circumstances surrounding the donation for the purchase of the theatre, so that they might discuss it and have the position clarified. They were also asked once again to help with the numerous decorating and cleaning jobs in the building. At the last committee meeting of the year it was announced that *Carousel*, notwithstanding the grumbles of the press, had managed to make a profit of around £180, so despite all the trauma the December meeting ended the year on a high note. That meeting saw the acceptance as a member of the bass-voiced Clifford Walker whose wife, Dorothy, had joined the Society for *Carousel* (along with her cousin, Audrey Bowen). This began yet another dynasty, for their daughter Alison and son Michael eventually became members, as did Dorothy's sister Margaret Harsley and Clifford's nephew Nigel Walker. The same meeting also introduced Susan Swift's destiny – Kenneth Robinson. They were to marry in 1966.

1962 began in a spirit of calmer optimism – the Committee even felt able to give a donation to Bondgate Youth Club to help offset a severe loss on their pantomime! The newly-constituted company Darlington Civic Theatre Ltd., which was leasing the theatre from the Corporation, now consisted of eighteen people. Fred Thompson was still Chairman, with W. P. B. Croft of Lloyds Bank as Hon. Treasurer and Miss Vera Seymour as Hon. Secretary. The Council of Management was composed of Lady Starmer, Miss W. B. C. Jewsbury (Headmistress of the Girls' High School), E. W. Hammond, A. B. Little (solicitor), C. J. H. Park and Canon P. N. Wansey, together with Ken Bodden, Wilfred Downing, Sam Herdman, Frank Murray, Jim Fraser Murray, Bernard Sanderson, Norman Thompson, George Todd and Jim Willans; the last nine, of course, being from the Operatic Society.

A good deal of redecorating work had been done on the theatre building by the Operatic Society members and by other organizations. A modern amplification system had been installed and a sounding board built over the stage for use during orchestral concerts. This, it was hoped, would encourage increased lettings which would supply much-needed cash to plough back into the theatre. With this more secure background in mind the theatre was booking a professional pantomime for late 1962 so the Society decided to concentrate on two big musicals each year, though they would still only run for one week each. (It was not until 1970 that longer runs were instigated.) It had been originally agreed to try to produce a small show, Sandy Wilson's *The Boy Friend*, in January 1963 but the pantomime rendered this unnecessary.

Sundry problems connected with the next three shows were presently being ironed out. There were seven children to be selected for *Kismet*, and there were difficulties in obtaining scenery for *The Belle of New York*; plans for *Song of Norway* had fizzled out completely so the Committee had decided to fall back on Gilbert & Sullivan, which was a shrewd move as Fred Sinden was now available as a producer. He lived very close at hand, in West Hartlepool, and had been one of the D'Oyly Carte company's principal tenors from 1949 to 1960; after leaving the D'Oyly Carte company he had given lectures on, and recitals of, Gilbert & Sullivan all over the country and had just been elected (in 1961) to NODA's panel of producers. Although he had done a great deal of private coaching he had never produced a show for a major amateur society before, and it would be good experience for him, as well as good for the Society to have a Gilbert & Sullivan expert.

The Annual General Meeting of 15 March 1962 emphasized one or two valuable lessons which had been learned during the year. A television item on *Aurora* – despite the power of television and the excellence of the show itself – had not produced any significant rise in ticket sales and so the onus undoubtedly devolved upon the sales efforts of the members themselves; also it had proved more costly for the Society to design and build its own scenery than to hire it. Fred Thompson urged for even more voluntary services to the theatre to boost its appeal. (It was also at this meeting, incidentally, that it was mooted that a full history of the Society should be written and published, though it has taken until the 1990s for this to happen.)

It had been a difficult year of chairmanship for Bernard Sanderson; though he said at the next meeting that he had enjoyed his year, he must, in a way, have been glad to hand over office to Ken Bodden.

So, on to *Kismet*. The cast numbered 60, plus the seven children, so it was a big show to do and several people had to play more than one named part as well as being in the chorus.

Clifford Walker had his first named part in this show playing Hassan-Ben, and Muriel Jones, a tall, auburn-haired former High School girl, who had joined the Society for *Aurora*, now played a rather more prominent role (as the Ayah to Zubbediyah). As to the leading roles, Kenneth Richardson was playing Hajj, the poet around whom the story centres, with Vicki Tringham as Marsinah, his daughter. Jawan, the brigand chief, was played by Ken Bodden and the wicked Wazir by Bernard Sanderson. Lalume, the pride of the Harem, was played by Glennis Beresford, the Caliph by Brian Thorpe, and Omar (as in Omar Khayyam) was played by Wade Cobban. The dancers were trained by Adela Iveson who, with Irene Skippon and Ann Thompson, also danced as one of the three Princesses of Ababu. The children included Fiona Bishop, Philip Murray, and Peter and Stephen Sanderson. This show also needed a large stage crew and it was here that the help which had been given by the Society's stage staff to the Boy Scouts for their Gang Show paid off, for several of the scouts came to reciprocate. These included Eddie Brown who, as well as having been a very young chorus member in two earlier shows, *Magyar Melody* and *The Gondoliers*, had been one of the stars of the Gang Shows in the days when his soprano voice had been of outstanding quality. The stage crew also included Alf Common, son of the famous Middlesbrough footballer of the same name (and uncle of Ann Parker – née Appleton – a present-day member). There was no alcohol ban on the stage crew at that time and Alf acquired a one-gallon whisky bottle which he would have filled with beer over at The Greyhound (the 'actors' pub' over the road from the theatre) for the refreshment of the workers. The snag was that Alf worked in the fly gallery above the stage and the bottle was very heavy, but he surmounted this little difficulty by installing an extra rope and having his bottle hauled up on it!

Kismet was a visual delight. The scenery, costumes, and dancing (especially that of the Princesses of Ababu) were a feast for the eyes, and the principals, especially Kenneth Richardson, Vicki Tringham and Brian Thorpe, justified their casting. The *Northern Despatch* extravagantly said of Kenneth Richardson, 'He is a man to build even a Shakespearean production upon!'[13] Glennis Beresford was a sizzlingly glamorous Lalume. The chorus, according to the *Northern Echo*, could have remembered to smile more and to look as though they were concentrating on the action being played out before them, but the *Darlington & Stockton Times* summed it up by saying that Joy Beadell should be well satisfied and '. . . should feel proud to have directed players of the resilience and capacity of those who were carrying on the tradition of this fine organization.'[14] Surprisingly, none of the papers mentioned the two Afghan hounds featured in the Caliph's procession. Still, 'We enjoyed *Kismet*,' said the *Northern Echo*, 'Allah be praised!'[15]

Yet still it lost money – £169. After the initial burst of enthusiasm on the part of the public engendered by that appeal for Vice-Presidents and

Patrons in the programme for *South Pacific* the numbers of these had dropped a little, possibly owing to the poor notices for *Carousel. The Belle of New York* simply *had* to do well so that the level of donations to charities could be kept up, although the donations now amounted to £11,000 since 1945. To this end it was decided that the ladies in the cast could save the Society money by providing their own modern dresses for the show as far as possible, with help, if necessary, from the Ladies' Committee (under the Chairmanship of Peggy Todd) in making them. Various social events would also be taking place – for instance, a Car Treasure Hunt, since these were much in vogue at the time. (Unfortunately the Hunt did not make money and had to be subsidized by the Ladies' Committee whose funds would often bail out loss-making events in the future.) The following two shows were also decided upon. *The Maid of the Mountains* was scheduled for autumn 1963. This was the first time the Society had repeated a production since 1945 – it had been performed by the pre-war society in 1937. *The Music Man* by Meredith Willson was to be given in the spring of 1964 and Joy Beadell was invited to produce it. Joy had been treated by the Society to attendance at the NODA Summer School which deals with all aspects of show performance and production – and very valuable these Summer Schools were and are. By the time of the committee meeting of 17 October 1962 the floorwork for *The Belle of New York* was under way, though another much-loved face was now missing. Edith Kershaw, that indefatigable, enthusiastic and cheery lady who had been a founder-member and accompanist of the Society had died shortly after the previous show. Tribute was paid to her in the programme and the tribute pinpoints the qualities needed in an accompanist for an operatic society. 'Edith,' it said, 'must have spent thousands of hours thumping out the tune at practices and rehearsals, but she always remained bright and cheerful and showed no signs of boredom or monotony' – being an accompanist is not easy. Frank Murray, as well as being Deputy Musical Director to Bob White for this Arthur Garside production, now took on the job of accompanist, for this show only, with Winifred Graham and Joan Beard to assist him. Then Winifred Graham became Hon. Accompanist in her own right. Happily the ticket bookings were going well for the show so it looked as though it would ultimately sell well, and Kenneth Bodden was to be invited to produce *The Maid of the Mountains*, for the usual reason: it was less of a burden on the Society's finances if a good local producer could be obtained.

Happily *The Belle of New York* did do well. The takings were in the region of £1,700 and of this £250 was profit – it equalled the record of *The Merry Widow* – not bad for a musical which had come to London from Broadway as long ago as 1898! None of the critics described it as 'dated' (though

The Belle of New York 1962 – Chorus. *See page x for full list.*

they did mention that it had been modernized in various ways); on the contrary, they were very much entertained. Sam Herdman was outstanding as Ichabod Bronson, the hypocritical father of the young male lead – Brian Thorpe's credible and creditable Henry Bronson. Sam gave a performance which excelled in every department. The *Northern Despatch* and *Darlington & Stockton Times* even praised his dancing – encouraging news for an ex-rugby player! As Salvation Army girl Violet Gray, Dorothy Matthew was a suitably delightful and demure heroine, while Lorrie Boddy as Cora Angelique proved to be her hardened-yet-not-too-coarse antithesis. Ken Bodden, in a slapstick role as Karl von Pumpernickel, drew enthusiastic appreciation from the audience as did Glennis Beresford as the soubrette Fifi. The audiences had not been slow in recognizing talent; this was to be Glennis's last appearance with the Society because her next move was of 'fairy-tale' proportions. Though not specifically trained for the professional stage, she decided to go to audition for *How to Succeed in Business without Really Trying*, a new American musical by Frank Loesser and Abe Burrows, which was to open at the Shaftesbury Theatre in March 1963. She won a part in that show and continued with her career on the London stage by appearing in seven West End musicals including *Funny Girl*, *Little Me*, and *Bless the Bride*, as well as on film in

Oliver! (For those who are interested, she eventually married a doctor in 1972.)

The usual praise was given to the dancers in *The Belle of New York* and the only problem was seen as being the common one of the lack of balance between the orchestra and cast – a balance which was always extremely difficult to achieve. Perhaps it is as well, though, that the reviewers were not there after the first night, for who knows whether they would have been amused by Richard Sampson's extra-special effect. At one point there had to be an explosion offstage but Richard thought he could do better than produce a common-or-garden sort of explosion. So he placed his explosive in a dustbin for greater effect. An informed source reports: 'Nobody needed laxatives for a month . . .' This was a great introduction for one of the stage staff, Ernie Mann: this was his first show. It says much for his stamina that he remained among the stage crew for so many years – until 1988 in fact, though he did return to help backstage for *Annie* in 1991. His wife, Fran, became a pillar of the Ladies' Committee and worked hard for the Society for many years until she had a stroke – the company sometimes used to think that Fran was born with a book of raffle tickets in her hand!

At the end of 1962 things were looking reasonable for the Society. Although it had lost on *Kismet*, *The Belle of New York* had kept it in the black. Not only had it been able to keep up its customary donations to charity, it had even been able to do a little more financially for the Civic Theatre, (and practically, too, by way of Bill Jones, Richard Sampson and Brian Thorpe joining the theatre's council). To add to the 24 chairs, the electric steam iron and the ironing board donated by the Mothers' Committee of Joy Beadell's School of Dancing, the Society's Ladies' Committee had donated curtains and an electric tea boiler. The successive tea boilers were presided over by Miss Evelyn Berry (who had been a member of the Society since before the war and on the Ladies' Committee since its inception) and her sister Lilian. They made the most efficient security firm look like amateurs. At one point the then-current appliance was nicknamed, by an irreverent Society member, 'The Sacred Tea-Urn of the Miss Berrys' and it was treated with the utmost respect. The Miss Berrys commandeered any member with a car and transported all the Society's crockery and cutlery back and forth for each performance. The tea-towels were even embroidered with the Society's logo and every item was meticulously accounted for – the non-return of so much as a teaspoon was regarded as a capital offence. There is no doubt that the saying 'fear concentrates the mind wonderfully' held true, for very few items ever went missing.

1963 opened optimistically, with *Trial by Jury* and *The Pirates of Penzance* well into rehearsal. *The Maid of the Mountains* was to begin rehearsals on 18 April, shortly after the end of the Gilbert & Sullivan run, under the musical directorship of Bob White and the producership of Ken Bodden. Ken had directed plays – though never a musical – and had done quite a lot of radio broadcasting. Arrangements for *The Music Man* for spring 1964 were going as planned, though no producer had yet been appointed. The Treasurer had taken two hundred of the Society's National Savings Certificates, which had now matured, and invested the proceeds in a Building Society account. Meanwhile Jim Willans threw caution to the winds and squandered, on the Society's behalf, the princely sum of £5 on Premium Bonds.

The mood of elation was shortlived, however. By mid-March, with the show only two weeks away, the Treasurer reported that ticket sales were very poor. What was more, the quotation for scenery for *The Music Man* from Empire Scenic Studios of Smethwick was £165 plus carriage, whereas for *The Maid of the Mountains* it would be £100 less than that from the same firm. There was obviously a need for discussion about this. These matters notwithstanding, the Treasurer was able to report at the Annual General Meeting that the finances of the Society were strong; he was of the opinion, however, that it should keep substantial amounts in reserve. This was very sound thinking – it was on this very point that the pre-war committees had been guilty of misjudgement and left themselves with far too little money to fall back on. *Trial by Jury* and *The Pirates of Penzance* lost over £70, mainly because members did not sell enough tickets. It has to be said, though, that a number of new members joined from Barnard Castle, Richmond and Shildon societies to play in the Gilbert & Sullivan and had probably not yet been properly initiated into the Darlington-style 'ticket-selling mode'. Still, the Darlington society had never before been blessed with such a large male chorus; there were 21 of them, if you count Sam Herdman, who also played the Usher in *Trial* and the Pirate King in *Pirates*, Roland Wigington (the Learned Judge and Sergeant of Police), Gordon MacFall (The Defendant), and also Denis Quinn, Edward Sinnott, and Robert King who all played 'bit parts'. A very pleasing aspect was that a number of the people who joined the Society for this show appeared in at least one or two more shows, though Jeffrey Wragg, Gordon Clarke and Sam Goldberg stayed for much longer with the Darlington society. The *Northern Echo* and the *Northern Despatch* were taken mainly with the producer and the company's sense of comedy, especially in the persons of Sam Herdman, Roland Wigington and Ken Bodden, though the whole show was described in the *Northern Despatch* as being 'brilliantly produced'[16] by Fred Sinden. The only real grumble was that the lighting was too dim in the second act of *Pirates* – just as well that it was not quite bright enough to expose the joke played by Bill Curr on Roland Wigington and Vicki Tringham, the Judge and the Plaintiff in *Trial*. They were to be hidden behind a newspaper and Bill had written on it, in thick black letters, 'No snogging with Vicki', before handing it, folded, to Roland. Unfortunately the joke misfired because Roland opened it the wrong way so that the writing faced the audience and he didn't see it. The orchestra did, but no one realized what was amusing them so much!

The *Darlington & Stockton Times* was rapturous about the whole show. The reviewer called it a 'double triumph'[17] and adjectives such as 'superb', 'polished', 'exciting', and 'colourful' are scattered like confetti over the article. The *Northern Despatch* made particular reference to the unaccompanied rendering of *Hail Poetry* in *Pirates* and this began a tradition in the Society, instigated by Ken Robinson. *Hail Poetry* is his *forte*, as members will testify, for at any Society gathering Ken will herd them together to sing it. What is more he will also personally conduct the piece. Quite possibly, when the Society's centenary comes round, the story of these legendary renditions will still be keeping his memory green!

It was a great shame that the Gilbert & Sullivan production had not sold better, particularly since John Reed had sent a special message wishing the Society luck. It was also sad that Eileen Young and Kenneth Richardson missed the show. Eileen had broken her leg and Kenneth had a long illness which forced him to miss out on this show and the previous one – his first absence since he had joined in 1947. Still, the Society could look forward to his return for *The Maid of the Mountains* and, as always, hoped for a financial success with it.

Richard Sampson took over the Chairmanship of the Society after the Annual General Meeting in April with some trepidation. Ken Bodden would be a hard act to follow for he had managed successfully to combine the offices of Chairman and Ticket Secretary as well as being a playing member. (It is quite a feat but it *has* been done since then. One instance which springs to mind is the occasion when Tom Kent, as Chairman of the Society in 1983, commented in a lively last-night-of-the-show speech from the theatre stage that the smallest of the dressing-rooms was quite crowded because there were crammed into it the Chairman, the Programme Manager, the Ticket Secretary, the Assistant Treasurer, the Minute Secretary and two members of the cast – and then revealed that this crowd in reality consisted of only two people: himself and John Lloyd!)

Despite the trepidation, however, Richard Sampson was looking forward to his term of office, though as it turned out he did not have an easy year. Indeed, the first problem occurred later in that same meeting over the musical directorship. Bob White had been Musical Director for eleven out of the past thirteen shows and must have felt that the position was very much his own. Now Frank Murray stated that he would like to be considered by the Committee as Musical Director for *The Music Man* the following spring. Frank, though he had no formal qualifications in music, had tremendous musicality and flair and was a perfectionist. In his youth he had won a scholarship to study music at Durham School, but instead entered the family bakery business as his mother wished. After discussion it seemed feasible to appoint Frank for that show and to ask Bob White to do the autumn 1964 one: *The Arcadians*, which had not been performed by the Society since the pre-war group had done it in 1934. A special meeting was called to discuss the subject again a week later, but it was agreed that the decision should stand.

General chorus rehearsals had begun for *The Maid of the Mountains*: the Committee aimed to give it maximum publicity, trying a pilot-scheme of blanketing two areas in the town with publicity material.

Joy Beadell, meanwhile, had not been letting the grass grow under her feet. As well as her dancing, her talent for producing was apparent and she had been developing it assiduously to become a professional producer. This meant, though, that she had to resign from the Committee since the rules state that no member of the Society may be paid professional fees. Wade Cobban was therefore co-opted until the next Annual General Meeting. Joy was much in demand in the North-Eastern area as a producer. It stands to reason; she was good at it, she could do all her own choreography, and she was local and therefore much cheaper to employ than, say, someone coming from London, whose fares and accommodation had to be paid for. As an example, in spring 1961 Arthur Garside had cost 125 guineas (£126 5s. 0d.) for four weeks of floorwork and attendance at the show for one week, plus his board, lodging and travelling expenses, and the Society also had to supply a choreographer. Two and a half years later Joy Beadell was asked to produce *The Music Man* and charged only £120 for doing the entire production including the choreography, helped voluntarily by Greta Sanderson, Ann Thompson and Julia Thornton as Ballet Mistresses. In contrast (even though Frank Murray had gone to a different firm – Scenic Display Services Ltd. of Bradford – and secured the scenery from them at a lower rate than from the previous firm the Committee had considered) the hire of the scenery was still going to be £120 plus £30 carriage, and the costumes from Chas H. Fox were to cost £281 6s. 0d. plus carriage. So Joy was excellent value.

Happily, two weeks before *The Maid of the Mountains* opened ticket sales were going much better than they had for the Gilbert & Sullivan. Moreover, the number of Vice-Presidents and Patrons had rocketed from 183 for *Trial* and *Pirates* to over 250 – the highest since the end of 1960. According to the *Northern Despatch* it played to a completely full house on

The Maid of the Mountains 1963. *Left to right*: Brian Thorpe, Ray Simmons, Mollie Jaques, Sam Herdman, Susan Swift, Adela Iveson. *Seated*: Bill Jones.

the first night and three performers were outstanding, namely Sam Herdman ('virile and commanding')[18] as the brigand chief Baldassare, Susan Swift ('comical' and 'thoroughly in character') as Vittoria, the newly-rich wife of another brigand (Tonio, played by Bill Jones), and Kenneth Richardson as General Malona. The *Darlington & Stockton Times* felt that the Society had made a mistake in choosing this particular show because although it '. . . had some very good tunes the dialogue was mostly too corny for modern audiences who perhaps like their comedy a little more sophisticated. As it was the cast found themselves struggling with material that at times touched rock bottom.'[19] Still, it was felt that the cast had made the best of it despite a certain amount of weakness among the singers and the reviewer added Mollie Jaques (who played the title role) to the *Northern Despatch*'s list of excellence. Nevertheless, the *Northern Echo* could only describe the show as a whole as 'fair'.[20] This must have been very disappointing for Ken Bodden and for the cast, but the show made enough money to give a healthy donation to charity and to increase the Society's back-up funds.

They now looked forward to *The Music Man* and its two 'firsts': Joy Beadell as a professional producer and Frank Murray as Musical Director. Sam Herdman was to be Publicity Manager and pull out all the stops to bring in the public, and Ken Bodden and Ray Simmons arranged for the Society to see the film of the musical (which had been released in 1962) to get an overall view.

There was, however, an undercurrent of unrest among the members over the autumn show for 1964. At an Extraordinary General Meeting on 21 November it was made clear to the Committee that the members emphatically did not want *The Arcadians* and the proposal was carried by a large majority so a re-think would have to be done.

An eventful three weeks then followed for Richard Sampson when considerable Committee reorganization took place. Jim Fraser Murray resigned owing to business commitments, and Frank Murray had to resign as Secretary because of his duties as Musical Director; George Todd then became Secretary and Alan Gamble took on George's job as Property Master. Bill Jones resigned as Assistant Secretary – he was to be Chairman the following year – and Cliff Walker succeeded to the job. Ken Bodden and Richard Sampson changed places so that Richard did tickets and Ken stage-managed. Amid this upheaval, however, the autumn 1964 show was fixed as Johann Strauss's *The Gipsy Baron* under the direction of a London producer, Freddie Collier (who had played professionally in musicals and organized ENSA shows from Drury Lane before moving on to produce amateur shows around the country), assisted by Greta Sanderson as Choreographer. Even the spring show for 1965 was chosen – Offenbach's *La Belle Hélène* with Joy Beadell to produce it and under the baton of Frank Murray, now firmly established as a Musical Director. Thus 1963 closed with a flurry of activity.

By the meeting of 15 January 1964 Ken Bodden and Richard Sampson both appear to have adopted the principle of 'better the devil you know' because they changed places and reverted to their previous jobs. There was also a considerable amount of discussion taking place over the hiring-fee for the theatre – it was felt that £385 was £85 too much, as it was, after all, nearly a 200% increase on the 1960 rental. By March, however, that had been resolved in the Society's favour and £300 had been agreed. The theatre was about to undergo considerable improvements – £6,000 (of which £3,000 was given by the Arts Council) was to be spent on structural alterations, including improved public toilet facilities and water heaters in the dressing rooms. The members looked forward keenly to this! They still had one more show to do without these facilities, however.

The Music Man was going on with a cast of 73, including Philip Murray as Winthrop Paroo and Fiona Bishop as Amaryllis (the two leading children), thirteen new chorus members, and four new dancers. Among the new chorus members were Joan Reynolds, who had come from

Shildon, and Eunicé Cockburn, a teacher from Sedgefield, who was soon taking leading soprano roles. Allene James (now Allene Norris, journalist and grandmother of triplets) had also joined the Society and was playing the 'bit part' of Mrs Squires in this show – though she was to deliver a knock-out performance in the title role in *Annie Get Your Gun* two years later. There were three other children in the show, apart from Philip and Fiona, and one was a new face. Along with Peter and Stephen Sanderson there appeared Michael Walker, son of Clifford and Dorothy. (Cliff was taking a lead in this show, as Charlie Cowell, a travelling anvil salesman, and Dorothy was in the chorus.) Large numbers of backstage staff were beginning to be needed for the shows. For this one there would be 24 scene changes using 'flying scenes' lowered on ropes from the flies so Richard Sampson had a crew of fourteen including Bill Curr (Managing Director of a local engineering company) who had crewed for *Trial* and *Pirates*, and who had press-ganged his son Sandy to join him backstage for *The Maid of the Mountains*. Cecil Grieveson was there and so was Ken Haigh (who was a member of The Bondgate Players and who now acts with The Festival Players). Ernie Mann and John Murray also helped, as well as Jack Rowell, who was to do sterling work on the Committee for a number of years. Alan Gamble, the Property Master – who took over from Brian Thorpe when Brian and Carol moved to Manchester – had four people to assist him while Bernard Sanderson – who was the electrician – had three.

The reviews of *The Music Man* were so enthusiastic that they should have prompted the public to rush for tickets. 'Traditional musical comedy,' said the *Northern Despatch*, 'is knocked for six at Darlington this week . . . *The Music Man* is really ALIVE. The show should set up a merry tinkle at the Civic Theatre box office.'[21] Raymond Simmons, who played the lead, overshadowed his comparatively weak singing voice with exuberant acting and Joyce Elliott, playing opposite him, acquitted herself well. The close-harmony singing of the School Board Members, as played by Jeff Wragg, Roland Wigington, Bernard Sanderson and Horace Wilson, was outstanding and the laughter engendered by Sue Robinson as Eulalie McKechnie Shinn with her 'ladies' dancing class' – comprising Muriel Jones, Jean Herdman, Allene James and Eileen Young – showed this to be the comic highlight of the evening. Joy Beadell's whole production of the piece, especially the chorus work, received lavish praise. This *should* have caused a rush for tickets but again the show lost money – just over £200. Inexplicably there were 70 fewer Vice-Presidents and Patrons, though it is true that in the years up to this point the spring shows in general had – for some reason – drawn fewer people in this capacity. So it remained to be seen what sort of a job would be made by Freddie

Collier of *The Gipsy Baron*, and how it would be received. Richard Sampson was to take a year off from being Stage Manager and Tony Cambell took over for this show and for *La Belle Hélène*.

By the middle of the year things were looking good on the surface. Most of the parts were cast for *The Gipsy Baron*. Eunicé Cockburn was to play her first leading role as Saffi and Fred Sinden was back to play opposite her, as Sandor Barinkay, as a change from producing. The 'opposition' to this hero and heroine was Sam Herdman as Zsupan the scheming pigbreeder and Mayor. (Sam had a brainwave when he got this part. He had a farmer friend, Percy Alderson, who lived at Over Dinsdale, so Sam went there and had a programme photograph taken of himself amid a group of apparently admiring pigs.) Dorothy Walker played Arletta his daughter, and Kenneth Richardson Count Kanska, a Civil Commissioner. Cliff Walker played a more benevolent character than he had in *The Music Man*, taking the part of Graf Peter Homonoy, Governor of the mythical province of Zrinyi. Other leading roles were played by Denis Quinn as Otto, Lorrie Boddy as Mirabelle, Joyce Elliott as Czipra (a gipsy queen), and Jeff Wragg as a Captain of Hussars. As a bonus Jim Willans's modest flutter on the Premium Bonds won £25 which encouraged him so much that he immediately reinvested the winnings in more bonds.

Behind the scenes, though, things were not going so well. Freddie Collier was causing discontent with his handling of the production. He had not begun well by requesting the cancellation of one of the Sunday floorwork rehearsals – Sunday is always a very heavy rehearsal day once floorwork begins. Now things were getting worse. He was not satisfied with the accommodation arranged for him and the company felt that he did not fit in easily with them. There were other difficulties besides. Denis Quinn had badly wanted the larger of the two comedy roles – the one which had been given to Sam Herdman – and he never spoke to Sam offstage after that. There was a problem with some members of the orchestra too. So it was an uneasy company which took to the stage on 26 October. The Committee, however, after writing to NODA expressing their dissatisfaction with Freddie Collier, had to look ahead to future shows and future producers: they decided upon the Ivor Novello classic *King's Rhapsody* for autumn 1965 as a contrast to the quirky comedy of *La Belle Hélène*, followed by *Kiss Me Kate* in spring 1966, though *Kiss Me Kate* was not definite because of potential problems with the performing rights. As to the matter of producers the most recent experience had been a salutary one. What better, then, than to look to home and ask Joy Beadell to produce the next two shows? She had, after all, never failed the Society in all the work she had done for it. In fact, once Joy had agreed, she had set herself on the road to producing almost all the Society's future productions for many years.

The apparently ill-starred production of *The Gipsy Baron* went ahead despite all its problems. It was visually very attractive. Dorothy Walker remembers what lovely clothes she had to wear but also remembers having her own special moment of horrible embarrassment when she did a little twirl during her solo and lost a shoe. Peter Henderson, who was dancing, had the presence of mind to sink to one knee, pick up the shoe and hold it out reverentially, but there was no way to replace it and make it look like part of the action; Dorothy still regrets that 'dot-and-carry-one' exit!

The press regarded the show with modified rapture though two people wrote to the papers to say how much they enjoyed it. Basically the reviewers did not think much of the show itself – in fact the *Northern Despatch*'s headline of 27 October was 'This Gipsy on road to nowhere',[22] while that of the *Darlington & Stockton Times* read 'Darlington Operatic Society shine with mediocre material'[23] and the *Northern Echo* was the best of the bunch with '*Gipsy Baron* takes a colourful bow'.[24] The overall view was along the lines of the *Darlington & Stockton Times* headline: that the cast had made the best of what was at their disposal. The leading players were all singled out for praise though it was felt that Eunicé Cockburn was a little on the demure side – and *this* time it was said of Sam Herdman that 'there was something of Falstaff lurking in his portrayal'! The *Northern Echo* paid tribute to the orchestra under Bob White – nice for him since most of the time, even nowadays, orchestras are castigated for drowning out the singers. This was such an unusual tribute that the Committee recorded its special thanks to him in the minutes of 18 November. The *Darlington & Stockton Times* reporter concluded by saying '*The Gipsy Baron* in no way detracted from the great reputation that Darlington Operatic Society enjoys. We look forward to their May production . . .'

The May production was the subject of discussion in the Committee towards the close of 1964, but problems such as the design of the scenery and the procuring of a rehearsal pianist were still to be resolved. By the end of the year, though, the majority of parts in the show had been cast. Helen was to be played by Eunicé Cockburn, giving her a chance to prove false the press's complaints that she was 'too demure', and Philip Logan, formerly with a Northallerton group, was to be Paris, her leading man. The scheming and comic Calchas the Augur was to be Kenneth Richardson, with Cliff Walker as Philocomus his sidekick. The four Kings, Menelaus, Ajax, Achilles and Agamemnon were to be Ken Bodden, Sam Herdman, Roland Wigington and Bernard Sanderson. Nesta, Helen's handmaiden, would be played by Joyce Elliott, and the frivolous Orestes,

Leona, and Cressida were to be Jean Herdman, Enid Spencer, and Betty MacFall, with Peter Henderson as Mercury and Lorrie Boddy as the goddess Minerva. So by the end of the year only the casting of the two remaining goddesses (Juno and Venus) was yet to be done and *La Belle Hélène* was well into rehearsal with the high hopes of the whole company resting on it.

The Society's second decade had been full of uncertainty and upheaval and the company had needed great tenacity to keep live theatre going in Darlington. Now that the Civic Theatre seemed secure, at least for the time being, and now that Joy Beadell was available as a highly competent resident producer, they had to maintain that tenacity and try to draw in new members to safeguard the Society's future.

Chapter 6

1965–1969

As 1965 opened the Committee had to consider carefully its financial position. *The Music Man* had lost money and so had *The Gipsy Baron*, though not very much. The autumn Dinner Dance had also been run at a loss but the Ladies' Committee had a reasonable sum in hand and was prepared to offset this. The Utopian Society was offering some dancers' costumes for £5 which might be suitable for *La Belle Hélène*, a money-saving offer worth considering, and George Todd and Richard Sampson had organized a visit to the scenery designers. It was agreed that one measure which would help the Society would be to increase members' annual subscriptions – to double them, in fact – so the Committee decided to put this before the Annual General Meeting. Still, at least the hire of the main wardrobe for *La Belle Hélène* had been arranged with Mutries and the Secretary had managed to secure scenery for *King's Rhapsody* from Scenic Display Services of Bradford for £120 plus carriage.

So there came the Annual General Meeting on 16 March. The Chairman (Bill Jones) and the Secretary (George Todd) reported first, outlining the brighter side of the state of the Society, but there was also some sombre news: the death of Wilfred Downing, who had worked hard for the Society for a number of years, and the impending demolition of Beaumont Street School which had been the meeting-place of the Society for so long. Jim Willans then delivered a report which laid on the line the financial problems of the Society. He drew attention to the fact that for the first time for a number of years there had been a reduction in the Society's assets and warned that unless immediate steps were taken this could become a regular feature. On average, he said, six items alone – the rent of the theatre, hire and carriage of costumes, professional fees, royalties, orchestra fees, and pianists' fees – cost £1,500 for a show. At current prices, maximum box office takings were £1,750, leaving only £250 at the outside to cover the many and varied incidental expenses and to produce a profit. Not only that, but fewer Vice-Presidents and Patrons were being enrolled so that donations were dwindling, and the profit on programme sales was decreasing because of increasing printing costs. He appealed urgently to members to help by selling more tickets, publicizing the shows as much as they could, attending the social functions to make them profitable, and recruiting more members. A vote was taken on doubling members' annual subscriptions to one guinea and the proposal was carried by an overwhelming majority.

This was the background to which George Todd succeeded as Chairman in April (he remained Secretary, too, with Cliff Walker as Assistant Secretary). Some relatively minor problems also had to be sorted out. Betty and Gordon MacFall had both had to drop out of the cast of *La Belle Hélène*, and Peter Henderson was forced to withdraw on medical grounds, thus depriving him of the opportunity to make a grand first entrance on a moped! (It was *that* sort of show!) Ann Holland, who had acted as prompter for the previous two shows, had written to say that she was unavailable for this one. Fortunately these problems were cleared up without too much difficulty: Betty MacFall was replaced by Maureen Gamble as Cressida and Sam Goldberg took over Peter Henderson's part as Mercury. The other two goddesses were also cast – Lorrie Boddy as Minerva and Dorothy Walker as Venus. Pat Knowles agreed to prompt. The ongoing problem of finding an accompanist, this time due to Winifred Graham moving to Scotland, was temporarily solved by Tom Homer stepping into the breach.

Bob White then resigned as Vice-Chairman and from all active participation in the Society. He had been a very active member for fifteen years and Musical Director for eleven shows, but his health had been deteriorating for some time and sadly he only lived for another eighteen months. He was greatly missed throughout the County Durham and Teesside areas where he had entertained so many people as a raconteur and musician. Sam took over as Vice-Chairman and it was decided that henceforward the committee member serving the longest time from his or her last term as Chairman or appointment to the Committee should be appointed Vice-Chairman, becoming Chairman the year after that. This arrangement still holds good, though any person may decline the Vice-Chairmanship should he or she so wish.

La Belle Hélène began its week's performance on 3 May. This show had even more people on properties and electrics. Bill Curr, in the absence of his son Sandy for *The Gipsy Baron*, had drafted in his daughter Judith to help with props, and for *La Belle Hélène* he had roped in both of them. Ernie Mann had got his son Stuart* in to help the electrics staff, so there were 25 Society members simply to help with the staging. Bill Bishop, Joy Beadell's elder son, had designed the scenery in the end, the construction being done by Scenic Display Services. Bill was studying art and drama

* Stuart died tragically, in a car accident, at the age of only 22.

La Belle Hélène 1965 – Dancers. *See page xi for full list.*

at the West Midland Training College at the time so this was good practice for him! *La Belle Hélène* is a wonderfully satirical piece, open to inventive production and played for fun. It was written by Jacques Offenbach in 1864 and here it was, 101 years later, recently removed from mothballs and (with its libretto brought up to date by Phil Park) released to amateurs. The Society hoped that other societies would come to see it for this reason. The press gave it wonderful reviews and praised the Society for its courage in breaking away from the usual 'safe' musicals. The *Darlington & Stockton Times* called it 'one of the most tuneful, colourful and amusing shows the Civic Theatre has seen',[1] and awarded full marks to Joy Beadell for her handling of it. These sentiments were echoed by the *Northern Echo*, and as for the *Northern Despatch* reviewer's effusion – well, considering he called it 'the biggest, brashest, laughter-raising crowd puller to be plonked on the Civic's stage for many a moon',[2] there is no doubt that he enjoyed his evening of escapism! Eunicé Cockburn was in excellent voice and gave a superlative performance as Helen of Troy – definitely worth starting a war for – and she was well supported, particularly by Kenneth Richardson as the wily Calchas and by Philip Logan as Paris (complete with blonde Beatle-style wig). The Kings, especially Sam Herdman and Roland Wigington, provided plenty of hilarity and Jean Herdman had been a happy choice as Orestes despite this role's being originally written for a man. Altogether the show was voted a winner. The Secretary of the

Hartlepool Gilbert & Sullivan Society wrote to George Todd saying that she found it '*the* most entertaining production, professional or amateur' that she had seen during the past few years. But still it lost money – just over £217 – and the Committee surely wondered just what it had to do to make some profit, for it was still giving the usual donations to charity. Jim Willans said at the committee meeting in July that it might soon become necessary either to realize some of the Society's investments or carry an overdraft. Hopes of getting the rights to perform *Kiss Me Kate* seemed to have sunk without trace, so it was decided that *Annie Get Your Gun* would have to be substituted for this as the spring show for 1966 in the hope that it, along with *King's Rhapsody*, might recoup some of the Society's lost assets. The Committee did not really want to have to increase the seat prices because theatre-going in general was in a decline. Even the appearance of a world-class star – Anna Neagle – appearing amid rave reviews in a thriller called *Person Unknown* had not managed to fill the theatre. The Council, however, appointed Mr Donald J. Hamilton-Moore as full-time professional Theatre Manager in September 1965 and it was hoped that this injection of new blood might give a much needed boost. A group called The Friends of the Civic Theatre was also formally established to try to help.

So *King's Rhapsody* was cast and the Society waited to see if romance and sentiment could accomplish what high comedy had failed to do. In the lead was Joyce Elliott as Princess Cristiane with Kenneth Richardson playing opposite her as Nikki, the reluctant King of Murania, and Roula Murray as his paramour, the glamorous Marta Karillos. Shirley Dodd, though about fifteen years younger than Kenneth, was actually playing his mother. That's what you get for being a good character actress! Sixty-six people appeared in the show and even more backstage staff than ever were needed to effect the fifteen scene changes. The Society had really gone all out to make *King's Rhapsody* as spectacular as possible – the Committee hoped that the public would flock to see a show which would normally be too ambitious to be put on in the provinces. By the time the show opened, however, it was obvious that there was no hope of making anything but a financial loss, even if every seat was sold for the whole run, since the expenses were so high. The production cost £1,800, £500 of which was for the costumes – the original ones from the London production. One of the measures taken to help offset the projected loss was to raise the price of the souvenir programme by 50% to 1*s*. 6*d*. – a shrewd move, as programme sales showed a profit of £95 as opposed to sales for *La Belle Hélène* which had only made £33. Fortunately the advertising costs for *King's Rhapsody* were also reduced by £100 owing to Sam's careful handling. So although the production lost £124 it was still

£93 less than the loss on *La Belle Hélène*. The press made much of the large expenditure on *King's Rhapsody*, questioning whether it had been well spent. Consequently they gave the show a lot of attention. The *Northern Despatch* took up half a page with photographs and its review. The reviewers in all three papers felt that the risk had ultimately been worth taking as the show went from strength to strength, albeit after a slightly weak start. There were pluses and minuses in the performances of individuals but overall the spectacle of the show ensured its success and the chorus work and dancing had been very effective. Barbara Brown's and George Sharratt's dancing was particularly mentioned. (George was a nurse at Darlington Memorial Hospital and was an exceptionally talented dancer.)

Immediately after *King's Rhapsody* the pianist problem arose again after Tom Homer declared himself unable to help with *Annie Get Your Gun*. Rehearsal accommodation for after the forthcoming demolition of Beaumont Street School had not yet been found, either, though negotiations had been opened with Firth Moor School.

It was decided that it would be practical to have an independent Patrons Secretary again and also an independent Ticket Secretary so Mrs Peggy Eynon was appointed as the former and W. Arthur Clarke as the latter. (The idea of an independent Ticket Secretary turned out to be impractical, however, and only lasted for one show before the job reverted to Ken Bodden.)

In general, though, 1966 opened with a lot of problems to be solved, finance being paramount. Nor had an autumn production yet been chosen and time was getting short. Franz Lehár's *Gipsy Love* and also his *Land of Smiles* had been considered along with another Offenbach piece, *Orpheus in the Underworld*, but at the beginning of January a more 'operatic' show, Johann Strauss's *Die Fledermaus*, emerged as favourite, and this was the show chosen. A month later a new pianist had been found. Although Graham Laws was the Hon. Accompanist, Brian Sheppard – music teacher at Eastbourne School – had been appointed as his assistant. Brian is still one of the Society's accompanists, though he retired from teaching in 1988. His vocal score is accompanied, on the music stand on the piano, by his omnipresent book of word puzzles for filling in idle moments. He has not yet tried to play a word puzzle instead of the score, but one of these days . . . ! Two 'old' faces were back in the Society as well as six new ones – Margot Newell and Nancy Greenwood (née Bertram) had returned to the company.

Because of the continuing money problems ticket prices were adjusted a little – they had, after all, stayed the same for five years. For the Monday night all seats in the stalls and circle would be reduced to 5s. from the

7s. 6d. (front) and 6s. (back) which they had previously been. For Tuesday to Friday, circle and front stalls would be increased to 8s. 6d. (from 7s. 6d.) while the back would stay at 6s. For the final night they would remain at 10s. and 7s. 6d. The upper circle, which had had a single price (2s. 6d.), would now be 3s. 6d. (pre-booked) and 2s. The Committee hoped that in this way they could sell out the first night and get a little extra money in over the other nights. At least the costumes and scenery would be considerably cheaper for the 1966 shows than they had been for *King's Rhapsody* – even the fairly lavish costumes for *Die Fledermaus* cost much less than half of what had been paid for the *King's Rhapsody* ones.

So George Todd, in his opening report at the Annual General Meeting in February 1966, was able to speak in optimistic vein saying that although the recent shows were 'financially a bit of a disaster' they were in other respects very successful. He also interpreted the various divergences of opinion which had occurred through the year as being signs of a 'virile and forward-looking society'. There was no doubt that it was a healthy society. It had over 70 members and despite the Treasurer's awful warnings its financial state was not bad at all: there was a balance of well over £2,000 even after the losses on the shows and the charitable donations. Great care would have to be taken to choose the right shows to appeal to the public, though, because, while it had cost around £1,500 to mount a show in 1965, that figure had risen to nearer £1,700 in just one year.

In March there was elected to the Committee another female member (only the third since the war): Susan Swift's appointment set a precedent, for she was succeeded two years later by Muriel Jones. Meanwhile, little problems were already cropping up over *Annie Get Your Gun*. Ray Simmons and Colin Hauxwell, who were both playing named roles, dropped out. So did Bernard Sanderson, and then Wade Cobban fell ill and also had to withdraw. However, Horace Wilson took over Wade's part as Pawnee Bill, and the others were replaced by Denis Quinn, Roy Tatman and David Todd respectively. There were also changes in the air for the theatre, for moves were afoot to transfer its management from the Civic Theatre Council to the Darlington Corporation. There had been some talk of building a brand new theatre and cultural centre but this soon died a death when it turned out that even partial modernization of the existing theatre would cost around £150,000! Given that the general public's support for live theatre in the town could best be described as lukewarm, the likelihood of the Corporation's spending so much money on modernization was remote. The Committee was aware of this but was determined to put on shows which were as good as possible to keep the audiences coming in.

Annie Get Your Gun certainly brought them in. The show contained a

Annie Get Your Gun 1966
Allene James, Roland Wigington.

host of memorable songs and had been the greatest box office triumph of Irving Berlin's rich Broadway career. It ran for over 1,300 performances when it came to the London Coliseum in 1947, which augured well for the Darlington society, but the burden of the show rested largely on the shoulders of the female lead. She would have to be outstanding – and she was. Having gone even to the extent of taking rifle lessons to add authenticity, Allene James gave a firstclass performance, a fact acknowledged even by the *Darlington & Stockton Times*, which was less enthusiastic about the show itself, describing it as 'excellent out-of-season pantomime for the town's children'[3] and 'a change from watching adult (?) and uninspiring plays on television'. (And no, the critic didn't like the orchestra either!) He did admit, however, that Joy Beadell's and the cast's handling mitigated the show's 'imbecilities'. The *Northern Echo* remarked that the storyline was thin but could not imagine that anyone would care in view of the way in which it was performed. The *Northern Despatch* said that the Society had taken two major gambles: the staging of such a lavish production and the choice of Allene James, in her first role of any note, to take a leading role which had been 'beyond many professionals'. 'Both decisions,' it said, 'paid off handsomely.'[4] Roland Wigington was the ideal leading man in the role of Frank Butler and Cliff Walker as Chief Sitting Bull gave an intelligent portrayal of that imposing figure, with fine support from Sam Herdman as Buffalo Bill, Kenneth Richardson as Charlie Davenport, Audrey Dunn as Dolly Tate and Denis Quinn as Foster Wilson, together with Greta Sanderson as Winnie Tate and Peter Henderson as Tommy Keeler. Philip Murray and George Sharratt were again among the dancers who, of course, were always prominent in Joy Beadell's productions. The *Northern Echo* claimed, in its review of 3 May 1966, that this show was '. . . a slap in the face of those who claimed live theatre in the town is dying.' This was all very well but despite the revised ticket prices *Annie Get Your Gun* was not quite a sell-out and the number of Vice-Presidents and Patrons had fallen, since *King's Rhapsody*, from 231 to 212, so the show only made around £50 profit. Still, at least it had not made a loss. There was further good news at the committee meeting of 18 May: the Society had received – from Weinbergers, the rights holders – permission to give the northern première of *Orpheus in the Underworld* in spring 1967. The enthusiasm of the society members was kept up by Jim Fraser Murray's organizing a one-day drama course under Max Miradin, a founder member of the Bristol Old Vic, to which members of various operatic societies in the area were invited. Jim, as North Regional Representative of NODA, had taken advantage of the fact that Mr Miradin lectured at the annual NODA Summer Schools to get him to spend a day at Darlington.

The Committee hastened to make enquiries about costumes and scenery for *Orpheus*. Again Bill Bishop designed the scenery and Scenic Display built it; Weinbergers suggested that a Miss Mary Payne should be contacted to supply costumes – which she did, in accordance with Joy Beadell's designs, at thirty shillings each, which was very reasonable. There was no question as to who should be producer for the future shows as Joy Beadell's professionalism was indubitable and she and the company gelled – they were not anxious to have any more friction with producers. The Committee decided that Vivien Ellis and A. P. Herbert's *Bless the Bride* would follow *Orpheus* but in the event there were problems over this and *Gipsy Love* was substituted in the autumn of 1967. *Bless the Bride* eventually followed in the spring of 1968.

Die Fledermaus, however, had to be the immediate concern. There were problems with floorwork rehearsals: some members felt that Joy had arranged too many of them. Also the leading lady, who had already been changed once, was not turning up for rehearsals. She had only recently joined the Society and cannot have been used to Joy's zeal for getting as near as possible to perfection in teamwork. In the midst of this – on 4 September – Bob White died. He had worked hard in the service of the Society and a minute's silence was observed for him at the committee meeting of 21 September. At this same meeting the problem of a leading lady was solved – Shirley Dodd, after taking character parts in so many shows, now got the Big One! It was a great part to get but proved to be a major headache for Shirley, who had only three weeks in which to learn the whole thing. So for her the show passed in something of a blur and she really only enjoyed it in retrospect! Her leading man was Ray Sollett, who was imported from another society, and in the supporting roles were Eunicé Cockburn as Adele, Denis Quinn as Alfred, Sam Herdman as Dr Falke, Ray Simmons as Prince Orlofsky, and Cliff Walker as Frank (the prison governor). Greta Sanderson appeared as Ida (Adele's sister), Denis Lochtie as Frosch the drunken jailer, Kenneth Richardson as Dr Blint (the lawyer), and John Kindleysides as the Major-Domo. There was a chorus of 37 and a *corps de ballet* of twelve including Fiona Bishop, George Sharratt and Susan Mann. Susan, daughter of Fran and Ernie, had joined the dancers for *King's Rhapsody* a year earlier and, according to various sources, was something special in the way of dancers. She was a Royal Ballet Scholar though she did not ultimately take it up as a career.

Just before the show – on 1 October 1966 – control of the theatre passed from the Civic Theatre Council to Darlington Corporation, so the Society was anxious to make a good job of this, its first show under the new regime. The Committee also considered the possibility of making the Society into a Limited Company to obtain tax advantages but this did not, in the end, happen. They did, however, decide that it would be a good idea to have official Legal Advisers, and Tony Little's firm – Latimer, Hinks, Marsham & Little – was appointed. *Die Fledermaus* was performed in an atmosphere of romance; Susan Swift and Ken Robinson had married, and so had Mollie Jaques (who became Mollie Moor). Eunicé Cockburn and Jeff Wragg had become engaged. Although it was a more 'operatic' piece than the normal run of musicals the show sold well enough for the costs to be cleared comfortably. George Todd felt that perhaps the well-received *Annie Get Your Gun* had helped to sell it as the audience numbered about the same. Eunicé was singled out by the press for her superb performance – her voice was so clear and powerful that it was able to dominate even when the orchestra was at its most enthusiastic, making the other characters seem 'vaguely insipid'[5] said the *Northern Despatch*. Shirley, however, though her voice was less strong, had given a delightful 'character' rendering of Rosalinda and the rest of the cast all contributed to a show which, as far as the reviews were concerned, sparkled as much as the champagne which figures so largely in the action. The acting – particularly by Denis Quinn, Ray Simmons and Cliff Walker in the scenes where they were 'inebriated' – gave much amusement to the audiences, who left feeling that they had been well entertained.

Before the end of 1966 the Society's new rehearsal home was Firth Moor School and *Orpheus in the Underworld* had been cast. This time there were no subsequent alterations to that first casting, which must have been a relief all round. Presenting a première poses enough problems of its own without running into casting difficulties. For one thing, it attracts a lot of extra publicity which, while being encouraging, also puts a great deal of pressure on the producer and performers to make a first-class job of it, so as to set as high a standard as possible.

The Darlington society had been asked by George Welford, the organizer of the town's Charter Centenary Celebrations (of the County Borough of Darlington) and sometime Producer for the Society, if it would acknowledge the celebrations in some way. In return for some financial help (with advertising) the Society – or rather, Sam on behalf of the Society – designed a special programme for *Orpheus*, incorporating the Centenary motif and the town's crest and motto (at that time *Floreat Industria*). It carried no other advertisements and consisted of an orange-coloured folder with the motif on the front, credits on the back and the story of *Orpheus* on the inside fold. Inside was a single large folded sheet decorated with the crest and motto and giving the cast list.

The beginning of 1967 saw the final winding-up of the Civic Theatre Company; its remaining assets – around £84 – were returned, as originally agreed, to the Operatic Society.

At the Annual General Meeting on 20 February Sam, coming to the end of his year as Chairman, commented on the enthusiasm shown at rehearsals for *Orpheus* and remarked that performing shows of the calibre of *Die Fledermaus* and *La Belle Hélène* was good for the Society because it would help to improve its standards. He also suggested that the members should watch professionals as much as possible and learn from them. George Todd, as Secretary, followed this by remarking on the good attendance at the NODA Summer School, which also helped to raise the standards of individual performers. Financially the Society had done reasonably well over the preceding year and this also held true for the Ladies' Committee which with various fund-raising events had, said Margaret Hardaker (the Chairman), increased its capital account considerably.

The Ladies' Committee, despite having been formed in 1962, had never been properly constituted, and it was proposed that in view of their magnificent work they should become a fully-constituted committee of the Society. The motion was carried unanimously and the nine serving members were elected *en bloc*. The Ladies' Committee is still thriving, still topping up the Society's assets with fundraising events, and still providing refreshments at floorwork rehearsals and during shows. Of the members of the Ladies' Committee on 20 February 1967, six of them had been on it from the beginning: Evelyn Berry, Ada English, Emily Hardy, Margaret Hardaker, Eileen Young and Peggy Todd, and four of these had already received medals for being associated with NODA, as active members, for 25 years. Margaret and Peggy were about to have their medals presented at a Supper Night on 3 June 1967, along with Lorrie Boddy's husband Fred, by Lady Starmer who had herself held the award for three years. Meanwhile the new committee elections were held and Frank Murray took over as Chairman.

Ticket sales for *Orpheus* were looking promising: a number of other societies, anxious to see the première of this show, were already contacting Ken Bodden (still the Ticket Secretary). There were enquiries from Leeds,

Motherwell, Ayr, Bradford and Tynemouth, as well as from local societies and from a producer from Edinburgh who was travelling down specially to see it. Even a representative from Weinbergers, the rights holders, was coming. Bill Jones was to be 'front-of-house' and arrange hospitality for these visitors.

Orpheus opened on 1 May and everyone was concentrating so hard on it that the April committee meeting had to be cancelled since most of the members were engaged in the production. This included the Chairman, who was, of course, Musical Director, and thus in charge of the twenty-strong orchestra, some of whom were travelling from Newcastle to play for this show. Eunicé Cockburn played Euridice with Denis Quinn as Orpheus and William Foster as Pluto, God of the Underworld. Shirley Dodd was Calliope the Muse, and other gods and goddesses were played by Dorothy Walker, Ann Bennett, Adela Iveson, Bernard Sanderson, Ken Robinson and Gordon Clarke. Denis Lochtie was the unfortunate Icarus (he of the melting wings), and Roland Wigington was Styx the ferryman. Juno and Jupiter were played by Lorrie and Sam, while George Sharratt, dancing at his best, provided a startling Bacchus, the God of Wine. George, ever the perfectionist, had not only designed and made his own cos-

Orpheus In the Underworld 1967
Denis Quinn.

tume when he felt that the one from the costumiers was unsuitable, but had also insisted on having real grapes rather than plastic ones, which, despite causing a certain amount of chaos when a good many of them were scattered and splattered on the stage, gave his performance a lot of *élan*! There was a chorus of 37 (including Mollie Moor – née Jaques – who had returned to the company after a three-year absence) and a *corps de ballet* of ten ladies and four men.

Among that *corps de ballet* there appeared for her first show Patricia (Tricia) Porteus, a member of yet another family that is very close to the Civic Theatre. Her father, Ray, worked in the Stage Door office for a number of years and her mother, Kath, is an expert seamstress who also worked in the dressing-rooms for many professional shows as well as for the Operatic Society. It is Kath who has made various new curtains each time the theatre has had refurbishments, including the elaborately-swathed ones for the circle boxes, and she also helped to re-upholster the thick padded rim of the front of the dress circle. It is amazing that she does not suffer from red-velvet phobia . . . ! Tricia has a brother, named Ray like his father, and Ray Junior now stage-manages for the Society as well as helping out with the professional shows at the theatre. Ray's three daughters Claire, Sarah and Amy have also appeared on the stage in Operatic Society shows, as have Tricia's daughter Brigitte and her son Patrick. Tricia's face is probably the most familiar to the audiences as she has been in most of the shows since *Orpheus*, though she almost missed out on this first show because of knee trouble. It was because of this cartilage problem of Tricia's that Kathleen Hunt came to join the Society. Kath was in *Rose Marie* at Shildon and the show was being choreographed by George Sharratt. He suggested that Kath should go to Joy Beadell for dancing lessons and she took his advice. Kath knew nothing of Darlington Operatic Society until Tricia's problem arose, when Joy asked if Kath would take Tricia's place if necessary. As it happened Tricia was able to dance and Kath therefore stepped down but offered her help backstage.

£2,000 was spent on staging *Orpheus*, and with new scenery, new costumes, and a newly-released show, the cast enjoyed themselves immensely, though Eunicé had one or two sticky moments. One of these was every lead's nightmare and it occurred in the opening scene of the show. Orpheus emerged from the 'cornfield' to make his first speech to Euridice, who was awaiting him by the proscenium arch. Looking like the answer to a maiden's prayer in his little tunic, laurel wreath on head and stuffed felt parrot on shoulder, Denis opened his mouth to speak and promptly forgot his lines. He solved his problem by simply saying blithely, 'Well, I'll hand it over to you, Euridice!' Eunicé, as one might expect, was momentarily nonplussed but fortunately not struck dumb. She instigated a brief chat with him and managed to incorporate the cue which would lead him into his next speech, by which time he had recovered his memory, but Eunicé's troubles were not over yet. One night after singing the 'fly duet' (this is where Euridice is in her bath and Jupiter has turned himself into a fly to gain access to her bathroom through the keyhole) Eunicé was in her bath on a front cloth, wearing nothing but a costume with bubbles in strategic places. She and Sam sang their duet, which should have ended with a blackout as soon as the applause began, upon which Eunicé would stand up in her bottomless bath and carry it off around her waist. The applause was even more resounding than usual on the night that the Stage Manager's attention was diverted for a moment and Eunicé was left to walk off, brilliantly lit, with her bare feet pattering along under the bath . . .

Though they were not there to relish these moments the members of the press had mostly enjoyed what they had seen. The *Northern Echo*'s review, though short, was sweet – it reported that the show was 'a triumph . . . a superbly imaginative and spectacular production'[6] as well as being extremely funny and having brilliant tunes. The *Darlington & Stockton Times* gave it a full column and expanded on views of a similar sort. It was particularly impressed by the dancing, and singled out George Sharratt for his stunning performance. (This was especially interesting, as George had, in fact, never danced a step until just over four years previously; he simply had natural ability and was largely self-taught.) The *Northern Despatch* reviewer was more critical. She picked out the costumes as the most memorable ingredient of the show and remarked that there were not many 'all-rounders' who were proficient at both singing *and* acting – she felt, for instance, that Eunicé was more singer than actress and Shirley was more actress than singer. For her the musical highlight was Roland Wigington's rendering of *I Was a King*. Nevertheless she did conclude by 'adding the jam to the powder' and said that although there was plenty to criticize there was plenty to enjoy and that audiences would enjoy a stimulating evening. One member of the audience, at least, was exceedingly impressed. Bob White's niece, Margaret Teasdale, had returned to Darlington to work, a year or so after qualifying as a teacher. Margaret was a fairly shy girl but was interested in joining the Society if her uncle would take her along to a rehearsal. Bob, however, had died without doing this and Margaret had hesitated to go alone; but now *Orpheus* settled the issue – the experience promised to be too good to miss and Margaret went along and introduced herself. Now Margaret Cunningham (her late husband Ian was also in the Society for a while), she is the headmistress of a junior school – and is still in the Society. Margaret was not the only one to be highly impressed by *Orpheus*: so was Kath Hunt. She thought it was wonderful and that the choreography in particular was out of this world. There was no doubt in her mind that she should join the dancers for the next show. Letters were received by the Committee from other societies who had attended the show and all were highly complimentary. The NODA councillor wrote to express his enjoyment and even the representative of Weinbergers wrote to congratulate the Society on the production. So the Committee, at its May meeting, was able not only to bask in all this praise, but to rejoice in the fact that *Orpheus* had made £90 profit – once more not a great deal, but satisfactory, the box office takings being only £4 short of those for *Annie Get Your Gun*.

It was at this juncture that difficulties arose over obtaining scenery for *Bless the Bride* in the autumn and the order of the next two shows was hastily switched so that *Gypsy Love* would replace it. This sounds easy but it is the poor perspiring Secretary who must make all the re-arrangements, rebooking the scenery and costumes and making arrangements with the rights holders – George Todd was not having an easy time. It had also been decided that, in view of the present difficulties in getting backstage helpers (most of those who were available for *Die Fledermaus* having moved on to pastures new), professional labour would be used to a large extent for future shows and he had that to arrange too. Nevertheless, within the next four weeks he had effected the changeover of the shows though the nagging problem of getting pianists for all the rehearsals was still there. Also, *Kiss Me Kate* had come under discussion again, and since the Society did not, in fact, manage to present it until 1971 the constant recurrence of abortive attempts to secure the rights must have been a thorn in George's flesh. At least one of his problems had been solved: that of a place to store the Society's properties which were presently stored at the theatre. A place had been found in Clark's Yard off High Row on reasonable terms, George having haggled to good effect over the rateable value, so the props were to be moved there in August, which would be a relief.

In the mean time, Society members were able to enjoy another of Lady Starmer's garden parties before getting down to the hard work for *Gipsy Love*, most of which was cast just after the garden party. Eunicé was chosen to play the lead as Miranda, the society girl in love with Antonio, a gipsy (David Carter of the Apollo Male Voice Choir at Stockton) but pledged to marry a member of the gentry, the Hon. Lawrence Lyall (Ray Simmons), son of Lord Lyall (Cliff Walker). Sam would play Eunicé's father, Marie le Mare (who had been in the chorus for several shows) would play her younger sister Lucinda, and Peter Henderson would play Oswald, Lucinda's boyfriend. Dorothy Matthew, newly returned from Kenya where she had been teaching for four years, would play Dilaia, a gipsy girl, with Constance Overend – a new member – as Ria, the gipsy queen. Shirley Dodd had another character part as Lady Phoebe, a widow who eventually marries Miranda's father, and Nancy Greenwood (née Bertram) was once more in a named part, as Kathy, Miranda's former nurse. A sad little note appears in the minutes of the committee meeting on 16 August 1967, and also in the programme for *Gipsy Love*. This records the death of Blanche Dunn who had been a loyal and unsung worker backstage, particularly in Dressing Room 6, and whose son Bert and daughter-in-law Audrey were also staunch members of the Society. It was at this same meeting that the death of Tom Gilchrist on 9 August was reported.

However, life goes on and the company was getting geared up for *Gipsy Love*, while the Committee was thinking ahead to spring 1969 and the possibility of presenting yet another Offenbach piece, *La Vie Parisienne*, on the strength of the press reaction to the other two. The pianist problem was still in evidence. The Secretary had managed to secure the services of Mrs Irene Cooper but now she was ill. Fortunately Mrs Sylvia Pursey (née Martin, yet another former High School girl) was able to help out. (She was, and is, a teacher, now dispensing first-class education in maths at Darlington's Sixth Form College.) The ticket prices for *Gipsy Love* remained the same as they had been for *Orpheus* but the programme reverted to its original format with information and photographs, the only difference being that, since Wm Dresser & Co. had closed, it was now printed by The Parkgate Press.

Of course *Gipsy Love* was the antithesis of *Orpheus*. It was romantic and sentimental with a far-fetched plot, so the atmosphere in the theatre was quite different. The cast of 70 gave it all they'd got and the press acknowledged this, but perhaps it was too much of a contrast, at this point, to the hectic pace of *Orpheus*. The *Northern Echo* critic gave it a good – if rather stilted – review and picked out the performances of Peter Henderson and Marie le Mare for their comedy (all three papers commented favourably on them, in fact), and the consensus seems to have been that the Society made a very good job of a potentially unpromising show. It also *looked* beautiful, and the choreography and all the stage movement was well handled – 'splendid'[7] was the word used by the *Northern Echo*. The singing had been all it should be though some of the acting was marginally less so, but in general the show was well received even though it was unlikely to set the world on fire. However it brought in record takings – £53 more than for *Orpheus* – and, at around £1,600 to stage, it had cost £400 less than *Orpheus*. There were more Vice-Presidents and Patrons than for *Die Fledermaus* (due to the different programme format for *Orpheus* they were not listed, so it is not known how many there were for that show) and their donations were fixed at 12*s.* and 6*s.* respectively. Thus the income was greater in this respect too, and the donations to the customary charities were assured.

Among the new faces to appear as Society members after the staging of *Gipsy Love* were Barbara and Gordon Toft of the Bondgate Gilbert and Sullivan Society. Gordon was chosen to play a lead in *Bless the Bride*, though Barbara did not appear in it because of the imminent birth of their daughter. John Hurlstone, a baritone, was also accepted and went on to sing many leading roles with the Society. In the mean time, though, *Bless the Bride* was the new focus of attention, for there was no break from rehearsal: then, as now, rehearsals for a show began as soon as the previous show ended in order to get as much polish on it as possible. Frank Murray had also managed to get Joan How and Brian Sheppard back to play the piano for rehearsals so that problem was temporarily solved.

Since the Society was in funds again there was a move afoot to offer to pay for alterations to the orchestra pit at the theatre, although the theatre's fate was still uncertain despite the Corporation takeover, and Frank Murray and Jim Willans were lobbying the members of the town's Arts and Library Committee to support its continued use until a new theatre should be built. So 1968 began on an optimistic note, even though there was still no joy for *Kiss Me Kate*, and after 'long discussion' in the committee room *My Fair Lady* by Lerner and Loewe was chosen instead: they would try again for *Kiss Me Kate* in autumn 1969. They were nothing if not tenacious – they had booked the scenery and costumes several times already and had to cancel them: a measure of how keen they were to present the show.

Despite the improvement in the Society's financial status Frank Murray introduced a note of caution in his 'Chairman's Remarks' at the Annual General Meeting on 22 February, warning that though the financial situation was improving with the continued improvement of the Society's productions it was much easier to fall from the top, and he stressed the point that the Society must at least maintain its present standard because it could take years to recover from one poor show. He also pointed out that, since each show cost in the region of £1,600 to put on, it cost £25 to put each cast member on the stage, so every member should aim to sell £25 worth of tickets. This *pro rata* rallying cry has been heard at regular intervals down the years but it did at least give a solid point of reference to the members as to what was expected of them in return for the enjoyment of appearing onstage and being rewarded by applause for their efforts. Jim Willans spoke of the lamentable occurrence of members' returning unsold tickets after the performance – this is a nightmare for the Ticket Secretary as they are already recorded as sold by the box office and royalties have to be paid on them, but it still happens, nearly 30 years later! The Committee had already decided that henceforward seats in the gallery would be unreserved and the tickets would simply be on a roll from which the Ticket Secretary could tear them should anyone request them in advance. The remainder could then simply be given back to the box office.

Following this meeting Jim Willans took over from Frank Murray as

Chairman and the new Committee was elected ready for the run-up to
Bless the Bride, Joy Beadell's thirteenth production for the Society. A month
later everything was safely booked for *My Fair Lady* and it had also been
settled that Joy Beadell and Frank Murray should be Producer and Musical
Director for *La Vie Parisienne* the following spring, though Mr J. R. Robson,
the NODA Regional Councillor, was pessimistic about *Kiss Me Kate* for
autumn 1969, and rightly so, for everything had to be cancelled again.

Bless the Bride ran from 29 April to 4 May 1968 and every bookable seat
was taken. It was a fairly frothy and sentimental piece but, with the spice
of A. P. Herbert's wit, not as saccharine as it might have been. The *Northern
Echo* review called it 'insipid'[8] but had to admit that Eunicé Cockburn, in
the part of Suzanne Valdis (the French actress) was 'perfect' – other than
that the show did not do justice to the 'immense capabilities of Darlington
Operatic Society'. The other two papers were less adversely critical. The
Darlington & Stockton Times was of the opinion that although *Bless the Bride*
was basically a less entertaining show than *Annie Get Your Gun*, which had
been so enjoyed, it excelled as far as the Society's efforts in professionalism
were concerned.

Bob Page, the *Northern Despatch* critic, had no reservations. He had a
very high opinion of the whole venture, choosing to highlight the performances first of Eunicé Cockburn and Adela Iveson (who played the
heroine, Lucy Veracity Willow – a part which suited her well, as she was
a very 'ladylike' girl). Gordon Toft as Pierre the actor hero, Sam (this
time a 'society veteran'![9]) as Lucy's father, Shirley Dodd as Lucy's mother
and Bill Jones as Lucy's unromantic fiancé had also played their parts
convincingly. He enjoyed the vignette of Ken Bodden and Eileen Young
as the octagenarian grandparents – the 'golden-wedding-day couple' –
and Lorrie Boddy's accomplished performance as the Nanny, together
with young Freddie Bynoe's joyful portrayal of Buttons, the page with
whom the heroine changes clothes to provide herself with a disguise. He
also referred to the orchestra and the musical directorship of Frank
Murray as 'impeccable' – which must have given Frank a warm glow as
critics almost always seem to find fault with orchestras and accuse them
of drowning the singers. The dancers, as always, received a lot of praise,
though Philip Murray and George Sharratt were not among them this
time. Philip was back in the autumn but George had left Darlington to
take up a new post in Tripoli so quite possibly Darlington's loss would be
Libya's gain. Fiona Bishop had also left the town to study speech and
drama at the Guidhall School of Music and Drama, but Norma Willey
had joined the dancers as had Anthony Armstrong, Maurice Cook and
Russell Dunn, though only Russell stayed in the Society after this show.
Dorothy Matthew was also leaving after her brief reappearance (as one

of Lucy's six sisters) for she had become engaged and was going to live in London.

Bless the Bride was a great success with the audiences and it looked as though the financial trend was continuing upwards, though Jim Willans, at the committee meeting on 15 May, was still only cautiously optimistic in spite of high box office takings, lower expenses, £132 of programme takings, and a continued rise in numbers of Vice-Presidents and Patrons! At the meeting there also came the pleasing news that Lorna Jackson, who had joined the Society for *Orpheus* and *Gipsy Love* in order to use the experience towards attaining her Duke of Edinburgh Gold Award, had been successful and was to receive the award at Buckingham Palace the following month.

Singing rehearsals had already begun for *My Fair Lady* and auditions for named roles were imminent. The royalties for this show would be higher than usual as it was only ten years old, so with 15% to be paid and the £500-plus payment towards the theatre's orchestra pit in the offing it had to sell well. It had been a smash hit in London, making more than £3½ million at the Drury Lane box office, so the show was intrinsically excellent and the Darlington production would succeed or fail on its cast. Therefore even the general acting members were carefully selected as well as the seven leading roles. Twenty-four ladies and twenty-four men were required to play bit parts and to be the chorus (though only twenty men were eventually secured – man-shortage was still the norm). Ticket prices had been static for two and a half years so they were to rise to 10s. for circle and front stalls and 7s. 6d. for back stalls (with a 2s. 6d. rise all round on the final night), and concessions would only be made for children and pensioners in the stalls, their tickets costing 6s. The upper circle would be 5s. (booked in advance) and 3s. 6d. (at the door). There was also to be an innovation for *My Fair Lady*: The Rotary Club, under the chairmanship of Basil Noble, was to book the whole theatre for the Tuesday night of the show to make it a special charity gala performance. At the conclusion the Club would make a presentation of a cheque to its chosen charity. This was the first of many such gala evenings and since then the Society has also given a number of concerts in aid of specific charities, beginning with one at Christmas that same year for the Lions Club. There was a lot of hard work ahead, for alongside the *My Fair Lady* rehearsals members were also rehearsing the chorus work for *La Vie Parisienne* in the autumn.

By July the principals were cast for *My Fair Lady*, the date of which would mark Joy Beadell's 21st year with the Society. Eunicé was to play Eliza Doolittle, with Kenneth Richardson as Professor Higgins and Shirley Dodd as his mother – yet again! Alan Round, in a rare onstage appearance with the Society (he worked backstage for several shows), was to be Alfred Doolittle, Eliza's father. Ken Bodden was cast as Colonel Pickering, Jeff Wragg as Freddy Eynsford-Hill, Eileen Young as Mrs Pearce the housekeeper, and Bill Jones as Zoltan Karpathy. Casting completed, Jim Willans had a meeting with Frank Murray, Jack Rowell, Richard Sampson and George Todd at which Frank Murray's suggested programme for the Lion's Club concert was examined and approved. Joy Beadell was chosen to be the narrator, the title would be *Music Round the World* and it would be given on 15 December. There was, shortly after this, a certain amount of unease among a number of members of the Society who felt that the visiting singers who would be in the concert were performing solos which could well have been sung by Society members, but this was solved principally by the Committee's receiving a letter from dissenters, noting it and then allowing the issue to die quietly! That settled, all attention was turned to *My Fair Lady* which opened for its week-long presentation on 28 October.

The photograph of Eunicé for the programme cover was taken on the steps of the covered market in the town centre. It represented Eliza Doolittle before her transformation into a 'lady' by Professor Higgins, and Eunicé perched on the steps, suitably grubby and bedraggled and surrounded by baskets of flowers. She was left in no doubt as to the effectiveness of her costume and make-up, for the voice of an elderly woman was suddenly heard. 'Ee, I say!' it said piercingly. 'Look at that mucky woman up there!'

Sadly, the show's opening was marred by the sudden death, a week before opening night, of Alan Gamble. Alan had been on the Props staff for nine shows and the Hon. Property Master for another nine, as well as the current one. Despite this terrible shock, however, the show had to go on, looking as though nothing was amiss – and it did. Not even the most determined critic could vote it anything less than a smash hit with its wonderful music, its well-chosen cast, and its beautiful costumes, made to original designs by Mrs Zena Devine of the Little Theatre at Middlesbrough and augmented with some from costumiers C. & W. May Ltd. The *Northern Echo* called it '. . . one of the most outstanding shows the Society has ever staged,'[10] paying tribute to 'superb characterization', and concluded by saying, 'Full marks to the Society – who must rank supreme among amateurs.' 'The Society has had many triumphs but this must be the greatest yet,'[11] said the *Darlington & Stockton Times* before it went on to praise Eunicé ('cannot be faulted'), Kenneth ('a meticulous performance'), Alan ('sheer robust vivacity'), Jeff ('would have delighted any debutante'), Ken Bodden ('gentle and reasonable, pointing up Higgins' insensitivity') and Eileen ('warm and homely, with a rich voice, modelled rather on

Renée Houston').* This reviewer was of the opinion that the show could have run for two weeks instead of one. The (Middlesbrough) *Evening Gazette* could not fault the show, and Bob Page of the *Northern Despatch* was thoroughly smitten, paying tribute to all – leading players, chorus and dancers – and calling it 'a company triumph'.[12] That Professor Higgins's front door had, after several mishaps, finally fallen flat on its face was swept aside in the glowing reception of the piece; that Eunicé had to sing *Show Me* while holding her dress together, after a quick change was not quite quick enough, fortunately went unnoticed!

The show was a lucrative as well as a visual delight, too. A triumphant Jim Willans reported at the November committee meeting that, for the first time in the Society's history, takings had gone well over the £2,000 mark – to £2,385 in fact, which was £550 up on the takings for *Bless the Bride*. Although this was a monumental breakthrough, the higher royalties due to increased sale of tickets and the higher percentage taken by the rights holders, together with the large expenditure on costumes and scenery and the cost of paying professional stage hands, would result in a loss on the production as a whole. It was a very small loss – only around £36 – but it did show the necessity for continuing to plan carefully and produce shows as economically as possible. Nonetheless, the Society was still able to donate £200 to charities that year.

Planning of future shows was very much in the minds of the committee members when they came together for the last meeting of 1968. Following the success of *My Fair Lady*, Frank Murray had been scrutinizing Lerner and Loewe's *Camelot*, the show based on *The Once and Future King*, T. H. White's book about King Arthur and the Knights of the Round Table, and the Committee thought this a good idea for the autumn of 1969. Ken Bodden also pointed out that autumn 1970 would be the silver jubilee of the re-formed Society so it was decided that the show which had marked that re-formation – *Merrie England* – would be repeated. Meanwhile the concert sponsored by the Lions Club had been well received and Frank Murray had shrewdly included a 'taster' from *La Vie Parisienne* to tempt the public.

Christmas came and went and the first meeting of 1969 – on 15 January – saw the confirmation of the casting for the male roles in the show, accomplished three days earlier (though three of the cast members changed before the show went on). Only one lady was definitely cast, though, and that was Eunicé, again to be the leading lady in the part of

---

* Renée Houston was a wonderful variety performer and actress who made her first stage appearance in 1916 and died in 1980. She had a rich, low-pitched voice and a trenchant wit.

Gabrielle. There was concern over the small number of people who had auditioned – it was almost unheard of, and quite disturbing, for the male roles to be cast before those of the ladies.

More disturbing was the fact that there was talk of making alterations to the theatre's auditorium – £20,000 worth of alterations – which would include the complete closure of the upper circle (or gallery) and the removal of a third of the stalls to give an area to be made into a bar. This would reduce the seating capacity from 1,150 to 601 and so could affect takings very seriously. However, future shows were agreed upon from autumn 1969 up to the end of 1972. The agreement had been signed for *Camelot*, for autumn 1969, at 12½% which meant that the show would cost less in that respect than *My Fair Lady* and so the seat prices could stay the same. *Summer Song* and *Merrie England* had been chosen for 1970, *The Grand Duchess of Gerolstein* and *Kiss Me Kate* (at last) for 1971, and *Lisa* and *The Sound of Music* for 1972. (Only four of these were to be performed at these times – and two of them have never been presented at all – but the Committee was not to know that at the time, and ignorance is bliss, so they thought they were well ahead.) *Camelot* did not have much chorus work, but Frank Murray thought it might be a good idea to put chorus members to learning some opera choruses which might possibly be used in a future concert, so they would not be allowed to be idle.

The Society proceeded on its way towards *La Vie Parisienne*. Susan Robinson had retired from the Committee to give birth to her only child, Julie, in February – the first time any committee member had retired for this reason! She was replaced by Muriel Jones. At the February meeting the casting of the ladies' roles was approved, the scenery had been ordered and the provider of costumes was being discussed. There was, however, a falling-off in attendance at rehearsals and this would have to be reme-died.

The Annual General Meeting on 13 March gave a review of the previous year's work. George Todd was pleased to point out the areas of new ground which had been broken – the Sunday night concert, the idea of two shows being rehearsed at the same time so that the chorus would be constantly occupied, and the innovation of having a gala performance for charity on behalf of another philanthropic organization. It was also pleasing to be able to speak of Jim Fraser Murray's election as NODA Councillor for the Northern Section and Frank Murray's as NODA representative for the region. Even Jim Willans in his capacity as Treas-urer was cautiously optimistic and his economically orientated heart was delighted by the fact that the theatre rental was still only £325 for a week's hire and that the Society was lucky enough to have Joy Beadell as a producer at very reasonable fees. As Chairman he referred slightly to some malicious gossip which had gone on in the Society (but then, when did such an organization *not* gossip?) but in general it had been a happy year for him. Lorrie Boddy had now joined the Committee to serve for two years, keeping up the number of ladies to two, and she took up her position at the following meeting on 19 March.

It was here that the first of the projected future shows bit the dust; at Frank Murray's suggestion, Wright and Forrest's *Song of Norway*, based on the life of the composer Edvard Grieg, was substituted for *Summer Song*. *Merrie England* was, however, definite for the Silver Jubilee. Frank had also negotiated a new agreement with the Musician's Union simplifying the orchestra's fees and clarifying things considerably, but the props were on the move again – this time having to be shifted from Clark's Yard, which had not been wholly satisfactory, to Education Department premises at Albert Road.

Jim Willans had ventured further into the field of high finance, having consulted a stockbroker on the subject of investment-for-growth by individuals on behalf of the Society, and he hoped that there would be more money to invest after *La Vie Parisienne*. It must be remembered that the Society was under a self-imposed obligation to use its money as wisely as possible to safeguard its charitable donations as well as having financial back-up in case of any show proving to be a disaster – at this stage it was like continually treading on eggshells because of the public's lacklustre attitude to live theatre in general. Public reaction to *La Vie Parisienne* was anxiously awaited. In the programme some interesting statistics were printed concerning the production: there were 64 in the cast, who had spent 60 hours on singing rehearsals plus 110 hours on floorwork, there were 200 costumes, and the production had cost £2,250 to put on. The cast was backed up, of course, by the Committee and Producer, who planned the rehearsals and arranged for publicity, programmes, costumes, scenery and furniture hire, extra lighting hire, props construction, booking of the theatre seats, rehearsal rooms and voluntary helpers (for example prompters and a call boy – the latter in this case being Peter Sanderson, Bernard and Greta's second son) and all the myriads of tiny details – and all for one week on the stage. It was to be hoped that the public would appreciate it!

The press certainly did. This show is not largely dependent on one or two principals but is essentially a team production so it must have several equally outstanding players and, according to the press, the Society was well able to provide them. As well as Eunicé as Gabrielle, Denis Quinn was the eccentric and lighthearted millionaire Brazil, Ray Simmons and Jeff Wragg were Raoul and Bobinet, the men-about-Paris, and Margaret Umpleby was Baroness Gondremarck with Sam ('dependable'[13] this time) as her husband. Marie le Mare was Pauline the flirtatious housekeeper, and Pat Durkin, a talented singer who had joined the chorus for *My Fair Lady*, was given a great deal of praise for her part as Metella the fashionable cocotte. Two of the dancers, Jane Hope and Susan Mann, were missing, but the troupe of Jacqueline Batey, Judith Dunn, Hilary Greenwood, Kath Hunt, Pauline McMain (née Keogh), Tricia Porteus and Norma Willey had been augmented by Sally Robson, Janet Thompson, Norma Willey's sister Susan, and Sandra Williamson. Margaret Taylor (now Margaret Singer) also joined for this show and became one of the hard core of regular dancers. In addition to having so many equally good performances the show was beautifully dressed, being set in Paris in the 1860s; it had good music, it was elegant, it was colourful and it was very well produced – all ingredients for success. All the rehearsal had been worthwhile and the public who came loved it, but Jim Willans was a worried man again. This is easily understandable. It was all well and good that the income for the show was £2,000 but that had still meant a loss of around £200, £40 of which was on programmes, and with the prospect of the closure of the gallery, plus the removal of five to eight rows of the back stalls for the refurbishment of the theatre, the outlook was grim. The Society's social events were not being supported as well as they could be, either. There was no option but to raise the prices of the seats for *Camelot* to 11s. 6d. for Monday to Friday and 15s. on Saturday, with no concessions. In view of the coolness of theatre-going support it was very risky but the film of *Camelot* had been released in 1967 and it was hoped that this would bring the public in.

Meanwhile there was the usual shortage of men and you can't have a Round Table with hardly any knights to grace it. Strenuous recruiting efforts, as well as seat-selling efforts, would have to be made. A matinée would also be performed (Kenneth Richardson's employers, Doggarts Ltd., had given permission for him to be away from work as he was playing the part of King Arthur) and Jim Willans said that, with the additional costs for a matinée standing at around £80, he was encouraged to hope for a profit of about £100 on the show. There was a shortage of one other man – a Stage Manager – as Richard Sampson was unable to help this time though he was willing to advise as much as he could. Ernie Mann was approached and agreed, though with some trepidation for he could not read music and did not wish to be involved with lighting. However, he was to be helped with the music cues and he had fifteen people to help with stage/electrics/props duties. At least he *should* have had fifteen but there was one notable absentee: Tricia Porteus's cartilage problem had now become acute and she was unable to dance in the show but had gamely volunteered to help backstage. When the time came, however, she had had to undergo surgery and was on crutches. (Tricia says she thought she would never dance again – but she was back for *Song of Norway*.)

During the summer break Lady Starmer gave her annual garden party for the Society. It was a particularly special occasion as Fred and Doris Thompson had both been in NODA for 50 years and Lady Starmer presented them with their 50-years bars to their NODA medals. Casting for *Camelot* had been completed just before the break and some new members had been admitted to the Society: Tom Kent, Lynne and Warnock Kerr and Avril Sowerby (though only Tom was to appear in *Camelot*), while Susan Wishlade, who was later to take some leading roles, joined the dancers. Michael Walker, Cliff and Dorothy's son, played his first notable role as Tom, the small boy whom King Arthur tells, at the very end of the show, to tell the world about Camelot. (Years later, Mike was to become the Society's youngest Chairman, at the age of 31.)

Eunicé was to be Guenevere to Kenneth's King Arthur, Denis Quinn was Merlin, Sam Herdman Pellinore, Philip Murray the evil Mordred, and Muriel Jones the sorceress Morgan le Fey. Nimue the nymph was played by Pat Durkin and John Hurlstone took his first major role with the Society as Sir Lancelot. By the time the October committee meeting came round the news of ticket sales was encouraging. The Rotary Club had taken the whole of the theatre for the Tuesday evening and it was fervently hoped that all their tickets would be sold. Other than that there were only seats left for the matinée, apart from one or two 'restricted-viewing' seats on odd nights. An irksome matter concerned dress rehearsals and the number of spectators brought in by members to them, which was getting out of hand. If they wanted to see the show they really ought to pay to do so. As a matter of fact, though, the show was oversubscribed for some nights and some members were not able to have the number of tickets they had requested. This of course was due to the reduction in seating capacity and there was no way round it, though the matinée helped a lot. Jim Willans hoped for a profit of around £200 so half of that was donated to the Society's usual charities. Nevertheless the £100 left over was not a fortune and could easily be swallowed up in little bits and bobs of expenses – for instance the return transport of the scenery had cost an extra £10 and the timpani needed repair which would cost £7 10s. od.

Camelot, though, was another smash hit and the press were not present on the night on which Peter Sanderson (as call boy) forgot to call the Act II beginners so that the curtain rose on an empty stage while he rushed frantically round the dressing-rooms shrieking that they were 'on' (they covered it up by drifting on in groups and singing as they came).

The *Northern Echo* could not fault it, saying that 'there were few superlatives adequate to describe it',[14] that the professional expertise of the cast was evident from the moment the curtain rose, and that Kenneth and Eunicé 'achieved perfection' with King Arthur and Guenevere while John Hurlstone was an impressive Lancelot and Philip Murray an insidious Mordred. The *Darlington & Stockton Times* said the same and added praise to Muriel Jones who had looked impressively evil. She certainly did, in a tight purple spangled costume, her auburn hair frizzed out into a bushy tangle and with very skilful make-up masterminded by Dorothy Waterfall (who was a producer for a drama group in the town). Sam also had an honourable mention ('doddery', 'motheaten')[15] but the reviewer was thoroughly impressed at the whole spectacle (the costumes were the original ones from the Drury Lane Theatre) and the polished production. Bob Page of the *Northern Despatch* agreed wholeheartedly, adding that King Arthur was in his opinion the finest part Kenneth Richardson had ever played and that this also went for Denis Quinn's portrayal of Merlin. The impact of Sam Herdman and Philip Murray was also outstanding for him, and all in all it had been a superlative production.

As 1969 drew to a close, therefore, a great innovation was being considered since so many people had been disappointed by not being able to get tickets for *Camelot*. Why should not *Song of Norway* run for nine nights instead of six? It should be a viable proposition since the hire of the costumes and scenery would not be very much more for the extra nights, and takings could be considerably increased. Granted, the orchestra would have to be paid and the theatre hire would double to cover the two weeks, but there would not be the usual mad rush to accomplish the get-in of scenery and there would be the luxury of extra dress-rehearsing. There would also be the possibility of selling another 1,800 seats – though of course there was also the terrible possibility that they might *not* be sold. There would be a concession, the Committee decided, to OAPs and children on the first night when their tickets would be 6*s.*, instead of the 11*s.* which would be the norm, with 15*s.* for the Saturday nights. It looked as though the Lions Club would like to take the whole theatre for one night, as the Rotary Club had done previously.

These things were in the minds of the Committee when the year came to an end. Doing nine nights of a show was a big step to take and it might land the Society in deep water. On the other hand it might do it a world of good. The theatre, in any case, would be much improved as the refurbishment would be complete in January 1970, with its rear stalls area converted to a new licensed bar and coffee bar and all of the seating replaced. It was to have a front-of-house manager too: John Wackett from the Octagon Theatre at Bolton. So the Committee decided to take the plunge and to look beyond any difficulties to the future – Sam was looking into new designs for the Society's official notepaper, for instance – and they daringly booked the theatre for another nine-night run for the production of *Merrie England* to mark the Silver Jubilee.

Chapter 7

1970–1974

1970 arrived and the Society was discussing ways, apart from the anniversary production of *Merrie England*, to commemorate its Silver Jubilee. There was no shortage of ideas – it was just that each one met a stumbling-block and had to be abandoned. Bill Jones suggested that a portrait of Lady Starmer, as President of the Society, should be commissioned. Lady Starmer expressed her gratitude for the thought but declined to sit for a portrait. Bill then hit on the idea of applying for a floral display in the South Park, but unfortunately the displays had already been planned for 1970. The televising of *Merrie England* and the making of a record were also eventually abandoned. Other ideas included presenting a piece of silver to the Council or a brooch to Lady Starmer but in the end it seemed more appropriate that some enduring memento for the Society as a whole should be sought. Some kind of Chairman's regalia seemed to be the answer and after sundry ideas had been inspected and designs considered over the year, a Chairman's Jewel and Ribbon was commissioned from Northern Goldsmiths, to be presented to the Chairman after a special performance of *Merrie England* which it was hoped a number of the cast of the 1945 production would be able to attend. (The Chairman's Jewel consists of a one-inch-wide loop of royal blue medal-ribbon with a shield-shaped pendant bearing the masks of Comedy and Tragedy in silver-gilt on a royal blue enamelled background. The words 'Chairman' and '25th Anniversary' appear on the top of the shield and the dates and name of the Society at the bottom. Silver-gilt plates bearing the engraved names of all of the Chairmen from 1945 onwards are attached to the ribbon.)

The Committee then turned its attention to *Song of Norway*. The Lions Club had booked one performance as a charity evening in aid of the Special Care Baby Unit at the Memorial Hospital and the Committee had agreed that the price of the programme should be raised by 6*d.* to 2*s.* They also adopted the idea of a reduction by 1*s.* in the price of tickets for block bookings of twenty or more.

By the time the Annual General Meeting was held in mid-February the show had been cast apart from the children. A pianist – Brian

Sheppard – had been chosen to perform Grieg's *Piano Concerto in A Minor* which was one of the central features of the show.

Ken Bodden, as Chairman, told the meeting that he was happy to confirm that the standard of productions was improving, though he also had the less happy duty of announcing a decrease in the number of playing members. It was good to have a nucleus of seasoned performers but new members were always needed lest the company become stagnant. Jim Willans stressed the need for members to sell more tickets which seems strange given that some of them had not been able to get all the tickets they wanted for *Camelot*: it was probably just force of habit!

Richard Sampson took over as Chairman after this meeting and the various committee jobs were sorted out. The children's parts were also cast and 'operatic' families were drawn upon. Alison and Michael Walker, Cliff and Dorothy's children, were there, and Peter Sanderson; there was Judith Todd, daughter of George and Peggy's son David, and Zoë, Sam and Joan Herdman's younger daughter, in her one and only appearance with the Society. Even Barbara Riding, daughter of the caretaker at Firth Moor School where rehearsals were held, was pressed into service as 'call boy'. Kath Hunt was playing a named part for the first time with Philip Murray and Russell Dunn in the Concerto Ballet.

There was no overture to *Song of Norway*, only a Prelude which would be much disturbed if there were late-comers so it was decided that they would not be admitted until the Prelude was ended. Moreover, the Committee cunningly arranged to start the performance five minutes later than stated on the tickets, just to make sure!

The press all agreed that it was an ambitious venture but one which was fully justified. 'Operetta at its best,' read the *Northern Echo*'s headline, and the review went on to say that it had 'spectacle, enchanting melodies, and fine dancing and singing', and that it was 'full of life and colour'.[1] The reviewers were partisan, having their favourite performers. For the *Darlington and Stockton Times* Eunicé Cockburn's performance as the glamorous and temperamental prima donna Countess Louisa Giovanni was one of the greatest triumphs of her career with the Society (though the memory which first comes to mind for Eunicé is somewhat more mundane. It is that of being towed hell-for-leather onto the stage by Ken Bodden's two poodles, borrowed for the occasion; the percussionist must have had some fascinating quality, as the dogs always headed directly for 'stage left' which is just above the percussionist's corner in the orchestra pit and at the far side of the stage from which Eunicé entered!) The other two reviewers took it rather for granted that Eunicé would give a fine performance and gave a good deal of praise to Pat Durkin as Nina, the girl whom Grieg (Ray Simmons) marries but whom his poet friend

Richard Nordraak (David Carter) also loves. The men fared less well in the reviews though Sam Herdman as Father Grieg ('jovial')[2] and Ken Bodden as Count Peppi le Loup received praise for their comedy. So did Bill Jones who played the gesticulating and ebullient Maestro Pisoni – his characterization was especially enjoyed by the *Northern Echo*. The cameo parts – taken by Kenneth Richardson as Tito, the mincing proprietor of a chocolate shop, William Foster as the dignified playwright Henrik Ibsen, and Kath Hunt as the superbly bitchy prima ballerina – were brilliant and exploited to the full, said the *Darlington and Stockton Times*; but the lasting impression, after all the colour and glamour, was of Brian Sheppard's excellent performance of the famous piano concerto on a grand piano in one of the circle boxes, with orchestral backing and with the Concerto Ballet taking place on stage.

Once the show was over the sums began. The nine-night run had boosted box office takings to £2,917 and even after the extra expense of theatre rental and orchestra the show showed a profit of £150, which was not bad at all. So the extra three nights of the run were justified, auguring well for *Merrie England*. A few problems had to be sorted out before then, however. One of them was that decimalization of currency meant that conversions had to be made before the next lot of ticket prices could be stated. Wardrobe had been a problem, too, for the hardworking Lorrie Boddy, for some of the costumes had not been satisfactory and there had been a certain amount of grumbling. Also some aggravation had been caused by practical joking: some of the food used on stage had been tampered with on the final night of the show. In this case the cream buns which were to be voraciously consumed by Bill Jones had been doctored with salt. (However, a number of tricks tend to be played in most societies, usually not to any serious extent, and since they are almost always played on each other by 'old hands' who can give as good as they get, the matter is not generally a serious one.)

As the summer of 1970 approached the Treasurer produced his decimalization conversions ready for 1971. Under the new system Vice-Presidents' donations would be 60p and Patrons 30p; OAP and children's tickets would be 30p with ordinary tickets at 55p (block booking 50p) and for Saturdays 75p (blocks 70p); programmes would be 10p. Members' annual subscriptions would be £1.05.

Preparation of the projected cost of *Merrie England* was also being worked out. It seemed likely that it would cost around £2,600 for this special occasion. No expense was to be spared on the production of the programme and there was to be a blaze of publicity. Sam had also had his new letterhead approved for the Society's stationery. The Rotary Club was having the Tuesday as its Gala Night, so one night was already sold for the show.

Even the advent of a Silver Jubilee celebration cannot allow future planning to take a back seat and though *Kiss Me Kate* had been chosen as the autumn show, the spring show had yet to be finalized. It was later decided to stick with the one originally selected and Offenbach's *The Grand Duchess of Gerolstein* was duly booked.

The Committee put a great deal of thought into casting *Merrie England* but this was accomplished before the summer break, apart from the role of Queen Elizabeth I. The only hiatus was over the part of Raleigh, which had been offered to Michael Hunt (whose only mention this is in the annals of the Society). He had a previous engagement so Jeff Wragg, Eunicé's husband of a year by now, took on the role. Some new faces appeared for this show. Trevor Harder, who had been keen to join the Society for a while, was accepted to play Silas Simkins, one of the two 'London actors' (Kenneth Richardson played the other). Ann Appleton, after a long break, rejoined the dancers, though Tricia Porteus was missing again. She was no longer Tricia Porteus for she had married and was now Tricia Freeman; she was in the Shildon society's production of *Oliver!*, and felt that trying to be in Darlington's show as well was not practical. Tricia was lucky not to have been one of those who had to present themselves at Raby Castle on the bitterly cold day on which the programme photographs were taken. Eunicé remembers it only too well. It was so cold that the cast shivered even in their heavy Elizabethan finery. Kenneth Richardson had on a pair of blue-grey tights and his face was almost the same colour by the time the session was over; one might say that the entire cast of principals was blue with cold around the ramparts!

Backstage there were some new arrivals to support existing members of the company – props and stage staff had numbered only sixteen for *Song of Norway* and Lorrie Boddy had attempted to look after both make-up and wardrobe, which was really too much work for one person. For *Merrie England* there were 25 props and stage staff, including Hilary Greenwood (Nancy, her mother, was still in the chorus). Cecil Grieveson's son Barry was helping, along with Marie le Mare's husband Derek, Betty MacFall's husband Gordon, George and Peggy Todd's son Barry, Susan Wishlade's husband Peter, and his fellow-solicitor, John Parker, who was later to make a considerable mark on stage in leading roles. There was also Parkin Raine who was to do much hard work backstage for the Society. John Simpson, who had joined the props staff two years earlier, was appointed Property Master. Lorrie originally withdrew from the production, but she was persuaded to stay on to do make-up, and a tiny dynamo – Elsie Campbell – was asked to be Wardrobe Mistress. Elsie accepted and is still wielding her tape-measure at every show. There was still no Queen Elizabeth I by September but eventually Nancy Chilver, a contralto from

Teesside Operatic Society, came to play the part. Nancy was to make an exceptionally regal Queen but she is one of those people who, though dignified, strait-laced even, in looks, is gifted with a great sense of comedy. She has since played, for Darlington, such Gilbert & Sullivan comedy roles as Katisha in *The Mikado* and The Duchess of Plaza Toro in *The Gondoliers*, and the Society was very fortunate indeed to get her.

The Committee wanted this Jubilee not only to be memorable but to be shared with as many people from the original 1945 cast as possible, so they sought them out and sent two complimentary tickets to each of them for Friday 30 October. For one of them, of course, they did not need to look far, for Nancy Greenwood had played Bessie Throckmorton in the first production. She was brought forward from her place in the chorus to be reintroduced to the audience, a memory much cherished by Nancy. Finally, at that same performance, the presentation of the Chairman's Jewel was made to Richard Sampson by Lady Starmer.

Much was made of the production in other ways. The theatre foyer was decorated with flowers by the town's Parks Department and a special banner was made to be displayed there, and Bill Jones entertained lots of visitors in the office at the theatre. So overall the show cost more than expected – around £3,000 – but the press thought it was money well spent (indeed, apart from the first Saturday there was a full house for each performance). The *Darlington & Stockton Times* remarked that the expense was justified by the pleasure it gave the audience to see a show where 'the ha'porth of tar had been gladly bought'.[3] The principals had all given fine performances and Nancy Chilver 'might have stepped from a portrait of Queen Elizabeth'. The *Northern Despatch* (by now called the *Evening Despatch*) referred to the show as a 'three-hour spectacular'[4] and said that it captivated the first-night audience by its verve, speed and alternating solemnity and gaiety.

Unexpected comedy was not mentioned, for it was fortunately not on the first night that Cliff Walker made his all-too-easy gaffe. With great dignity he escorted Pat Durkin (as the May Queen) onto the stage immediately after the interval for *The Month o' May*. It was only a matter of seconds before it dawned on him that something was unusual: he could see the audience – which meant that he was still wearing his thick-brown-horn-rimmed spectacles . . .

The costumes were spendid and the scenery was new (from Clifford and Brown of Nuneaton). Since this was the modern Sadlers Wells version there were a few extra bits of business, including a masque of St George and the Dragon which was comically carried out by Kenneth Richardson and Trevor Harder. (Some unrehearsed business was also necessary, remembers Joan Reynolds, because the theatre roof was leaking, and

Merrie England 1970. *Left to right*: Trevor Harder, Eunicé Cockburn, John Hurlstone, Nancy Chilver, Jeff Wragg, Pat Durkin, Kenneth Richardson.

mopping-up operations were taking place backstage while the cast tried to sing and dodge the rainfall at the same time. Large amounts of age-old dust were coming down from the flies with the rain and those members of the cast who had to stand still had to contend with dirty water splashing onto their make-up and costumes. John Parker recalls that a message went out to the cast after the first act: 'Umbrellas will be worn in Act II!')

The press picked out a number of cast members for special mention: Eunicé was an appealing Bessie Throckmorton and Marie le Mare a delightful Jill-All-Alone, while John Hurlstone was a gallant Essex and Pat Durkin a most attractive May Queen, but overall there was, they agreed, no weakness in the company either in principals or chorus and dancers. Joy Beadell and Frank Murray were much praised for their efforts. It was a shame that the *Northern Echo* did not review the show but when the Society performed *The Grand Duchess of Gerolstein* the following spring the reviewer from that paper confessed to not liking light opera so perhaps that was the reason. He was, at least, honest!

Of course the show had been bound to lose money because of the high cost of putting it on but it was felt it had still been worthwhile as a landmark in the Society's history.

Hard upon the end of the run of *Merrie England* there came the annual

25th Anniversary Celebrations, 1970. *Centre front:* Glennis Beresford, Kenneth
Connor, Lady Starmer. *See page xi for full list.*

dinner-dance. This was also a gala occasion and was well attended. Isabel
Farrage came, having been invited from her home in the South, and Mr
Harry Cook, immediate past-President of NODA, came to propose the
toast to the Society and brought his wife. To add to the festivities Kenneth
Connor, the film and television star, came and performed in a cabaret.
He brought with him Glennis Beresford, who was now regularly appearing in West End musicals and who had appeared with Harry Secombe
and Connor himself in *The Four Musketeers* at Drury Lane two years earlier.
Chris Fox and Colin Tarn (he of the last-minute scribblings of the score
for *Aurora* in 1961) completed the cabaret cast of four. The occasion was
a most lively and enjoyable affair, though there was a cloud hovering over
the Society because Frank Murray was not well and had gone into hospital
after the end of the show. Sam was to take over the rehearsals until Frank
was fit again. The Committee was unsure of what to do for the best. The
weight of two heavy musical shows a year was a great burden on Frank
– and perhaps the members of the Committee closest to him suspected
how ill he was. However, Frank gave them a draft of what he considered
to be the requirements of cast and chorus for *The Grand Duchess*, and it
was agreed to see if this looked like being met after the first two rehearsals
before further moves were considered.

The Society distributed £110 to charity at the end of the year and then
it was back to Offenbach and *The Grand Duchess*. 1971 opened with the
casting of the show. Eunicé played the title role with Trevor Harder as

her suitor Prince Paul. George Dixon, a newcomer, was chosen to play Private Fritz, the main (and unwilling) object of the Duchess's flirtatious attentions, and Sam (who else?) played General Boom. The object of Fritz's fancy, Wanda, was to be played by Pat Durkin, and Marie le Mare, Muriel Jones, and Dorothy and Cliff Walker (the latter as Baron Grog) were there too. Also appearing were Kenneth Richardson as Baron Puck, Bernard Sanderson as Kras the Duchess's *aide de camp* and Denis Lochtie as the Sergeant Major, with Roy Tatman, Jeff Wragg, David Todd, and Horace Wilson as the officers: Spatz, Spitz, Spotz, and Sputz respectively. Shirley Dodd was chosen to play Olga, one of the ladies-in-waiting, but injured her leg and had to be replaced by Ann Wood, and Bernard Sanderson also withdrew and was replaced by John Kindleysides. Elsie Campbell and Lorrie Boddy had both settled into the niches they occupy today as Wardrobe Mistress and Make-up Supervisor.

The Annual General Meeting, with only 49 members present, was held on 2 March and had an air of mixed feelings about it. Although the audiences which had attended the last two shows had apparently enjoyed them immensely, Richard Sampson feared for the Society's future. As in the previous year there was a drop in the playing membership (though the remaining members were enthusiastic about performing) and only three nominations had been received for four vacant places on the Committee. Even the Ladies' Committee numbered only seven instead of nine.

The question of nine-night runs was raised. According to Jim Willans the cost of playing three extra nights was so far just about balanced by the extra income in the end, and potentially a lot more people could see the show. So the extra nights were to be preserved for now, and the rehearsals of *The Grand Duchess* continued with gusto.

The Society then received yet another blow. Frank Murray died on 6 March, just fifteen months after his brother, John, had been killed in a car accident. It is a measure of his popularity that well over 300 people attended his funeral and there was no doubt that he would be greatly missed. The Society, to show its appreciation of him in tangible form, immediately set up a fund – the Frank C. Murray Memorial Fund – to donate money to the newly-formed local association for the National Society for Cancer Relief.

Once again, though, the show had to go on and a great deal of effort was put into gaining publicity for it, one venture being participation in the Round Table carnival by means of an Operatic Society float designed by Wade Cobban.

Of course the company now lacked a Musical Director, but fortunately Joseph Lee agreed to take on the job. He had been an army musician for

22 years and was a conductor with the Royal Signals Band at Catterick Camp. He was no stranger to amateur operatic society work for he had spent some time with the Richmond Amateur Operatic Society and had then been with Stockton Stage Society for a number of productions. He asked only that expenses should be paid to him.

There would be no Gala Charity Night for *The Grand Duchess* because the Round Table were busy planning their carnival, so members would have to be even more diligent in selling tickets and organizations making block bookings would be encouraged by being given a special mention in the programme. There was also discussion about the possible placing of advertisements in the windows of shops standing empty, as well as a window display in the Nationwide Building Society.

It was at this juncture that the Committee co-opted another lady member to fill one of the two gaps created by the resignation of Lorrie Boddy and the death of Frank Murray: Eunicé Cockburn was elected. So what with her new duties and her leading role in the show she was kept busy.

Twenty-seven large parties of theatre-goers from various organizations came to see *The Grand Duchess* as well as the usual attenders. The *Evening Despatch* and the *Darlington & Stockton Times* voted it a hit, the *Despatch* (in its report on 7 May) saying that the first night's house loved it, and singling out Trevor Harder's clever handling of the role of Prince Paul along with Eunicé's capricious Duchess, George Dixon's peasant soldier and Sam ('veteran bass') in his role as the bumbling old commander-in-chief. 'God bless Ruritania,' said the *Darlington & Stockton Times* wryly, 'for without it many an operetta would never have seen the light of day.'[5] The review was good, though, the critic seeing that below the frothy exterior the show demanded rather more, musically, than many operettas; the solo work was more technically exacting, and the choruses were '. . . something more than the gay-singalong type.' The paper singled out the same players for praise as the *Evening Despatch*, with the addition of mentions for Pat Durkin's Wanda with her 'voice of ease and clarity' and Kenneth Richardson whose Baron Grog owed 'more than a little to the Mad Hatter'. The *Northern Echo*'s piece revealed more about the critic than the show – which he described as 'silly and tiresome', calling the music 'little more than sub-Sullivan mind rot'[6] – but he was forced to admit that even if it was rubbish it was well-performed rubbish! Joseph Lee and the orchestra had acquitted themselves well – he would continue to be Musical Director for the next five shows.

The cast enjoyed doing the show as much as was possible after the loss of Frank Murray, and there were moments of fun backstage. Kath Robinson (née Hunt) remembers that the show contained a very elegant and pretty ballet which the dancers performed in traditional white ballet dresses. The dancers, however, were fascinated by the flamboyant and luxuriant black false moustaches worn by the men. When Greta Sanderson entered the girls' dressing-room shortly before their cue one night she was greeted by a small sea of dancers, clad in pristine white ballet dresses, each startled little face turned towards her adorned with a sumptuous black moustache.

Eunicé has many memories of the show, but it is not the tuneful music, the colourful costumes or the applause which stands out; it is the boots – the boots which she wore with her military costume. They were so tight and they pinched her toes so cruelly that her predominant memory is of marching in sprightly fashion, and wearing a glowing smile, while searing agony throbbed through her feet. For nine nights!

The overall takings for *The Grand Duchess* were just over £2,107 and the show lost money even though the royalties were only 10%. The Committee hoped that *Kiss Me Kate* would make up for it and provide a silver lining, particularly after all the struggling to get this Cole Porter piece onto the Darlington stage; a Gala Night would help if one could be held. Experimentation would have to be made to minimize losses on future shows so the Committee decided to try running spring shows for only six nights while keeping the autumn ones (when the nights were drawing in) to nine. Accordingly the decision was made to stage Jerry Herman's *Hello Dolly!*, based on Thornton Wilder's book *The Matchmaker*, for six nights in May 1972, then *Pickwick* in the autumn. They would follow this with Grainer and Miller's *Robert and Elizabeth* (based on the love story of Robert Browning and Elizabeth Barrett), and Frank Loesser's *Guys and Dolls* in 1973. At the same time the Committee was eager to produce Jerry Bock and Sheldon Harnick's *Fiddler on the Roof* as soon as it was released to amateurs, and so decided that any of these shows could be replaced by that if necessary.

Happily the Rotary Club wanted to hold a Gala Night at *Kiss Me Kate*. Better yet, it wished to donate the profits to the Frank C. Murray Memorial Fund – a most welcome offer – and meanwhile the Society's investments were showing a small profit. On the ticket front Ken Bodden had announced that he wanted to withdraw from the office of Ticket Secretary and someone else would have to take on the job after *Hello Dolly!* Nobody wanted it, of course – nobody ever does – so the Committee put off the evil moment and hoped, like Mr Micawber, that something (or rather someone) would turn up.

At least the number of Society members seemed to be on the increase again. At the auditions preceding the committee meeting in July, eleven new members had been accepted, including John Parker (who had hitherto only helped backstage), Pat Port and Barbara Riding, both of whom had come into the Society to be 'call boys'. Sadly, though, three of the eleven only stayed for one show and two were never in a show at all but Christine Coates (the singer rather than Christine Coates the dancer, who did not join until 1976) stayed on for many years, Lawrence (Jimmy) Hall remained until his death in 1989, and John Parker (who married the dancer Ann Appleton) is still on the scene, helping backstage when he can.

By now the Society was carrying an overdraft of around £20 and Jim Willans had the unfortunate task of transferring some money from the deposit account to cover it, which went against the grain. The huge size of the loss on *The Grand Duchess* had become apparent when the bill for the programmes came in – the total loss amounted to over £600. If any impetus was needed to make a tremendous success of *Kiss Me Kate* then this was it.

They had most of the show cast, however, though one or two changes had to be made. Eunicé Cockburn and John Hurlstone were playing the leads, Lilli Vanessi and Fred Graham, with John Lavelle and Marie le Mare as the secondary leads, Bill Calhoun and Lois Lane. John Parker and Sam Herdman were cast as the two comic gangsters and Eileen Young was to play Hattie the maid. Wade Cobban designed the scenery (Billingham Forum Theatre were to build it) and was also playing Ralph. The cast was completed by Kenneth Richardson as Harry Trevor, Alan Round as Paul, Bert Dunn as the Stage Doorman, and Ken Bodden as Harrison Howell. The 'play within a play' cast contained, as well as the players from the main cast, Jimmy Hall as Gremio, Jeff Wragg as Hortensio, Cecil Grieveson as the Haberdasher, Roy Tatman as Nathaniel, Gordon Clarke as Gregory, and John Kindleysides as Philip.

At the committee meeting in July 1971 the autumn show for 1972 was abruptly changed. *Pickwick* was not a very practical choice because of the difficulty of casting the title role. Harry Secombe, who had starred in the original West End show in 1963, was a hard act to follow. What was more, *Fiddler on the Roof* was due to be released to amateurs in October 1972 and should be seized upon if possible.

The Committee did not have a summer break. Instead it turned its attention, in August, to the matter of a Ticket Secretary to take over after *Kiss Me Kate*. A victim had been found outside the Society in the person of Reg Ekins, a local businessman, so a weight was lifted from Ken Bodden and Wade Cobban (who had helped Ken). Jim Willans, meanwhile, having failed to get a grant from Northern Arts to offset the loss on *The Grand Duchess*, had had to withdraw a further £450 from the Society's building society account to transfer to the current account. The page where this minute is recorded is not tear-stained but it gives off doleful vibrations!

A month later, though, a triumphant George Todd had secured from Chappell and Co., the rights holders, permission for the Society to present *Fiddler on the Roof* only a month after its release, which would be a tremendous coup.

There was no Stage Manager as yet for *Kiss Me Kate* and Richard Sampson was not sure whether he would be available but Bernard Sanderson knew that Gordon Holton, from Hurworth, was interested in helping backstage. Gordon immediately declared himself willing, thus beginning an association with the Society which lasted until his death in 1993, and which is continued by his daughter Liz (who has been a very active member ever she was old enough to join, beginning as a dancer and later taking major roles) and his wife Betty, who supports the Society without taking part in shows.

A week before opening night the outlook was considerably brighter. An anonymous contribution of £100 had been received to help offset the costs of *The Grand Duchess*, and *Kiss Me Kate* was selling well. Thirty-two parties had made block bookings to see it and smaller parties were coming from Cheshire and Leeds Operatic Societies. Moreover, it was hoped that the newly-constructed scenery could be sold to one of the hire-firms for around £300 once the show was over – possibly this could be used against the hire-charge of the scenery for *Hello Dolly!* from the same company. However, there was a certain amount of anxiety about some chorus members' not having attended as many rehearsals as they should (they were to be watched carefully); also there was anxiety about the shortage of men, for a number of 'waiters' would be needed for *Hello Dolly!*, to perform the 'Waiters' Gallop'. The men in *Kiss Me Kate* cast modesty aside as they donned the knitted woollen tights which condemned them to over-exposure, and the mood was, in the main, optimistic on the opening night.

The show's press write-ups justified this optimism – so did the takings which were over £750 up on those for *The Grand Duchess*. The review by the *Northern Echo* critic (not the same person who had been so scathing about *The Grand Duchess*) was short but sweet. 'A fine cast of players star in this rip-roaring musical,'[7] said Peter King. Bob Page of the *Evening Despatch* remarked on the difficulty of dealing with a 'story-within-a-story plot' and said that the Society came through with flying colours, Eunicé Cockburn and John Hurlstone being first-class in every department, and Marie le Mare confident and professional. The press liked Sam Herdman and John Parker in their James-Cagney-style *Brush Up Your Shakespeare* scene, too. The potential of the 'machine-guns' they carried was too good to miss since they were actually water-pistols. On the last night they put them to good use by using them liberally during the curtain calls, which resulted in some very damp people, including the Musical Director. All in all it was a good show, well presented in all aspects. Kath Robinson remembers this show well for a different reason. Dancing is hot work and Kath imbibed a little too freely of some alcoholic refreshment at the interval. Consequently, when the rest of the dancers ran, holding up their arms, from one corner of the stage to the other, Kath, who had gone to the wrong side, found herself running forward to meet them . . . John Hurlstone, on the other hand, had cause for self-congratulation on his *ad lib* when Eunicé slammed the door of her room in Petruchio's house and jammed it solid. 'I' faith!' said John. 'The maiden has shot her bolt!'

The Committee expressed satisfaction with *Kiss Me Kate* at its November meeting, which followed the show, and it was gratifying that Leeds Operatic Society had written in appreciation of the production, going so far as to ask if the Darlington principals would be willing to consider acting as understudies for their own production of it.

Less gratifying – in fact quite worrying – was the fact that the theatre contracts for 1972 had not been received, owing to the resignation of the Theatre Manager. John Wackett had moved to a new post, that of Head of Drama at Darlington College of Technology, during the customary three-month closure of the theatre from the end of May. (This closure was necessary because there was a lack of affordable live entertainment to fill the time in.) Not long after John Wackett left, Donald Hamilton-Moore also resigned so the theatre had no senior management at all and if the choice of a new manager was not a good one the theatre would have a gloomy future, if indeed it had a future at all. The Committee tried to shut out this grim prospect and proceeded with plans for 1972.

The sale of the *Kiss Me Kate* scenery only realized £175 instead of the hoped-for £300. However, the royalties for *Hello Dolly!* would be at a fixed rate of £70 for the first perfomance and £38 for each of the other performances together with a rental of £20 for orchestration, so at least the Committee knew in advance what they would have to pay in that respect. Naturally it was less than for *Kiss Me Kate*, which, though also at a fixed rate, had, of course, played for the extra three nights. George Todd, however, had been looking long and hard at the costings for *Hello Dolly!* and estimated that if the ticket prices and ticket sales stayed at the same level as they had been for *Kiss Me Kate* the loss on the show would be £400, for other costs had risen. A price rise, sufficient to go some way towards lessening the loss, while not acting as a deterrent to the public, might reduce that loss to £100, and a matinée might be a good idea when there was only a six-night run. After a good deal of soul-searching the Committee agreed on this and raised all the ticket prices by 10p to 65p for Monday to Friday and the matinée, and to 85p for Saturday evening.

The matinée performance would also allow children and OAPs a reduced price of 40p. There would be no reduction for block bookings, though. It was hoped that these steps would stop the rot, as it were, before it started.

At the last meeting of 1971 there was a gloom-inducing communication from the accountant in charge of the Civic Theatre business, proposing a rise in the theatre rent and asking to know the financial state of the Society. Jim Willans and George Todd went into 'clam mode' and refused to tell him, preferring to see what would happen when a new Theatre Director was appointed. It was a shock, however, considering the financial ups and downs of the last few years, so Christmas 1971 was not unalloyed merriment.

If miracles do occur, however, one surely did so early in 1972, and, though no one could have interpreted it as such at the time, the result of one action was like that of putting one's life savings on a rank outsider in the Derby and watching it romp home at 200 to 1! That action was simply that, out of the many applicants for the job of Theatre Director, the Corporation chose Peter Tod, who, at the age of only 24, became the youngest theatre director in the country. Within five years he was to turn an average attendance of 20% into an incredible 80%. While other theatres in the country were being forced to close, Peter Tod raised Darlington Civic Theatre from being semi-moribund to throbbing with life and enthusiasm. At the time, of course, the Operatic Society committee had no hint of this. Peter Tod wrote to the Society introducing himself, which was a friendly gesture and was warmly received.

A new contract had been negotiated with Evans Brothers and the royalties for *Hello Dolly!* had been reduced by £4 per performance, so that was a little ray of sunshine. The *Fiddler on the Roof* contract was signed with Chappell and Co. at 12½% and George Todd had managed to secure booking of the costumes, scenery and props of the touring company as a job-lot from Theatrical Costume House (Westcliffe) Ltd. for the two weeks, at £700 plus £120 carriage.

The desperate search for men was still on for *Hello Dolly!* although the casting was done apart from the role of Barnaby Tucker. It was suggested that Ferryhill Operatic Society should be approached to see if any of its male chorus would be willing to join in and committee members were all urged to join in the great man-hunt.

The local Jewish community had got wind of the *Fiddler on the Roof* coup and intimated that they would like to have a special performance of it in aid of their own charity work.

In the mean time, *Hello Dolly!* was well into rehearsal and by March there had been several developments, all but one being pleasant. On the plus side Joe Lee had applied to become a member of the Society, despite the fact that it had been pointed out to him that in accordance with the rules he would not be eligible to be paid a fee for his services, and he had declared himself willing, if elected, to fill the vacant place on the Committee; the part of Barnaby Tucker had been given to John Parker, and a new actor, Philip Bethell, joined the cast of this show to play the Judge. Philip was a part-time teacher of speech and drama at the Immaculate Conception School and at the Technical College, as well as running public-speaking courses for Sergeants and Inspectors at the Police College at Danby Wiske and later at Dishforth. (Though now retired he still takes the occasional pupil and is an examiner for the London College of Music and the Guildhall School of Music and Drama – this is what *he* calls 'retirement'!)

The unpleasant development was that Value Added Tax had reared its head, and this could prove detrimental to profits. The NODA Director had written to all societies urging them to write to both Terence Higgins MP and their local MP decrying the imposition of the tax, though the measure of success achieved equated with King Canute's abortive demonstration of stopping the tide coming in. Terence Higgins did point out that small companies with a turnover of less than £5,000 would be exempt which was a comfort for the time being, but naturally the ever-optimistic Society was hoping to do better than this before too long.

Hello Dolly! was performed in May and staging and props work was carried out by only thirteen people, but what they lacked in quantity they made up for in quality. Kath Hunt would support this view, for Philip Robinson came to work with the stage staff for the first time and he and Kath were married that same year. As for other newcomers, June Park joined the dancers and, though she did not know it at the time, would marry a future member, Guy Allen. Young Liz Holton had finally made it, too, after wanting to be involved for some time. Too young to be a full member she only came along as 'call boy' but it was a start. The name Peter Cutchie also appears for the first time, among the chorus. He was yet another member who went on to make the theatre his career, though at the time nothing was further from his mind. He was then a clerk with Lloyds Bank, which he left to become a landscape gardener before taking a post as Assistant House Manager at the Civic Theatre. This was during the directorship of Andrew Jowett (1979–1982), and when Andrew moved to the Arts Centre at the University of Warwick, Peter went too. (He is now Director of Queen's Hall Arts Centre at Hexham, Northumberland.)

The show was enlivened by the use of a sixteen-piece marching band (for *Before the Parade Passes By*) made up (by Joe Lee) of musicians from the

Duke of Wellington's Regimental Band from Catterick Camp. It was eminently successful. The press did not have a churlish work to say about the show – in fact the reviews were peppered with superlatives. The *Darlington & Stockton Times* called it '. . . a sizzling sensation which compelled the audience to demand curtain call after curtain call in what is probably the best amateur operatic production to be performed in Darlington.'[8] Some individual performances had been exceptional: Eunicé Cockburn, in the title role, was described as 'superb'[9] by the *Northern Echo* and 'truly fantastic' by the *Darlington & Stockton Times*. The *Evening Despatch* commented that she never faltered and her excellent singing was matched by her acting of the part which she performed with 'joyous abandon and humour'[10] (though Eunicé says she almost did falter when she came through the fringed silver backdrop at one point and the feathers in her hat threatened to become caught up in the silver strands). Even her American accent, added the review, had been admirably sustained. The papers agreed that all of the cast were outstanding in their own ways – Sam Herdman ('dependable') as Horace Vandergelder, the reluctant bridegroom, with his 'natural approach to acting' and Marie le Mare showing 'flair' as Irene Molloy. Sue Wishlade was 'superb' as Minnie Fay – happily the disaster of the dress rehearsal, when she caught her wig, while dancing, on John Parker's cufflink, leaving the wig dangling there, was not repeated – and John Parker himself ('what a performance!') was clearly outstanding as young Barnaby Tucker, another comedy part. Ray Simmons was commended for his performance as Cornelius Hackl, and Muriel Jones for her strident Ernestina, but it was the overall praise which was so gratifying. The chorus and dancers, the orchestra, the clever producing by Joy Beadell – this show had it all, but the Society itself, as a cohesive whole, won accolades too, from the *Northern Echo*: 'Darlington Operatic Society can always be relied upon to produce a first-rate interpretation with a professional polish of any material given them . . .', from the *Darlington & Stockton Times* came: '*Hello Dolly!* was near perfect and who can improve on perfection?', and from the *Evening Despatch*: 'Ambition never seems to outrun capability with this company.' Not all went as smoothly as on this opening night, for there was to be a potentially dangerous accident during the 'Waiters' Gallop' at a later performance. This was a very fast number executed by the 'waiters' who all carried items of food or drink on trays and crossed the stage diagonally, interweaving as they went. One of them – Jeff Wragg – had a large skewer and was supposed to spear the chicken carried by Ken Robinson. Unfortunately Jeff missed the chicken and stabbed Ken, who had to be rushed to hospital, still in full make-up and feeling foolish, to have a tetanus injection. He recovered perfectly well but probably still shudders at the sight of a kebab!

Hello Dolly! made between £350 and £400 profit which was wonderful news, but how do you follow a show which had hit the heights, as this one had? *Fiddler on the Roof* was a good choice because of its complete contrast to the razzmatazz of *Hello Dolly!* It was originally performed in New York from 1964 to 1972, where there were 3,242 performances, making it the longest-running musical in American theatrical history. It is the story of poverty-stricken and hard-working Jews in Tsarist Russia and their instinct for survival, and is based on stories by Sholem Aleichem.

The local Jewish community did not book the whole of the theatre for a night but nevertheless started the ticket ball rolling by booking 100 seats for the first Saturday of the show in aid of the charity *B'nai B'rith* which helped underprivileged children. A special charity brochure was produced for that one performance, to go with the programme. They also gave valuable advice to the Society on matters of ritual such as the wedding scene and the Sabbath prayer scene.

The pianist problem had arisen again as Joan How was ill and in hospital, and although the Society had Brian Sheppard he could not reasonably be expected to play for *all* rehearsals, both singing and dancing ones. Malcolm Sykes, a local professional pianist, was approached and pronounced himself willing to help, but he strained a finger and was unable to play. Advertisements were even placed in the press, all to no avail. So Brian Sheppard, helped by Sam Herdman, had to soldier on.

The shows for 1973 were under discussion again. *Charlie Girl*, by David Heneker and John Taylor, would just have been made available to amateurs by the spring and it would be nice to give yet another newly-released show, but it presented something of a dilemma. It had starred Anna Neagle and Joe Brown in its London run and had had 2,202 performances, even after the critic Bernard Levin had described it as '. . . harmless trash, somewhere between perfectly frightful and dead 'orrible,' and as '. . . determinedly second-rate.' [11] Godfrey Winn had defended it, saying he thought it was time the average playgoer was protected from '. . . the personal judgement of that small, acidulated, self-important group of highbrows who condemn everyone else's taste in theatre as being fit only for the coach trade.'[12] In light of these argumentative views *Charlie Girl* was probably too much of a gamble, so it was abandoned. Then it was suggested that perhaps *Guys and Dolls* should be brought forward and given in the spring instead of the autumn. Whatever the show, however, the Committee now decided to abandon the idea of a six-night-only run for spring as it was felt that nine nights could still be sustained, and the services of Joy Beadell and Joe Lee were retained once more for both 1973 shows.

Productions beyond these were also being mulled over and, as well as

Pickwick still being a possibility (if a leading man could be found), *Mame* and *The Count of Luxemburg* had been mentioned.

Peter Tod had proved to be most helpful over *Hello Dolly!* and was already popular with the Society, so much so that he had, by the time of the June committee meeting, been asked to be principal speaker at the annual dinner-dance. He was already beginning to put the Darlington theatre on the map, having first negotiated a prestige opening season of plays with the London-based Triumph Theatre Productions, organized massive publicity, secured a Government grant to revitalize the outside of the building, and got Janet Baker (now Dame Janet Baker) to give a Celebrity Recital. The Friends of the Civic Theatre, whose number had dropped to only 32 in 1970, began to build up support again. All of this was good news for the whole town and the Society was naturally delighted.

The Committee took every possible care in the casting of *Fiddler on the Roof*, which marked Joy Beadell's 25th year with, and 21st production for, the Society. The most curious event was probably the casting of Stephen Henley as Tevye, the leading man. He was from Yarm, had acted with Middlesbrough Little Theatre, and more or less walked in to the auditions saying he would like to play the role. The effect of his appearance was startling. He *was* Tevye, to the life, and there could be no doubt that he should have the part, despite the normal policy of only going outside the Society for leading-role players if it was unavoidable. Eunicé was to play Golde his wife, while his daughters – Tzeitel, Hodel and Chava – were to be Kath Hunt, Sue Wishlade and Fiona Bishop. Their respective suitors — Motel, Perchik and Fyedka – were to be Ray Simmons, Jeff Wragg and John Parker. Lazar Wolf, the butcher originally destined to be Tzeitel's husband, was Sam Herdman, and Fruma-Sarah, the ghost of Lazar Wolf's first wife, was Muriel Jones. (Muriel made quite an impact on the audiences. She was hideously made-up and the bilious green of her draperies was further enhanced by green stage-lighting. She was carried on the shoulders of six-foot-two tall Peter Wishlade who was hidden by her long and voluminous garments. Muriel herself is six feet tall so together they presented a formidable figure. She remembers a very unnerving moment as Peter was about to rush onto the stage carrying her during one performance. She was already on his shoulders and waiting in the wings when she swayed forwards and almost over-balanced. She says that she will never know how Peter managed to keep his balance and right them both, but that it must have taken an almost super-human effort!) Other cast members kept their feet firmly on the ground: Shirley Dodd was to be Yente the matchmaker, Susan Robinson was to be Grandma Tzeitel, and George Dixon, Ken Bodden and Kenneth Richardson were to be Mordcha, the Rabbi, and the Constable respectively. Meanwhile, Barrie Dargue, who lived at Shildon and was an operating-theatre nurse at Bishop Auckland Hospital, had just joined the Society. He was that perpetual-object-of-desire for any operatic society – a good tenor – and was warmly received, being given the small role of Mendel, the Rabbi's son. Other small roles were played by Carol Willey, Cliff Walker, Horace Wilson, Audrey Dunn, Peter Sanderson and Stephen Wragg. Peter Cutchie was to be the 'Fiddler' of the title and had the dubious honour of opening the show, sitting on the roof of Tevye's house. Peter Hydes made his first appearance with the Society in the chorus for this show and eventually continued the history of matchmaking in the company by marrying Hilary Greenwood, Nancy's daughter, who had been in the Society for some time by now. Several of the backstage staff also appeared in the list of chorus-members so that they could go unobtrusively about their stage duties – so Ernie Mann, Bernard Sanderson and Roy Tatman were able to be seen onstage without having to pay 'appearance-money'. (It is traditional that if a member of the stage-crew is inadvertantly seen by the audience he or she is required to buy drinks for the rest of the stage-crew.) Lastly, all three Holtons were involved in *Fiddler on the Roof*, for Gordon was stage-managing, Liz was 'call boy', and Betty was in the stage-crew.

Although *Hello Dolly!* had done so well, it was hoped that *Fiddler* would be an even bigger success financially, for the Society hoped to give sufficient money to the theatre to refit two dressing-rooms as well as making its customary charitable donations. The two dressing-rooms were to be called the Starmer Room and the Operatic Room.

Problems now arose again with the productions for 1973; the Society was having difficulty obtaining scenery and costumes for *Guys and Dolls* so eventually the show had to be left in abeyance (though it would be considered for the following spring) and *Robert and Elizabeth* was reinstated as the spring show. There was now a gap in the plans where an autumn show should be.

The rights for *Robert and Elizabeth*, however, were hastily secured from Samuel French at 12½% royalties, and though there was some initial difficulty in obtaining scenery George Todd did finally manage to get some from Midland Stage Decor.

These problems faded into insignificance, however, next to the immense success of *Fiddler on the Roof*. Though it had its humorous moments it was quite a different proposition from the usual type of show put on by the Society. It was not sumptuously costumed, it did not have a conventionally happy (or tragic) ending, and it was based on a very serious subject: gradual loss of tradition and community and the necessary compromise.

The critic in the *Darlington & Stockton Times* called it a 'musical with a meaning'[13] and one feels that it was not really his cup of tea. Despite observing that the performance in itself was good but not exceptional, he had, however, been enormously impressed by Stephen Henley's portrayal of Tevye – and also by John Parker's display of Cossack dancing! Judith Leckenby of the *Northern Echo* had been impressed with the cast's performances, recommending that the public, if its taste in musicals went beyond the hearts-and-flowers variety, should see this show, and Bob Page of the *Evening Despatch* was thoroughly taken with it and did not wonder that it had had such phenomenal success on stage and screen. He praised the chorus, the dancers and the individual characters, and felt that the Darlington society did the show full justice. Stephen Henley, in fact, impressed all the reviewers, and Eunicé had coped well with a part which was a total change from her usual roles. (Indeed Eunicé was much touched at one point, seeing tears in her husband's eyes and thinking how much she must have moved him with her portrayal of Golde. Unfortunately this was not the case – she had just inadvertently jammed his finger in a piece of scenery!) The other characters had been well drawn, too, said Bob Page, and the public must have agreed with him, for the box office takings amounted to over £3,500, despite a slight drop in the number of Vice-Presidents and Patrons. It meant that 1972 closed on a reasonably high note, financially at least.

1973, however, opened with further difficulties, one of which concerned the use of the theatre for an autumn show. (The question of that production had, of course, been a knotty one from the start, what with the chopping and changing, and still no show had been chosen.) Another amateur society wanted to use the theatre and it was a question of either altering the dates of one of the two societies' shows or having them 'back to back' which would not be good policy on Peter Tod's part. Peter had also indicated that he would prefer the Society not to use the theatre office for entertaining guests. Perhaps he did not quite realize what a firm tradition this was and that, had it not been for the Society, there would not even have been a theatre, let alone an office. So the Society committee stuck to its guns. Another problem concerned *Robert and Elizabeth*. Eunicé was to play Elizabeth and Stephen Henley was coming back to play her father Edward Moulton-Barrett,* but though some of the other parts were cast, there was still no leading man. What is more, the accompanist problem was no nearer to being solved – the Society had been much

---

* Coincidentally Lady Starmer numbered among her acquaintance another Edward Moulton-Barrett, a descendent of the family. She invited him to be present at the final performance but he wrote her a charming letter, regretting that he would be on his way home from Jamaica at the crucial time.

saddened by the death of Joan How. To pile on the agony, members were once more being dilatory over attendance at rehearsals. Jim Willans was happy in his own way, though, for the profit made on the last two shows had enabled him to replace the £450 which he had so reluctantly taken from the Society's building society account. So he, at least, felt a warm glow.

By the time the February committee meeting arrived the glow was beginning to spread a little further through the Committee. Peace had been made with Peter Tod and he had booked the dates at the theatre in the Darlington society's favour. Also there had been a favourable outcome from an inspection of the Society's accounts by HM Inspector of Taxes which suggested that a rebate might be claimable. Now that the financial situation was looking better Joe Lee had put forward the idea that the Society might repeat another show, suggesting that *The Merry Widow* be performed in the autumn and that it should be done as lavishly as possible with the best sets and costumes to be had. The Committee had taken up the idea, and even Jim Willans was in the happy position of being able to bring himself to admit that the Society was in a healthy state once more!

Then the glow receded. Andrew Taylor (from a Cleveland society), who had finally been cast as Robert Browning, withdrew, so now the hunt was on once more for a leading man. John Parker was suffering an identity crisis: he had been cast as Captain Surtees Cook but, when Peter Henderson was not able to take the part of Octavius, John was asked to take that part instead, while Ray Danby, who, like Stephen Henley, was a Middlesbrough Little Theatre player, was asked to play Cook. There was no one to play Henry Bevan, either, so the Society borrowed Geoff Heeley from Darlington's Kay Players to take on the role. All of the male chorus members eventually took named parts as well, but it had been a struggle to make up the male numbers and the Committee probably wished that Mr and Mrs Barrett's family of twelve had been weighted more heavily on the distaff side!

The glow was further dimmed by the sad news of the death of that longstanding member, Bert Dunn, on the very afternoon of the committee meeting of 22 March. He had been in *Fiddler on the Roof* and had been expected to be in *Robert and Elizabeth*. Also Jack Rowell was ill and had to refuse the office of Chairman. (George Todd was next in line but felt that he could not fulfil both that role and his job as Secretary so eventually Bill Jones agreed to be Chairman for a further year and Sam Herdman was willing to be Deputy Chairman.) There were some bright spots, however, for several problems were solved. For one thing a Robert Browning had been found. Cliff Walker had been in a production at

Bondgate Chapel and knew that one of his fellow-performers had played the part of Robert at Hartlepool sometime during the past year. Thus it was that Keith Tate was, at short notice, to rescue the Darlington society from great difficulty (and would do so more than once). The Committee must have breathed a collective sigh of relief – not only did they have a leading man, but he was a *tenor* – and now they knew where to find him when they were in need! Also, after considerable searching, a dog had been found to play the part of Elizabeth Barrett's dog Flush. Tess was a little golden Cocker Spaniel who was sure to appeal to the audiences (although in the end she became so interested in the audience that she lost her concentration!) A certain amount of dissent among the members over performing *The Merry Widow* was quoshed when it was pointed out that everything had already been booked for the show and it would be too costly to renege at this point. Finally, Noël Coward's *Bitter Sweet* had been chosen as the show for autumn 1974 – *Guys and Dolls* was still the tentative choice for spring.

Robert and Elizabeth proved to be a mixed blessing as far as reviews and box office takings were concerned. The reviewers' opinions were divided. The *Northern Echo* referred to 'strong script and pleasant music',[14] but added 'To achieve the Society's usual professional polish requires first-class singing and acting, not always apparent.' The *Darlington & Stockton Times* spoke of 'mediocre music, songs and script',[15] and the *Evening Despatch* only said that it was an appropriately romantic choice for spring. Stephen Henley and Eunicé Cockburn were praised as being first class, while Keith Tate, though a little hesitant at first (and no wonder, considering the short time which he had had in which to rehearse), improved as the show went on. Ray Danby had made a very good impression in his first appearance with the Society. It had been Kenneth Richardson's 50th show with the Society, which was quite an achievement, and Richmond Operatic Society had then asked him to play the lead for them in *The King and I* so he was obviously in fine form.

Sadly, though, *Robert and Elizabeth* did not capture the imagination of the public as *Fiddler on the Roof* had done, and the takings were £500 down, while Joy Beadell's fees were to go up for the 1974 shows. She was undoubtedly still a great bargain, though, and the Committee agreed to the new fees without hesitation.

It was fervently hoped that *The Merry Widow* would prove a more attractive proposition to the public, so instead of dwelling on past difficulties the Committee looked ahead.

The ticket prices now had to be raised, of course, because of VAT, and the 65p ones went up by 10p and the 85p and 40p ones by 5p. The scenery was hired, the contract (at 12½% royalties) was signed, and the auditions were set for mid-June. By 26 June the casting was complete. Eunicé was a 'natural' for Anna Glavari and John Hurlstone was to play opposite her as Danilo. Kenneth Richardson was to be Baron Zeta with Carol Biggin as his flirtatious (but 'highly respectable') wife Valencienne, and Jeff Wragg as her admirer Camille. John Parker had another comic role as Njegus, Baron Zeta's factotum. So things were set fair for this show, but the Committee remained concerned about the lack of men in the Society and, with *Guys and Dolls* in mind, the consequent casting problems. There were, for instance, only eight men in the chorus for *The Merry Widow* – just half the number of the female chorus, which now included two more 'society wives' who had both been roped in for *Robert and Elizabeth*: Peter Cutchie's wife Rowena and Tom Kent's wife Judi. Also – at last – it included Liz Holton, who was now old enough to be a full member of the Society!

The idea of reducing the Society's output to only one show per year was brought up again, this time by Ken Bodden, but after 'lengthy discussion' it was clear that no one really wanted this to happen and members were urged to make every effort to attend all rehearsals to make up in quality for what was lacking in quantity. Besides, the Society was paying for the decoration and carpeting of the Theatre Director's two offices, as well as giving the usual donations to charity, so it was necessary to continue to raise as much in the way of funds as possible. Fortunately the scenery problem for *Guys and Dolls* had been solved: James Fredericks were able to supply it, and Ernie Mann had declared himself willing to construct the requisite props if necessary, so the show was assured for the spring of 1974. Ernie was already engaged in building props for *The Merry Widow* with John Simpson, but sadly John was not to see how successful these were for he died only a month before the show opened and Wade Cobban stepped in to help Ernie.

The Merry Widow went on without too many hiccups, though John Hurlstone had an unfortunate encounter with a wrought-iron chair. The frogging on his elaborate uniform became inextricably caught in the chair's scrolling when he sat down and he had no alternative but to appeal for help, saying to Eunicé, 'Madam Glavari, I appear to be stuck.' Eunicé was so intent upon remembering her lines that he had to say it several times, with increasing emphasis, before the message got through to her. John Parker was in some pain, having gone to give his new fiancée, Ann Appleton, a kiss backstage and having got his nose speared on one of the heated rollers in her hair!

The show was a general success though yet again the reviews were mixed. The *Northern Echo* said that if the Society thought it necessary to repeat one of its previous productions then this show was the one which lent itself to revival better than most. The *Evening Despatch* was much more enthusiastic. Its reviewer said that the revival (it was fourteen years since the earlier production) was well worth waiting for; she was thoroughly entertained, agreeing with the *Northern Echo* that the leading players gave superb performances. She had also greatly enjoyed the high-kicking performance of the can-can by the Grisettes – Ann Wood, Hilary Greenwood, Norma Willey, Ann Appleton, Kath Hunt and Sue Wishlade. The *Darlington & Stockton Times* was more reserved. 'Good but not brilliant'[16] was the verdict, and, though Kenneth Richardson, Eunicé Cockburn, Carol Biggin and John Hurlstone had given good value (especially the first two) and though it provided an enjoyable evening's entertainment, for some reason that extra 'something' was lacking.

Behind the scenes, however, all was not well, for something of a crisis was developing. The night after the opening of *The Merry Widow* the Committee was obliged to have a special meeting after the show – at 10.45 p.m. Joe Lee had written to George Todd saying that he would have to stand down as Musical Director for *Guys and Dolls* because of business commitments. Fate, however, had already taken a hand. John Beagle, a lecturer in music at the Stockton/Billingham Technical College, had written to the Society introducing himself, and Jim Willans and George Todd had already had a meeting with him. This did not go down too well with some of the Committee who felt that George and Jim had jumped the gun in taking things this far without consultation. They took a week to mull it over and held another meeting immediately after the close of the following Wednesday's performance, at which they decided to invite John Beagle to be Musical Director for *Guys and Dolls* and see how it went. George, in particular, was much hurt by the criticism of his course of action and felt it his duty to offer his resignation as Secretary, which he duly did, and which the Committee accepted with regret when he declined to reconsider. (He remained Vice-Chairman and temporarily took over the job of Ticket Secretary left vacant shortly afterwards by the resignation of Reg Ekins.) The Committee was very much divided over the issue, so much so that Richard Sampson and Ken Bodden also resigned and an Extraordinary General Meeting was called so that as many of the members of the Society as possible should be able to consider the question and make their views known. Some indication of the involvement of the members is given by the fact that 77 were present at this meeting, but the occasion was an unhappy one, with the members divided as much as the Committee. Eventually, after much discussion, a vote was taken and in the end the majority of the members – 70% – came out with a vote of confidence in the Committee's decision.

There was yet another special meeting of the Committee a week later regarding the wording of the Society's rules for tax reclamation, and it was agreed that three of NODA's model rules should be substituted for the original ones. This had, however, to be put to members of the Society, so yet another Special General Meeting was held in mid-December at which the members agreed unanimously with the Committee and some harmony was restored.

This was all just discomfort, however, compared with the real tragedy which had occurred in the mean time. On the first Saturday night of *The Merry Widow* the news came through that Joy's son, Bill Bishop, who was now living in Holland and who was due to come back for the last night of the show, had died very suddenly at the age of 28. What made it worse was that it had been going to be a family reunion, for Eoin was also coming, from New Zealand, and Fiona was going to New Zealand for a year in the near future. The entire membership was devastated, for Joy's loss was very much their loss too. It was a terrible blow which had to be borne somehow, and Joy threw herself into her work, both with her own dancing school and the Society, determined not to let the company down whatever she might feel like inside.

So at the start of 1974 the healing processes had to begin on all fronts. Two of the gaping holes in the Committee where Joe Lee, Richard Sampson and Ken Bodden had been were now filled by Gordon Holton and Shirley Dodd. They were both re-elected (and joined by Ken Robinson) at the next Annual General Meeting. John Beagle appeared to have settled in well as Musical Director and rehearsals for *Guys and Dolls* were going well. The booking of scenery and so on was in hand, as was the contract for *Bitter Sweet*, which went through at only 11% for the performing rights. Props were a problem, as C. & W. May had gone bankrupt, but Ernie Mann came to the rescue and built them himself.

Adjustments were made to Vice-Presidents' and Patrons' donations to allow for VAT – they were raised to 80p and 40p respectively.

Some new members had been accepted, too, all with good voices: Florence Woods, Christine Swales, and Christine and John Hacking. The Hackings had arrived just in time for John to join the stage crew for *The Merry Widow*. (They had both been members of the Lancaster Red Rose Operatic Society before John's job caused the move to County Durham.) Not only did John have the voice necessary to handle major-role material, but that voice was also a light baritone – which could be used to sing *tenor* if the need arose! His job involved a good deal of travelling, however, and he and Christine had two young daughters, so they were rarely able to be in a show together. There was no doubt whose show *Guys and Dolls* would be: John was cast in the lead as Sky Masterson, the gambler, and Christine Swales was cast opposite him as the Salvation Army girl, Sarah

Brown; Ray Danby and Sue Wishlade were the secondary leads, Nathan Detroit and Miss Adelaide, while Jeff Wragg played Nicely-Nicely Johnson and would sing the show-stopper *Sit Down, You're Rocking the Boat*. Cliff Walker was Arvide Abernathy and Sam Herdman was Big Jule, the gambler who would only use his own dice which had had the spots rubbed off them '. . . but I remember where the spots formerly was'! Eileen Young, who had not been in a show since *Kiss Me Kate*, played the Salvation Army General, Matilda B. Cartwright (and, incidentally, distinguished herself by managing to put her fist clean through her tambourine during a performance). The show, in fact, was fully cast by mid-February and all the omens seemed promising – even to extent that pianists had been successfully booked for all rehearsals, the work being shared between Brian Sheppard and Janet Day. This was the first show for which Ray Porteus joined the stage staff, and Christine Hacking was helping back-stage when she could, too, along with Peter Cutchie, two Danbys (Ann and Norman), George Davidson, Geoff Heeley, Harry Hodgson, Ron Pearson, Ken Robinson, Colin Singer (who was to marry the dancer Margaret Taylor), Jim Taylor and Mike Williams (who married Susan Mann). Mike was also helping to augment the chorus. Since there were so many named parts for men in *Guys and Dolls*, the men's chorus line consisted of only six of them as well as Mike. The ladies numbered 22.

Future shows were being discussed, for the Committee was only one show ahead, as it were, with *Bitter Sweet* booked for the autumn. The short-list consisted of *La Perichole, Mame, Sweet Charity, Lisa, Waltzes from Vienna, Summer Song* and *How To Succeed in Business Without Really Trying*. It is probably not coincidence that that last show received its first mention in Society annals shortly after John Hacking joined, for it was one which he fervently wished – and still does – that the Society should present. In the event, none of those suggested shows was performed but this has often been the case, for the course of show-selection, like that of true love, seldom runs smoothly!

(Jim Willans announced at the mid-February committee meeting that Fred Thompson was ill and in hospital; Jim had sent him a plant on behalf of the Society. Once more this apparently proved to be fatal. At the Annual General Meeting three weeks later the 68 members of the Society who were present observed a minute's silence for Fred. He was com-memorated by the Society's donating money to the theatre towards the alteration and decoration of the coffee-bar there.)

Sure enough by mid-April, following the formation of a sub-committee to prepare show suggestions, a fresh provisional list of shows had been put forward: *Sweet Charity* and *Oliver!* for 1975, *The Sound of Music* and *The Count of Luxembourg* for 1976, and *The Boy Friend* for spring 1977. It was also suggested that at Christmas the Society might do some carol-singing on High Row in aid of the Mayor's Christmas Appeal.

Happily the theatre contracts had been signed for *Guys and Dolls* and *Bitter Sweet* at the usual terms of payment, but there was a rise in the theatre's charges in the offing. George Todd expressed concern, two weeks before the opening of *Guys and Dolls*, that only 60% of the tickets had been sold, so a plea was urgently made to members to try to sell more seats. At least he had more encouraging news on the personal front, however, for he had been asked to stand as NODA Councillor for the Northern Section, which would be a feather in the cap of the Society.

Guys and Dolls was a good show, splendidly presented – the reviewers were in full agreement on that score. The *Northern Echo* said that it was well worth seeing '. . . even if you normally can't stand brash American music hall.'[17] The atmosphere of Damon Runyon's New York had been captured admirably by the whole cast and all the leading players were commended, particularly John Hacking, Christine Swales, Ray Danby and Sue Wishlade. The whole show had polish and style and the *Evening Despatch* summed it up by saying of the cast '*Guys and Dolls* is a big test of amateur skill and they come through with flying colours.'[18] John Beagle received praise for his first venture with the Society and the paper made reference to his 'stylish conducting', so he had good cause to be pleased. What is more, the special effects had been so spectacular that there had been spontaneous applause for these alone.

Critical acclaim, though helpful, does not guarantee box office success though: the show only attracted 49 people to be Vice-Presidents and 89 to be Patrons, and the box office takings were down £400 from *The Merry Widow* and £550 down from *Fiddler on the Roof*.

The inquest was held at the May committee meeting four days after the show ended. Jim Willans's distress is evident from the minutes of that meeting. He asked the members of the committee to consider a number of points for discussion at the next meeting. First, he wondered if a ten-night run might be a good idea for *Bitter Sweet*. Second, since members had questioned the higher cost of seats on the first Saturday as well as the second, he pointed out that though there was an emptier house it took more money – though perhaps children should have a reduced ticket price of 50p. Third, he pointed out that some members did not sell enough tickets and he wondered if there should be a rule that every member should sell at least ten-pounds-worth. (This is an old chestnut, having cropped up both before and since, but it would be an exceedingly difficult rule to enforce.) Fourth, more foresight was needed in the ordering of costumes. Some of the costumes ordered for the show had not been used but £60 had had to be paid for them just the same, and this was money wasted. Fifth, there was no doubt that advertising costs had been very high for the last show and some cutbacks would have to be made somewhere. Finally, he thought that hospitality for visitors in the Committee Room at the theatre was costing too much. Any money-saving ideas from members would be welcomed.

Since the mood of the meeting was already sombre, Gordon Holton thought he may as well add his twopenn'orth, and took to task those members who had been guilty of 'amateurish' behaviour. It was thought that members had been wandering around at the back of the dress circle and leaning on the rail during the show. Though, as it happened, the offenders turned out not to have been members of the Society, it was perhaps a timely reminder. Also behaviour had been 'unprofessional' backstage, with people taking flash photographs from the wings during the production, and stage passes were not being produced at the stage door, either. He was worried about the scenery for *Bitter Sweet*, too. The Billingham Forum Theatre had been asked for a quote to build it but were dragging their feet. If they did not come up with something soon, the alternative would be for Clifford and Brown to build a new set which would cost £200 to hire plus £125 carriage. With VAT the total would be £357. He was doomed to disappointment over the cost in the end: the Forum Theatre won through, but their scenery turned out to be only £7 cheaper than Clifford and Brown's. Still, at least they were nearer home!

The next committee meeting was almost as gloomy. The points Jim Willans had made were thoroughly discussed, with the result that an extra night's presentation of *Bitter Sweet* was to be given, thus setting a precedent for ten-night performances. They agreed that tickets for children should be 50p for the first Saturday and that sherry or tea only would be offered to guests in the Committee Room. (A further suggestion that the value of the beer tickets, customarily given to members of the stage crew, be cut to the value of half a pint of beer per night, instead of a pint, was defeated!)

Financially the Society was now in serious trouble – it looked as though the loss on *Guys and Dolls* might be as great as £600. Another increase in ticket prices would be an unwise move, it was felt, but the losses had to be recouped somehow. The future shows underwent a reshuffle. The idea of bringing forward *The Sound of Music* to be the spring 1975 show would seem to be a shrewd one. It was almost certain to be a money-spinner – shows with children in them usually are – and *Bitter Sweet* seemed likely to do well (though fingers were firmly crossed). If members could be chivvied into trying to sell at least £10 worth of seats each the day might yet be saved. One thing at least could be done. The format of the programme could be changed for *Bitter Sweet* to reduce costs, and a local company could be asked to sponsor it. The Society was, as always, woefully short of tenors and would have to look elsewhere for someone to play Carl Linden, but if a 'name' could be found to take on the role this might prove an added attraction and the cost of such a venture might be justified. John Gallagher, a semi-professional from Middlesbrough, was approached and auditioned but a number of other commitments meant he had limited availability and the Committee had to think again. The summer passed, and though *Bitter Sweet* was mostly cast and Gordon Holton had been to see Billingham Forum's scenery for it and been pleased with what they had done so far, there was still no Carl Linden.

The September meeting of the Committee produced a possible answer. What about asking a professional? John Larsen was known to some members of the Society and Peter Tod could help to get him. John Larsen was a Northerner, born in North Shields, and, though trained as a teacher, he had competed in a number of Northern Musical Festivals. His success in these had encouraged him to turn professional as a singer, and in this he was very successful too, becoming a member of the Sadlers Wells Opera Company before touring extensively in Australia in starring roles. He toured in *Bitter Sweet* with June Bronhill and appeared in the West End in *Man of La Mancha* and *Showboat*.

Things, it seemed, were beginning to look up from all aspects at this point. John Larsen agreed to come and was warmly welcomed by the Society. He was pleasant, unassuming and easy to get on with. John Smith's Tadcaster Brewery had agreed to sponsor the programme, which consisted simply of a cast-sheet within a single-fold cover which contained the credits, a short profile of John Larsen, and the storyline of the show. The John Smith's advertisement was on the back. The Rotary Club had booked the whole theatre for the first Friday, so that was one night's tickets sold.

As always Joy Beadell produced the show and John Beagle was Musical Director although he had indicated that he would not be available for *The Sound of Music*. Gordon Holton stage managed, and though he, too, expected to be unavailable for *The Sound of Music*, he was willing to put in the preliminary work.

So *Bitter Sweet* was presented from 30 October to 9 November, with a cast of 65.

It was a good show, superbly sung, and Eunicé Cockburn and John Larsen, as the leads, gave outstanding performances; several people normally in the chorus were given the chance to play named roles, including Ann Parker (née Appleton) as Dolly Chamberlain, Alan Adams as Mr Bethel, Judith Gott as Honor, Tricia Freeman as Helen, and

Elizabeth Jackson as Jane. Peggy Todd played Lady Devon, and Edna Ford, of The Pilgrim Players, played her only role for the Society, as Mrs Millick.

Despite all the splendour of the production (though the scenery had not, in the end, lived up to expectations) the reaction of the press was mixed. The *Evening Despatch* printed a piece about John Larsen three weeks before the show and its subsequent review, apart from a little grumble about backstage noise, was a good one, giving John and Eunicé great credit for their performances and singling out Shirley Dodd and Kenneth Richardson for their character acting. No press photographer came on Civic Night, however, and the *Northern Echo* gave it scarcely more than a dozen lines, calling the piece 'dated'[19] while enjoying the actors' performances. The *Darlington & Stockton Times* gave it 44 lines, which, though short, were at least sweet. John and Eunicé and the rest of the cast excelled themselves, it said, and the quality of the dancing could only be compared to that of the professional shows, while the duel scene had been particularly well handled.

The loss on *Guys and Dolls* had turned out to be even greater than at first thought because there was a considerable loss on programme sales and the total loss on that, coupled with a loss on *Bitter Sweet* – for which the Committee had had such high hopes – turned out to be the startling sum of £1,400. In the face of such apathy what was the Society to do? Well, it soldiered on, of course.

By the end of 1974 the Committee had pulled itself together again and was planning its next moves. The last five years had been very trying from a financial point of view, but things might have been very much worse had it not been for the appointment of Peter Tod; but for him, the theatre might have gone the way of so many others and eventually had to close. For the Committee it was a matter of getting the formula right. An extra night's performance had seemed to be justified in terms of takings versus expenditure, and if *The Sound of Music*, with Brian Sheppard as Musical Director, turned out to be a crowd-puller, as expected, then that extra night's takings could go a long way towards pulling the Society out of the mire. If *The Sound of Music* could then be followed up with a tried and tested favourite which the Society could depend on to be a success, and if, say, a one-night concert or two could be given, this would be lucrative and not too expensive. *The Desert Song* was decided upon for the autumn 1975 show, with *Oliver!* – another show containing a lot of children – to follow in spring 1976.

Jim Willans reported, at the last committee meeting of the year, that Guisborough Rotary Club had asked him for a block booking of 80 seats for *The Sound of Music*, and that the Darlington Rotary Club had asked to have the theatre for the Tuesday evening's performance of *The Desert Song* for its Gala Evening, so at least ticket sales got off to a good start. Gordon Holton squared his shoulders and volunteered to approach the manager of North of England Newspapers about press coverage, Joy Beadell was appointed Producer for *The Desert Song* with John Beagle as Musical Director, and the Committee braced itself to face 1975 and its fourth decade.

Chapter 8

1975–1979

After the recent losses on shows 1975 opened, naturally enough, with finance as the Committee's primary concern, and for the first four months a large amount of time was spent in discussing ways of saving money and making money. The Society was becoming less able to fulfil one of the purposes of its existence – donations to charity – and this situation had to be remedied somehow.

Nothing, however, seemed to go right.

It was agreed that the programme for *The Sound of Music* would be of very basic design – just a triple-folded card, eighteen inches by eleven inches – but no company could be found to sponsor it, as John Smith's had done for *Bitter Sweet*. They tried to get some help from Northern Arts but none was forthcoming at this stage – *they* were on a tight budget, too. The rental for the theatre was rising steadily as its own costs rose; for one thing, vastly increased business meant that more staff had to be employed and more room had to be found for those staff.

At the Annual General Meeting money-saving ideas were discussed but there were problems with each of the suggestions put forward. Should members' annual subscriptions be raised? Preferably not, as they were subject to VAT. Could the orchestra be reduced? It was already reduced as far as possible and any further reduction would mean a lowering of the shows' standards because the orchestra would sound thin. Could amateur musicians be used? No, because all musicians playing in the theatre had to be Musicians' Union members. Could there be cutbacks in scenery and costumes: for instance, could impressionist scenery be used? This would be impractical because the Society would have to construct its own scenery, which could be an expensive business. Besides, it would have to be stored, and storage was a perennial problem.

A *Melodies for You* concert was given in March 1975 and it attracted around 500 people who paid £1 each. John Beagle was Musical Director and was offered an honorarium to cover his expenses, but he declined it, which was a kind gesture. So, once the bills were paid, there was a profit of around £300. The press attended in force and gave the concert good reviews, suggesting that such concerts were rather refreshing, particularly when they were so well performed. The revenue was a great boost to the dwindling assets of the Society, and Jim Willans cashed in the National Savings certificates and put the money into the Building Society. He was disenchanted, too, with the uninspiring state of Unit Trusts and vowed to sell the Society's holding if they went up even a little.

The Sound of Music was to run from 30 April to 10 May and on 16 April the new Ticket Secretary, Ken Robinson, informed the Committee that sales were not as good as expected. This was a blow because they had all thought that it would do exceptionally well, so Sam Herdman went all-out to get as much publicity as possible. At least the casting had been accomplished with only one or two hiccups. Carol Biggin was Maria and Kenneth Richardson was Baron von Trapp. Hilary Greenwood had her first significant role as Liesl, with Enid Allison as Elsa Schraeder, and Barrie Dargue as Max Detweiler – a part he would play again when the Society repeated the show in 1989. Mollie Moor, who had not been on stage since *The Grand Duchess* in 1971, played the part of the Mother Abbess. This show was unusual in that it was one of the few in which Sam Herdman did not appear, but two new members joined and are still regular performers with the Society: June Aiken and Ian Whitfield.

Ian joined because of visiting his local pub – the Duke of Wellington at High Coniscliffe – on a Thursday night. The members of Darlington Operatic Society who lived at Barnard Castle would call there and have a sing-song after rehearsal, and Ian was gathered in by them.

June and her husband, George, had moved to the area from Lincolnshire, where June had been in an operatic society since she was sixteen. It so happened that their very first social night out after their move was to the Civic Theatre where the Darlington society was doing *Bitter Sweet*. June remembers that, as she looked at the company on the stage, she could see in the cast the same sort of people as she had left behind and was sure that she would feel at home among them. The following morning she and George went to their local church at Sadberge. The Vicar welcomed them and June told him about their visit to the theatre, whereupon he introduced them to Alf Robinson, an older man who had just joined the Society.* Alf took June to the rehearsal the following week and all was as she had expected – it was, she says, just like being at home!

Ian's speciality is small roles – the more the merrier – and June is a born comedienne.

There was some alarm about the scenery for *The Sound of Music*. It was ordered from Clifford and Brown, it was the set used in the original West End production, and it was vast. When Gordon Holton saw the

---

* Alf continued to appear in shows until he was in his seventies.

measurements on the plans he thought it would not fit on the stage, but fortunately Clifford and Brown had made a mistake in their description: it did fit, but only just. One item alone, a large set-piece forming the von Trapp living-room, took four men four hours to build and was only used for three of the show's twenty scenes, Together, the scenery, props, costumes, and stage furniture made up four large van-loads and needed all the backstage workers' ingenuity and patience to cope with it all. They hoped their efforts would be instrumental in ensuring a successful show. Press reaction to the overall appearance of the show justified their hard work: all agreed that it gave a professional-looking finish. As far as the cast was concerned the reviewers' individual preferences were well to the fore. Carol Biggin was outstanding in the eyes of all, and Kenneth Richardson had acted well, though the reviewers felt that he was not quite the right type for the part – they would, of course, have seen it played by Christopher Plummer in the film. Barrie Dargue was described by the *Darlington & Stockton Times* as '. . . dashing . . . but a shade on the young side, and though he had many other desirable qualities his singing was not the strongest point.'[1] The *Evening Despatch* said he had 'improved considerably since his debut on the Civic stage' and he '. . . was confident and competent as Detweiler.'[2] The *Darlington & Stockton Times*, while admiring Mollie Moor's performance, felt that her voice had too much *tremolo*; the *Evening Despatch* thought that she was just right. All the reviews agreed that the children (who included John Murray) were most attractive and Joy's production was, as always, impeccable. The audiences loved it – they always love a show containing children (though not all *producers* do!) – and they became so caught up in the action that they even booed the Nazis. (The Nazis were even less popular with the theatre staff after certain of the male cast perpetrated a practical joke which went wrong. They obtained a dummy, dressed it in a Nazi uniform, placed it on the ladies' toilet near the top-floor dressing-rooms, and awaited the girls' reaction. None came. Unfortunately no one went in there before the cleaner arrived the next morning – *her* reaction was all that could be wished, though the malefactors were not there to witness it. Peter Tod was not amused.) It was wonderful to have such quality in the audiences, but the big question for the Committee at this point was whether they had attended in sufficient quantity to produce a profit.

The takings averaged £500 per night and since the highest price was £1 on each Saturday, 85p for other nights, 60p for OAPs and children on the first night, and 60p for children on the first Saturday it seems to have played to nearly-full houses. The net profit, however, only amounted to £118, of which £80 stemmed from programme sales. There seemed no alternative but to raise the seat prices for *The Desert Song*. At first a general rise to £1 was suggested but there was some disagreement about this. A price of 90p on weeknights and £1 on Saturdays seemed better, but once costings were worked out for the show the enormous price rises all round meant that 90p would not be enough. The Committee decided, reluctantly, that they would have to charge 95p for weeknights and £1.10 for Saturdays, with children and OAPs at 70p for the first Wednesday and Saturday. There could be no concession for block bookings.

Radio Tees had now opened and Gordon Holton was its Contributor to the Arts so he was able to get even more publicity than usual for the show. Nevertheless, *The Desert Song* was beset with difficulties from the first. Clifford and Brown's scenery was booked but, by June, Gordon learned that it had been damaged during another society's production, and Scenic Display's scenery had to be booked instead, at a cost of £320 (which, at least, was £40 cheaper). John Beagle, who was to be Musical Director again, reported that with his permitted allowance for an orchestra he could only get eight musicians. There was no alternative but to allow him an extra £175. He and Joy, who was to produce as usual, felt that ideally there should be only twelve dancers and twelve chorus ladies in the show, which could be difficult considering that there were 36 ladies to be chosen from. This caused 'much discussion' but of course there would be plenty of room for all in *Oliver!*

By mid-July *The Desert Song* was cast, with Eunicé Cockburn as the leading lady, Margot, and John Hacking as Pierre (The Red Shadow). John Parker and Sue Wishlade took care of the comedy as Benjamin Kidd and Susan (following in the comic footsteps of John Reed and Eileen Young 25 years earlier). Sam Herdman was back again to play Ali Ben Ali. Barrie Dargue and Tricia Freeman were not in this show but June Aiken was playing Edith, and Kath Robinson the seductive Azuri. There were yet more new members, however, some of whom would be with the Society for a long time and some of whom are still in it – despite forays into other societies from time to time – like Arthur Ellis who played Captain Paul Fontaine, Margot's spurned suitor. Margaret Lowther made one of her intermittent appearances as Clementina, and Avril Sowerby, who had joined the Society at sixteen and abruptly had to leave it again because of her schoolwork, was back again to be in the chorus. Now she was married, and her husband, Steve Blain, also joined. So did Chris Noble, son of Basil Noble who had helped to start the admirable practice of Gala Evenings for the shows. Among the new dancers was Betty Cooke, who, though no longer taking part in shows, still supports the Society (and is fondly remembered as being one of the best high-kickers the company ever had, maintaining that ability into her fifties); two years later she was to bring in her daughter, Janet, who danced in shows until she had her family. Glynis Johnson also joined the dancers for *The Desert Song*. Glynis is profoundly deaf but no one seeing her on stage would ever have suspected it, her sense of rhythm and timing is so acute. It is a measure of her skill that people mostly forgot that she was deaf anyway! She married and became Glynis Wilkinson, and, like Janet Cooke, ceased to dance with the company when she had her family. These new members were all very good for the Society but the difficulties continued. The Committee wanted to have a live donkey in the production for John Parker and Sue Wishlade to ride on, but this posed two problems: first, they had no donkey and second, Peter Tod would not have one in the theatre because it needed a special permit. Peter was mollified by assurances that the donkey would only be in the building for a very short time each night and that a permit would be obtained. Getting a donkey was not so easy. Gordon Holton arranged an appeal on the radio and had pieces put in the *Northern Echo* and the *Evening Despatch*. Eventually, via Ann Parker, a Mr Middlemiss of Hurworth agreed to loan a beast of equable temperament, which rejoiced in the name of Cedric. It was impossible to insure Cedric as a fully fledged thespian but Jim Willans prudently doubly insured John and Sue in case of accidents!

Then another bone of contention was raised. A flag had been commissioned, bearing the logo of the Society, and Peter Tod had given permission for it to be flown outside the theatre during the runs of Society shows. The Ladies' Committee was prepared to raise money by extra activities to pay for it but Jim Willans was angry over what he obviously considered an extravagance and felt that if the Ladies' Committee was to make extra money it should go to him to help balance the books. There was 'much discussion'. Finally a vote was taken and Jim was defeated. He then asked about the design and was unhappy about that, too, but the project went through and the Society got its flag, in the light and dark blue colours of NODA.

Two weeks before opening night 88% of the tickets had been sold, probably because of the massive publicity arranged by Gordon Holton, who had blanket bombed every possible target. Such success was encouraging, while the show itself was looking very promising indeed. No effort had been spared. The men who were to be Legionnaires had even reported to the barrack square at Bradford Armoury in Neasham Road for the Territorial Army Drill Instructors of the 50th Northumbrian Signals Squadron Volunteers to put them through an intensive course in foot and arms drill.

Then there occurred what every society dreads. The leading man developed laryngitis just in time for opening night on 29 October. John Hacking was not about to chicken out. He went on regardless, on the first night spending his time between appearances gargling to bring temporary relief to his badly inflamed throat, but naturally his voice lost some of its power. The other cast members helped him along when he was singing with them and John Beagle and the orchestra toned down the volume so as not to overstrain his voice. He sang the role again on the second night but was quite unable to continue after that in case he produced a more serious condition. In desperation the Committee contacted John Larsen, who was singing with John Hanson's company in London. John Larsen averted the crisis, temporarily at least. He came to Darlington on the Friday morning, calling at Homburg's in Leeds to collect costumes on the way, had a quick rehearsal with such of the company as were available, and went on stage at night. He and Eunicé, of course, had played opposite each other the previous year in *Bitter Sweet* (Eunicé says that he was very easy to work with) and he knew the part of The Red Shadow well, having played the role in an extensive tour of Australia. John, however, could only take over the part for two performances because he had other commitments, and by the Monday John Hacking had still not recovered. Then someone had a brainwave: Murton Amateur Operatic Society had just completed a one week run of the show. How about asking if *their* Red Shadow, George Peart, could fill in for a night or two? George Peart could and did, and the production was saved, for John Hacking was able to return on the second Wednesday to complete the run, and was particularly touched when, on the night on which he returned, George Peart rang him up to wish him good luck. Everyone heaved a sigh of relief. Good as John Larsen and George Peart were, they were bound to play the part in their own ways and it cannot have been easy for the cast, particularly for Eunicé, who had done all the floorwork with John Hacking and who had to adapt herself to the acting styles of the others before returning to the original when John Hacking came back. So many things can go wrong in any production without having to contend with feelings of uncertainty as well. Sue Wishlade was seriously uncertain about the donkey. She was terrified of riding him, and he reinforced her doubts by careering across the stage on the first night, but Cedric was a quick learner and soon perfected his stage technique, trotting composedly each night to his designated place.

The bouquets of flowers and the other gifts presented to cast members on the final night of the show were well deserved, as was, undoubtedly, the large bunch of carrots presented to the donkey. Cedric was offered for sale following his theatrical triumph. It is not known who bought him, but it was certainly not Chris Noble, who had been appointed by Joy to what Chris called 'guano duty'. Chris half-hoped that he would receive The Call and achieve overnight stardom by becoming eminently noticeable, but sadly the donkey refused to oblige except at the dress rehearsal – and Chris remained doomed to obscurity. Cedric did, however, leave generous deposits in a box at the stage door, which Jim Cooper (the theatre's stage manager) and Tom Kent used on their roses, with spectacular results.

Best of all, the audiences enjoyed themselves. Despite John Hacking's reduced vocal power on the first night, the press gave the show excellent reviews. Much was made, of course, of John's throat problem over the whole run, keeping it constantly in the public eye, but the show had been enjoyable and entertaining, and special mention was made of Eunicé, John Parker, Sue Wishlade, Kath Robinson (though the *Darlington & Stockton Times*, for some reason, called her Judith Aitken!), Colin Raine (who played Sid El Kar), Arthur Ellis and Sam Herdman. The show was slick and the chorus well-drilled, especially the men – their square-bashing had paid off. It played to very full houses and if anyone in the audience noticed that one of the Riffs had suddenly become a hunchback, it was never mentioned. To Elsie Campbell, responsible as she was for the look of the costumes, it stuck out like a wart on the face of the Mona Lisa. Some of the Riffs were doubling as Legionnaires and for quick-change purposes had slipped on their djellabas* over their uniforms. When Elsie had seen the last of the Riffs safely onto the stage she found that she was one Legionnaire-hat short. It was then that her horrified eyes lit upon the hump, and suddenly she knew where the other hat was. Its owner remained blissfully unaware.

The Desert Song had more than its fair share of misfortunes and it cost £5,000 to put on – but it made money, and suddenly there was light once more at the end of the tunnel for Jim Willans, who was able to report '. . . seating capacity for the show, virtually 100%.'[3] It was music to the Committee's ears. After struggling to find money for charitable donations in 1974 it was able to give something to Cancer Relief, St John of God's Hospital, and the League of Pity, without putting the Society in dire straits. Even more to the good, a great deal of money would be saved on the scenery for *Oliver!*: Shildon Operatic Society were willing to loan theirs (which had, incidentally, been designed by Bill Bishop a few years earlier) for £75 plus carriage, which would save about £250 on the probable cost of hiring it from one of the major companies. They also helped by building a special fireplace to house Fagin's jewels. They made a beautiful job of it, says Ernie Mann, but when the Darlington stage crew went to get it it was too big to be got out of the workshop and had to be sawn in half.

---

* Loose, striped, dress-like garments.

Nevertheless, the scenery was cleverly constructed, so that for the stage staff it was simply a case of adding to, and taking away from, a basic 'build', and Gordon Holton hired a special backcloth from the Robert Luff Organization in London, to reflect the sophisticated use of light which the show required. The costumes would be comparatively cheap for *Oliver!*, too. Homburgs had quoted £2.75 per costume, which was £1 each cheaper than those for *The Desert Song*. Rarely, it seems, did things stay on an even keel. Either everything went the Society's way or *nothing* did. The Ticket Secretaryship was a problem, though: Ken Robinson warned that he could not do this job for *Oliver!* Despite much discussion at the November meeting no conclusion was reached. The Committee left it over until December – quite possibly to see which of them would weaken first, because *somebody* had to do it! Ticket prices would have to rise again, however – differential pricing having been considered and rejected – so the general price would be £1 with the usual adjustments for Saturdays, OAPs and children. (The standard donations for Vice-Presidents and Patrons also rose, to £1 and 50p respectively.)

The minutes of the final meeting of 1975 are written in a different hand from any other minutes of the Society. Item 3 reads: 'At this stage Messrs E. Mann and J. C. Parker arrived and duly apologized to the Chair for their late appearance. As penance the last-named was appointed Minute Secretary in the absence of Miss E. Cockburn.' [4] John Parker had the pleasure of being able to record that the Society's props store (which had been threatened with reclamation by Durham County Council who owned the premises at Albert Road) was safe for the time being, that the annual carol singing had raised nearly £100 for the Mayor's Charity Fund, that Liz Holton had been accepted as a full singing member of the Society in addition to being a dancer, and that three other ladies had been accepted as singers, including Margaret Nicholls, a local journalist who might also be a help with publicity. He was further able to add that 24 boys had auditioned for the parts of Oliver and The Artful Dodger and that six of them were distinct possibilities. The problem of a Ticket Secretary was resolved, if only for the time being, because Bernard Sanderson said that he would take over temporarily after the run of *Oliver!* while George Todd said that he would be prepared to do the job for *Oliver!* only. Even the show for autumn 1976 had now been selected. The Committee's choice was *Oklahoma!* which had done so well when last performed in 1958. All this business was accomplished in under two hours and John Parker concluded his brief reign as Minute Secretary by recording that 'There being no other business the meeting closed at 9.17 p.m. (to the surprise of all concerned).' Things were looking very much brighter than they had at the same time the previous year.

1976 saw a change of auditor for the Society. *Oliver!* would be the 21st production for which Philip Bacon had been auditor and he now had to resign owing to other commitments. T. A. W. (Walton) Wedge took over and remained the Society's auditor for the next eighteen years, after which Mike Hudson took over in 1994.

1976 also saw a sad event early in the year. Isabel Farrage, widow of Robert, and the Society's only Hon. Life Member, died. Even though she had moved away to live with her daughter Vivienne she had retained her interest in the Society and kept in contact; she had, after all, been Hon. Patrons' Secretary for a long time. On the lighter side, in the same minutes which tell of that sad news it is recorded that a major problem had been solved. A grand piano was needed for the planned spring concert. Peter Stanley, of Williams music shop, had been unable to offer much, but Jim Willans had managed to obtain a baby grand 'from some other source!'[5] (*sic*) – which rather makes it sound as though it fell off the back of a lorry! The Committee wisely did not ask any questions; they kept quiet and arranged for a piano tuner.

The Civic Theatre charges were going up from 1 April and though Peter Tod said that he would not charge the higher rate for *Oliver!* the Committee had no option but to raise the ticket prices yet again for *Oklahoma!* to cover the extra costs. A rise of 10p per ticket was agreed for weekdays and 15p for Saturdays, OAPs and children to remain at 75p. In general, though, the state of affairs was much happier and the Society had just about recouped the losses of the previous years.

A Sunday evening concert entitled *Music to Remember* was given in March. It contained a broad spectrum of songs ranging from opera to 'middle-of-the-road popular' and played to a full house. Its success enhanced further the mood generated at the Annual General Meeting which had been held ten days previously and which was a much more cheery affair than the previous year's. The Society had, over the last two years, weathered heavy financial loss, illness among the Ladies' Committee, and the trauma of doing a show with three different leading men, and had come through it all safely through effort and teamwork. Bill Jones who, as Secretary, had borne a good deal of the burden, congratulated the members and remarked that if the same enthusiasm was shown by them in the forthcoming year as had been demonstrated in 1975 the Society could be sure of a rosy future. Meanwhile Tom Kent made a valid point. He suggested that as finance was healthier a souvenir programme might be considered again; the triple-fold card ones were rather drab and, though cheap, were not very attractive. The Committee compromised. The card programme was kept for *Oliver!* but a souvenir one would be produced for *Oklahoma!* and then a card one for the spring 1977 show. After that they would see. The members were also informed that it was proposed that Rule 13 of the constitution be altered so that it did not state a fixed amount for members' annual subscriptions but would be worded so that the rule allowed flexibility. This was perfectly reasonable and was agreed.

At the next committee meeting George Todd handed over the Chairman's chain of office to Jim Willans for what would be Jim's 30th and final year on the Committee. No one had served on the Committee for as long as Jim. He had been Ticket Secretary for twelve years and Treasurer for eighteen, and it seemed fitting that, after all his hard work over so many years, he should go out in a blaze of glory. He was cheerful at this meeting because he estimated that the concert might have made as much as £400 – in fact what it made in the end was £300 clear profit – and because *Oliver!* had been cast and was well into rehearsal. John Beagle and Joy Beadell were secured to take care of both the productions for 1977 and even the pianist situation was well under control; as well as Richard Pearson there were Christine Purvis, David Garrood and Joanne Monaghan who would accompany at rehearsals. The last three were all connected with John Beagle at the Stockton/Billingham Technical College. David was a lecturer there and was teaching harmony and counterpoint to Christine, who already had her LTCL* in piano and was doing a further diploma in singing. Christine greatly enjoyed accompanying so she was glad to help with rehearsals. (She has done a considerable amount of accompanying since, in the early heats of the BBC Young Musician of the Year competitions.) Joanne Monaghan was studying for the same diploma as Christine. David was a particularly valuable person to have around, as it happened, because John Beagle was taken ill a few weeks before the show; although he was much improved by early April the show was to open on the 28th, and David could have taken his place, though this was not necessary in the end.

Apart from the two boys who played the leading roles in *Oliver!*, eighteen others were recruited for 'Fagin's gang', one of them being Nigel Walker, Cliff and Dorothy's nephew. (Cliff was playing Mr Brownlow and Dorothy was playing Mrs Bedwin, his housekeeper.) Another was John Murray, understudying Simon Treadgold who was playing Oliver. (Simon is the son of the Reverend John Treadgold who was Vicar of Darlington at the time but went to St George's Chapel, Windsor, to become Chaplain to Her Majesty the Queen, and is now Dean of Chichester.)† Andrew

---

* Licentiate of Trinity College of Music, London.
† Simon went from Barnard Castle School to Marlborough and then to Sandhurst. He is now a Major and a Company Commander in the Welsh Guards, serving in Northern Ireland. He still has the photograph of himself as Oliver which was presented to him by the Society.

Wallace, understudied by Stephen Harrison, played the Artful Dodger (the first understudy was Simon Heritage but he dropped out), while Fagin was played by Ray Danby (in an extraordinary wig) and Bill Sikes by Arthur Ellis, who was made up to look thoroughly evil and the antithesis of his real personality. Arthur has a highly-developed sense of humour and is probably the most active practical-joker in the Society, though he can take it as well as dish it out, as they say. (Arthur was to play the same role again for the Society in 1993 by which time his daughter, Louise, was grown up and consequently did not re-enact the tear-jerking performance she had given to a party of pensioners sitting behind her and her embarrassed mother, Vivienne, in the dress circle, when she thought her Daddy had really been shot!) Nancy was played by Judi Bond (of the Pilgrim Players) who had joined the Society for *Bitter Sweet*, with Sue Wishlade as her friend Bet. Mr Bumble, the wicked beadle, was played by Sam Herdman, with Sue Robinson as Widow Corney, Barrie Dargue and Muriel Jones as Mr and Mrs Sowerberry the undertakers, and Steve and Avril Blain as Noah Claypole and Charlotte.

Linda Egginton joined the Society at this time and became the sort of loyal, if unsung, member who helps to provide its backbone, being in the chorus or helping backstage, much as Edith and Fred Dawson do: Edith in the kitchen during shows, making tea for the cast and visitors, and Fred doing 'front of house'. They remain in the background but are sorely missed when they are not there. Steve Luck also joined the Society to be in the chorus for this show. No one who has met Steve is ever likely to forget such a lively and colourful character, and no doubt a large number of people in professional theatre would agree with this! He had several jobs before deciding that theatre was his spiritual home and he joined the staff at Darlington Civic Theatre in June 1985. He was Publicity Officer there before moving to the Grand Opera House at York in January 1993. It is from Steve's book about the Civic Theatre, *Nine Hundred for the Nineties*, that much of the information about the theatre itself has been obtained for *this* book.

By the time the Committee met on 8 April everything was well in hand for the performance of *Oliver!* No one was better prepared than Jim Willans: a master of forward planning, he had already purchased the liquid refreshments for entertaining his guests at the next two shows, in anticipation of an increase in the price of alcohol in the government's forthcoming budget. It is painful to have to record that the guests drank the lot during the run of *Oliver!* and poor Jim had to buy more for *Oklahoma!*

Oliver! was tremendously popular with both press and public. Margaret Nicholls was not in this show but reviewed it for the *Evening Despatch*. She recognized the difficulties presented by the show itself and mentioned Judi

Bond and Ray Danby in particular for their fine performances, and Simon Treadgold and Andrew Wallace for their endearing qualities. She also had admiring words to say about the set and the chorus groupings. Judith Leckenby, in the *Northern Echo*, regarded this show as 'Darlington Operatic Society's most imaginative show for some time'.[6] She added Arthur Ellis to Margaret Nicholls's list of special mentions, but also said that it was some of the minor characters – Muriel Jones, Sue Wishlade and Barrie Dargue – 'who had the most style'. Allene Norris broadcast her views on Radio Cleveland on 29 April, and Allene, of course, had seen the Darlington society from both sides of the footlights. She felt that what she considered was a slow start was probably due to first-night nerves and was rather disappointed with Ray Danby's performance as Fagin; however she, too, picked out Barrie Dargue and especially Muriel Jones as being outstanding in a cameo scene with Steve and Avril Blain. Judi Bond and Arthur Ellis had also played their parts exceptionally well. All in all she thought that the Society had tackled an ambitious show very well, and also had kind words for the stage crew (who are often ignored) and for the scenery. The *Darlington & Stockton Times* voted the show a 'smash hit'[7] and had praise for all the participants including Sam Herdman ('salacious'), Susan Robinson and Cliff Walker. If something goes wrong on a first night the press are sure to mention it, and, sure enough, Tricia Freeman's skirt fell off during the energetic dancing – but she was praised for the way in which she slung it over her shoulder and carried on: that word 'trouper' cropped up, as it so often does! On the other hand the press were not present on the night that Avril Blain had her disaster. During the scene in the undertaker's shop in which Oliver escapes, Muriel had to pretend to faint and Avril had to pour water over her from a jug. As arranged, Avril jumped over a coffin with the jug, but two things were her undoing: she miscalculated the jump and the jug was not only very full but was covered in hairline cracks. Avril landed on Muriel and the jug smashed to smithereens, soaking them both and cutting Avril's hand quite badly. As soon as she was able to leave the stage Avril was taken, still in make-up and costume, to the Hospital's casualty department. She suffered the indignity of a tetanus injection in her backside and had to have her hand stitched, but was back again for her next appearance after the interval. (Joy was her usual imperturbable self: 'Lovely, dear,' she said, 'fine, perfect' – and those who know Joy will be able, in their mind's ear, to hear her say it!) The spillage did not do Barrie and Sam any good, either. As they rushed on after the commotion Barrie slipped on the water, tore the ligaments in his ankle and knocked against the scenery, which collapsed onto them both.

Still, *Oliver!* was a tremendous box office success and managed to make a profit of over £900 – wonderful news for a Society which had, so comparatively recently, been in the financial doldrums. It was hoped that the momentum could be kept up with *Oklahoma!* which was to start its ten-night run on 27 October. Once again the Society was in luck as far as scenery was concerned, for it was loaned relatively cheaply by Scarborough & District Light Opera Society. More was spent on this show than on *Oliver!*, however. There was double the number of chorus members and double the number of people dancing so a lot more costumes were needed. There was also a souvenir programme which sold for 15p, though its expense turned out to be well covered because George and Peggy Todd did sterling work in attracting advertisements to finance it, actually managing to get almost £400 worth. George Sharratt, by then living in London, came specially to dance the counterpart of Curly in the Dream Ballet. Joy Beadell was originally going to dance Laurey but this would have increased her workload to intolerable proportions so Sue Williams did the dancing. Jim Blenkhorn, a well-known Darlington gymnast, danced the part of Jud Fry. Two members recreated the parts they had played in the 1958 production: Sue Robinson was Aunt Eller, of course, and Kenneth Richardson was Ali Hakim. Hilary Greenwood, who had by now married Peter Hydes, took her first leading role as Laurey, and June Aiken *her* first lead as Ado Annie, with John Parker playing opposite her as Will Parker. Curly was played by a new member, Cambridge-University-educated Graham Saunders, who, as a boy, had sung the leading role in a production of Gian Carlo Menotti's *Amahl and the Night Visitors* on television. Arthur Ellis was playing another 'baddie' role as Jud Fry, and, like the Bill Sikes role, he would play this part again – in the 1991 production. Peter Hydes was cast as Slim, Sue Wishlade as the hideously-cackling Gertie Cummings, Tom Kent as Cord Elam (the Sheriff), and John Hacking as Andrew Carnes, father of Ado Annie (the girl who 'cain't say no'). Sam Herdman had originally been cast in this part but he had to attend a conference during the run, so it was one of the few shows he missed – and then, to his chagrin, the conference was cancelled at the last minute. The cast did not even take a summer break – rehearsals were continuous – and there was also rehearsing to be done for a joint Christmas charity concert with the Sedgefield Sinfonietta, in which Klaus Zoll, the pianist, and John Reed had promised to appear. (John's last appearance on the stage of the Civic Theatre had been 26 years earlier and he had just completed a quarter of a century with D'Oyly Carte.) Both were to give their services free. The show for spring 1977 was discussed in the summer and the Ivor Novello piece *Glamorous Night* was chosen. So it was a busy summer and a fairly contented one, though in July the Committee was startled to find that the rise in the theatre rental was a steep one: over £200. However, Jim Willans had discovered that Northern Arts gave £25 to any society producing a show whose composer was still alive, and he promptly claimed this for *Oliver!* as Lionel Bart was only 45 and very much alive.

Things proceeded smoothly towards *Oklahoma!* Ernie Mann was unable to give as much time as he wished to the show, but he agreed to act as Property Master in an advisory capacity, and Bob Jarratt came in as his Deputy. Bob had first been involved with the Society in a small way during *The Desert Song.* He was an electronics technician at Darlington's Memorial Hospital and had met Gordon Holton by chance when a show was being put on there. They were having some problems with the staging of the show and someone suggested that Gordon should be consulted since he stage-managed for the Operatic Society. Bob, of course, knew quite a lot about the electrics side and this close association with Gordon led to Gordon asking if he would like to help out backstage for Operatic Society shows. Bob and his woolly hat became an institution in the Society. Indeed, if Bob did not appear, the woolly hat would probably have made its own way to the theatre through force of habit. It has since disappeared and for all anyone knows it may have gone to ground and taken up residence in some remote corner there, so Bob has had to resort to a baseball cap – which is serviceable but lacks the charm of its snug predecessor.

At the committee meeting immediately before the show Bernard Sanderson gleefully reported that all but 500 of the 6,000 seats had been sold (though his glee was mixed with chagrin since he had had to return money to people who could not be accommodated because they had failed to give an alternative night on their booking forms). He was confident that the box office would not have much difficulty in selling most of that 500, and in this he was quite right: they were sold before opening night.

So *Oklahoma!* went on – in the bi-centennial year of the American Declaration of Independence, with the good wishes of the Governor of the State of Oklahoma to help it along; a kind letter from his Press Secretary was received in response to a letter sent to him by John Parker, then the Society's Press and Publicity Officer. A copy of the Governor's letter was printed in the programme.

Oklahoma! was an immense success; one member of the public went so far as to write a letter of appreciation to the press about it, rather than just to the Society. Margaret Nicholls was in the show this time but Sue Lewis, reporting in the *Evening Despatch*, said that the Society was given a warm welcome and that she had enjoyed the show herself, referring to it as 'a spectacular'.[8] For her the highlight was the Dream Ballet (though she did pinpoint Hilary Hydes, Graham Saunders, June Aiken and John

Parker, and also the chorus generally) which she said 'held the audience spellbound'. The *Northern Echo* described the show as 'delightful',[9] choosing – as well as Hilary and Graham – Arthur Ellis's characterization as its favourite. The paper also praised the chorus singing and made special mention of the very high standard of the choreography. Bill Duff, in the *Darlington & Stockton Times*, called the show a 'vintage performance'[10] and was much impressed by Graham Saunders's singing. He enjoyed the performances of all the principals and described Jud and Curly's duet (*Poor Jud is Dead*) as 'a gem'. For him, too, the dancing was 'immaculately done' and he regarded the *Many a New Day* ballet – danced by Tricia Freeman, Margaret Singer (née Taylor) and Sue Williams – as 'an unexpected bonus'. Little did he realize that among the dancers was a 'new girl' who was to add even more elegance to the dancing in the future. Her name was Christine Coates, she was tall, slim and dark-haired, and, like other dancers from the Joy Beadell School, she had unmistakable style.*

The show made money. In spite of the considerable extra expenditure it still made over £430 clear profit which must have been very heartening for the Committee. They should have known better than to bask in the glow of success, though, for 'Murphy's Law'† is always with us. Soon after the show things began to go sour and a whole list of irritations surfaced at the committee meeting on 17 November. Massive rent increases for rehearsal rooms at St John's School were announced. (This is one of the charges which members of the Society probably never think about, yet it is quite expensive. For 1977 the cost of rehearsal accomodation went up to £500 per show.) There were letters of complaint from people who had failed to obtain seats for the show (even though this was largely their own fault). Parkin Raine, who had joined the stage-crew in 1970 and helped with stage management since 1973, became at odds with the Society and this was taken as a form of resignation. The Society flag had not been flown during the show but no good reason had been given. The Radio Tees report on the show was received with displeasure as it appeared detrimental to Joy. Some members had proved to be disruptive and were asked to leave the Society, which left a nasty taste in many mouths. The company objected to being told at the dress rehearsal that they could not sit in the auditorium to watch the parts of the show they were not in, and finally there was criticism from the members because the American National Anthem had been played instead of the usual one. On top of

* Christine later married John Murray and they have, the Society hopes, produced two potential members: Jonathan and Abigail.
† 'Anything that *can* go wrong, *will* go wrong.'

all this the ticket prices would have to go up yet again to keep the profits up. All in all, it was a stormy committee meeting and there were only three bright spots: scenery and costumes and the other essentials for *Glamorous Night* had all been safely ordered, Bob Jarratt was willing to take on the job of Property Master with Ernie Mann to help him, and Klaus Zoll and John Reed had given final confirmation that they would participate in the *Music at Christmas* concert on 12 December.

The concert was a huge success. John Reed, known so well to Darlington audiences, had proved to be a tremendous draw and every seat was sold, so the Operatic Society's share of the profit amounted to £200, which was given to St John of God's Hospital.

Productions for autumn 1977 and for 1978 were discussed at the final committee meeting of the year. A repeat of *The Student Prince* was chosen for autumn 1977 and seven shows were suggested for 1978, including, for the umpteenth time, *Sweet Charity*, but, as was often the case, plans were to go awry and the programme had to be altered.

Then, at the beginning of the new year, three weeks into rehearsals, came yet more misfortune. The scenery for *Glamorous Night*, booked from Scenic Display, turned out to have been double-booked for one of the weeks, and the other society had made its booking first. Valiant efforts were made by a helpful person at Stagesets to obtain a set of scenery from the touring company, all to no avail. After 'much discussion' the show was changed to Sandy Wilson's 1920s pastiche *The Boy Friend*, chosen because it did not require a lot of chorus work and rehearsal time was short. To keep the chorus occupied, singing rehearsals would begin immediately for *The Student Prince*.

In the new year there came the loss of two members who had been with the Society since the end of the war: Connie Murray (Jim Fraser Murray's wife) and Ada English both died and their loss was much mourned. Overall, however, the year produced quite an increase in membership – and a number of these people would be with the Society for some time. At the beginning of the year Linda Roots, Alf Robinson's daughter, joined, bringing with her her friend Vivienne Robson, and Ron Egginton, brother of Linda Egginton, came too. Some who were later to marry into the Society also arrived. Alan Davison, who was to marry Margaret Nicholls, was one. So was Guy Allen, who later married June Park who had joined the dancers for *Hello Dolly!* in 1972. Chris Noble's friend, Lindesay Steel, was yet another who would marry a dancer: Janet Scruby who joined the Society at the same time as he. There was imminent romance among the stage crew, too: Peter Cutchie had introduced Frances Harman to the backstage life of the Society, and Frances later married Stephen Sanderson, going on to start another generation of little Sandersons – Anthony, Helen and Jennifer – to take their part in Society affairs. John Lloyd also joined (though he was long-married already!) because of a chance meeting with Ken Robinson in the Gents' toilet during the interval of *The Boy Friend*. Ken had taken to heart a desperate appeal by Sam Herdman at a committee meeting to try to get more men for *The Student Prince*. John had been having a difficult and depressing month or two, owing to the fact that he had found his comparatively young next-door neighbour dead; it had been a considerable shock. At Ken's suggestion he joined the Society in time to be in *The Student Prince* and has been deeply involved ever since, proving himself to be unique in being a *willing* victim for the job of Ticket Secretary from 1981 to the present day.

There was 'a vast number of applicants'[11] for parts in *The Boy Friend* and it promised to be a good show. It was to be hoped that it would do well for there was news of a further massive price increase: on application to Homburg's for costumes for *The Student Prince* the Committee learned that the prices had gone up to £5.95 per costume. Also the Society wanted to help pay for the extension of the theatre offices into what had been the fish shop next door, and to turn the old offices into a special Function Room where guests could be entertained. The Society would pay for the decoration and carpeting of this room. They also commissioned a portrait of Lady Starmer, the Society's President, from Risbey's, the Darlington photographers (who would process it to look like an oil painting), and this would be hung there. To add to the general expense, the Committee discovered that Musicians' Union rates of pay had gone up by 4%!

Two members of the cast of *The Boy Friend* were selected even before the general auditions. There was to be a speciality Spanish dance in the third act and George Sharratt was giving up some of his annual holiday to come back to perform it, with Joy Beadell as his partner; George also choreographed three of the numbers in the show. *The Boy Friend* was cast in February (leaving only nine weeks in which to rehearse) and Avril Blain was chosen to play the leading role of Polly Browne, with Hilary Hydes, June Aiken, Sue Wishlade and Judi Kent as her four girlfriends. Her leading man, Tony, was played by David Lynch, who made only this one appearance with the Society, as he had just been accepted as a student by RADA.* Craig Gaddas also made *his* only appearance with the Society, as Bobby, but he, too, went into showbusiness and appears on television from time to time. Eunicé Cockburn played the flirtatious Madame Dubonnet, angling for Polly's father Percival Browne, played by Arthur

---

* The Royal Academy of Dramatic Art.

Ellis. Kenneth Richardson played the equally flirtatious Lord Brockhurst, with Sue Robinson as his Lady-Bracknell-like wife. Shirley Dodd was Hortense, the French maid, and Alan Davison, Steve Luck and Peter Cutchie were three eligible Frenchmen. Ian Whitfield, Tom Kent, Betty Cooke, Tricia Freeman, Liz Holton and Ron Egginton made up the rest of the cast: Ian as a gendarme, Tom as a waiter, and the other four as guests. John Beagle was Musical Director and also played the piano in the six-piece orchestra. They all had to work very hard, as time was so short.

Before the show went on, however, Jim Willans told the members attending the Annual General Meeting on the last day of March that the total profit on the production account for the previous year had been just over £1,366. (How fortunes had reversed since the gloomy report at the Annual General Meeting two years earlier!) He was peeved that no more had been won with the Premium Bonds, but you can't have everything. Even so, Jim could hand over to the next Chairman a Society which was in good shape. The incoming Chairman was to be the first lady ever to hold that office – Eunicé Cockburn – and there were now two more ladies on the Committee: Audrey Wigington (later to become Audrey French) had been elected in spring 1976 and June Aiken had just been elected. Eunicé took on her responsibilities with a certain amount of trepidation but there is no doubt that she was a good Chairman (as well as being a decorative one). Her first duty was to entertain the Society's guests during the production of *The Boy Friend*.

Two weeks before the show opened there was concern at the committee meeting because a lot of seats remained unsold, so it was decided that there would have to be more advertising in the press. There was also some difficulty over getting a Musical Director for *The Student Prince*. John Beagle had said that he would not be available; David Garrood said he thought he could do it, then found that his other commitments would not allow it. Peter Oversby was appointed and then that did not work out either. The uncertainty continued for the whole of the summer until finally John Beagle was approached again and managed to fit it in. Amid such uncertainty the production of *The Boy Friend* took place. Much had been sacrificed by some members of the cast for this production. After the onset of 'Beatlemania' in the 1960s long hair had become fashionable for men and this fashion had persisted. This would not do for a musical set in the 1920s, though, so the male members of the cast had to sacrifice their flowing locks. They accepted the fact when they were warned at the auditions but grew increasingly more reluctant as the show drew nearer. Despite making a lot of fuss they finally had to bow to the inevitable when a hairdresser was summoned and a mass shearing-session took place. (The girls had to have

1920s hairstyles too, of course, but were much more calm about it.) The sacrifice was worthwhile for they were rewarded with wonderful reviews. The *Northern Echo*, despite a little gripe about overacting, called the show 'splendid' and said it had '. . . vim, vigour and enthusiasm and some first-rate ensemble dancing.'[12] From the two other papers the word 'professional' stands out. The *Evening Despatch*'s review was fairly short and the word appeared three times; the reviewer added that the show was 'a joy to watch!'[13] The *Darlington & Stockton Times* devoted three-quarters of a column to it, and gave full marks to the whole company for presenting a show which was 'polished, vital and colourful'.[14] Avril Blain was ideal as the delicate Polly Browne and David Lynch was a perfect foil for her, bringing out the humour in his part; his dancing, singing and acting '. . . could not be faulted.' Eunicé Cockburn, said the paper, was 'spectacular' as Madame Dubonnet – what is more, she was able to sustain the French accent admirably – and Shirley Dodd portrayed the French maid in exactly the right manner. Kenneth Richardson (who won all hearts in the fancy-dress party scene when he appeared, dressed as a bee and with a completely deadpan face, for the song *It's Never Too Late to Fall in Love*) had given a good characterization, too, and Arthur Ellis, as Polly's father, had been all that was 'correct' in the true British fashion – until the stage crew got at him, that is. At the moment when his character decided to succumb to the charms of Madame Dubonnet he had to turn and fling his champagne glass into the wings. This manoeuvre had to be carried out without leaving broken glass on the stage so he had to throw it out through the tabs where it would be caught in a sheet by two of the stage crew. Beside them was Steve Blain with a bucket containing broken glass which he shook to give the effect of the glass breaking. At the first dress rehearsal Steve duly 'broke the glass'. At the second dress rehearsal Joy wanted the noise to go on longer so he added broken bricks to the glass in his bucket to get a better effect. On the first night he poured the mixture into another bucket, giving an even more sustained effect. The audience roared with laughter and Arthur remained frozen in the throwing position until the noise ceased. Each night the 'effect' got longer, as Steve warmed to his task, and the audiences laughed more. Then the stage crew added even more refinements. One night they held up, in the wings, a large notice for Arthur to see, saying 'Three shots for £1'. Another night the notice said 'Sandy Wilson is in the audience', and the next night it said '*Harold* Wilson is in the audience' (a reference to the Prime Minister, who had recently resigned). This was all very well but they cunningly made the writing smaller and smaller each night, and Arthur became more and more fascinated to see what each fresh notice would say, so that on the last night of the show, when they excelled themselves and wrote a long message in very small writing, Arthur's comeuppance for sundry tricks played was complete because it took him all his time to get back into the scene without the audience being aware that he had been distracted. Avril, too, had her moment of cringing on the last night, when she was dancing the Charleston in a pierrot costume and the huge pompom flew off one of her shoes; it disappeared right up into the lights and came down with enough speed to produce a noticeable thump when it landed on the largest of the percussionist's drums.

Still, it was a fine production, and one of which Joy, George, John and the cast could be justifiably proud. Financially it did very well, making a profit of nearly £750, so Jim Willans, who had volunteered to stay on in the position of Treasurer until July before handing the job over to Sam Herdman (who is still doing it!), was able to retire happy and was made Honorary Vice-President the following year. For his last encore he claimed back, and received, the £25 fee from Northern Arts for the performance of a work by a living composer!

That summer the Society managed to land another 'first'. *Sweet Charity* had been chosen for the spring 1978 show but an exciting possibility then arose: Alan J. Lerner and Frederick Loewe's *Gigi* would be released for amateurs on 1 January. Bill Jones, as soon as he got the go-ahead from the rest of the Committee, was onto it like a flash, and secured the rights to present the northern première of the show. So *Sweet Charity* underwent its first cancellation.

By mid-summer *The Student Prince* was more or less cast. Eunicé Cockburn was the female lead, Kathie, John Hacking was Count von Mark (Prime Minister of Karlsburg), Sam Herdman was Ruder (the innkeeper), Keith Tate was back again to play Dr Engel (tutor to Prince Karl Franz) and Alan Davison was Captain Tarnitz. The leading three students were Arthur Ellis as Detlef, Ian Whitfield as Lucas, and Jeff Wragg as von Asterburg. The Prince's aunt, Grand Duchess Anastasia, was Greta Sanderson, who had not been in a show for three years. One important individual was missing from the list though: there was no leading man. Again the Committee talked of contacting professionals for it was important that *The Student Prince* should do well and provide some extra financial back-up for *Gigi*. *Gigi* was going to be an expensive show. Although the costumes, despite being brand new, would be about the standard price from Homburg's (£5 each plus VAT), the scenery, if hired from Stagesets, was going to cost nearly double the usual sort of price: £600 plus carriage and VAT. The props would cost well over £300 and the royalties would be at a fixed rate rather than a percentage and would amount to nearly £1,000. Nevertheless it was decided not to raise the ticket prices for *The Student Prince* but to put up the price of the programme to 20p.

It took most of the summer to find a leading man for *The Student Prince* but, in the end, the Committee asked the Society's old friend and some-time saviour John Larsen to come, and he agreed willingly. There seems to have been some dissatisfaction over the auditions for the part of Princess Margaret (to whom the hero is betrothed) but eventually Sue Wishlade got the part and that was that. Thankfully the whole show was now cast, and not a moment too soon, for opening night was only seven weeks away and Joy liked to start floorwork rehearsals in plenty of time. Kath and Phil Robinson had neatly fitted in the birth of their only child, Sally, between *Oklahoma!* and *The Student Prince*, so Kath only missed *The Boyfriend* – at two months pregnant she had been high-kicking as one of the 'card girls' in *Oklahoma!*

A second Aiken was drawn into this production: Sharon, the eldest daughter, was 'call boy'. Since the departure of Parkin Raine, Ray Porteus had become Stage Manager, with Stephen Sanderson as Assistant, oth-erwise the 'old faithfuls' were still on duty: Gordon Holton as Stage Director, Bob and Ernie doing props, Lorrie doing make-up and Elsie on wardrobe. In all there were thirteen stage staff to help with scenery and so on, as it was quite a heavy show in that department. (George Todd's workload was also getting heavier as this point, too – as well as his committee work with the Society he had now been elected Vice-President of NODA.)

After the last-minute casting (as Toni the waiter) of Philip Bethell when Peter Henderson had to drop out, *The Student Prince* was performed, with some attractive little additions to the programme from Helmut Humm, official photographer of the city of Heidelburg. These were three photo-graphs, one of an old postcard showing a scene setting of the play *Old Heidelburg*, on which the musical was based, the second of the old Heidel-burg University around 1900, and the third of the original playbill an-nouncing the première showing of the play in 1901. Herr Humm also sent some posters for the Society to use for publicity purposes.

Unfortunately there were no newspaper reviews of the show because of a journalists' strike which affected all the local papers, but there is *some* information to he had, for Bill Duff, of the *Darlington & Stockton Times*, went to the show and wrote some copy in case publication was resumed. He enjoyed the show and commended Eunicé Cockburn and John Larsen for their performances, also picking out John Parker and Tom Kent (as the Prince's valet and the valet's assistant) for their comedy, and Keith Tate for his sensitive performance as Dr Engel. He also laid stress on the 'notable vocal ability' of Arthur Ellis, Sue Wishlade and Alan Davison. He felt that '. . . as long as Darlington Operatic Society produces such works as this . . . and does so with the musical and acting skill that has

The Student Prince 1970. *Left to right:* Guy Allen, Chris Noble, Graham Dove, Lindesay Steel, Alf Jackson, Ian Dods, Kevin Mooney, Ron Egginton.

gone into this production, then the society will continue to flourish and be well patronized.'[15] Debbie Davis, of the programme *Housecall* on Radio Cleveland, said that she had never seen the show before but had enjoyed it. She also said that the first night had been a sell-out and the audience were showing every appearance of enjoyment. She commended Eunicé, John Larsen and John Parker in particular but said that the chorus was a bit weak in places. (John Beagle had expressed concern over this, too.) The first night accident was also pointed out – one of the tables fell over, smashing a decanter and glasses – but it had not spoiled the audience's enjoyment and the show was visually very pleasing.

Backstage one night, Arthur Ellis engineered one of his notorious practical jokes. To a top-floor dressing-room containing eight of the ladies' chorus he went, towards the end of the interval, bearing a tray of water. He interrupted their consumption of meringues (sugar for instant energy?) and swore that if each girl placed a single strand of her hair on top of the water whoever's hair continued to float was the sexiest. When they had each placed a hair on the water and were looking closely and eagerly to see whose was floating (yes, they *were* gullible, weren't they?) Arthur banged the tray from beneath and they were all drenched. Avril Blain suffered the most. Not only was she on the receiving end of most of the water, but, being very slim, had had to pad out her bosom with cotton wool in order to fill out her dress. And once cotton wool is soaked the water tends to percolate. It percolated all through the next scene leaving Avril in a soggy state for some considerable time – which, she freely admits, served her right for allowing herself to be taken in by the infamous Arthur. Arthur, however, did not get away with it. At first there were vengeful mutterings from the girls but after two nights these ceased and he was lulled into a false sense of security. The main men's costume for this show consisted of a pair of thick white nylon tights with a strap under the foot, braces to hold up the tights, boots, and a short tunic – altogether reminiscent of the ballet dancer Rudolf Nureyev. As the time drew near for Arthur to change into this delicious costume, some of the girls kept him talking so that he had to rush. He was encountering immense difficulty with pulling up one of the legs of the tights when the horrible realization struck him that the foot part had been sewn up tightly with a good thickness of thread. He had no option – he was playing Detlef and had lines to say, so the tights would have to go on. He heaved them up and tightened the braces to strangulation point, but still he was left with a sad little membrane-like piece of cloth stretching diagonally across about eight inches south of where the crotch should have been. To complete their revenge the ladies felt that water should also be involved somewhere, so they laid on a suitable denouement by waiting until he was in the shower on the last night, in Dressing Room One, and tipping a bowl of flour over the top, leaving him covered in a wonderfully glutinous flour-and-water paste. As the proverb says, revenge is sweet.

The jollity was dampened, though, when the accounts were finalized. 97% of the seats were sold for *The Student Prince* and there were virtually the same numbers of Vice-Presidents and Patrons as there had been for *Oklahoma!* at the same time the previous year. It is a measure of how much costs had increased that *Oklahoma!* made a profit of over £400 and *The Student Prince* made a considerable loss, although more than £6,700 had been taken in ticket money. So after the previous year's financial high it looked as though lean times were returning, though the Society *had* been able to give away £1,400 over the year. It was not just the Darlington society which was in difficulties. Even NODA was having a bad time and was launching a £35,000 appeal.

The loss on *The Student Prince* was not the only worry. The scenery for *Gigi*, which had been ordered from Stagesets, was far too big for the Civic Theatre stage. Gordon agonized as to how it could be fitted in, but there was no way round the problem. Clifford and Brown would have a set ready by the time the show was due but there were no stage-plans available from them when the matter was discussed by the Committee in November. However, the size was right for the theatre and it was £150 cheaper than the Stagesets set. All they could do was wait for the plans. At least they were able to settle on a show for autumn 1978. David Heneker's musical *Half a Sixpence*, based on H. G. Wells's novel *Kipps*, was chosen. John Beagle said he could not be Musical Director, but gave plenty of notice so that there was time to cast around. There was a new Ticket Secretary, too, by the end of the year. Peter Cutchie, with his wife Rowena as his official assistant, was led as a lamb to the slaughter! The ticket prices would have to go up yet again for 1978 and they were set at £1.40 for weeknights, £1.50 for Saturdays, £1 for OAPs and children on the first night, and £1 for children on the first Saturday.

1978 opened with everyone trying to look on the bright side. John Parker, who was still Publicity Officer, went all out to give *Gigi* as much publicity as possible since it was going to cost around £8,000 to put on (though, as it turned out, it cost considerably more than that). He even wrote to Maxim's, Paris's most famous restaurant, where some of the action in the show is supposed to take place, to see if they could offer any help. Maxim's was even more helpful than he could have hoped. The Press and Public Relations Officer, Madame Boyer, sent, at Monsieur Louis Vaudable the proprietor's request, a colour picture showing the restaurant's decor (unchanged since 1899), a postcard of Maxim's, and a menu with its cover drawn by SEM, the cartoonist, around 1907. She also sent two photographs taken at Maxim's when MGM shot the film of *Gigi*, as she thought that they would help the Society to choose the right costumes, hats, jewels and so on. Not only did she send all these things, but Maxim's allowed the Society to use the SEM menu cover as the cover design for the programme, and also sent twelve genuine Maxim's menus to be used on the tables in the scene which was set there.

Preparations for *Gigi* were gathering momentum as early as February, when the leading parts were cast. Sue Wishlade was to play the title role and Arthur Ellis would play opposite her as Gaston Lachailles. Sue Robinson was to be Mamita, Gigi's grandmother, and Shirley Dodd her Great Aunt Alicia. Kath Robinson was cast as Liane, Gaston's latest, faithless love, and a newcomer to the Society, Stan Lloyd, was to play the part made famous in the film by Maurice Chevalier: Honoré, Gaston's uncle. Stan is an ex-RAF Group Captain who served in the Middle East during the Second World War and who, he says, spent his leisure time '. . . shuffling up and down the stage at the Royal Opera House in Cairo while Rommel was shuffling up and down the desert.' He was in a number of productions there and also performed in Hong Kong and '. . . any other stage I could set my military feet on.' He loved the whole atmosphere of theatre and is what actors call 'a natural'. Backstage, Christine Smith had brought along her twin, Linda, to help – a most fortunate move, for Linda is now the backbone of the Props department, though Christine died suddenly, in 1984. She was only young and her death put the whole society into a state of sorrow and shock. June Aiken got her husband George involved, too, to help backstage, and George is now one of the mainstays of the stage crew, doing stage management as well as crewing.

There was progress on the *Half a Sixpence* front, too. The contract had been signed with the rights holders at 12½%, and Arthur Berwick, a teacher of French from Hurworth Comprehensive School, had agreed to be Musical Director. The scenery, costumes and props were all booked but the ticket

Gigi 1978 – Stan Lloyd.

prices would have to go up once again, by 10p for weeknights and by 25p on the two Saturdays, partly because the cost of the printing of the tickets by the theatre had risen quite considerably, and partly because the theatre rental was to increase for 1979. Still, at least the show was settled in all departments. What to do in 1979 was the next question. It had been suggested that, since concerts always seemed to be successful financially, perhaps it would be a good idea to stage one concert and one musical a year instead of two musicals. Concerts were usually one-night-stands, though, and besides, musicals were, in some ways, more fun for everyone to do. So the Committee decided to try to keep on with the two musicals and to give a concert as well, if possible. Accordingly, it was decided at the February meeting that the spring show would be *The Mikado*. Later it was changed to *The King and I*, but by April, owing to difficulties with booking both of these shows, it had transmogrified into Dorothy Reynolds and Julian Slade's *Salad Days*, which was a similar sort of show to *The Boy Friend*, had a small cast playing a lot of parts and wearing easily-contrived costumes, and might therefore be expected to make a similar sort of profit

Arthur Berwick

to *The Boy Friend*. It was also decided that a concert would be given a month or two after *Salad Days*. There was a good reason for this. Consider the Society's position: by that April committee meeting only 62% of the tickets had been sold for *Gigi*, the costs would be considerably higher than for *The Student Prince*, and even though 97% of the tickets had been sold for that, it had still made a considerable loss. There was much anxiety; the Committee even agreed, at one point, to seek information on lotteries with a view to raising funds (though this never happened).

In the end 96% of the tickets were sold for *Gigi* and it *did* lose a lot of money – in fact it cancelled out all the profit *The Boy Friend* had made (£750) and £25 more. But what a splendid show it was! The scenery was brand new, and so were the costumes, of course. Homburg's had done the Society proud, for the costumes were very well made in the most beautiful styles and colours. Every detail had been attended to in the women's dresses, and the men's suits were spectacular, ranging from rich dark green to peach in colour (all with matching top hats) and from tail coats to lounge suits.

The media went into ecstasies. The *Northern Echo* called the musical 'ambitious' and said that the company had more than done it justice: '. . . without exception the cast performed excellently backed by a superb chorus. The dancing was a delight and costumes and set quite spectacular.'[16] The *Evening Despatch* said '*Gigi* can't help but win the hearts of visitors to Darlington's Civic Theatre . . . last night's production was fast, funny and very colourful with only one or two hitches to mar a splendid first night.'[17] This critic felt that, at one point, Sue Wishlade sang off-key (though no one else in the press had appeared to notice) but had enjoyed Stan Lloyd's performance. She felt that the star was Shirley Dodd, who had excelled herself. The show was summed up as '. . . a good light-hearted night's entertainment, yet another feather in Joy Beadell's cap.' The *Darlington & Stockton Times* devoted a whole column to it. 'Congratulations,' it said, 'to the intrepid Darlington amateurs who dared to scale the heights of one of the truly greats of all musicals, with its extravagantly opulent sets and costumes and its memorable collection of tunes . . .'[18] The reviewer went on to refer to a 'whirling kaleidoscope of colour, action and sound' and said that Maurice Chevalier 'somewhere in those celestial wings' must have been applauding Stan Lloyd who gave a 'really accomplished, delightful performance'. Arthur Ellis's accent, acting and singing were described as faultless and he managed to make the prodigal Gaston a very likeable character. Susan Robinson and Kath Robinson also received praise (though Kath maintains to this day that her performance left a lot to be desired). The *Darlington & Stockton Times* agreed with the *Evening Despatch* about Shirley Dodd's portrayal of Aunt Alicia but was more specific. 'Shirley's performance,' said the report, 'was completely professional – I would run out of superlatives if I had the space to go into more detail of her wonderful characterization. Her timing, gestures, knowing how to judge the laughter pauses – all West End stuff.' There was also a special mention for Debbie Traice and Richard Boucher* who played the two children in the piece. Jan Verrall, speaking on Radio Cleveland,[19] told the listeners 'There are still a few tickets left, so do go and get them. It certainly was a trip into nostalgia and what a wonderful trip it turned out to be . . . some of the scenes were breathtaking, and . . . oh, the costumes!' Even so, she was staggered by the sum which it had ultimately cost to put on the show – £9,000. She paid a very special tribute to Joy Beadell, saying 'she surely reigns supreme as the Society's professional director' (this was Joy's 27th show for the Society) and added '. . . she's a great little lady with a giant-sized appetite for good theatre, and so humble with it. In her own words she says "I'm always striving to do better next time".' This was quite true – Joy invariably aimed higher for each show and was indefatigable. Jan Verrall also had very appreciative words to say about the slickness and speed of the stage crew and about the orchestra, and it is obvious, looking at a transcript of the broadcast, that it was not just said out of kindness.

Some things *did* go wrong, of course. Poor Tom Handy (in his fourth show – he had joined the Society for *Song of Norway*) had to sit on a circular

* Richard made the theatre his career. After becoming a dancer in the Operatic Society shows he went to RADA and studied stage management and theatrical studies. He now works for Theatre Project, part of the Very Light Group, which provides lighting for many West End and touring shows.

sofa seat in the centre of the stage in the Hotel Lobby scene, reading a magazine, just before Honoré and Mamita sit on that same seat to sing the well-known duet *I Remember it Well*. Tom became quite engrossed in the article he had begun reading and forgot to leave the stage. Fortunately John Lloyd had the presence of mind to go back on, greet Tom as though he were an old friend, and walk off with him so that it looked natural, before Tom found himself playing gooseberry! It is one of those occupational hazards if there is any 'reading' to be done on stage. Several years later, for *The Music Man*, lots of books were required for a library scene, because the heroine is a librarian. The present writer borrowed a large number of books from Darlington Public Library, but, knowing the hazards, chose elderly non-fiction volumes, the most racy of which dealt with the theory and practice of the operation of beam-engines!

When *Gigi* was over the Committee was delighted to receive letters from the Mayor of Darlington, and Shildon Operatic Society, as well as from members of the public, offering congratulations on a wonderful show. However, as the proverb says, 'Handsome is as handsome does', and the aftermath in the cold light of day showed that the cost of the production was not covered, even if the profit from the programmes and the Vice-Presidents' and Patrons' donations were taken into consideration. *Gigi* had been an indulgence, but nonetheless the Society hoped and believed that it was a worthwhile indulgence in terms of getting support for future shows.

In the mean time, Ken Robinson, as Social Secretary, was trying to organize as many social events as possible to bring in extra revenue. According to the minutes of the committee meeting for 15 May 1978, for instance, a number of activities were planned. There was to be a spring dance at the Masonic Hall, a car rally (another name for a treasure hunt), a wine and cheese evening, a barn dance and the annual dinner-dance.

For *Half a Sixpence* it was hoped that the orchestra could be reduced (by two) to fifteen, plus Christine Purvis on piano, in order to try to save some money but Arthur Berwick was not very happy about this. Some members of the Society were not very happy about *Salad Days*, as the number in the cast was strictly limited, but those not in *Salad Days* would at least have the chance to be in the concert shortly after the show.

In July there was more unrest, this time about the casting of *Half a Sixpence*, partly because some people who wished to be considered for parts had been on holiday when the auditions were held and the parts had been cast in their absence, and partly because not all of the parts had been auditioned before the whole Committee. However, after prolonged discussion the Committee, as a democratically elected body, reserved its right to do things in its own way, though Arthur Berwick finally prevailed and got *his* own way over having the number of players he had originally wanted in the orchestra.

As for *Salad Days*, the cast would save some money by providing their own everyday costumes, with special character costumes being supplied by Homburg's. There was some difficulty in getting a Musical Director, but George Hetherington, from Durham, was approached and agreed to take the job on. He had done the show four times before, was a pianist, and had already worked with Joy Beadell.

Two happy events occurred towards the end of that summer. The first was that Connie Reeves, who had come from Burnley to live at Hurworth, joined the Society. She had been a member of Colne Operatic Society, was full of life and very gregarious, and was leading-role material. The second was that George Todd was to be made President of NODA in September. This was a great honour for the Society and a just reward for George's hard work for the Association over so many years. For George himself it was a mixed blessing, for NODA was still in dire financial straits and there was some talk that it might have to go into liquidation, though by October it had been reorganized and seemed to be safe once more. It was not in such a bad state that it was unable to recognize quality: the programme produced by June Aiken for *Gigi* was Highly Commended in the customary programme competition run by the Association.

A week before *Half a Sixpence* opened Peter Cutchie was able to report to the Committee that only 275 seats remained to be sold over the whole run, which was very good news.

John Parker was leading man for the first time as Arthur Kipps, with Hilary Hydes as his leading lady Ann Pornick. Sue Williamson played Helen Walsingham, the upper-class beauty by whom Kipps is briefly dazzled, with Muriel Jones as her mother and Guy Allen as her wastrel brother. Hilary's husband Peter played the part of her brother in this show and, together with with Warnock Kerr and a lugubrious Steve Luck, made up Kipps's trio of workmates. Warnock and his wife, Lynne, had acted with the prestigious Minerva Club in their native Glasgow and had been made Life Members of it, but were now living in Richmond and were members of the operatic society there. Lynne was involved in *Half a Sixpence*, too, playing one of the minor roles. Kenneth Richardson played Chitterlow, the actor/playwright who makes Kipps's fortune for him the second time around; Stan Lloyd was Mr Shalford, the shop-owner, with Sam Herdman as his assistant Carshot and also as the photographer in the well-known *Flash Bang Wallop* number. The four shopgirls were played by June Aiken, Kath Robinson, Avril Blain and Sue Wishlade, and the cameo roles were taken by Greta Sanderson, Judi Kent, Chris Noble,

Half a Sixpence 1978. *Left to right:* June Aiken, Warnock Kerr, Kath Robinson, John Parker, Peter Hydes, Avril Blain, Steve Luck, Sue Wishlade.

Steve Blain, John Hacking, Lindesay Steel and Linda Roots. The final 'named character', Edwin, was played by Ebony. Edwin was the shop cat and Ebony belonged to Arthur and Pat Berwick's children, Robert and Helen.* Peter Sanderson, Bernard and Greta's middle son, who had returned to the stage for *The Student Prince* after a five-year break following *Fiddler on the Roof*, was also on stage. Peter had a particular interest in this show. He worked in Murrays, the family catering business, and each day of the show he spent half-an-hour making the pane of glass through which Kipps accidentally puts his hand, cutting it and bringing him to the notice of Helen Walsingham. The nineteen-by-ten-inch pane of glass was made from sugar and water and heated to the exact temperature which would allow it to set in a block which looked like a window pane. What is more, he got it exactly right every time!

The show was destined to have its problems. John Parker had an unfortunate experience which occurred when he had to quick-change his clothes and appear in white flannels and a blazer. This was done partly offstage and partly behind a small chorus ensemble on stage. It worked like a charm until the final performance when the zip on the flannels

---

* Ebony was still alive, very fit, and seventeen years old, in 1994.

finally gave up and John was obliged to stand alone on stage and sing *She's Too Far Above Me* with gaping flies. Steve did not fare too well either, on that same night, when John, flinging out his arm to point offstage, accidentally smacked him in the mouth so that he had do the next number with blood pouring from a split lip. Hilary Hydes's voice gave out, owing to an infection, after the first performance. Fortunately Sue Wishlade had recently played the part of Ann at Stockton and took over on the second night after only three hours' rehearsal. Thereafter Lynne Kerr and June Aiken shared the part of Flo Bates, the shopgirl, which Sue had vacated: Lynne portrayed the character but June spoke the lines since she already knew them and Lynne had no time to learn them.

It was an interesting initiation for the eight new members of the Society: Anne Bainbridge, Maggie Barnes, Elizabeth Connagh, Rebecca Hauxwell, Kim Keeler, Connie Reeves, Lisa Rossiter and Sue Hewgill (Sue was a dancer), though Connie had probably seen similar scenarios before. Still, from the audience's point of view the transition was achieved quite smoothly.

The press reviews were diverse. The *Northern Echo* called it 'another colourful production with no expense spared',[20] mentioning only John Parker ('excellent . . . brings quite a professional touch to his singing and dancing') and Hilary Hydes ('provides humour and charm') in particular: the critic felt that the chorus, dancers and orchestra deserved the best of the praise. The *Darlington & Stockton Times* said '. . . everything about the show was a delight to experience.'[21] It also said 'John Parker left nothing, but nothing, to be desired in his interpretation . . . He could dance, he could act, he could sing . . .' John received a loudly cheering ovation at the final curtain '. . . he well deserved it – they all did,' opined the critic, and went on to praise Hilary (for an 'enchanting' performance), and also Stan Lloyd, Sue Williamson, Muriel Jones, Guy Allen and Kenneth Richardson. Even the cameo parts were described as 'admirably played'. By contrast, one would not think that the *Evening Despatch* critic had attended the same show. To be fair, the review said that the cast '. . . gave a bright, polished, and energetic performance.'[22] Nevertheless this critic could only say 'If the stage version of *Half a Sixpence* was twice as good then Darlington Operatic Society's opening night at the Civic Theatre would have been a roaring success.' (This person had probably seen the film, which starred Tommy Steele and Julia Foster; some of the songs in it differ from those in the stage version.) The show, she thought, was very slow-moving, and several scenes too long. John Parker was given a very good review, and Steve Luck, as Buggins the eternal pessimist, also got a special mention, as did Kenneth Richardson. The audiences reacted well to it, however, and there were letters of appreciation.

Half a Sixpence 1978 – Chorus. *See page x for full list.*

There was a new item in the programme for *Half a Sixpence*: a feature called 'Society Notes' had been introduced which gave snippets of news to the public about the members. This programme sadly records the death at the beginning of the year of Gordon Clarke, who had been one of the Duke of Wellington pub crowd who had annexed Ian Whitfield. Jim Fraser Murray had been awarded a gold bar to his NODA medal, for 50 years of service to the amateur stage, and Eileen Young had a second bar; George Todd's election as NODA President was proudly mentioned, too. Then there were such items as Audrey Wigington's marriage to Bob French (Audrey was Assistant Secretary to the Society), the birth of Sue and Mike Williams's daughter Nicola, Stephen Sanderson and Frances Harman's engagement, and the appearance of Philip Tsaras (né Murray) in the West End musical *Bubbling Brown Sugar* after his recent London appearance in *Jesus Christ Superstar*. There was a one-page feature on Kenneth Richardson, for this show marked the 40th anniversary of his first appearance on the Civic Theatre's stage: he had been in the chorus of *Tom Jones* which opened on 7 November 1938. (Sam remembers that Peter Tod presented Kenneth with a book on behalf of the theatre.) There was also news of Society activities and of the fact that £1,485 had been distributed to charities in 1977–78. It was hoped that this feature would make the audiences feel more of a bond with the Society.

At the end of the year the Committee took stock. *Half a Sixpence* had not done too badly, with only 98 seats left unsold. True, it had made a loss, but only £158. There was *Salad Days* to come, and a *Melodies for You* concert in June. The decision was made – and stayed firm – that the autumn show for 1979 would be *White Horse Inn*, which had a bit of everything in it and Arthur Berwick as Musical Director. In spring 1980 Ivor Novello's *The Dancing Years* would be repeated with John Beagle as Musical Director – the Committee would then see what a bit of lyricism and sentiment would do for the public.

It can be difficult to ring the changes to suit the public mood: they may say 'I don't like American shows', and will stay away from, say, Jerry Herman's *Mame*, but will turn out in force for *South Pacific*. They tend to be suspicious of a foreign title like *La Belle Hélène* but will willingly go to see *Gigi*. It is one of life's imponderables, like the present Ticket Secretary's question of why, for thirteen years, did the Tuesday and Wednesday of the second week of the show always sell out first, until the spring of 1994 when the pattern changed abruptly and the Thursday and Friday of the first week became the most favoured nights?

The Committee's New-Year resolutions had to be to try to organize more fund-raising events and to work hard to produce shows which would not lose money. This was going to be difficult because the cost increases were gathering momentum. For one thing the theatre rent per night was going up by £15, and the Producer's and Musical Director's fees rose with the cost of living, as did Musicians' Union wages. At least in Joy the Society was lucky to have a Producer and Choreographer combined. One problem looked like being solved at any rate: the ongoing search for a good props store, because the Society had been offered a property in Borough Road, very near to the theatre.

The Committee then cast *Salad Days*, in late February. It was an unusual show, designed to use a cast of only twelve (though Joy swelled the total number to eighteen by adding six dancers). Between the twelve of them they played 54 parts, so it was a show which called for a lot of talent and a lot of discipline. The stage staff numbered seventeen, almost as many as the cast. The dancers were Christine Coates, Sue Hewgill, Tricia Freeman, Kath Robinson, Peter Sanderson and Michael Walker. The actors consisted of nine of the Society regulars: Barrie Dargue, Sue Wishlade, Connie Reeves, Warnock Kerr, Steve Luck, June Aiken, Stan Lloyd, Avril Blain and Shirley Dodd. Then there were three young men who were with the Society just for this production: Ian Corner, Stuart Parsons and Peter Topping (though Ian made a return visit to be in

Brigadoon in 1981). Avril, Stuart and Steve basically took only one part each, as Avril and Stuart played the central two characters, the university students Timothy and Jane, while Steve played the other key role, that of Troppo the deaf-mute who has in his keeping the magic piano which will make everybody dance.

The Society had not only a large membership by now – well over a hundred – but also a number of people who were keen to be on the Committee. It was a far cry from that unhappy year when there was the unfilled vacancy. At the Annual General Meeting there were nine nominees for only four places – a healthy sign – but this was not selling tickets. By 29 March, when Bill Jones took over from Bernard Sanderson as Chairman, only 41% of the tickets for *Salad Days* had been sold and the cast were doing everything possible to save money. The costumes were 1950s style so the girls were borrowing clothes that various of their friends had hung onto from years back, and were making some of the clothes themselves. Steve Luck also designed and made some. Barrie Dargue's abiding memory is that he borrowed Avril's father's dinner suit for this show and it was sent back to Homburg's with the rest of the costumes by mistake. It was never seen again and it still lies heavily on Barrie's conscience!

Sam had prepared an item to go in the programme: a chart showing how much of the price of a £1.60 ticket went on each item of expenditure for a show. It was quite interesting to look at. Of the £1.60, 36p went on the orchestra, 29p on the hire of the theatre, 22p on costumes, 19p on scenery hire, 18p on royalties, 14p on professional fees, 12p on VAT, 4p on advertising, 4p on rehearsal expenses, and 1p each on printing and insurance. He hoped that this would help the public to understand the need for the planned ticket price-rise in the autumn and also encourage more of them to become Vice-Presidents and Patrons. There was another niggling worry, too: Peter Tod was leaving the Civic Theatre to go to manage the Bristol Hippodrome, and the members were wondering if his successor would be as sympathetic to the Society.* (They need not have worried. Andrew Jowett took over from Peter and then, of course, Peter Cutchie joined the theatre staff as Assistant Manager, so all was well.)

In the end, just under 78% of the tickets for *Salad Days* were sold. It was well short of what had been hoped for, but the economies that had been made meant that the show managed to make a profit of £716.

The *Northern Echo* did not print a review but the *Evening Despatch* and *Darlington & Stockton Times* headlines were composed of variations on the

---

* Peter is now at the Birmingham Hippodrome.

same sentence – 'Hard work pays off' – and both critics urged the public to see it. It was a versatile cast, they agreed, and Joy had delivered a good, lively production. The *Darlington & Stockton Times*, as usual, gave the fuller of the reviews and praised Stuart and Avril's performances, and that of Steve Luck. Stan, Shirley and Barrie were especially mentioned for the way in which they had managed to change their personalities, as well as their clothes, for their various roles. Stan had an actor's nightmare on the night when Ian Corner was late for his cue. With enormous presence of mind, Stan managed to sustain a telephone conversation with an imaginary character for some two and a half minutes until Ian arrived. Even a minute alone on stage, not knowing when someone will appear, feels like years, so it was quite a feat.

The next function, of course, was the *Melodies for You* concert on 8 and 9 June. Three weeks before the concert ticket sales were poor. There were 52 people in it, and they and other members as well were urged to try to sell more tickets so that enough profit would be made to back up *White Horse Inn*. The Committee had already agreed on the 10p rise in ticket prices for that show and did not want to raise them any further, despite an increase in VAT.

The concert had a good variety of items. There were songs by Gilbert & Sullivan, Ivor Novello, and Lerner and Loewe. There were excerpts from *The Boy Friend* and *Die Fledermaus*, some light popular songs, and some choral singing; there were a couple of duets, one operatic (from *The Pearl Fishers* by Bizet) and one amusing (the *Cat Duet*, commonly attributed to Rossini but actually by Robert Pearsall, an Englishman). There was also the *pas de deux* from *Giselle* danced by Catherine Peabody and George Sharratt. Pat Berwick and Christine Purvis played, as a piano duet, *The Skaters' Waltz* by Waldteufel. Contrary to expectation all 600 seats were sold and the concert made a profit of about £215, so that, plus what had been made on *Salad Days*, could go some way towards covering any loss on *White Horse Inn*. Even so, the Committee had to do a rethink on ticket prices when the show had been re-costed to take into account the large increase in VAT, and the £2 tickets had to be raised to £2.10. They were also looking ahead towards expenses for *The Dancing Years* in the spring. For one thing, Stagesets were quoting £570 plus carriage for the scenery, and Clifford and Brown £450 plus carriage. This was a huge difference and the Committee was going to have to decide whether the extra money should be spent on what would obviously be the more lavish set provided by Stagesets. (In the end they had no choice but to book the expensive set of scenery since no plans were received from the other firm; however, after negotiation, Stagesets did reduce the hire charge by £70.) As one problem receded, though, others approached: Joy had said that her workload was very heavy and she really wanted to produce only one show each year. (It should be borne in mind that she produced for other societies as well as Darlington.) Also, a number of members had dropped out of the production of *White Horse Inn* by mid-September, which was disappointing, but 38% of the seats had been sold, which was not too bad. The cast members who remained were rehearsing hard. John Hurlstone and Eunicé Cockburn were playing the leads, Leopold and Josepha, with Sam Herdman as Grinkle (the manufacturer) again, and Anna-Maria Wilson, from Stockton Stage Society, as his daughter Ottoline. Barrie Dargue was playing Valentine Sutton, and Steve Luck was to be Sigismund Smith. Philip Bethell was pressed into service again to play Professor Hinzel, with Lynne Kerr as Gretel, his daughter – the part played by Greta Sanderson in the *White Horse Inn* of 23 years earlier. Kenneth Richardson, who had played Leopold in that show, was this time playing the part of the Emperor. Connie Reeves played Kathie the postwoman and her young son, Garry, was playing the boy waiter at the inn. Sue Hewgill was playing the part of Zenzi, the goatherd, and there would also be a goat and a St Bernard dog to add verisimilitude!

In mid-October, a week before the show, the Society had sold 87% of the tickets, and, of the remaining tickets returned for sale at the box office, a further £550 worth (4.5%) had already been sold. The Rotary Club Gala Night had not been supported as well as had been hoped, though. They had booked the whole theatre for one evening and then had 300 tickets left over so it was up to the theatre to sell them if possible. In the end 98.2% of the tickets were sold but there were extra expenses to be met. For one thing, the show was a long one, with two intervals, and it therefore went on after 10.15 p.m. meaning that the members of the orchestra had to be paid overtime. But did the audience get value for money? The answer is not clear from the newspaper reviews. The *Northern Echo* did not print one, the *Evening Despatch* reviewer did not care for the show itself, though she said it was technically good and there were some nice songs, and the *Darlington & Stockton Times* thoroughly enjoyed it! Both papers spoke of the high cost of mounting the production: £10,000 (though in fact it eventually turned out to have cost over £12,000). The *Evening Despatch* said that by the end of the show 'the audience . . . were wilting in their seats'[23] and the *Darlington & Stockton Times* called it 'an evening of delightful entertainment', saying also that the opening night was a 'great success'.[24] The *Evening Despatch* chose for special mention Steve Luck and Eunicé Cockburn – and Sam Herdman's knees! And the goat. The *Darlington & Stockton Times* gave an opinion on each of the leading characters and found them all technically good and pleasing in their interpretations. It spoke of the very high quality of the singing, acting and dancing.

White Horse Inn 1979 – Dancers. *See page x for full list.*

It also mentioned the St Bernard dog. And the goat. Sue Hewgill and Kath Robinson had a torrid time with the animals. The dog, handled by Kath, was beautiful but enormous. Care had to be taken that goat and dog did not meet face to face in case of animosity, though they had to cross the stage diagonally in opposite directions in fairly quick succession. The dog kept trying to speed things up and there was some doubt, between it and Kath, as to who was controlling whom. Sue is very small and slight (in fact she was just the right size to be Wayne Sleep's partner when they were at the Royal Ballet School together) and is not built to control headstrong animals. There were, in fact, two goats – the Committee was hedging its bets, goats being of an inherently capricious nature. Both would be waiting in the wings and Sue would take on stage whichever seemed the less likely to be either stagestruck or consumed by stage-fright at the time. The goats, however, though beautiful to look at and innocent in appearance, were also secretive – they did not communicate clearly to Sue which mood was prevalent from night to night, so she was in a constant state of uncertainty, which, granted, makes for a flow of adrenalin, but is not good for the nerves. On the first night the goat she selected was stagestruck; once on stage it became enthralled by the experience and had no wish to leave. The second night she fared no better; her Chosen One got a little way onto the stage, decided that enough was enough, slipped its lead, and departed precipitately towards the wings where its owner was standing. This was particularly unfortunate as the hapless goatherd was supposed to sing and talk to the goat, so Sue was left addressing an empty collar and lead – still an indelible and toe-curling memory for her. At least, in the end, the dog and the goats *were* prevented from meeting, but it was a close-run thing. John Parker also got more than he bargained for in this show. He and John Hacking were filling out the 'band' on stage and John Parker was given a tuba. What he did not realize was that it had a proper mouthpiece, so he was thoroughly disconcerted by the unearthly noises which it produced when he blew it. Arthur Berwick had his own little fiasco; the Mayor of Amiens (Darlington's twin town) was to be a guest at the show and Arthur was asked to make some special arrangements. Since he taught French he translated the story of the show and a potted history of the theatre for the visitor's delectation. He even went to the trouble of organizing band parts so that the Marseillaise could be played in the Mayor's honour. And then the plane bearing the illustrious guest was diverted to Edinburgh. Arthur was thoroughly deflated!

Anyway it was all over now, and as the end of the year approached the Committee sat back to think about that show and those to come. Despite all the worry and the high costs *White Horse Inn* had made a profit of £575, but *The Dancing Years* would be an expensive show and ticket prices would have to be raised by 25p this time. (Members of the Society would have to pay rather more for their subscriptions, too, to keep in line with inflation. These went up to £5.)

The question may be asked: when lavish shows cost so much to put on, why did the Society not do something cheaper? The answer was, to enable the public to see at comparatively low cost the sort of show which was becoming increasingly difficult for professionals to put on because of the enormous cost of paying a large number of cast members. There were 60 people in *White Horse Inn* and there would be 52 in *The Dancing Years*. Backers would have to be very confident indeed to put on shows such as these with professionals.

The Committee toyed with the idea of presenting *The Dancing Years* for eleven nights instead of ten, but decided against it; they also decided on *Showboat* for autumn 1980, but this was soon scotched by the members, who did not want to perform it. *Brigadoon* was chosen instead, therefore, with *Sweet Charity* to follow in spring 1981.

The end of the year brought a very heavy blow. The last meeting of 1979 was held on 19 December and Bill Jones opened it by paying tribute to Lady Starmer, who had died that morning. The whole town would miss her but the Society would feel her loss particularly badly because she was very much loved. She had not just been a figurehead as President for so many years but had always taken a keen and active interest and had been so generous with both her time and her hospitality. Now she was gone and it was the end of an era.

Looking back over the five years it is the tremendous financial see-sawing that stands out. The first five shows made a respectable profit but the losses on *The Student Prince* and *Gigi* were substantial. The last two shows made a combined profit of nearly £1,300, though, and the Society also had a large and enthusiastic membership to carry it into the 1980s so there was every reason to be optimistic.

Chapter 9

1980–1984

1980 opened on an encouraging note with the auditions for *The Dancing Years* for which the standard of contenders was 'very high'.[1] Less encouraging was the fact that Gordon Holton was concerned that he would be very short of stage staff and urged the Committee to try to interest some men in helping with this. By mid-February the show was cast and the Committee at last had the knowledge that the concert and both the shows in 1979 had shown a surplus, enabling £600 to be given to charity, so they lived in the hope of a good public response to the current production. There appeared, alongside Christine Purvis and David Garrood for this show, a pianist who had done some accompanying for *White Horse Inn* and who had played the clarinet in the orchestra for that show. His name was Stephen Sild and he had two degrees in music. Having taught at Conyers School at Yarm, he was about to become – at the age of 27 – Head of Music at Brinkburn School at Hartlepool (now Hartlepool Sixth Form College). He, like Christine Purvis, was a born accompanist and any singer will know what this means – an accompanist can make or break a performance.

Steve Luck had got the lead in *The Dancing Years*, playing the part of the composer Rudi Kleber, though he was chagrined at having to have his hair cut and restyled again, having grown it back to its former luxuriant state after *Salad Days*. He had only taken comedy parts before, so this serious role would be something quite new to him. Eunicé Cockburn played opposite him as Maria Zeigler, with Kath Robinson as Grete Schone his young admirer. Kenneth Richardson, who had played the lead in 1954, now took the part of Prince Charles Metterling, and Margaret Lowther was back to play Cacille Kurt. Sam Herdman, Greta Sanderson and Cecil Grieveson, who had all been in the 1954 show, were in the cast, too. The elder of the two Kent children, Jonathan, was making his stage début at the age of ten and playing Maria and Rudi's son Carl. Young Garry Reeves (Connie's son) was understudying him as well as playing a cameo role.

The primary topic at the Annual General Meeting in March, at which Bill Jones handed over the Chairmanship to Sam Herdman, was, of course, the death of Lady Starmer. The Society was very deeply affected by this and it was too soon to contemplate seriously the appointment of a successor. The other main topic, as usual, was finance. For one thing, the commission charged by the theatre for sales of tickets at the box office was to rise. For sales in excess of £1,000 it would be 15%. With ticket prices increasing it was necessary that the Society should continue to present quality shows which gave the public value for money. Wise investments were also a prime factor so that returns from them would help to provide financial security. The Ladies' Committee continued to help to raise money by way of jumble sales, raffles and similar activities, though Peggy Todd had now resigned after twenty years of hard work in its cause; the resultant vacancy was filled by Eileen Hogg. There was also another notable resignation: Gordon Holton decided to call it a day. He had work commitments to consider and had worked very hard on a lot of shows as Stage Director, but the days of having an amateur Stage Director were coming to an end. The theatre had its own professional stage staff and the march of progress was producing more and more technical refinements and more demarcation rules. He was Stage Director one last time, for *The Dancing Years*, and then bowed out.

By March *The Dancing Years* rehearsals were going well, and there was *Brigadoon* to be thought about. Arthur Berwick was booked as Musical Director for that, the arrangements for costumes, scenery and props were agreed upon, and all seemed to be going smoothly. There seemed to be a lack of costumes available for *Sweet Charity* but Bill Jones was still looking around and there was no reason for even a hint of unease – yet. The unease – it follows as night follows day if one becomes too comfortable – began to set in three weeks later, at the next committee meeting. With less than two weeks to opening night only 53% of the tickets had been sold for *The Dancing Years*. Ivor Novello was not attracting public interest as much as had been hoped. Publicity was increased; the price of the programme was increased too, though this was to cover a further rise in printing costs.

Hitches and more major problems came thick and fast both during and after the show. *The Dancing Years* was a lavish show and was well performed, with a cast of 53 which now included in the chorus the decorative Margaret Webb, who managed to make any old costume look wonderful just by putting it on, and also Heather Wane, who had joined the Society just before *White Horse Inn*. (Heather likes to cook and has always kept up a constant supply of delicacies to be eaten – with enormous relish – in the dressing-rooms.) The show needed 23 stage staff (including Nicholas Sanderson doing his first show) to make it run smoothly, which gives some idea of the complexity of the scene changes. The scenery was very large and very heavy, and this gave rise to one of the hitches. At one point

John Hacking, who was one of the crew, averted a major disaster, turning himself into a 'human cleat' by wedging himself in to hold two large pieces of scenery together and upright for the whole of one scene when they threatened to fall disastrously onto the actors! Christine Purvis admits responsibility for another hiccup. Steve Luck was supposed to run his fingers idly up the keys of the piano on the stage in a *glissando* during a contemplative and poignant pause. Christine, who was playing the piano in the orchestra pit, provided the sound, since the piano on the stage had a dummy keyboard. She confesses that on one occasion she was really not paying attention as she should have been. Consequently Steve's silent *glissando* preceded her audible one by a number of seconds. The ensuing roar of laughter from the audience did not do a great deal for the mood of the moment and Christine made sure that she gave the score her full attention after that. Poor Eunicé had a difficult time during the second week when she contracted a tummy bug – stage heroines do not suffer from anything so indelicate as tummy bugs – but to her great credit she managed to conceal her misery remarkably well.

Then there were the major problems. Only the public who were present knew anything about the show. There was a journalists' strike at the crucial time which was a great pity, as the journalists' prepared copy makes it aggravating, even in retrospect, that it was never released to the public. The *Evening Despatch* said that it would be impossible for the Society to better such excellent entertainment, and that even the smallest roles were expertly handled. The *Darlington & Stockton Times* said that it was a magical three hours of entertainment given by a talented and utterly professional group of performers, particular reference being made to Jonathan Kent. Even a jokey (and anonymous) Radio Cleveland reviewer admitted to counting himself lucky to have been able to see such a show. However, there were no reviews which might have tempted the public to buy tickets, and some of the people in the show sold no tickets at all, so in the end only 82.9% were sold, leaving 1,031 empty seats over the ten-night run. The show lost over £800.

Peter Cutchie had been working at the theatre before he had to deal with the tickets for *White Horse Inn* and his workload in trying to do both jobs was hopelessly heavy. He and Rowena therefore decided to resign as Ticket Secretaries after *The Dancing Years* so the job was vacant again. Fortunately George Todd volunteered to fill in, but only temporarily. To pile on the problems there was no scenery and no costumes to be had for *Sweet Charity*. Homburg's were willing to try to concoct a set of costumes but the scenery problem was insurmountable, so *Sweet Charity* bit the dust for the second time and the Committee voted to give *The Mikado* a second outing in spring 1981 instead. (There was a move to try to get John Reed to come to play the part of Ko-Ko, which was one of his most celebrated roles with the D'Oyly Carte company, but he was not available.)

No sooner had one problem been resolved than another cropped up. In June, when *Brigadoon* had been in rehearsal for three weeks, the costumiers notified Bill Jones that, just before receiving confirmation of Darlington's booking of the costumes, they had received a firm booking for them from another society, and they were therefore no longer available. Bill tried other costumiers, all to no avail. Fox's had now closed and their *Brigadoon* costumes had been sold to Southend Operatic Society, who would be giving their production about two weeks after the Darlington presentation.

The Committee gave up the idea of *Brigadoon* and decided to do *Camelot* instead, so Bill had to rearrange everything for that, as well as book everything for *The Mikado* – and it had to be done quickly. Bill rose to the occasion. In just under two weeks he had booked scenery, props and costumes for both shows, getting Stagesets to agree to accept the deposit already paid for the *Brigadoon* scenery as a deposit on the scenery for *Camelot*. Within the next month he had sorted out some confusion over the hire price of the *Camelot* costumes from S. B. Watts and agreed a price of £7.50 each, and had also secured costumes for *The Mikado* from Homburg's at £5.95 each, including one wig per person. He had also been in touch with the Southend (Leigh-on-Sea) Society and arranged to buy from them, for £500, the *Brigadoon* costumes which they were buying from Fox's, so that Darlington could do the show the following year instead.

By mid-July *Camelot* was cast. This time Connie Reeves was taking the part of Guenevere. Warnock Kerr, playing his first leading role in a musical, was taking the role of King Arthur which Kenneth Richardson had had the previous time, and Kenneth was playing Merlin. Steve Luck was playing a thoroughly unsympathetic part this time – that of the evil Mordred. Muriel Jones and Sam Herdman were recreating the roles they had played in the 1969 production: Morgan le Fey and King Pellinore, and a newcomer to the Society, Sue Ledger, the possessor of a pure, clear soprano voice, was cast as Nimue. The four principal knights, Sir Dinadan, Sir Clarius, Sir Lionel and Sir Sagramore were played by Cliff Walker, Ian Whitfield, Chris Noble and Keith Tate; Dorothy Walker was Lady Ann, Tom Kent was Squire Dap, and Garry Reeves took the part of the young boy, Tom of Warwick, which Mike Walker had played the last time. Barrie Dargue was the ballad singer, and little June Park, the dancer, was a Page. Judi Kent was one of the two Heralds, the other being Eileen Oliver, who had joined the Society for *The Dancing Years*. It will be apparent to the careful observer that once more there is a character missing from this list: there is no Sir Lancelot. The part was to have been played by Maurice Dobson, whose name had not been linked with the Society before, but during the summer break he dropped out and by mid-September it was crisis time again as the Committee looked in vain for a replacement. In their hour of need they once more turned to John Larsen, who declared himself not only able, but happy, to work with the company for one month. There was relief all round and rehearsals continued with the company's minds set at rest. Beneath the surface turmoil other business was under way. In her will, Lady Starmer had left her home, Danby Lodge, to the Abbeyfield Society to establish an Abbeyfield House as accommodation for the elderly in memory of Sir Charles Starmer. The cost of converting the house was estimated at around £80,000 to £90,000, and it was hoped to raise £50,000 of this by public appeal. Since the Society wanted some kind of memorial to Lady Starmer, the Committee decided to launch an appeal fund account to help with this, though, to be fair, it was really only a memorial to Sir Charles; still, at a later date, a portrait of Lady Starmer was presented by the Society to be hung in the Town Hall, so there was, in the end, a satisfactory conclusion in that there were memorials to them both. Although the Rotary Club booked the theatre on the first Saturday for a Gala Night at *Camelot* in aid of the appeal, ticket sales were otherwise disappointing, with only 60% of the seats sold before going to the box office. They were not going particularly well there, either, with only a week to go before opening night.

Camelot, which ran from 22 October to 1 November, had its fair share of incident, one way and another. The costumes for the ladies were very beautiful, particularly Connie's. One of her dresses was so beautiful that when the theatre held an 'open day' on the Sunday following the first week, a member of the public was discovered in Connie's dressing-room trying it on! The men, on the other hand, had considerable difficulty. (A personal memory stands out here, from the night of the 'costume call', for not many people can say that they have come home after visiting a friend and fallen over a suit of armour in their hallway.) The knee-joints of the armour were difficult to cope with, and the long velvet cloaks had their hems weighted with lead to make them hang as they should. It is as well that the men had their backs to the audience when the rank and file went to King Arthur and knelt to be knighted, because the extra weight, combined with the jointed knee-pieces, caused some agonized facial expressions. The idea of carrying the cloaks over the arm instead was discussed, but this idea was speedily dismissed by Joy when she inspected the back-view of some of the knights with their cloaks off: the armour covered fronts only, from knee to waist, and the tights on some of the taller men were not over-long, so it looked as though they had taken the concept of the plunge neckline and applied it to the back of the tights. The verdict was: keep the cloaks on and suffer!

The actual performance of the show brought its own problems. The special flash effect on Merlin's carriage turned out to be more of an incendiary device. A column of marching knights was simulated by employing the age-old method of having pikes nailed to a long board carried by two people, only the tops of the pikes being visible at the back of the stage (or 'upstage', as it is called in the theatre); Connie had, at one point, to exit at one side and hurry round the back to appear next time from the opposite side after a quick change of costume, and she collided with the board almost knocking herself unconscious. She was hastily picked up and dusted down, went back on stage and completed her scene looking and sounding quite normal, but without, in reality, being fully aware of what she was doing. Connie remembers that one night she completely forgot the words of one of her songs and made up a whole verse as she went along – which temporarily mesmerized Arthur Berwick who was Musical Director. Warnock, too, had an unnerving experience. As the story draws to a close, Guenevere is to enter a convent and the armies of Arthur and Lancelot are to do battle with each other. Arthur bids farewell to Guenevere and has a moving speech which he concludes by telling young Tom of Warwick to pass on to future generations the story of Camelot. Warnock had to leave the stage briefly before these events and have his armour buckled on. There was not much light at the side of the stage, but he was quickly dressed by two of his 'knights' and went on stage to say farewell to Connie. This complicated manoeuvre went remarkably well until the second Thursday night. It was when he put out his arm to put his hand under Connie's chin and raise her face that the awful realization dawned: the elbow-pieces of his armour were buckled on the wrong way round and he was quite unable to bend his arms. Within a second or two Connie realized what was wrong and had the presence of mind to lower her chin onto his hand as he reached out, but it was a nasty moment. To his eternal credit, Warnock delivered his final speech with great sincerity (and in pure Queen's English) despite the restriction in his arm movements. There was not a dry eye in the house and one can only be thankful that the audience could not hear the burst of broad Glaswegian vituperation to which Warnock gave vent as soon as he came off stage. He can laugh about it now, along with everyone else, but he did well not to be thrown off his stride at the time.

The press, of course, knew nothing of this – what a field-day they could have had – but even so the show again had mixed reviews. The *Northern Echo* pronounced it a 'magical spectacle' and '. . . a lavish show, full of vivid pageantry, costumes and sets.'[2] Kenneth was described as 'win-some'(!), Warnock as 'lovable', John as 'impressive', and Connie as 'sweet', and the critic (who *can* it have been?) loved it all. Bill Duff gave a slightly more critical review in the *Darlington & Stockton Times*. He praised the dancers and the chorus before going on to write about the principals. His only criticism of Warnock and Connie was that their voices were not powerful enough, and that the front-of-stage microphones were not much help. John, he said, was excellent, and Kenneth and Sam were splendid. Muriel Jones and Steve Luck had really got into their roles, personifying evil, and their costumes and make-up enhanced their performances. All in all he regarded the show as a '. . . colourful production, magnificently dressed and staged.'[3] The *Evening Despatch* critic was not at all impressed by *Camelot* as a show and referred to '. . . the general shoddiness of the show as historical pastiche.'[4] Though he owned that there were some fine musical numbers he concluded that 'it has anybody with a feeling for history in a continuous cringe of embarrassment' (which is all very well if one discounts the fact that most historians regard the story of King Arthur as mythical). He then added some jam to the powder. 'It is to the credit of Darlington Operatic Society,' he concluded, 'that they do as well as they do with it. Musicians, singers and dancers make the numbers go with a swing and Connie Reeves is a charming Guenevere.' Regardless of whether the press liked it or not, however, only 74.5% of the tickets were sold. The Committee braced itself for a large loss, and it was just as well, because they got it. *Camelot* cost between £13,000 and £14,000 to put on, and it lost a staggering £2,830, which turned out to be the greatest loss ever in the Society's history.

This was particularly sad because it was an entertaining show and very well performed. All in all the choice was probably justified for the reason mentioned earlier: the chances of seeing a professional company put on a show as spectacular as this in the North were negligible. The loss would take some recouping, though. The show had had, of necessity, to be chosen in haste, but the massive loss reinforced the need to cost shows very carefully. At the committee meeting following the show it was decided that careful costings should be done for the next two shows and that each department be given a budget which was not to be exceeded. At the same meeting the still-shocked Committee decided that only one show would be performed in 1982, in the autumn.

At the last committee meeting of 1980 – on 17 December – a new Ticket Secretary was appointed: the 'new boy' of two months on the Committee. The lot, as they say, fell on John Lloyd. 'Oh, and by the way,' he said to his wife on returning home after the meeting, 'you're the Assistant Ticket Secretary.' With those few words came the end of normal life as she knew it. They were both to discover that there is no such thing as 'simply' selling tickets. There are bad legs, claustrophobia, smallness of stature, tallness, impaired sight and impaired hearing to be catered for when allocating seats. There are people who ask for specific seats and there are people who are so easy-going that they leave the booking-form blank and write a note saying 'Any night will do as long as we are in the fifth (or sixth, or even back) row in the stalls' – and they enclose a blank cheque to allow for price differences. There are those who love the upper circle and those who will not sit there at any price. There are one or two people who send a cheque and leave the form completely blank, blandly assuming that the Ticket Secretary knows from the surname on the cheque exactly who they are, which night they want to attend the show, and where they want to sit. There are often bizarre exchanges on the telephone, for instance:

> 'Have you any seats in the circle for the second Wednesday?'
> 'Only restricted viewing, I'm afraid.'
> 'What does that mean?'
> 'There are supporting pillars at each side of the circle and the view is partly obstructed by them.'
> 'Oh. Well, have you any for the next night, then?'
> 'Only the same seats, I'm afraid.'
> 'And is the pillar still there?'

Or this:

> 'Have you any tickets left for the last night?'
> 'I'm sorry, there are only restricted viewing left.'
> 'And are those *facing* the stage?'

(From the theatre itself Stephen Sandford, the House Manager, came across a classic. A customer asked for two tickets and on being told that there were only single seats left asked for 'two singles together' . . .)*

Some people are also under the impression that Darlington Operatic Society's Ticket Secretary knows all about other societies' shows. He has even been asked the curtain-down time of another society's show elsewhere in County Durham. It is a great burden to be considered omniscient!

1981 opened with Committee thoughts focused on how to reduce costs while keeping up high standards. They decided to cut down on expenditure on *The Mikado* by not having car stickers to advertise it and by not

---

* All these examples are true!

having two different sizes of poster. Yet again it was resolved to abolish the tickets entitling the backstage staff to a pint of beer each night but again this minute was speedily rescinded. When Sam, as Treasurer, costed out the show, taking into account the economies, he estimated that to run it for six nights would cost £6,300 – less than half the cost of *Camelot*. Ticket prices, it was thought, need not be increased for the show, and *Brigadoon* should be costed as soon as possible so that the prices could be fixed for that. Various fund-raising activities were arranged, too. A new member, Mavis Wilson (who had sung with Sue Ledger in the Bondgate Gilbert & Sullivan Society and who was another member brought in by Cliff Walker) immediately said that she and her husband Michael would have a pâté and wine evening in the summer, after the May Treasure Hunt and before Ann and John Parker's barbecue.

By March *The Mikado* was beginning to take shape. Yum-Yum was to be played by Sue Ledger, and Connie Reeves and Mavis Wilson made up the remainder of the 'three little maids from school'. Nancy Chilver was to be Katisha and Kenneth Richardson Ko-Ko, while Sam was resurrecting and honing the Herdman sneer to play Pooh Bah again. Pish Tush was to be played by another newcomer, Ian Kirkbride – a Customs and Excise man – who was a good all-rounder, able to sing, dance and act, and who had a very good stage presence. (Ian was once asked, as a joke, to broadcast on Radio Cleveland, purporting to be a Second World War pilot, Ginger Johnson, who talked about his wartime experiences. Despite the fact that Ian was too young even to remember the war he made the character seem so real that one broadcast became a series of several, and people took him seriously and got in touch with the radio station to take issue with him on minor points. Ginger Johnson acquired the same credibility as Grace Archer for whom wreaths were sent to the BBC when the imaginary character died in a fire in *The Archers*. Ian even went so far as to appear at Darlington Show as Ginger Johnson, complete with flying-helmet and gauntlets – and got away with it.)

John Hurlstone was delighted to get the part of The Mikado. It was a role he had longed to play for years and he had, over a long period of time, practised and perfected an explosive and chilling outburst of maniacal laughter to use in the build-up to the refrain of The Mikado's only song in the piece (*A More Humane Mikado*) in the hope that he would one day play the part. (He was, in the event, lucky to be alive to play it, for during the second week of the show he was standing by a friend's broken-down car, having brought a mechanic to see to it, when a wooden packing-case lid flew off the back of a passing lorry, re-bounded off the open bonnet of the car and caught John a glancing blow on the head, knocking him out. Had it not hit the car first he could well have been very seriously injured. He still went on stage in the evening, though!)

The notable exception to the cast list was, yet again, the leading man, for no Nanki-Poo had yet been found. On 5 March they got someone from outside the Society. He turned up to begin floorwork on 11 March but refused to have any actions set for him because, he said, he did not bother with that until he was in costume. Joy insisted that she did not work that way; she liked to have everything set as soon as possible and then polish it until it was as near perfect as she could get. (This is borne out by Sue Kirkbride, formerly Sue Ledger. She and the other 'little maids' made their first entrance carrying schoolbags and had to place these on the stage at the front. At one rehearsal without these props Joy was not satisfied and sent them off again. They were almost off when they automatically returned, with one accord, picked up the imaginary schoolbags and made their exit. This is called 'conditioning'!) It would not do for Nanki-Poo, however. He flung his vocal score on the floor and walked out. Keith Tate was minding his own business and singing peaceably in the chorus at the time. Those members of the Committee who were at the rehearsal swooped upon him, and almost before he knew what was happening he had been induced to audition and was given the part on the spot, thus rescuing the Society for the second time.

Amid all these fireworks the Committee had discussed the election of a fitting President to follow Lady Starmer. One person stood out by virtue of long association with the Society and of the constant hard work which enabled it to have the excellent reputation which it enjoyed: Joy Beadell. They put it to the vote at the Annual General Meeting on 12 March and Joy was elected unanimously. Joy was very conscious of the honour and felt that she had an awesome task in following Lady Starmer, but there is no doubt that she filled the position admirably and was as much respected and loved as her predecessor.

George Todd was once more installed as Chairman and the members proceeded with the task in hand – *The Mikado*. They also gave some thought to the one show for 1982, though there was a possibility that a concert might be given as part of the opening activities for the new Arts Centre which had been set up in the old Teachers' Training College building in Vane Terrace.

Two weeks before *The Mikado* opened 84% of the tickets had been sold, so things were looking promising; *Brigadoon*, however, was to run for ten nights rather than six, and was going to cost about £12,000. Ticket prices had not been raised for *The Mikado* so for *Brigadoon* they went up to £2.75, and to £3 for the Saturdays, with the usual concessions. An experiment

The Mikado 1981.
Left to right: Ian Kirkbride, Keith Tate, Sam Herdman.

would also be tried: the theatre was to be given 50 good seats and 50 restricted viewing seats to sell for each night.

At last, at a specially-called meeting, the show for 1982 was chosen, together with two shows for 1983; *Kismet* would be given in 1982 for ten nights, and they would try out a week-long run of *Mame* in early 1983 with *The Arcadians* for a ten-night run in autumn. Or so they thought. Two weeks after the meeting at which this was decided the news came through that Schwarz and Tebelak's *Godspell* was to be released to amateurs. It might be advantageous to produce such a show in the spring rather than just a concert and, since it did not require very elaborate costumes and scenery, it should not be too expensive to put it on for just a week. Bill Jones hastened to investigate.

Meanwhile *The Mikado* had been a roaring success with the public – 98% of the seats had been sold. The press also voted it a hit. The *Northern Echo* did not so much review it as report it, but called it 'quite a lavish production'[5] and mentioned that there were some 'new ideas' in it (Joy had made the entr'acte into a ballet, 'Yum-Yum's Dream Ballet'). The paper added that Sue Ledger was a sweet Yum-Yum and the rest of the cast supported her and Keith Tate superbly. The *Evening Despatch* said that the whole of the production worked very well and that the company did '. . . an all but professional job which allows the charming absurdity of [the] opera to come across at full strength.'[6] Margot Whiting wrote the review for the *Darlington & Stockton Times*. She had not only seen the show 'countless times'[7] but had sung in it herself, and she was most enthusiastic about this production. It was a pity, though, that since the show was only on for a week her review appeared on the day of the last performance – the other 2% of the tickets might have been sold on the strength of it! She referred to the company as '. . . a group of amateurs whose perform-ance was anything but amateur and who gave the whole show that unstinting joy and enthusiasm and sheer affection that no professional company could ever achieve.' She added that everything about the show was 'sheer delight'. Kenneth Richardson was 'a Ko-Ko to remember' and Sam Herdman's Pooh-Bah 'one of the funniest I have seen', and they both sang superbly. Keith Tate was described as 'that happy combination of good looks and good singing' – which must surely have brought maiden blushes to his cheeks! Sue Ledger was 'enchanting' in every way and Nancy Chilver was 'splendidly menacing', interpreting exactly the Gilbert & Sullivan conception of Katisha as a character whom one could hate and love at the same time. John Hurlstone's rendering of The Mikado was eminently successful and Ian Kirkbride's characterization of Pish-Tush was greatly admired. Perhaps, in retrospect, it could have been run for ten nights – after all, a good many of the 98% of seats sold would have been restricted viewing. Still, it was done now, and Sam was eventually able to report that it had shown a surplus of £1,076, which went over a third of the way to making up the loss on *Camelot*. More good news followed: Bill Jones had managed to book *Godspell* for the spring – to be performed for a week – so the outlook was somewhat more prom-ising. Disaster was never far away, though. Just as the renting of a new props store was being negotiated the old one was burned down and the Society lost a great many items, most of them irreplaceable, and Ernie Mann lost some of his tools. The props were insured, it is true, but placing a value on many of the items was extremely difficult.* It made up the Committee's minds, however; the new props store, owned by Burts of Gladstone Street, would have to be used and the essential roof repairs would have to be done as soon as possible. They could at least be thankful that there *was* a replacement props store available – considering the

---

* Among the items incinerated were the treasured menus from Maxims which had been used in *Gigi* in 1978.

John Beagle

difficulty the Society had had over the years with this storage problem, even before this latest disaster, they had been very lucky. But luck often breeds luck, they say, and this held true. Homburg's were interested in buying the *Brigadoon* costumes, so they offered to provide the four extra costumes (for dancers) needed for that show, plus the whole wardrobe for *Kismet*, free of charge in exchange. This was a good deal as there would be a lot of exotic costumes needed for *Kismet*. A producer had also been found for *Godspell*. Joy was not available but Bill Jones had heard good reports about Paul Kerryson, a lively young producer/director from Manchester Library Theatre, who had appeared in the show in the West End and on tour. Paul was fortunately free and the Committee snapped him up. John Beagle was willing to be Musical Director. To add icing to the cake Tom Kent had been to the NODA National Conference where he was presented with the Owen Peacock Memorial Trophy as winner of the NODA Souvenir Programme Competition for the *Mikado* programme, and one of the performances of the show had been recorded and was to be broadcast on Radio Cleveland on New Year's Day 1982.

It was no good becoming smug, though. There was still most of the previous year's loss to be made up, and five days before the opening of *Brigadoon* there were still 2,000 of the 6,000 seats left unsold; the Committee began to discuss the possibility of running autumn shows, like the spring ones, for only six nights. There was plenty to think about; the Society was to give a concert in February in aid of the British Diabetic Association, to buy an Argon Laser. There was also *Godspell* to be considered.

It was fortunate that the older members of the Society would be kept occupied with the concert because *Godspell* was going to be a show containing mostly the very young, and it was hoped that this would serve an added purpose by attracting new young members. *Godspell* required only fourteen people including a backing-group of singers, and in the end nine of them were teenagers. Paul Kerryson arranged the auditions himself. In the normal run of things, to enter the Society the prospective member has to do an audition in front of the whole Committee. This consists of singing a song of the candidate's own choice, and what is sought is someone who can sing in tune and have enough power in the voice to be able to make a significant contribution to the strength of the chorus. One would think that this would go without saying, but it is surprising how many people turn up to auditions with nothing prepared, or unable to hold a tune, or with a voice which is barely audible. Increasingly now, though, although they are accepted or rejected according to the quality of the voice, members cannot just get away with singing *or* dancing *or* acting. They have to be able, to a greater or lesser extent, to do all three. (For instance, for *Anything Goes*, in autumn 1994, most of the cast members were required to be able to tap-dance. Some of them had to learn from scratch and a good deal of perspiration and concentration was expended by a great many people. The town practically echoed with the sound of tapping feet and muffled swearing as steps went wrong!) For the *Godspell* auditions Paul wanted each prospective cast member to sing a song from the show and also to perform a piece which would show all facets of his or her talent. They had to have personality, versatility and a great deal of stamina, and an item was printed in the *Evening Despatch* inviting people over sixteen to audition.

While all this organization was going on the cast of *Brigadoon* had rehearsed assiduously and were in good form to open the show on 28 October. The two sisters, Fiona and Jean MacKeith, were played by Sue Ledger and Kath Robinson, with Sam Herdman as their father, the role he had played in 1960. Chris Noble was Charlie Cameron, Jean's fiancé. The two Americans were Barrie Dargue as Tommy, and Ian Kirkbride as Jeff. The comical, man-hunting Meg Brockie was played by June Aiken who tortured her hair with wire into sticking-out pigtails in the cause of her art. The maladjusted Harry Ritchie was Steve Luck. Jane Ashton, Tommy's girlfriend-back-home, was Mavis Wilson, and Mr Murdoch, the village elder, was played by Kenneth Richardson who had been in the chorus last time. Mollie Moor, who had played Fiona in the 1960 production, was acting as prompter for this show, as was Eunicé Cockburn – it is one of the pleasing features of the Society that many people who have played a lot of leading roles are still willing to help out with prompting, dressing, selling programmes, or working as stage crew. The photographs for the programme were taken at the Toytop picnic area near Richmond, causing a certain amount of disquiet to picnickers who had gone out for a peaceful afternoon and were rather startled to find a local invasion of persons in kilts, flitting round and peeping out of bushes, with bits of heather stuck in their hats.

Only 82% of the tickets were sold for the show – it would have needed

Brigadoon 1981 – Chorus. *See page xi for full list.*

90% to break even – but there were a few more Vice-Presidents and Patrons than for *The Mikado*. The *Evening Despatch* did not review the show but the paper did print a preview to whet the public's appetite, stressing the '. . . lavish costumes, the attractive sets, the sword dancing and even a Scottish piper.'[8] (This job was undertaken by the Middleton brothers, Arthur and Tony, who took turns.) After the first night the *Northern Echo* proclaimed the show 'a happy choice'[9] and commended, in particular, the performances of Barrie Dargue and Sue Ledger, and of Ian Kirkbride and June Aiken. It also wrote in admiring vein of the look and sound of the whole piece. The *Darlington & Stockton Times* went further. It was, it said, '. . . the ideal tonic to banish the blues on a cold winter's night.'[10] Ken Jackson went on to say of Joy's direction '. . . it is her professionalism and vision of how the musical should and does appear to the audience which makes it as good as the efforts of many professional societies.' He gave good reviews to all of the principals and special mentions to Sam ('tackles his role with ease and professionalism'), Chris Noble ('his singing voice comes over very well, especially in the tender, slow ballads') and Steve Luck ('gives the best performance I have seen from him'). Mention was made by both the reviewers of the dry-ice effect and of the cost of the carbon dioxide used – £30 per night. One night it must have seemed that the stage crew used much more than the night's quota in the scene where Harry Ritchie tries to run away from Brigadoon and is hunted

Brigadoon 1981
Barrie Dargue, Sue Ledger.

down and killed. Great clouds of icy fog rolled across the stage, enveloping the orchestra, the first five rows of the stalls, and also the fugitive, who could not be seen by the audience. Neither could he be seen by his pursuers – they only knew where he was because they saw it at rehearsals! John Lloyd, who played McGregor, did not have an easy time during the show, for when Harry was 'killed', John had to carry him onto the stage by himself before handing him over to four others who placed him on his grassy bier. He practised at home by carrying his wife round the living-room, which gave the neighbours food for thought, but in those days she weighed ten stone, while Steve was around thirteen stone. It made a lot of difference. John had to stand holding Steve as 'deadweight' for a short while before handing him over and as a result lost several pounds in weight over the ten nights.

By the end of the run it looked as though, once the financial side of the show was worked out, there would be a surplus of over £500, which gave an added fillip to the antics at the after-show party at which Keith Tate, Ian Kirkbride and Mike Walker enhanced the usual cabaret by giving a somewhat ribald version of the song *The Heather on the Hill*. Suffice it to say that Keith, dressed in drag, was Heather, and there was much laughter. What is more, a jokey reference had been made during the show to the coach-hire company Ellerman Beeline, and they had sent a donation, which was very gratefully received.

The Society divided the surplus made on the show between the Mayor's Fund, the Samaritans, the NSPCC, and St John of God's Hospital, and continued with the plans for 1982. The final auditions for *Godspell* were held in January and Paul Kerryson was pleased with the casting. By February there was good news and bad news. The good news was that the concert, *When Vienna Sings*, in aid of the Argon Laser, had done exceptionally well, and the Society raised more than £1,200 for it. The bad news was that Teesside Operatic Society planned to give *Kismet* in the spring of 1983 and they felt that a production at Darlington only a few months earlier could well affect their box office receipts. Because Teesside had been granted their licence-to-perform earlier than Darlington, Darlington had to step down gracefully and choose another show. Since the costumes from Homburg's would be free because of the exchange for the *Brigadoon* ones, the Committee decided that a show on the same scale of lavishness as *Kismet* would have to be given, so they chose *King's Rhapsody*. They also hastened to book *Mame* for spring 1983 lest they be forestalled again. The other piece of news was much worse. Just a few days before he was due to take part in the Argon Laser concert, Kenneth Richardson died very suddenly at the age of only 61. The *Evening Despatch* printed a piece about him, calling him 'The Man of Many Faces' – he had probably appeared on the theatre's stage more times than any other man. Joy Beadell, in an interview for that article, said, 'He was one of the best actors we have had or ever will have. He could play drama or musicals, which is not very usual. He was a wonderful actor.'[11] He was sorely missed by everyone in the Society, and it is a fitting tribute to him that his name lives on in the Kenneth Richardson Memorial Trust. The Society also refurbished the foyer and dressing rooms at the Civic Theatre in his memory for the theatre's 75th Anniversary.

Kenneth's was the fourth in a series of deaths, for Shirley Dodd's father Neville had also died during the year as had Emily Hardy, who had been in the Society since 1945 as a chorus member and also on the Ladies' Committee. Lorrie Boddy's husband, Fred, had died early in 1981, so four loyal and longstanding members were now gone in just over one year. Like all other actors, though, their motto would have been 'The show must go on'.

The cast of *Godspell* pressed on until March, when two of the young men in the cast dropped out. With such a small and young cast this could have proved to be a further disaster. They even considered cancelling the show, but this would have been a terrible waste when the cast had been rehearsing so hard and when Terry Coleman (of the Civic Theatre) and Ray Porteus had already put in so much work on constructing a set. Nevertheless, things were looking most insecure; only 1,000 of the 7,000 seats had been sold (there was to be a matinée) just one month before the show opened.

Peter Cutchie would bear the brunt of the problems since he had become the new Chairman when George Todd handed over to him in March and finally stepped down from committee work after 23 years of service. George had been Chairman three times, Property Master for five years, Secretary for nine years, and Ticket Secretary for several productions. He had also done a lot of work for NODA, of which he was now an Honorary Life Member.

Gradually things were righted, though. Paul Kerryson had auditioned a boy named Geoff Stevens who lived at Billingham. He was seventeen and was at the Stockton/Billingham Technical College preparing to enter the Guildford School of Acting and Dance. So he joined the cast, while Paul himself undertook to play the part of Judas. In fact, Paul made his 1,000th appearance in *Godspell* during the Darlington run of the show. He was versatile, easy to get on with, and injected enormous enthusiasm into the cast, bringing much relief all round.

Bill Jones had meanwhile made all the arrangements for *King's Rhapsody*, with the same costume deal from Homburg's as had been agreed for *Kismet*. He had also managed to get the scenery for it from Stagesets using the deposit sent for *Kismet* and had secured the performing rights for *Mame* for spring 1983. The big task now would be to sell *Godspell*, which would not be everybody's cup of tea. In spite of all efforts only 68% of the tickets were sold in the end, though a number of those were sold to people who came back to see it for a second – and even a third – time, for it turned out to be a superb show. Paul had put many original ideas into it, both serious and funny, and he got the mixture just right. True, only 116 Vice-Presidents and Patrons supported it, whereas 198 had given donations during *Brigadoon*, but it was hoped that the absentees would return for *King's Rhapsody*, which was more in the tradition of the Society. The costumes and scenery for *Godspell* had not been expensive and some of the cast bought their costumes from the Society at half price at the end of the run. Furthermore the scenery was being stored in the new props store with a view to hiring it out – Paul Kerryson himself started the ball rolling by asking to hire it for two separate weeks. It seems a pity that *Godspell* did not reach a wider audience, though quite a lot of the tickets were sold after the first two of the reviews appeared. The *Northern Echo* called it an 'excellent effort' and 'a very vibrant production' and said that it was clever and well mimed with some nice topical touches. John Beagle's four-piece band had put in some 'very hard and skilful work'.[12] The *Evening Despatch* pointed out that it is a sign of a show's success when a stream of smiling people come away humming the songs, and though by this measure alone this *Godspell* was successful the production scored on many other counts. Paul had brought the script up to date so that it was 'as fresh as the original'. The timing was 'simply excellent' and the show was 'never preaching but certainly not irreverent'.[13] As that reviewer pointed out, it was not a vehicle for anyone to star in – it relied on the characters interacting – but Ken Jackson, in the *Darlington & Stockton Times*, could not help but pick out Steve Luck for his portrayal of the 'Jesus' character, for Steve had excelled himself. Ken Jackson confessed to having something in common with many others: prejudgement of the show. He expected not to enjoy it and that it was just going to be 'an irreverent piece of hokum'. 'Thankfully,' he said, 'I was proved wrong, and no doubt many older people in the audience were, too.'[14] This turned out to be true. The vitality and zest of the company was so infectious that it was impossible not to be carried along with it, and it really did come across as a marvellous piece of theatre. Of the core members of the Society only Kath Robinson, Steve Luck and Mike Walker were in the cast, with Janet Cooke (Betty's daughter, now Janet Watson) and Kim Keeler (now Kim Oldham) in the backing group. Sadly, none of the other cast members stayed with the Society, though they were very talented, but some who were teenagers hoped to go into higher education, which would take them away from the town, like Sarah Goddard, Donald Beaverstock and Jonathan Keighley. Carol Burton, Rosemarie Dodd, Jill Rowcroft and Geoffrey Stevens lived out of town to begin with, and the next show, *King's Rhapsody*, would not be Chris Thorns's cup of tea. So the Society lost most of them, but it had been good experience for them, it had been great to have them around, and they certainly livened things up!

Despite the relatively low attendance *Godspell* did show a surplus of nearly £700, which was one in the eye for the sceptics. The question now was: would *King's Rhapsody*, the antithesis of *Godspell*, do as well? The company began the singing rehearsals.

Andrew Jowett had by now left the Civic Theatre and gone to Warwick, and that spring William McDonald was appointed as the new Director. He seemed keen to keep up a good relationship with the Society, and he and Bill Jones came to an agreement about the cost of the hire of the theatre and the price of the tickets; the Committee also agreed that William should attend committee meetings when appropriate.

Ticket prices were altered slightly for *King's Rhapsody*. The standard price was £3, the same as for *Godspell*, but the final night would be £3.50, and the concessionary prices, which had been lowered from £2.25 to £2 for *Godspell*, would now rise to £2.40. It was a constant juggling act to try to balance ticket prices with show costs, and of course the show was running for nine nights instead of ten, or six, or six plus a matinée – complicated stuff.

Mame was still on line for spring 1983 but *The Arcadians* had come to grief. Quite simply, the members of the Society did not want to do it – well, perhaps nymphs *were* a bit *passé* – so the Committee decided to re-run *The Music Man*; although it had lost money last time, the intervening nineteen years might have altered its fortunes.

The summer passed quite peaceably, apart from a jolt over the very high price of props hire for *King's Rhapsody*, but Bill Jones settled that, and got the bill reduced from nearly £1,500 to just over £1,100. The show was short on publicity because the posters were not printed soon enough, and the Committee felt that the show should have appeared in some of the theatre's advertising material. The cast was completed in September by the addition of John Hurlstone to play Count Egon Stanieff, and Steve Luck and Eunicé Cockburn were playing Nikki and Cristiane. Mavis Wilson was Marta Karillos and Nancy Chilver returned to play Countess Vera Lemainken. Shirley Dodd and Sam Herdman were playing the roles they had played in 1965: Queen Elena and Vanescu, while Simon Cutchie, Peter and Rowena's eight-year-old son, would play the boy-king, just before their move to Warwick. Eunicé counted herself lucky to be able to take part after she and Jeff were involved in a very bad car accident when on their way to the South of France for their summer holiday. Eunicé recovered comparatively quickly, but Jeff had to undergo several operations on his arm and hand. Considering the severity of the accident both of them were lucky to be alive.

Another piece of good fortune concerned the *Godspell* scenery. It had been hired out to the societies at Buxton, Harrogate, Sunderland, Scarborough and Lincoln, and was finally sold, so it had more than paid for itself.

A week before *King's Rhapsody* about 70% of the tickets had been sold, but it was becoming clear that it was going to lose money. For one thing, an extra expense had been incurred by the necessity of having a professional flyman, because it was a very heavy show to stage. It was also a very long show – three acts – and as soon as the first night was over the problems from this became apparent. The show ran past 10.15 p.m., so that overtime payments had to be made to the orchestra. Cuts were made in the show, but of course this entailed the removal of lines as well as parts of songs, so some people who had minor speaking roles were bereft of these altogether, which caused considerable anguish. So the Committee decided to restore the lines, pay up, and look pleasant!

In the end, only 80% of the tickets were sold, so the takings were just over £13,000 gross, and it lost nearly £2,300. It had mixed reviews, which were unanimous in their opinion that it had been a courageous under-taking and that Steve had played his part exceptionally well. The *Darlington & Stockton Times* said that Shirley was 'first class' and that Mavis had captured the character of Marta Karillos 'to perfection'.[15] Eunicé, as always, had been a good leading lady, and Sam Herdman and John Hurlstone had been as reliable as ever; there was a special mention of Mark Lawrence, a young black dancer, who showed superlative ability and agility in his role as the Tartar Chief in the Mu-ranian ballet sequence, but the chorus was weak in places, and the brass section of the orchestra came in for some criticism. The Society has not given an Ivor Novello show since.

King's Rhapsody 1982
Shirley Dodd.

To sweeten the pill the Commit-tee did gain a great deal of pleasure at the meeting following the show, on 11 November, for it was then that Bill Jones read out the letter from the solicitors dealing with the affairs of Kenneth Richardson's mother, informing him of her be-quest to the Society of the money to set up a fund in memory of Kenneth, to help with the vocal training of young members. The Committee *gave* pleasure, too, by making George Todd an Honorary Life Member of the Society.

Late in the year *Mame*, which was to run for six nights, was causing some anxiety. Through all sorts of fund-raising efforts, the Society had managed to remain in the black over the year, but the costs for *Mame* had reached a level where it would be difficult to cover them except by excessive ticket price increases. Costume hire was one of the big items – though Steve Luck was designing some of them for Homburg's to pro-vide – and whoever played Mame would alone have eighteen changes.

Eventually it was decided that the opportunity to do the show was too good to miss. Savings could be made here and there, and ticket prices could be raised a little, to reduce the inevitable loss. This is where a pattern begins to show: the talk is not of making profit at this stage, but of minimizing loss – costs for everything were rocketing and there was a dip in the audience attendance figures. Interestingly, the Vice-President and Patron numbers were not fluctuating very much, except, understandably, for *Godspell*. *The Dancing Years* attracted 210, *Camelot* 191, *The Mikado* 189, *Brigadoon* 198, *Godspell* 116, and *King's Rhapsody* 189, but of course the levels of the standard donations (£2 and £1) had been the same for many years, and, indeed, are still the same now. Ticket prices, at any rate, had to go up, and were raised, in most cases, by 25p. In the mean time Dorothy Walker and Ian Kirkbride (both newly elected to the Committee since Warnock Kerr and Peter Cutchie had left it) would have to dream up some good ideas for publicity.

The end of the year had once more brought doleful news: the death, on the last Friday of *King's Rhapsody*, of Ken Bodden. He had been a faithful member of the Society for 28 years and had served on the Committee for fifteen of those years. He had been Chairman twice (and been Ticket Secretary for 22 shows) as well as producing and playing roles, and, like Kenneth Richardson, he would be remembered with affection.

The first thing to do in 1983 was to cast *Mame* and book everything for *The Music Man*. The lead in *Mame* went to Connie Reeves, with Shirley Dodd as her 'bosom buddy' Vera Charles, and Kath Robinson as the mouse-like Agnes Gooch who eventually blossoms more like a peony than a rose. John Lloyd was to be the tight-fisted killjoy banker Dwight Babcock, a part which his fond family, as is their wont, cruelly remarked required no acting ability on his part whatsoever! Chris Noble was playing his son, the awful Dwight Junior. Young Patrick, the ten-year-old nephew of Mame, was played by twelve-year-old Melvyn Dawson, son of Edith and Fred, and the grown-up version of Patrick was played by Steve Blain, the transformation being effected by the ingenious use of a stage-revolve. Avril Blain played Pegeen, who becomes Patrick's wife by the end of the show, and a bright little boy called Paul Dodds played the cameo role of Patrick and Pegeen's son in the last scene. Ito, Mame's Japanese servant, was Mike Walker, and other roles were played by Joan Kirkwood, Sue Robinson, Greta Sanderson, Mavis Wilson, June Aiken, Ian Kirkbride, John Hacking, Sam Herdman and Ian Whitfield. It was a promising cast, which lacked only two members: the male lead, Beauregard Burnside, and his horrible old mother. When these last two were found they complemented a very good cast, for Eileen Young came back to be a tiny but formidable Mother Burnside, and Ken Horsley, a member of Billingham Upstairs Theatre, was imported to play Beauregard. He had played leading roles in musicals and had guested for Middlesbrough Operatic Society, as well as being a member of the Billingham Barber Shop Quartet.

Once *Mame* was cast and Joy and John Beagle had got the rehearsals into the familiar pattern, it was time to think about shows for 1984. *No, No, Nanette* was mentioned, as well as *How to Succeed . . .* (again), *The King and I* and *The Quaker Girl*, but finally a repeat of *The Gondoliers* was chosen for the spring, and *Orpheus in the Underworld* for the autumn.

Then came the Annual General Meeting in early March. At a meeting which lasted two and a half hours Tom Kent, as Chairman, told the members of the massive costs of producing shows and urged them once more to make every effort to sell tickets, to attend the social functions, and to attract more members. Bill Jones reinforced this, and Sam Herdman went still further, impressing on the members that the Society did not have limitless funds and also that what *was* in reserve was now earning less, owing to lower interest rates. He was grateful that there was a Social Account which had supplemented the funds, but Customs and Excise had informed him that VAT should be paid on that, as well as on the General Account. Jim Willans, who was still there like a guardian angel, although no longer an active member of the Society, was worried about the cost of commission on tickets sold by the theatre, but the answer really was to have the members sell more tickets and to publicize the address and telephone number of the Ticket Secretary to encourage the public to contact him for seats. (They did try this by having a 'booking form' printed in a local free paper, the *South Durham & North Yorkshire Times*.) Joy, as President, had some interesting things to say. She felt that changes had occurred over the last ten years and that the Society did not have the talent which had abounded then. She stressed the fact that theatre was an important creative art and that ten years previously there was a great deal of competition for parts. Not only that, but members also tried to improve on the talents they had by taking lessons where necessary. She also mentioned that the stage and props crews had helped out with professional shows at the theatre and gained valuable experience that way. She, too, urged members to sell more tickets. In view of the recent losses perhaps the pep-talk was timely for the newer members, and perhaps it also inspired them to see five long-service awards presented: to Peggy Todd for 40 years, to Greta and Bernard Sanderson and Bill Jones for 35 years, and to Sue Robinson for 25 years. (Later in the year Cecil Grieveson and Margaret Hardaker got their awards for completing 35 years.)

By mid-March it was clear that the cost-cuts that had been hoped for for *Mame* had not materialized. So far only 55% of the tickets had been sold – the public was suspicious of a show that, in the main, they knew nothing about – and the Committee would have to grit their teeth and brace themselves for a heavy loss. What a shame it was that there was no such thing as a press *preview!* The first two nights sold badly but once the first review appeared the tickets began to sell well – though of course they were sold from the theatre, so commission had to be paid. If the *Darlington & Stockton Times* review could have appeared the morning the show opened to the public it might well have been a sell-out instead of the 94% it actually achieved. For *Mame* was a smash hit. The *Darlington & Stockton Times* headline read 'If you can get a seat tonight, go and see this barnstorming *Mame*.'[16] The review went on to call it a 'bubbling cocktail', and said of the cast 'They get through adrenalin like it was going out of fashion.' Fashion was the operative word – the costumes were as wonderful as the ones for *Gigi* had been (though one or two of the wigs left something to be desired). Connie was the perfect Mame – she looked good, had a strong voice, and was well able to handle the comedy. Melvyn Dawson gave a remarkable performance, for Patrick is a very big part to play, and he played it with immense confidence, reacting very well to the other characters, and not being put off by the fact that Connie was his French teacher at Hummersknott Comprehensive School! The *Darlington & Stockton Times* would have liked to mention more individual perform-ances but lacked the space, though Shirley Dodd and Kath Robinson did get a special mention. The *Evening Despatch* agreed wholeheartedly. 'If you can still get tickets . . . grab them,'[17] said the critic, and followed this remark with one which mirrored the philosophy of the Committee exactly: 'otherwise you'll miss a rare opportunity to see the excitement and spectacle of a show which most professional companies could not afford.' As well as praising Connie, the review also singled out Melvyn, Kath and Shirley, but said that, overall, the show was '. . . a strong team effort with every department – singers, dancers, actors and musicians – offering 100% enthusiasm.' (The *Northern Echo*'s review was brief and vague, but this was not surprising since the critic was only there for the last fifteen minutes of the show.) It was very gratifying for the cast to know that their efforts were appreciated. Connie, in particular, had had a difficult time, not least with all the costume changes which were so speedy that they had to be done at the side of the stage with the help of Elsie Campbell. Elsie lost a false tooth in the process when she snapped it off in her haste to pinch together a hook which had come apart; time was too short to look for pliers, but teeth are not really designed to mould metal, and Elsie paid the price. Connie was very touched when the stage crew spent a lot of their valuable time constructing a little box of a changing room with a light in it at the side of the stage, to make one aspect of her role easier for her. Nothing, however, could prevent her from having an uncomfortable time in other ways. She suffered multiple contusions on various parts of her anatomy. During the show-within-a-show number, *The Man in the Moon is a Lady*, a crescent moon was suspended above the stage and Connie, as Mame playing the part of the 'Moon Lady', had to sit on it. She was supposed to look somewhat unstable but at the same time be 'acting' for all she was worth. She was supported by a nine-inch-wide wooden board fixed to the back of the crescent, which was all well and good to sit on but which scraped her legs horribly when she had to pretend to lose her balance. (The battery-pack stuffed down the back of her knickers to power her radio-microphone did not make for ease and comfort, either!) Fortunately, the incident at the dress rehearsal when she *did* lose her balance and slipped right round to hang under the crescent, displaying the Reeves underwear to the auditorium, was not repeated during the run of the show, but the massive bruising and scrapes on her legs took some time to heal.

Kath Robinson also suffered injury. After the transformation of her character from frumpishness to glamour, which incidentally produced a *very* startling contrast, she had to sashay down a long staircase wearing very high heels. She stumbled and fell one night but carried on as though nothing had happened even though she had torn the ligaments in her thigh. There were no understudies, of course, and in any case the part of Agnes Gooch is arguably one of the best portrayals Kath has ever done; she continued to play the role but at the end of the run her thigh was all colours of the rainbow and it was some time before she made a full recovery.

Chris Noble and Mike Walker had to put up with a good deal of teasing. Chris remembers that, as Junior Babcock, he had to smoke a cigarette – and Chris was always an avid anti-smoker. At the after-show party he was presented with a packet of cigarettes 'for performance over and above the call of duty'. Mike was teased unmercifully because of his hair – or lack of it. Although only young he was what would be called, in this age of political correctness, 'follically challenged', and the thick black wig he wore as Ito, Mame's Japanese servant, probably afforded him more hair than he had ever had in his life! However, he gave a bravura performance and for some time the company, when convened, would perform what they called 'mass Ito impressions', trying to reproduce the giggle which he had perfected for the part.

Mame was a wonderful show and the questions that hovered over the Committee were: 'Could we have run it for ten nights in view of the number of people who tried to get tickets when there were no more available?' 'Would it have made money with a longer run?' Many people who had seen it had wanted to come again and could not get in. It was irritating, because *Mame* did lose a lot of money – over £1,500 – though, of course, this was £800 less than the loss on *King's Rhapsody*. Still, it was over now, and too late for regrets.

It was decided, after *Mame*, that a different ticket price experiment would be used for *The Music Man*. Though the general price would remain at £3.25 (£3.50 for the final night), children would be admitted for £2.50 for the first three nights instead of just the first night, and the same would go for OAPs, their price dropping from £2.75 to £2.50 in the hope of attracting more of them. There would also be a concession of 25p per ticket for blocks of ten or more, except for the final night.

Already there was a problem with the show scheduled for autumn 1984. *Orpheus in the Underworld* was to be given in Stockton in the spring, so the Committee decided upon a repeat of *My Fair Lady* for the autumn instead of *Orpheus*. *The Gondoliers* remained all set for spring, with Arthur Berwick as Musical Director this time. John Beagle felt that he wanted a break before returning to do *My Fair Lady*.

July brought some good news and some bad. The good news was that, though there had been ongoing problems with the latest props store, a new one had been found, unexpectedly quickly, behind the Foresters Hall in Northgate, and a group of volunteers led by Ray Porteus Senior and George Aiken were to repair and decorate it after the show. Also lots of social events were taking place and, since the pep-talk at the Annual General Meeting, were being well supported. *The Music Man* was cast, and the appropriate bookings of scenery and so on had been made for both *The Gondoliers* and *My Fair Lady*, so all was taken care of for the shows in the foreseeable future. The bad news was that Ernie Mann and Bob Jarratt resigned from the props staff, Ernie owing to ill-health (his own and Fran's), and Bob because of family commitments (he had married Liz Fern, a widowed hospital social worker with two young sons, just the previous year). Bob also resigned from the Committee, but both he and Ernie did manage to turn up to help backstage at many future shows, without having to make the absolute commitment which had been necessary when they were Property Master and Deputy Property Master. By way of thanks for all his work over the years Ernie was made an Honorary Life Member of the Society. During the summer Steve Blain was persuaded to take over as Property Master and George Aiken (who had by now got his son, Stephen, drawn in to work backstage, just as Mavis Wilson had inveigled her husband, Michael) was poised to saturate the town with publicity.

A week before the opening of *The Music Man* about two-thirds of the tickets had been sold and the company hoped fervently that the show would be a great success, though there were some last-minute things to be put right. One difficulty had at least been solved already, though. History was repeating itself for Sam Herdman. The last time *The Music Man* had been performed, in 1964, Sam had changed roles from being Mayor Shinn to being Marcellus Washburn when the actor who was to play Washburn moved away from the area. This time, at two weeks' notice, he took over the role of Charlie Cowell, the anvil salesman, when Cliff Walker, who was to play the part for the second time, fell ill and had to drop out. Sam had been looking forward to taking life easy, as he had just retired as regional secretary of the National Association of Master Bakers, but it was not to be. It was just as well that he had some extra free time in which to learn his lines!

Another difficulty concerned a piano which had been sold to the Society and was to be played on stage by Brigitte Freeman, who was cast as Amaryllis. At the first dress rehearsal it was found to be a full semitone down in pitch, and a piano tuner had to make a mercy-dash the following day to put it right. (The piano tuner – Gavin Atkins – swore he had heard that a Broadwood cottage piano, which was also to be used in the show to represent a pianola and which was borrowed from the Police Social Club, was wheeled on a trolley to the theatre with a flashing blue light on top, but this story may be apocryphal . . .)

If, as they say, a bad dress rehearsal makes for a good show then *The Music Man* should have been a winner. Joy liked to have two dress rehearsals, on the Monday and Tuesday, ready for the Wednesday opening. On this occasion the first one lasted till midnight and the second till 11 p.m. before she was satisfied.

Connie Reeves was playing Marian Paroo the librarian, with Joan Kirkwood as her mother, and Ken Horsley was back again to play opposite Connie as Harold Hill. This time John Parker was playing Mayor Shinn (and managed not only to look and act like an elderly man, but to sound like one, too, though the rest of the cast were amazed that his vocal cords held out under the strain of the assumed voice for the whole run). Christine Murray and Janet Steel were playing his daughters, Zaneeta and Gracie, with Steve Luck as Tommy Djilas, Zaneeta's boyfriend. Ian Kirkbride was playing the lively Marcellus Washburn, and June Aiken was his partner – as Ethel Toffelmeier ('the pianola girl'). The barbershop quartet of schoolboard members consisted of John Hacking, John Hurlstone, Bernard Sanderson and Andrew Taylor (the counter-tenor from Teesside), with Shirley Dodd and Dorothy Walker playing the wives of two of them. Three Society members were playing the roles they had played in 1964. Bernard was one, and the other two were Sue Robinson as the Mayor's wife, Eulalie MacKechnie Shinn, and Eileen Young as Mrs Squires. The *Northern Echo*, in a preview, cruelly pointed out that between them they had '110 years active service on the stage'.[18] Paul Dodds and Melvyn Dawson were undergoing role-reversal, because this time Paul was playing a leading role, as Winthrop Paroo, and Melvyn was understudying him. But this show was really a family affair. Tom and Judi Kent were both in the chorus, their son Jonathan was call-boy and their daughter Zoë was understudying the role of Amaryllis. Amaryllis, of course, was played by Brigitte Freeman and her mother, Tricia, was dancing. Brigitte's brother, Patrick, was among the cast of children. Kath Porteus, Tricia's mother, was one of the matrons to the children, looking after them backstage. So were Paul Dodds's mother Margaret and Jennifer Hird, mother of Richard Boucher who was dancing. Greta Sanderson was also a matron, and as well as Bernard, her husband, her three sons were involved: Peter in the chorus,

The Music Man 1983
Ken Horsley.

Stephen stage managing, and Nick crewing. The only reason her daughter-in-law Frances was not there was because she had recently had her second baby. Ann Parker was not in the show but the Parkers' daughter, Emma, was another of the children, along with Sue Hewgill's younger daughter Joy, Michael and Mavis Wilson's daughter Helen, and Martin, son of Sue Ledger who had by now married Ian Kirkbride. It is all very involved but it shows how people are caught up and gathered in!

How did this family affair go? Very well, according to the press reports. No one from the *Evening Despatch* was able to be present, but the paper had published two pieces about the show before it opened. The *Northern Echo* outlined the story and said 'a bigger load of frivolous tosh you could hardly hope for' but added '. . . in the hands of the Darlington Operatic

Society it is a joyous and dazzling spectacle of a show . . . At times it is difficult to remember that this is an amateur show.'[19] All of the performances, the *Echo* thought, were hard to fault. The *Darlington & Stockton Times* enjoyed it, too, and gave excellent write-ups to Ken and Connie, Steve and Christine, and John Parker and Sue Robinson. The paper particularly liked the opening scene in the train, in which the men created the rhythm of the train movement using the dialogue (very difficult to do successfully), and Sue Robinson's wonderful comic ladies' dancing troupe (Eileen, June, Dorothy and Shirley). The ordinary dancing was done with great precision, too, the *76 Trombones* number and the dance in the library being especially memorable. There were some complaints, mainly about the dearth of proper American accents and the noise of the scene-changing, but it has to be said that the noise-level improved very quickly and if the accents were lacking the audiences did not appear to notice. Still, the *Darlington & Stockton Times* rated it 'a show not to be missed'.[20] 21% of a potential audience *did* miss it, though, as only 79% of the seats were sold, but five people, including a representative of Chester-le-Street Operatic Society, and Michael Fallon, who was MP for Darlington at the time, took the trouble to write and offer congratulations on the show. It made a loss of about £450, but this was a very small amount compared with the previous two shows, so the outlook was a little brighter. The Society managed to give fairly modest donations to five charities at the end of the year, and hoped for better things from 1984. They decided to keep the general ticket prices the same for *The Gondoliers* but to reduce the price of restricted viewing seats by 25p. Ian Kirkbride, now Publicity Manager along with Dorothy Walker since George Aiken had taken on joint stage managership with Stephen Sanderson, resolved to promote *The Gondoliers* as much as possible.

Sam opened the new year by presenting the Committee with budget estimates. *The Gondoliers* would run for six nights and *My Fair Lady* for ten. The bald facts were that, in order to produce a surplus from just the revenue from tickets, The *Gondoliers* would have to sell over 95% and *My Fair Lady*, if prices were raised by as much as 40p, would still have to sell over 90%. It was a grim outlook, and either money would have to be made in other ways, or costs would have to be cut somehow. One way in which the members did make money was by taking up Heather Wane's idea of a Sponsored Knit on St Valentine's night. The idea was that members should get people to sponsor them at so much per inch completed, with a time limit and a specified number of stitches on the needles. Eighteen ladies joined in, plus four brave men: George Aiken, Barrie Dargue, John Lloyd, and Heather's husband Arnold. How much experience the other three had in this field of endeavour is uncertain, but John

The Sponsored Knit (Valentine's Night), 1984.

had to be taught from scratch. The experience was about as rewarding as trying to teach a rhinoceros to knit with two telegraph poles. Blisters developed on hard-worked fingers and the gnashing of teeth was heard in the land. He had, however, plenty of willing sponsors, all of whom were, to say the least, doubtful about his potential expertise. On the night the end result was seven inches of rather wobbly knitting, with holes here and there which he swore were intentional and were actually buttonholes. Still, he had confounded the sceptics and they paid up amid much mirth, for they insisted on seeing the 'finished article' before parting with hard cash. Among the experts Gillian Marshall (a new member who worked as an area manager for Thorntons, the chocolate-retailers, and who had just moved to the area), knitted the most – she managed thirty inches in the set time and Fate, with a nice sense of irony, decreed that her prize was a box of Thorntons' chocolates! The evening raised the amazing sum of more than £220 for the Society.

The Gondoliers was having casting problems which went on well into February. A Duchess, a Luiz and a Marco were the most difficult to find, but, once found, turned out to have been well worth the effort. The rest of the cast was an exceptionally good one, and introduced some new faces into the Society, as well as well as some 'old' ones. Of the 'old', John Hurlstone came back to play Don Alhambra, Stan Lloyd to play the Duke of Plaza Toro, and Nancy Chilver to play the Duchess. The new faces were Gillian Marshall, whose golden soprano voice was ideal for Casilda, David Curtis – an exceptionally good young baritone – who played Guiseppe, and David's wife, Pauline, whose lovely voice displayed a maturity that belied her youth. She played Fiametta, and had a short solo near the beginning of the show. David Beall, a particularly good tenor, came from Teesside to play Marco, and Michael Geddes of Chester-le-Street – still only in his teens – came to play Luiz. He was an excellent choice, as he was very tall and slim and had a 'lyric tenor' voice – he was also nothing like the dim-witted character he played in the show! (There was a new face behind the piano in the rehearsal room, too, as Pat McIntyre, a teacher of Music at Polam Hall School, had come to help Christine Purvis and Brian Sheppard with accompanying.) The rest of the parts were taken by Society regulars. Connie Reeves and Sue Kirkbride played the leading roles of Tessa and Gianetta, Barrie Dargue was Antonio, and John Hacking played Francesco. The small roles of Vittoria, Giulia and Inez were taken by Jacqui Wright, Sharon Priestley and June Aiken, and Sam Herdman covered the two roles of Giorgio and Annibale. It was a splendid cast and the show deserved to do well.

At the Annual General Meeting, Tom Kent, in his last appearance as Chairman, acknowledged the fact that the Committee had accepted the principle that production losses, provided they were kept to a minimum, could be covered by money raised from social events. The previous year had shown that this could be done: the Society had still managed to remain in the black despite losses on both shows. The fact was that the public who did attend received the shows with every appearance of enjoyment; the Vice-President/Patron figures remained fairly steady – around 160 each show – and the number of organizations which booked blocks of seats also remained fairly constant – around 25. Also at that meeting Honorary Life Membership was conferred on six people, all of whom had been associated with the Society for many years and had given exceptional service. They were Eileen Young, Jim Fraser Murray, Margaret Hardaker, Evelyn Berry, Sam Herdman and Doris Thompson, widow of Fred (though unfortunately she could not be present as she was ill).

Once the Annual General Meeting was over, Ian and Dorothy set about the public with a vengeance, bombarding them with publicity. Dorothy managed to secure the big notice board on High Row for a poster and there was to be a cake stall in the town on Easter Monday, with people in costume. Ian arranged to be interviewed on Radio Tees in April and on Radio Cleveland sometime before the 14 May opening date. He posted large bills outside the theatre and then induced his wife Sue, Kath Robinson and Judi Kent to do the James Herriot run – a half-marathon (though at walking pace, which was very magnanimous of him) – their T-shirts bearing one letter on the front and three (or four) on the back of each so that the letters across their backs read GON DOL IERS and across their chests D O S – which meant that they had to be careful to stay in the correct formation! Finally, just before the show opened, Ian arranged for the press to take photographs of some of the cast in a boat in the South Park – or as he put it 'A stunt in a punt on the pond in the park for the press'.

The Gondoliers sold so well that John Lloyd instigated the ill-fated 'John Lloyd Memorial Matinée' mentioned in Chapter 2, and the meagre attendance at this reduced the overall percentage of ticket sales to 84.5%. Despite the fact that it was a very small audience it was a very appreciative one, and so the company felt that in that respect the extra performance was worthwhile, though the revenue gained was not enough even to pay the band for that afternoon.

The reviews were excellent. The press found no fault in the production, save that the *Darlington & Stockton Times* wished that Gillian Marshall's wig had been nicer, so the Society had every right to be proud of its efforts. The *Northern Echo* said that the company '. . . excelled itself in a joyous production which delighted the packed house.'[21] The singing was 'virtuoso' – Pauline Curtis's first solo set the standard, which remained tremendously high. The comedy was well executed, too, and Joy had had a lot of novel ideas for injecting fun into the show. Stan Lloyd's sandcastle-building episode went down well with the audiences as did his motley band of 'soldiers' (dancers made up to look like toy soldiers and exhibiting minimal intelligence). The *Evening Despatch*, as well as registering appreciation of the fine singing, dancing and comedy, remarked that '. . . Gilbert and Sullivan have ensured this is a slow-moving tale, I'm afraid. Yet this new version has the sparkle and enthusiasm to turn it into an eye-catching spectacle.'[22] The *Darlington & Stockton Times* gave the show sincere and whole-hearted praise (apart from the wig). All the principals received individual accolades and the paper summed them up by calling them '. . . the strongest line-up of principals I've seen in an amateur G & S show.'[23] The paper had also enjoyed the dancing and comedy enormously, and both it and the *Northern Echo* made particular mention of Arthur Berwick's orchestra.

The Society is frequently reminded of *The Gondoliers* even now. The men's costumes for the beach scene at the opening of the second act were old-fashioned bathing costumes, with short sleeves and legs, made out of horizontally-striped red, white and blue material. They were made especially for Darlington's production by Homburg's, and caused a gale of laughter when the curtain went up. In nearly every production since then, at least one of them seems to turn up with the costume order. The Society is waiting to see if one will be sent – and if so, how it can be fitted in – if they ever perform *Miss Saigon* or *The Phantom of the Opera!*

To everyone's surprise, despite the loss of revenue on the matinée, *The Gondoliers* showed a surplus – only £120, it is true, but at least things were looking up a little. The Committee looked again at the costing of *My Fair Lady* and at the state of the funds. Social and fund-raising events were doing well (the cake stall and the James Herriot run – or rather walk – had raised nearly £250) but *My Fair Lady* was going to be an expensive luxury. The cost of theatre rent, orchestra, props and scenery alone would be over £9,000, even before taking into account professional fees, rehearsal accommodation and those other items which had been listed in Sam's chart in the programme for *Salad Days*. They deliberated for some time and then decided that the only thing to do was to put up the ticket prices by the 40p which had been mentioned before. They restructured the charges, however, more or less into the format in which they are today. For a ten-night show they would have a cheap night for everybody on the first night and the Monday night; a cheap night for children on the first Friday; and a reduction for blocks of fifteen or more on all nights save the first, the Monday, and the last (when all the seats would be dearer). Restricted viewing seats would be cheaper in proportion on all nights but the last. (The only extra differences today are that there is a reduction for OAPs on the first Thursday, and the price of restricted viewing seats is reduced for the last night too.)

Having settled this, they had to choose shows for 1985. For the third time *Sweet Charity* was chosen for spring, with Joy and John as Producer and Musical Director, and for the autumn it was to be *South Pacific*, last performed by the Society in 1961 – the great man-hunt would have to be revived.

The immediate concern was to cast *My Fair Lady*. Auditions were held on 1 July, and by 18 July the show was cast, with the exception of Freddy Eynsford-Hill. Pauline Curtis was cast as Eliza Doolittle, with Ian Kirkbride as her dustman father. John Hurlstone was Professor Higgins, and Stan Lloyd was his friend, Colonel Pickering. Shirley Dodd was Mrs Higgins, Greta Sanderson was Mrs Pearce and Sam Herdman was Zoltan Karpathy. There were a good many small roles, too, so a lot of people had the chance to have a named part.

Gloom was cast over the summer, however, for Christine Smith died very suddenly at the beginning of August, and Jim Willans, who had had a stroke some months earlier, died at the end of it. Denis Quinn, who had been a member from 1958 to 1970, also died, two months later.

In September the Committee reconvened and assessed the situation in the run-up to *My Fair Lady*. Non-production items had managed to raise over £900 during the year, but the rental of rehearsal rooms was to rise by nearly £3 per session, and the cost of printing the programmes had risen. The cost of a programme would therefore have to rise to 50p. Still, at least the arrangements for *Sweet Charity* were going smoothly, and Bill Jones had discovered that Kentish Players Amateur Operatic and Dramatic Society had some scenery which seemed satisfactory, judging by the plans they had sent. A licence had also been obtained to perform *South Pacific* at 12½% royalties, and there should be no difficulty in getting scenery and costumes.

Greta Sanderson, who acted as the Society's delegate at the NODA National Conference, was able to report that NODA's affairs were going more smoothly, too. They had hit on the idea of a lottery with a car as first prize, and this had gone a long way towards easing the solvency problem.

Ian Kirkbride organized a lot of publicity for *My Fair Lady* by, amongst other things, arranging for press photographs of some of the cast in costume at Sedgefield Racecourse, and photographs of himself with some local dustbinmen complete with his young stepson Martin in a dustbin on his back, which Martin seemed to enjoy prodigiously!

A week before the opening of *My Fair Lady*, John Lloyd announced that 78% of the seats had been sold, but that the bookings for the first Thursday, Friday and Saturday were looking sluggish as usual. Bookings gathered pace rapidly during that last week, though, and eventually 96% were sold.

When the show went on it was worth all the money and trouble spent over it – even Pauline Curtis said in a newspaper interview that it was worth the effort she had put into losing some weight to look trimmer for the performance! Stan Lloyd felt that it had been worth the struggle he had had even to appear. He had a virus so severe that he had to stay in bed all day, get up and do the show, and then go straight home and back to bed again. It had also taken a long time to get someone to play Freddy, despite coverage of the problem in the press, but finally Colin Kerr, who was primarily a club singer and who had a very good tenor voice, appeared on the scene, which was a relief. John Parker extracted enormous enjoyment from this show. He played several 'servant' roles and took great delight in adopting sundry disguises and voices to do so. There is no doubt that the major hit, as far as Jeff Wragg was concerned, was the Irish accent and enormous red moustache which John affected for the role of Mrs Higgins's chauffeur. John knew that Jeff appreciated it – there was no mistaking the source of the mighty explosion of male laughter in the auditorium!

My Fair Lady 1984 – Chorus. *See page xi for full list.*

There were several letters of congratulation on the show from members of the public, reinforcing what the newspapers said about it. The headlines to each of the three reviews were fairly predictable: 'By George! I think they've got it!',[24] 'More than fair . . .',[25] and 'Oh! It was loverly'.[26] They were all exceedingly complimentary. The *Northern Echo* flatteringly said that '. . . there must be something in the Trades Descriptions Act . . .' (about the show) because '. . . it is supposed to be performed by an amateur group but Darlington Operatic Society has come up with a production that simply sparkles with professionalism.' Pauline was described as 'dazzling', John Hurlstone was 'excellent', Stan Lloyd 'charming', and Ian Kirkbride 'marvellous'. The *Darlington & Stockton Times* echoed these sentiments – 'so professional that at times it was difficult to believe all the performers were amateurs' was the verdict. Pauline's performance was described as having 'style, panache and humour' and her singing as 'stunning'. John was compared, inevitably, with Rex Harrison who had played the role in the film, but the reviewer felt that he 'made the part all his own'. Ian got a good write-up in general, and Colin was complimented on his superb singing voice. The *Evening Despatch* made the point that, at the age of just 22, Pauline had a fine voice and the makings of a great performer, which was a sound prediction, for that voice has grown better and better. Visually, the show was another stunning one. The Ascot scene was portrayed just as it was in the film. The lights went up on a motionless cast, a beautiful tableau of grey morning suits, and fabulous dresses and hats all in black and white; after a couple of seconds' awed silence there was enormous applause – Joy was a past mistress when it came to tableaux (or 'pictures', as she called them). Judging by comments overheard in the bar afterwards the audiences certainly thought they had had their money's worth, even with the extra 40p on the tickets, and that 40p, plus some careful management, meant that the show showed a surplus of nearly £1,800! The Committee must have been jubilant, though it does not show in the minutes – they were too busy organizing for *Sweet Charity*, having decided not to raise the ticket prices this time. *Sweet Charity* would run for one week, and auditions would be held on 20 January. It was likely to lose money, judging

Dancing Years, 1980
Eunicé Cockburn, Jonathan Kent.

by the costings, but at least the *My Fair Lady* surplus provided a cushion for that, as well as the means to donate £500 to charities at the end of the year.

Arrangements for *South Pacific* were also being made. Joy, of course, was to be asked to produce, and Arthur Berwick to be Musical Director, since John Beagle was doing *Sweet Charity*. Stagesets were supplying the scenery, and Homburg's the costumes. So, after all the uncertainties, the year ended well, with carol-singing at Holy Trinity Church and at Denton Church, with an excellent dinner-dance, and with Honorary Life Membership to be offered to Bernard and Greta Sanderson, Bill Jones, Cecil Grieveson, Marjorie Willans, Lorrie Boddy and Roula Murray.

The last five years had been testing ones. Though there had been bright spots, such as the large number of new members, some excellent productions and the appointment of the Society's first lady Chairman, there had been a lot of sadness at the deaths of several members and a lot of agonizing over finance. The company had done well to weather the heavy losses on five of its last ten shows, but the accounts for the last two had remained in the black so the decade ended with the Committee in a cautiously optimistic mood again. They knew very well that it did not do to be complacent – some of them had seen it all before and were well aware that smugness tended to be rewarded with a sharp lesson!

Chapter 10

1985–1989

Any prophets of doom would have been justified as things turned out, for the beginning of the Society's fifth decade was in stark contrast to the ending of its fourth.

The first half of 1985 had a nightmare quality. It opened with news of the deaths of Doris Thompson and Margaret Hardaker, both so recently made Honorary Life Members. There were niggling matters, too. One of the advertisers in the last programme had gone into receivership and the bill would not now be paid. A backcloth from Stagesets had gone missing and could not be found. For *Sweet Charity* a portion of an already crowded orchestra pit would have to be taken up with a pretend 'lake' in which Charity almost drowns, so John Beagle was trying to reduce the number of orchestra members. William McDonald was leaving the theatre, too, and there was difficulty in getting another suitable director.

Then Joy fell ill. Joy, who was the hub of the Society, had to pull out of the next production. Joy, who always seemed so fighting fit and full of energy and enthusiasm, had to have an operation and radiotherapy. Feelings of disbelief and concern swept like a tidal wave across the whole Society. Despite their anxiety the Committee had to keep moving with arrangements which had gone so sadly awry. As well as the monthly meeting that January, three Extraordinary meetings had to be held. Another producer would have to be found. Robert Marlowe, Paul Kerryson and Fr Ricardo Morgan were unavailable, and there were drawbacks to one or two other producers (for instance, those to whom *Sweet Charity* would not be the sort of show to appeal). Therefore, at the first of the Extraordinary meetings, on 20 January, *Sweet Charity* went down for the third time, and Stephen Sondheim and Jule Stein's *Gypsy* was chosen instead. Glynn Mills, from Scarborough, would be asked to produce. He had done a lot of acting in the West End and in the provinces, and had just returned from Canada where he had been in *Piaf*. A day later, at the second Extraordinary meeting, Bill Jones reported that although he could get the licence to perform *Gypsy* there was no scenery to be had anywhere. He had enquired what other shows were available, and *Hello Dolly!* was a possibility. It was only thirteen years since the Society had done the show but speed of choice was very important now. The Committee decided to go for *Hello Dolly!*, to ask Glynn Mills to produce it, and to ask the Brooklyn-born Sue Little, who had had her dance training in New York, to be Choreographer. Sue had taught dance in several London schools, was a founder member of the English Dance Theatre, and now lived in Darlington. John Beagle would continue as Musical Director. Of course it would be more expensive in every way to put on *Hello Dolly!* A lot more costumes and scenery would be needed and it would be dearer paying three professionals rather than two, so ticket prices had to go up yet again, by 30p.

Four days later the third Extraordinary meeting was held, by which time the licence, scenery, Producer, Choreographer and vocal scores had been obtained, and arrangements had been made to have a new set of tickets printed – an all-time record for Bill!

Less than four weeks later things were returning more-or-less to normal in the circumstances. *Hello Dolly!* was cast, and, best of all, Joy's treatment was proving effective and she was beginning to feel a little better, though she was very tired.

Connie Reeves was playing Dolly Levi in the show, with Sam playing opposite her, repeating his role as Horace Vandergelder. Christine Swales, who had not been in a show since she had played the lead in *Guys and Dolls* in 1974, was playing Irene Molloy, Avril Blain was Minnie Fay, Shirley Dodd was Mrs Rose, and June Aiken the strident, florid Ernestina. This time Barrie Dargue was playing Cornelius Hackl, and John Parker was Barnaby Tucker; both of them were more than double the ages of the characters they were playing but they can both be numbered among those lucky people who look much younger than they are.* Steve Luck was Ambrose Kemper and Tricia Freeman the lachrymose Ermengarde. This left only the parts of Rudolph (the Head Waiter), the Judge and the Court Clerk to be cast. Dorothy Walker organized publicity. She had sole responsibility now, as Ian Kirkbride's job had taken him and Sue and their extended family to Southend. They left a big gap in the Society for they were a very popular family as well as being valuable cast-members.

The Social and Fund-Raising Committee, comprising Eunicé, John Hacking and Mike Walker, was arranging lots of social activities to keep up the financial 'cushioning' and these social events were being very well supported, which was heartening.

The Annual General Meeting in March that year was a very happy one, apart from the obvious regret at the deaths of the five members during the previous year and the removal of Sue and Ian to Southend.

---

* The author is not open to bribes.

The Chairman (John Hacking) and the 88 members who were present were able to welcome back a fully-recovered Joy, and to rejoice in the fact that both of 1984's productions had been so enjoyable and so profitable – financially the Society had had its best year ever and the membership now totalled 121. Still more encouraging, the Kenneth Richardson Memorial Trust had been able to furnish six applicants with bursaries to help with singing lessons.

The Society now had no Honorary Vice-President since the death of Jim Willans, and Sam Herdman was unanimously elected to the position; Honorary Life Membership was bestowed, as planned, on Lorrie, Roula, Greta and Bernard, Marjorie, Bill and Cecil. Sam was elated over the fact that the Society had been able to give generous donations to charity over the year and hoped that even more would be available for distribution in the year to come.

Two weeks before the opening of *Hello Dolly!* the ticket sales were going so well that it looked as though Sam's hopes would be realized, but there was a feeling of anxiety among the cast. Relations between Producer and Choreographer were somewhat strained and the cast felt that they were under-prepared for the show and needed more precise direction. As far as the dancing was concerned, Sue was an excellent choreographer but was used to working with professionals who were not only able to dance with precision and athleticism but were easily able to make changes to their routines and, what is more, remember those changes without difficulty. This was where the amateurs fell short; it was not anyone's fault, but a simple fact of life. However, the cast, with the help of John Beagle, did their level best to overcome the problems and the show began its week-long run on 29 April. Connie has confessed to having felt very nervous, but, with hindsight, she need not have been. She gave a splendid performance – all the cast did – and the capacity audiences appreciated the show. With only eight weeks in which to rehearse, and with all the other problems there had been, a small miracle was achieved. The *Northern Echo* acknowledged that 'the experience of years'[1] showed through in the performance on the first night. Connie was commended for playing her part with 'a full-blooded enthusiasm', and special mention was made of Sam, Christine, and John Parker – who was, after all, playing the part of a boy half his age. The *Evening Despatch* and the *Darlington & Stockton Times* were in full agreement over the incredibly professional job the company had made of the show after such a short rehearsal period. The 'Waiters' Gallop' was singled out by the *Evening Despatch*, as well it might be, for it was a masterpiece of timing. Again there was an accident, though, for Jimmy Hall fell and received a back injury from which he never made a total recovery. The *Darlington & Stockton Times* declined to pinpoint a star performance other than to say that Connie was 'tremendous'[2] in her role, because the paper felt that the leading players were so well cast and the company all worked so well together. Of course there was the usual fair share of hiccups backstage; for one thing the explosion which had to occur in Barnaby and Cornelius's cellar in Vandergelder's store not only nearly deafened John and Barrie, but threatened to blow them straight through the stage before they had a chance to scramble through the trapdoor.

There were two people working with the Society for *Hello Dolly!* who would bear watching for the future: Charlotte Aiken, George and June's daughter, who had been 'call boy' for *My Fair Lady* and was doing so again for this show, and Kiran Singh, the young daughter of an eye specialist, who was in the chorus. The futures of both of them were in the world of professional theatre.

At the May committee meeting John Lloyd was able to tell the Committee that every ticket was sold for *Hello Dolly!*, including the circle boxes, which were only sold on special request or as a last resort. Nevertheless there was a loss on the show – nearly £600 – partly due to the fact that there had been no time to prepare proper costings, but some valuable lessons were learned, not the least of which was that it ill-behoved the Society to take Joy for granted. The Committee acknowledged this by voluntarily increasing her fee to produce *South Pacific*, for which Arthur Berwick would be Musical Director, and they further asked her to produce the two shows in 1986: *How to Succeed . . .* for spring, and *Kismet* for the autumn – if it was not likely to be too expensive. There would be nearly an extra 2,400 seats to sell for *South Pacific* because of its ten-night run, and the general ticket prices were to stay more or less the same for that as they had been for *Hello Dolly!* The price would be raised for only the first night, the Monday, and for restricted viewing seats. At this rate the show could produce a reasonable surplus with only an 85% attendance.

Over the summer, problems cropped up and were solved one way and another. The props store was proving to be unsustainable – it cost too much and had been broken into several times – so Steve Blain took the smaller items and stored them in his garage, and Bernard Sanderson put the larger ones in one of the packing sheds at his market garden. There was a similar problem at the rehearsal room, where members' cars were being broken into, but the Society was offered the Dance Studio at the Arts Centre for rehearsals, and though the acoustics were not ideal it was in a more central location than the school they had hitherto used. Finally, the question of ladies for *South Pacific* reared its head again – how should they be chosen? Would the ladies of 1985 be as reticent as those of 1961? The Committee boldly asked them to wear shorts for the auditions and this time there was no demur.

The Society had taken part in a concert given at the Dolphin Centre by Angela Jenkins and John Noble, a husband and wife professional team, and they agreed to a request to put on a weekend workshop for the whole Society. The fee would be paid out of the Kenneth Richardson Trust and it would benefit everyone instead of just a few.

By mid-July the main casting of *South Pacific* had been completed and

South Pacific 1985 – Mavis Wilson.

only the smaller parts remained to be cast by Joy in September. It was an interesting cast and the show contained a number of new faces in named roles. Mavis Wilson was to be Nellie Forbush and John Hurlstone Emile de Becque. Roula Murray, after a long absence from the cast lists, came back again to recreate the role of Bloody Mary, with Fay Nutting (sister of Pamela Carter) as her daughter Liat. Barrie Dargue was cast as Joe Cable (despite his protests that he was too old!), and the two US naval men – Captain Bracket and Commander Harbison – were John Hacking and John Lloyd. A new member, Keith Craney, was Luther Billis, and Emile's two children were played by Patrick Freeman and Nicola Whitfield, Ian's daughter (his wife Georgine came along to be matron to the children). All the Society's 'regular' men were involved and to the company's delight some new ones had been found, including Adrian Fawlk, Mike Taylor, Bob Lamb, Steve Emmerson, David Barkes, Allan Carver, Jillson Lawrence, Nigel Hayler and Jonathan Parkin. Jonathan Curren and Chris Lepingwell, both students at the Sixth Form College, also came along. Some new girls came into the show, too, and Lynn Coulson, Katie Sharp, Maxine Allinson, Ann Oxley and Linda Dawson (Edith and Fred's daughter) stayed in the Society, as did Jayne Tweddle, a dancer, who later took some leading singing and acting roles after she married and became Jayne Summerbell. Vera Davison, who had played many leading roles for the Newton Aycliffe society, also joined Darlington for this show. So a cast of 62 was finally assembled.

By mid-September rehearsals and ticket sales were going well but there were difficulties on the *How to Succeed . . .* front. There was apparently no scenery to be had, and no costume plot, and John Beagle felt that although it was a good show it was musically difficult; as he was also Musical Director for Stockton Stage Society's show in March he felt that he could not do it justice for Darlington. He did discover that a set of scenery *was* available – but at a cost of £900. The Committee discussed the matter and decided that the financial risk was too great. So they settled on *Annie Get Your Gun* for the spring show, reverting to a ten-night run in view of the fact that *Hello Dolly!* had sold so well and that *South Pacific* seemed likely to do so.

For *South Pacific* – the 80th production by the Society – there were 222 Vice-Presidents and Patrons, the largest number since *Half a Sixpence* in 1978, and the number of visiting organizations rocketed to a record 42. The show played to full houses every night – with all its memorable songs, its mixture of comedy, romance and tragedy, and its excellent cast, it was a tonic to the most jaded of eyes and ears. The newspaper reviews said it in their headlines: 'Sell-out',[3] 'Lively Amateurs Enchant',[4] and '*South Pacific* has 'em in love with a wonderful show'.[5] The only fault they could find was that the American accents were not flawless, but the rest was all enthusiasm. The *Evening Despatch* declared that the Society 'came up trumps again with their slick performance', while the *Northern Echo* said that it was 'slick, lively and colourful' and that the Society more than did the show justice. Mavis, John, Keith and Roula were mentioned by name, but the paper said that the rest of the cast all deserved credit. The *Darlington & Stockton Times* called Mavis an 'Angela Rippon look-alike' (Angela Rippon was a popular television newscaster at the time), and said that she was excellent, passing the ultimate test of continuing to look good even after washing her hair on stage. John Hurlstone looked the part of the hero and he acted magnificently, according to the critic, who also praised Roula, Barrie, John Parker (who was playing comedy again, as one of the seamen) and Keith Craney, who gave a masterly portrayal of Luther Billis. Both the *Northern Echo* and the *Darlington & Stockton Times* compared Keith's portrayal to the famous Sergeant Bilko, a cunning and devious character played by Phil Silvers on American television. In the *Honey Bun* number Keith sported a wonderful tattoo of a sailing-ship on his stomach. It looked authentic, but in fact it was painted on each night by his wife Denise's sister – he was made to lie on the floor for her to create this work of art so that she got as flat a surface as possible to work on! Keith was able to 'roll' his stomach muscles in such a way that it made the ship look as though it was pitching and tossing. The effect on the audience was mesmeric and won him a number of fans! The show made the Society a lot of fans, too. *South Pacific* produced a surplus of over £2,500, even though some of the costs were higher than estimated, and it ensured that the Society was able to make higher donations to charities. Over £1,500 was donated that year, bringing the total since 1946 to over £21,000. Also, using a legacy left to the Society by Margaret Hardaker, a new table and chairs were bought for the boardroom at the theatre.

No sooner was *South Pacific* over than rehearsals began for *Annie Get Your Gun*. David Garrood had accepted the position of Musical Director and Joy, of course, was Producer. There was one problem, though. The theatre now had a new Director, Brian Goddard, and he had informed Bill in November that he had so far been unable to arrange for the Society to have the two weeks which it wanted for the show. He did, however, want the theatre to promote a concert with Angela Jenkins and John Noble, backed by the Society, the proceeds to be split between the professionals, the theatre and the Society, 60%, 30% and 10% respectively, so it was agreed that this should take place in June. The year came to an end with a carol service at Holy Trinity Church with the Polam Hall School choirs, and a party at Michael and Mavis Wilson's house.

1986 opened with good news: Brian Goddard had managed to arrange things at the theatre so that the Society would be able to run *Annie Get Your Gun* from 30 April to 10 May. He had also advised the Society to inform the Council of its charitable status, which might give a reduction in hire-rates. This was most encouraging and the Committee hastened to do this and to make a final decision on an autumn show, plumping for *Carousel* when *Kismet* seemed likely to be too expensive. It had also become obvious that shows now had to run for ten nights in order to achieve any surplus on the production accounts.

In February the relief of getting the show cast was marred by the news of the death of Evelyn Berry, who had been such a permanent fixture of the Society until she had been taken ill a few months previously. It was almost impossible to imagine the tea-urn going for any length of time without Evelyn presiding over it and she would surely be missed. Also, George Aiken decided that he would have to resign from the Committee, as he had been made a Company Managing Director and could not promise commitment, though he remained with the stage crew. However, the show *was* cast – at least, all the major parts were. Kiran Singh won the part of Annie Oakley by doing a splendid audition, and with her dark good looks was set to be a wonderful leading lady, worthy of the precedent

Annie Get Your Gun 1986. *Left to right*: Emma Parker, Nicola Whitfield, Helen Wilson, Kiran Singh, Indra Singh, Patrick Freeman.

set by Allene Norris twenty years before. Allene was writing a book about the traders in the Darlington covered market* which was being illustrated with sketches by Yvonne Talbot, a newcomer to the town, and Yvonne was prevailed upon to do a sketch of Kiran for the programme cover. Mark Ellis came over from Teesside to play Frank Butler, and the rival Wild West/Far East show-owners, Buffalo Bill and Pawnee Bill, were played by Sam Herdman and Cliff Walker. Chief Sitting Bull was played

* *The Market* by Allene Norris. Illustrated by Yvonne Talbot. Talbot Print, 1986.

by Keith Craney, and the Tate sisters, Dolly and Winnie, were played by Greta Sanderson and Avril Blain, with Jonathan Curren as Winnie's boyfriend Tommy Keeler. There were five children in this show – Annie's brothers and sisters and another little boy. The little boy was Patrick Freeman and Annie's sisters were Emma Parker (John and Ann's daughter), Nicola Whitfield and Indra Singh, Kiran's younger sister. Annie's brother, Little Jake, was actually played by a girl – Helen Wilson, daughter of Mavis and Michael, who was to give a most convincing performance.*

Those were the main parts but the complete cast numbered 63 – several new people joined the chorus and dancers for this show, making a total of 21 new members over the past year. The show required complex staging and effects (guns and so on) so there were, in total, twenty stage crew and props staff, the latter of which included Charlotte Aiken.

The tickets were selling very well. In fact, 60% were gone by the second week in March, by which time all the accoutrements had been booked for *Carousel.* Joy was to produce it, of course, and John Beagle was to be Musical Director.

The minutes of the March Annual General Meeting take up six sides of foolscap. It was almost as though, after the period of harmony and solidarity among the members and Committee during the difficult times, the floodgates of grievance opened once the Society was seen to be prospering. There was discontent about the casting of shows and the fact that the Committee had imported people to play leading roles; some members felt that shows should always be cast from within the Society unless it proved totally impossible. (At this point a committee member drew the attention of these dissenters to the fact that there was a vacancy on the Committee and asked if any of them would care to be nominated, but there were no takers.) The Committee regularly runs into this sort of trouble from time to time over casting, as a balance has to be struck. It has a responsibility to fulfil the aims set out in the rules, the chief of which are concerned with furthering the development of public appreciation and taste in the operatic and dramatic arts, and assisting charities. To do this the Society is duty-bound to perform works to as high a standard as possible to attract large audiences and thus raise as much as possible to benefit its chosen causes. This means that the people chosen to play parts have to be the most appropriate available, and of the highest quality possible. This sometimes means getting someone from another society – the aims of which, after all, are substantially the same as those of the

---

* Tragically, Helen died at the age of 18 in 1994 after a road accident in 1991 left her badly injured and in a coma.

Darlington society. At the same time, the Society's own members should not be made to feel inadequate if they are not wholly appropriate for a part. (A performance of *La Traviata* by another amateur society, many, many years ago, springs to mind. The heroine was a lady of mature, not to say vintage, years, playing the young, beautiful and consumptive Violetta. Had she been at least young, and a high soprano rather than a mezzo-soprano, even the fact that she 'died' in a candlewick dressing-gown and wore a wig which looked as though it had been constructed from potting-compost might not have reduced the piece to the farce which it ultimately became – yet she *could* have been appropriate as, say, Katisha in *The Mikado*. This is an extreme example, but there is no doubt that the shortcomings of the central character caused the attributes of the rest of the cast to be ignored.)

Another point of discussion that evening concerned the fact that committee members who are relatives of people auditioning for parts are not allowed to be present at those auditions – but Rule 19 is quite clear about this so there was no real room for discussion. Nevertheless, the Committee had been given plenty of food for thought after this meeting and a variation on the first of the items was to cause a good deal of trouble in under eighteen months' time.

Meanwhile the company got on with *Annie Get Your Gun* and the Committee got on with arrangements to give further donations to four charities (at this time the Society was supporting MIND, the NSPCC, the Samaritans, and St John of God's Hospital) and with the choice of a show for the spring of 1987, which was to be *Guys and Dolls*.

With two weeks to go before *Annie Get Your Gun*, 87% of the tickets had been sold – it looked as though the idea of reverting to a ten-night run for spring as well as autumn was a sound one. This was borne out by the profitable result, as ultimately 97% of the tickets were sold. The public loved the show (much to the relief of the company, whose first dress rehearsal had gone on until 12.40 a.m.), and they loved Kiran as Annie. So did the press – though in its preview the *Darlington Advertiser* (a free weekly paper introduced after the demise of the *Evening Despatch*) made much of the fact that she experienced a certain amount of embarrassment at first over having to kiss Mark, whom she had never met before rehearsals, in front of an audience. The *Northern Echo* said that Kiran was '. . . on fine form . . . she sings and dances well and acts with great confidence.'[6] Mark Ellis was described as 'dashing', while John Parker (in the role of Charlie Davenport), Greta Sanderson and the children also received honourable mentions. Joy's production was described as '. . . slick and well organized.' 'Once again,' the review said, 'these amateurs have proved they can turn in a first-class show.' The *Darlington & Stockton*

Times particularly praised Mark, Sam ('society stalwart'), John Parker, Tom Kent (as Foster Wilson) and Keith Craney ('heap good depth of understanding'), but was especially impressed by Kiran's 'inspired' performance which was described as 'well-timed' and 'intuitive', aided by 'excellent deportment and telling facial expressions'. 'Kiran,' said the paper, 'gave the impression that she is doing what comes naturally to her.'[7] This was a most perceptive remark, for Kiran went on to make the theatre her career; she attended the Arts Educational drama college, and has appeared fairly constantly in theatre and on television, notably in *London's Burning* and *Children's Ward* (under her stage name of Kiran Hocking) as well as in advertisements.

At the committee meeting which followed the show, *Carousel* figured largely in the discussions. All the arrangements had been made but Stephen Sanderson and Ray Porteus, who were stage managing, were concerned about the size of the permanent carousel which was to come with the scenery. The stage at the Civic Theatre is relatively small and the carousel was twelve feet in diameter. They hoped to be able to resolve the problem, but one gets the impression that they were crossing their fingers and hoping that it might fit miraculously into the space available.

In the summer the Society was able to give some money to the Darlington Talking Newspaper Association, to the local hospice movement, and to the Samaritans, all of whom were most appreciative, and it was good to be in a position to be able to give donations more freely. Before the summer break the bookings for *Guys and Dolls* of scenery from Stagesets and costumes from Homburg's were finalized and most of the casting was completed for *Carousel*. The leads – Julie and Billy – were to be taken by Vera Davison, in her first major role for the Society, and Arthur Ellis, who had not been in a show with Darlington since *Gigi* in the spring of 1978 (although he had helped backstage for several shows). If he was running true to form the cast would have to keep an eagle eye on him to avoid falling victim to any practical jokes. Nicola Whitfield was to play their daughter Louise. Carrie Pipperidge was to be played by Mavis Wilson, with Barrie Dargue as Mr Snow, while Sam was playing Mr Bascombe, Julie and Carrie's employer, with Kath Robinson as his wife. Jimmy Hall was playing the Heavenly Friend, and Keith Craney had the unenviable task of playing the Star Keeper (unenviable because it is a part which can look like pure ham acting if not handled carefully), as well as the part which goes hand-in-hand with it, namely Dr Seldon. Connie was back, after missing two shows, as Nettie Fowler, and June Aiken was the jealous Mrs Mullins. Barrie and Mavis were given a full Society-family of children: Melvyn Dawson, Nicola Reeves (Connie's

Carousel 1986 – Principals and children. *See page xi for full list.*

daughter), Sally Robinson (Kath and Phil's daughter), and a 'full house' of the Freeman/Porteus family. It was a record attendance for them. For the Porteus side all three of Ray junior and Judith's offspring were among the children: Claire, Sarah, and little Amy, who was only four years old. Ray senior was stage doorkeeper at the theatre at the time, and Kath and Judith were matrons to the children along with Avril Blain (whose elder daughter, Romana, was also playing one of the children). For the Freeman side Tricia was dancing and Brigitte and Patrick were among the children. There was as yet no 'baddie' – the part of Jigger Craigin was still unfilled – but by September they had found him: Steve Blain would play the part as well as being Property Master.

A week before the opening, ticket sales were disappointing, for there were still 1,000 seats unsold, but in that last week and during the show business picked up and ultimately 97% of the seats were filled.

Carousel was not an easy show. Stephen Sanderson and Ray Porteus's misgivings were well justified. The roundabout was so enormous that it looked as though the cast would have to act round it, through it, and over it, and one of the horses was an equine Van Gogh in that one of its ears was missing. Once this edifice was on the stage it would have to stay put for the duration and the cast would just have to learn to live with it. This learning process took until nearly one in the morning at the first dress rehearsal, but by the second dress rehearsal the cast members were coping. Of course the audiences and the press knew nothing of this. They found the show very enjoyable and there was no feeling, as there had been the last time around, that it was intrinsically tedious. The *Northern Echo* declared that 'DOS have always been in the big league of the region's amateur companies and their production . . . maintains their high standard.'[8] Vera Davison 'who has a fine voice', said the paper, gave 'a sparkling performance', and Arthur, Connie, Steve, Barrie and especially little Amy received mentions. John Beagle also received special mention and the critic said that his '. . . fine orchestra . . . was the icing on the cake.' John would treasure this remark, particularly as there was a letter of complaint, not for the first time, about his rendering of *God Save the Queen*. John's special arrangements of the National Anthem are legendary – he liked to give it a different flavour depending on what show was being performed but such innovations were not always appreciated by the traditionalists! The *Darlington Advertiser*'s June Hawdon was captivated by the two smallest children, Amy and Romana, but she was generally impressed with the show – leads, dancing and sets alike – and was full of admiration for Steve's American accent in particular. She also thought that Nicola Whitfield's performance – Nicola was only fifteen years old – showed great promise for the future. (Nicola did not ultimately become a professional dancer – her first ambition – but contented herself by staying with the Operatic Society as a hobby.) The *Darlington & Stockton Times* had enjoyed Nicola's performance, too, and also mentioned Connie's rendering of *You'll Never Walk Alone* as being outstanding. Keith Craney was described as 'bearing a startling resemblance to Boss Hogg out of the television series *The Dukes of Hazzard*[9] and was commended for his comedy and his introduction of topical references into the part. The critic had some reservations, however – 'entertaining with a relatively high standard' was the final verdict – and one of these reservations concerned the lack of microphones. This was a problem which could not be addressed seriously by the Committee until some years later, because of the expense. The problem was insoluble until 'head microphones' became available;

chest microphones pick up rattling jewellery and breathing (though they are better, in the opinion of many, than nothing) while head microphones are fixed at the top of the forehead under the hair or wig and are very efficient. They also cost around £1,000 each!

The cast seemed to enjoy the show as much as the audience. Arthur, in particular, was not long in making his presence felt. Vera was his target and a foewoman worthy of his steel. On the second Thursday night he made careful preparations for the 'clambake' scene. Each night Vera would prepare her basket of food for the scene and include an apple, which she would take out and place on the stage beside her. That night not only did Arthur sabotage her basket by filling it with stage weights, making it incredibly difficult to lift without betraying the fact that it was about twenty times heavier than usual, but he also sliced the apple and pressed it back together again, so that when she placed it on the stage it fell spontaneously into neat quarters. Vera, however, could hardly complain, as she had thoughtfully provided a whoopee cushion to go under the blanket on which Arthur had to sit (Vera was also an old hand at this sort of thing!) Contrary to his expectations, though, she did not doctor the 'coffee' which she brought to him on stage, but enhanced the contents of the tray by furnishing it with a variety of interesting and unusual objects, some of which might have caused the composure of a lesser man to desert him completely. Honours were consequently even.

At the Committee's day of reckoning it was discovered that financially *Carousel* had done even better than *Annie Get Your Gun*. The programme sales were higher, perhaps because the price had remained at 50p. Moreover, the numbers of Vice-Presidents and Patrons had risen from 180 for *Hello Dolly!* through 222 for *South Pacific* and 254 for *Annie Get Your Gun*, up to 255 for *Carousel*, though the number of visiting organizations had fallen a little. At the November committee meeting it was decided that the ticket prices would stay the same for *Guys and Dolls*, which was already in rehearsal. There was a new version of *The Pirates of Penzance* now that its original copyright had expired, so they decided to give that show in the autumn of the following year if it was available, with Joy and John as Producer and Musical Director. They also scheduled another concert and another weekend workshop with Angela Jenkins and John Noble in between the two 1987 shows since the ones in 1986 had been such a success. So once more the year ended on a high note, with carol-singing in aid of the Multiple Sclerosis Society and over £3,000 given to other charities. Not only that, but *Guys and Dolls* was cast, all but the part of Nathan Detroit and those of one or two of the gamblers. Avril Blain was to be Sarah Brown, and Mike Stephenson, a local farming lecturer who had been one of the dancers in *Annie Get Your Gun*, was to be Sky Masterson.

Guys and Dolls 1987
Left to right: John Parker, Keith Craney, Joe Cooper.

Kath Robinson was cast as Miss Adelaide, John Parker as Nicely-Nicely Johnson, Sue Robinson as General Cartwright, and Richard Boucher, who had danced the part of the Carnival Boy so elegantly in *Carousel*, as Harry the Horse. Sam was playing Big Jule again and Cliff Walker was to have played Arvide again, but he had ultimately to pull out owing to ill-health, so Bernard Sanderson stepped into the breach. The Hot Box dancers were Judi Kent, Liz Holton, Janet Watson (née Cooke), Jayne Summerbell (née Tweddle), Fay Carter (reverting to her maiden name from Fay Nutting), her sister Pamela (now married to Mike Walker), Tricia Freeman, and June Aiken (though June later withdrew and was replaced by Sharon Emmerson). Joe Cooper, who had joined the Society for *Annie Get Your Gun* along with his wife, Elizabeth, was cast as Lieutenant Brannigan.

By January an evening of operetta with the Nobles had been arranged to take place in June and a contract had been arranged to perform *The Pirates of Penzance*, at royalties of only 7½% and with Joy and John at the helm. At the February committee meeting it is recorded that Keith Craney would play Nathan Detroit (although he and Denise and the family would be moving to Cambridge shortly after the show), Mike Walker would play Benny Southstreet and Jillson Lawrence Rusty Charley. (Keith grew a small moustache to play Nathan and became so fond of it that he kept it for nearly eight years. He had to shave it off, however, early in 1995, when he was offered the part of the Dame in a pantomime and felt that the opportunity was worth the sacrifice.) The final two members of the happy band of crapshooters were Cecil Grieveson as Society Max and Ian Whitfield as Liver Lips Louie. Stephen Sanderson, Ray Porteus and Steve Blain would get together and coordinate the lighting and stage management.

Guys and Dolls 1987 –
Bernard Sanderson

There then arose the question of scenery for *The Pirates of Penzance*; a York society had presented the show and had commissioned new scenery for it. Joy, Bernard and Greta had been to see the York show and enjoyed it, but they discovered that the Barrow society intended to buy the scenery and then hire it out to Lancaster; this need not be too much of a problem though, provided, of course, that the productions did not clash. The February meeting ended on a sad note as the minutes record the death of Vivienne Jackson who had been in several shows around eight years previously – her youth (she was only in her thirties) and the fact that she left a husband (Ken Jackson, who had given the Society such carefully-considered reviews in the *Darlington & Stockton Times*) and a young daughter made her loss even more keenly felt.

At the Annual General Meeting Ernie Mann received a NODA medal for 25 years' service, having done background work of immense importance for all those years. Sam highlighted the fact that, as well as doing his work backstage and on the Committee, Ernie spent many hours in a draughty old workshop to produce some very good props, which saved the Society a good deal of trouble and money. Eunicé Cockburn stepped down from the Committee at this meeting; she had done a great deal of work for the Society in various capacities and, in fact, continued to work in the background. Three members of the Ladies' Committee were also now retiring: Frances Sanderson, Heather Wane, and Eileen Young who had been a founder-member and had served for 25 years. Happily there were three ladies who were willing to replace them, so Eileen Singh (mother of Kiran and Indra), Dorothy Carter (mother of Pamela and Fay) and Denise Craney joined Elsie Campbell, Kath Porteus, Eileen Hogg, Linda Smith, Jennifer Hird and Edith Dawson. Denise was only able to serve for a short time until she and Keith moved, whereupon Heather Wane came back in to fill the gap. Heather withdrew from the Committee because of her husband Arnold's ill-health, but felt a responsibility to the Society as well. Arnold died a year later. Though he was not a member of the Society he was always willing to support it – viz. his attempts at sponsored knitting – and he was one of nature's gentlemen.

John Lloyd took over as Chairman for what looked like being a peaceful and profitable year. Like the curate's egg it was only good in parts, but at least it started well and finished well. It was only early March and the tickets for *Guys and Dolls* were being sold at the usual sort of rate for this time of the year. The Committee was aware that there were some shortcomings among the cast but there were still nearly two months to go yet; the publicity was well in hand, for a banner, which was Ian Kirkbride's legacy to the Society and was to be strung across Skinnergate, was being taken care of by Bernard Sanderson, and Tom Kent was getting on well with preparing the programme. The question of having relatives present at auditions received another airing but was finally settled – the answer was 'no', and the discussions came to an end.

By the time the April meeting came round the problems were beginning to manifest themselves. The Skinnergate banner had been damaged and had to be repaired, ticket sales were 7% down on those for *Carousel* at the corresponding time, and Joy and John had informed the Chairman that they both felt strongly that the Society ought not to attempt the new version of *The Pirates of Penzance* for various reasons – for one thing it would only use fourteen ladies and would need twenty young and agile men. There was 'lengthy discussion'. Finally it was decided that *Fiddler on the Roof* should be repeated instead. There was a good reason for this. John Lloyd had sent out a 'show suggestions slip' with all of the ticket booking forms, inviting people to say what would be the show they would most like to see the Society perform. Despite a huge wave of apathy sweeping over the public – only a third of the slips were returned – the response was interesting. The favourite was *The Merry Widow*, which had had such mixed reviews from the press in 1973; joint second came *Kiss Me Kate* and *Fiddler on the Roof*; fourth was *The Sound of Music* and fifth was *Seven Brides for Seven Brothers*. Then came *The King and I*, closely followed by *Kismet*. *The Student Prince*, *My Fair Lady* and *The Desert Song* were joint eighth, and *Oklahoma!* and *Showboat* joint eleventh. Surprisingly, Jerry Herman's *Mack and Mabel* came next – it *has* been discussed by the Committee from time to time but they decided that there was too little for the chorus to do in it. Fourteenth came *Song of Norway*, *Oliver!* and *Sweet Charity*. There were also many others – like *The Girl Friend* and *Chu Chin Chow* – but each of these had only a single vote. It was possibly the lack of sufficient 'oper-atic'-type voices in the Society that meant that *Fiddler on the Roof* was chosen in preference to *The Merry Widow* – but it shows that the Society *will* take notice of its public, for *Kiss Me Kate* was chosen for spring 1988 to follow *Fiddler on the Roof*, *Kismet* followed that (though not solely because of the questionnaire), and *The Sound of Music*, *The Merry Widow* and *Oliver!* have all been performed since then.

Guys and Dolls, however, was the current concern. It opened on 29 April and produced mixed reviews. The *Northern Echo* was underwhelmed – the paper, in a four-inch column, called it '. . . a decently staged and mostly well-sung show that's a thoroughly workmanlike job but lacks that vital indefinable something that lifts it out of the ordinary.'[10] It did admit that there were some 'splendid moments' but did not enlarge on this. John Parker stood out for this critic (though he called him John Parkson) and he was surprised that *Sit Down You're Rocking the Boat* did not get an encore. The *Darlington & Stockton Times* filled a whole column and expressed views on the show which were just the opposite. 'The very professionalism,' the paper said, 'hits you straight between the eyes, and the marvellously colourful costumes and excellent choral harmonies make it extremely appealing. The work,' it added, 'is just as smooth as a professional production. In fact the atmosphere is better, as professionals often come across as cold and clinical and just "going through the motions". Director Joy Beadell seems to cast a magical spell of calm and assurance and the result is a sparkling effort, brimful of wit and fire.'[11] The cast had all seemed at home in their roles: Mike Stephenson 'effortlessly conveyed the arrogance of the character', Avril 'played with sympathy and conviction', Keith 'played with consummate ease and conviction', and John Parker was 'perfectly at home'.

Of course the show was not without its problems. For instance, one of the dances was left looking totally inadequate since it had been choreo-graphed specifically to be done with strobe lighting (to give it the look of an ancient black and white jerky film) and the strobe light kept fusing.

(Little things like that can cause a certain amount of tension, but this can sometimes be relieved by playing a joke or two. Gary Winn, who had joined the Society for *Guys and Dolls*, took most of the punishment in this area, in the scene where he had to stick his head into a doorway which led offstage and whistle to warn the crapshooters of the police raid. A doorway like this is an irresistible temptation – Gary never knew what he was going to see when he looked through it, for the rest of the cast had evolved a programme containing a variety of delights! Determined on revenge on the last night he managed to spray water over the malefactors and then ran offstage – face-first into a custard pie which had been lovingly prepared for him.) Another problem was that some of the costumes were not very satisfactory – indeed Kath Robinson had sacrificed one of her own evening dresses for the *Take Back Your Mink* number, allowing it to be torn apart and fixed with velcro fastening which would allow it to be removed quickly. Poor Kath. She was a wonderful Miss Adelaide, but at a somewhat fraught dress rehearsal she had cause to be more fraught than most. She had a very quick change in the wings from a dress with shoestring straps, under which she could wear no bra, into a nightdress and negligée – only there was not enough time to put on both of them, so she opted for the negligée. It was a very pretty negligée. Pretty but transparent. Ready as Kath always was to throw herself into whatever part she was playing, there were limits. She cowered in the wings clutching the offending garment – what there was of it – round her and protesting that she could not appear. At least, not so *much* of her could appear. From her seat in the auditorium Joy commanded, in her inexorable fashion, that Kath should come out on stage so that *she* could form an opinion. Kath demurred but finally gathered up the tattered remains of her dignity and stepped out. The cheer which went up from the orchestra pit was ear-splitting. Kath had a different outfit by the time the public saw the show.

The summer concert on 21 June was a great success. The members then had to think about *Fiddler on the Roof*, which would mark Joy's 40th year with the Society and which would be her 50th show as Producer/Choreographer. The men were auditioned first, and this was where the trouble began. It was initially over that vexed question of going outside the Society – this time for someone to play Tevye, one of those leading roles on which hangs the success or failure of the whole show (*Sweet Charity* and *Barnum* are other examples). The problem was that the Society still did not have among its membership a thoroughly satisfactory Tevye, any more than it had had one last time, when Stephen Henley had made his unexpected appearance. There were two candidates from outside the Society, and this was where the second problem arose. One of these two was an amateur and the other was a professional who had already played the part. Both auditioned and the amateur was given the part, the general policy being that amateurs should be used. Then it was discovered that he would not be available for two full weeks of the floorwork. This put Joy in an exceptionally difficult position, for she felt that she could not produce a properly polished show if her leading man was going to be absent for so long. An Extraordinary committee meeting was held. It was more extraordinary than most and a major headache for the Chairman. Joy outlined her views. In essence her point was that, though the professional could not be there for all of the floorwork either, he knew the part thoroughly, and anyway professionals are, by virtue of their training, much more easily able to absorb and remember direction than are amateurs. (This sort of thing had already been amply demonstrated in the choreography for *Hello Dolly!*) A professional, however, commands a fee. Joy suggested that perhaps a different producer might be the answer and she was prepared to withdraw. There was much discussion. One member did not want to take part in a vote and left the meeting. Six of the others did the same. In accordance with correct committee procedure this constituted seven abstentions so the Chairman continued with the item. The remaining five declared confidence in Joy and it was decided to recheck the precise length of time the amateur would be absent. If this was as already declared the professional would be asked to play the part. The matter was investigated. The amateur *would* be absent for two full weeks and so the professional was engaged.

The Operatic Society committees over the years had had sundry differences of opinion, but never one so divisive as this – not that any of it was directed against the professional himself, for he had done a superb audition. Rather it was over a matter of principle. However, the decision had now been taken in a fashion which was procedurally correct, and frayed tempers had the summer break in which to simmer down. Who was this professional? His name was Beverley Jones, 'a great bear of a man (more teddy than grizzly) . . .' [12] as the *Northern Echo* put it in its review of *Fiddler on the Roof.* He lived near York and had been in the choir at York Minster before studying organ, singing and drama at the Royal Academy of Music for his LRAM* and between 1967 and 1970, for four consecutive years, he had won the Best Actor and Best Singer awards at the Waterford Light Opera Festival. He then turned professional in 1972, appearing in programmes on television and becoming Musical Adviser to Yorkshire Television. He had done cabaret and he had done musical arrangement and

* Licentiate of the Royal Academy of Music.

direction for Harry Secombe, Moira Anderson, Gracie Fields, Howard Keel and Eartha Kitt. He finally took up producing and directing in 1976, doing work for major operatic societies. Apart from all this, even if the Society had thought that Stephen Henley *was* Tevye, those fifteen years previously, then this man was, if possible, even more so. He grew a beard especially for the show though he shaved it off immediately after the last performance, which rendered him momentarily unrecognizable to the rest of the company! Beards were a feature of the show and many of the men grew their own rather than sport false ones. The greatest irony was that the only man who originally had his own beard had to trim it back to stubble – Tom Kent was playing the Rabbi and the requisite long grey beard would not fit over his own.

By the time the September committee meeting came round the cast was virtually complete. Connie Reeves was playing opposite Bev Jones, as Golde, with Christine Murray, Pamela Walker, Zoë Kent, Emma Parker and Nicola Reeves as their daughters Tzeitel, Hodel, Chava, Bielke and Shprintze. (Zoë was having a busy time – the fifteen-year-old was studying for two roles: one as the modest Chava and the other as the brash Miss Adelaide in her school production of *Guys and Dolls*.) Pete Sowerby (a dancer who had joined the Society for *Annie Get Your Gun*), David Curtis and Melvyn Dawson were Motel, Perchik and Fyedka, suitors of the first three daughters. Sue Robinson, Sam Herdman and Shirley Dodd were Grandma Tzeitel, Lazar Wolf and Yente, the characters they had played in the 1972 production, but this time Mavis Wilson was Fruma-Sarah, transported on the shoulders of Joe Cooper, who also played Nachum the beggar. He came in quite handy when the props staff dropped potatoes from one of the carts on the second night, for Joe neatly covered the gaffe by being given a bucket and made to 'scavenge' for them! The 'Fiddler' this time was a young dancer named Robert Rowell and the two other children in the production were Jennifer Hird's son Kristen* and Patrick Freeman.

The souvenir programme for this production was considerably enlarged by Tom Kent. The numbers of Vice-Presidents, Patrons and visiting organizations (which were listed in the back) were growing, and it was also helpful to have more space to print photographs of the people taking the minor, as well as the major, roles. There was space, too, for brief biographies of the leading players. It was a great improvement on the smaller programme and was so successful that the format has been retained.

---

* Kristen went to work in London in 1994 as an assistant waiter at Clarence House, the Queen Mother's home.

Fiddler on the Roof 1987
Clockwise from bottom left: Nicola Reeves, Pamela Walker, Christine Murray, Zoë Kent, Connie Reeves, Emma Parker, with Bev Jones.

The show opened on 28 October, and by 21 October 80% of the tickets had been sold. Bev Jones had fitted in extremely well with the rest of the Society and it was obvious to the company that he would be an excellent Tevye. This was borne out by the reviews of the show. The *Northern Echo* (which had attributed those ursine qualities to Bev) found plenty of both humour and pathos and said that he gave the production its heart and soul. The production, it concluded, was slick and polished. (That was not the night on which the brakes on the castors of Tevye and Golde's bed in the 'ghost scene' were left off, causing the whole contraption to start to roll towards the orchestra pit when Connie jumped onto it. She was, she says, much more economical with her acting-movements after that!) The *Darlington & Stockton Times* regarded the show itself as 'one of the great musicals of all time'[13] and felt that this production did it justice. Bev's rendering of *If I Were a Rich Man* 'brought the house down', the chorus work was 'especially fine', and the dancing 'a particular triumph'. 'When,' said the critic, 'did I last experience that tremendous sense of expectation from an opening number, with singing and dancing of almost West End class?' The review concluded by saying '. . . if there are any spare tickets you should go for them.' The audiences undoubtedly enjoyed the show – they said so – but the icing on the cake was provided by a gentleman from America. He was a Jewish businessman who was staying in a hotel in the town, saw the show advertised, and managed to get tickets for himself and a colleague. When the performance was over he was so thrilled with it that he rushed round to the stage door, burst in, and demanded to see Bev. Having greeted Bev like a long-lost brother, he said that he had enjoyed the show so much that he 'felt as high as if he had had eight glasses of wine' (he hadn't!) and told Bev that his daughter had been married under a canopy, exactly as the wedding on stage had been done, just a few weeks previously. Such approbation from someone who knew exactly what he was talking about was the best that it was possible to get. It had been an expensive show to perform since the professional fees were higher, but though it made £630 less than *Carousel*, it made around £1,500 more than *Guys and Dolls*. What is more, the programme sales were greater than for *Carousel*, so the Committee was well pleased.

Just as *Fiddler on the Roof* was about to go on, arrangements for *Kiss Me Kate* were finalized. Although availability of scenery was limited Stephen Sanderson had managed to get a set from Clifford and Brown (it had been decided that, since the Stage Manager was the person most closely concerned with the scenery, it should be up to him to organize its hire so that the most convenient size and set-out would be obtained). Homburg's were providing the costumes at a similar sort of price to that which they had charged for the last few years. *How to Succeed . . .* was looked at yet again, and was chosen as the autumn show. Then the Society lost both its Property Master and one of its leading ladies; Steve and Avril Blain were moving to Devon in the new year because of Steve's job-change. Though Bernard Sanderson was no leading lady he did agree to take over as Property Master, and a room in the Arts Centre was hired to house the small props which had been in Steve's garage. Steve and Avril were greatly missed.

Kiss Me Kate would have to have higher ticket prices – 15p higher, to be exact – for the box office commission charge had risen by 2½% and

Kiss Me Kate 1988
Left to right: Mike Stephenson, Liz Holton, Vera Davison, John Hurlstone.

the rental by 7%, as well as other incidental costs. In fact, in the last year, the commission had risen by 93% and the rental by 23%. Rehearsal-room rent had also risen considerably. Though the Society had been able to give £2,000 to charity over the year, more revenue was required just to keep running on the spot.

The arrangements for *How to Succeed . . .* had already begun – at least a contract had been signed with the rights holders – and Joy was to produce it. John Beagle did not want to be Musical Director this time, so other potential musical directors were approached, and Stephen Sild,* who had been an accompanist and played in the orchestra for several shows, was appointed. There were difficulties over scenery, though,

---

* Stephen was to marry Gillian Marshall in the spring of 1989.

reported Stephen Sanderson. He had heard that the Southend society had built their own and he had enquired about it, but it had now been disposed of and he was casting around in search of another set. The Royal College of Music at Manchester thought they could build one but it would cost about £3,000. Costumes were proving to be something of a problem too, so Joy, Elsie Campbell and Vera Davison were exploring the possibilities of home-made costumes. (Vera, as well as being a leading lady – she was to take the lead in *Kiss Me Kate* – is also a clever seamstress.)

In the mean time *Kiss Me Kate* was fully cast and the publicity for it was being energetically handled by the latest new committee members, Steve Emmerson (husband of Sharon, who had been one of the Hot Box dancers in *Guys and Dolls*) and Elizabeth Cooper (wife of Joe, who had played Lieutenant Brannigan in the same production). John Hurlstone was playing the Fred Graham/Petruchio part, with Vera, of course, as Lilli Vanessi/Katharine. (This was the fourth time John had played Fred Graham – his daughter had been named Katharine after the central character.) Liz Holton had her first major role as Lois Lane/Bianca and Mike Stephenson was back to play Bill Calhoun/Lucentio – a gambler once more! Cliff Walker was playing Harry Trevor and Barrie Dargue was Paul, with Janet Robinson 'blacked up' as the maid, Hattie, who opens the show with the number *Another Op'nin', Another Show*. The two gangsters were played by Arthur Ellis and Mike Walker (who was now Chairman of the Society). Sam Herdman was playing Harrison Howell and the parts of the other players in the 'show within a show' were to be taken by David Birkett, John Parkin, David Barkes, Pete Sowerby, Steve Berriman and Michael Mitton. They all combined to give an excellent show. 'Past experience of the society,' said the *Northern Echo*, 'leads you to expect a well-drilled, well-produced, thoroughly workmanlike show and Joy Beadell's presentation doesn't do anything to disappoint these expectations. John Hurlstone and Vera Davison,' the review went on to say, 'are well-matched sparring partners, both with good singing voices and a feel for the exaggerated, theatrical dramatics that their characters employ.'[14] Arthur and Mike were also commended for giving 'full value' to the *Brush Up Your Shakespeare* number. This item was also taken up by the *Darlington & Stockton Times*, which regarded it as 'one of the high spots of a thoroughly enjoyable evening'[15] and the paper was also appreciative of John and Vera. 'Not only is their singing of a very high standard,' said the piece, 'but their acting was lively and convincing.' Liz Holton and Mike Stephenson, as well as the gangsters, were mentioned as supporting the leads well.

Arthur Ellis and Mike Walker had to stand for a long time on the stage during dialogue, and the devil, as they say, finds work for idle hands to do. Especially Arthur's hands. He thought that he would try to put Mike off his lines when the time came, by blowing as large a bubble as possible with the gum he was chewing. It was only when the sight made no impression whatsoever that he realized that Mike did not have his glasses on and was consequently blissfully unaware. So that fell flat, as did also the bubble, for it burst lavishly over Arthur's face just in time for his own lines. Mike was made to notice something, however, on the last night of the show. When he fired his gun into the air there was no mistaking the fact that both a 'cat' and a 'chicken' fell from the fly-gallery. Arthur received his come-uppance, as expected, on that night. He had a huge papier-maché *Works of Shakespeare* – it measured three feet by two feet by one foot thick – from which he read one short sentence which apparently spread over to the next page, to which he had to turn. The book was very easy to hold, papier-maché being so light – except, that is, when it is filled with scrap iron! Mike had to make the customary Chairman's speech from the stage, too; when the time came for the bouquets to be presented he remained in his gangster character. 'Get the broads with the flowers,' he ordered, brandishing his machine-gun, so everyone crowded in, leaving Arthur jammed at the side of the stage – where the stage crew, plentifully armed with water pistols, were able, in a leisurely fashion, to soak him all down one side. (The stage crew have their own particular rites, dividing themselves firmly into two factions: Stage Left and Stage Right. Sue Kirkbride remembers that during *Brigadoon* in 1981 competition was particularly keen between them. Sticky notices were everywhere backstage, proclaiming the superiority of each side over the other. One side decided to demonstrate this one night by doing their crewing wearing evening dress and white gloves. The other side, promptly claiming that they were much superior because it was just like a holiday to them, came in shorts and shirts. On the final night, however, they called it a draw, turning their attention instead to Sue and Barrie in their last love duet. Sue was treated, as she sang, to the sight of the entire stage crew in the wings, dressed in kilts, sporrans and various assorted under-wear; if there were tears in her eyes that night they certainly were not romantic ones.)

Kiss Me Kate had, at any rate, been a success and produced a good surplus, which meant that the charitable donations would be maintained at as high a level as was usual, but there was no time to indulge in feelings of self-congratulation. Three days after the end of *Kiss Me Kate*'s run a special meeting of the Committee was called by Mike Walker. The unthinkable was about to happen: Joy – Producer, Choreographer, President, foundation stone almost – was leaving. She had decided to emigrate to New Zealand at the end of the year to be nearer to her family. Fiona and her husband and little Tiffany were there, as well as Eoin, Joy's remaining son, and Joy felt she should go 'before I'm too old' – though no one could quite imagine Joy ever being old. The Committee received a written request, signed by 38 members, asking them to reconsider the proposal to perform *How to Succeed . . .* in the autumn. The feeling seemed to be that Joy should be allowed *her* choice of what would be her last show for the Society. She chose the lavish *Kismet* and Bill Jones hastened to make the arrangements for the change of programme. Since Stephen Sild had already been appointed Musical Director for the autumn show he remained in that capacity; it was, in a way, a shame that Joy and John Beagle could not collaborate for one last time, but John made up for it by putting together a *Farewell to Joy* concert, to be given in her honour at the theatre on 11 September.

Kismet was going to be a big, expensive show, and the Society lost no time in putting it into rehearsal once the performing rights were secured and the scenery and costumes (which cost £1.50 per costume more than usual – they were gorgeous) safely booked.

Early booking had to be sought for a producer for the spring show of 1989, which was to be *La Belle Hélène*. Callous though this sounds so close to the news of Joy's departure, it was essential, and someone had to be found who would be in tune with the Society. Bev Jones was a distinct possibility because he had already worked with the company and had got on well with them as an actor. An alternative would be Robert (Bob) Marlowe. He had been a dancer, a singer, an actor, and a cabaret artist on board ship. He had specialized in summer shows and was justly famous for his successful 'end-of-the-pier shows' at Cromer. It depended on which was available, though obviously Bob Marlowe would be more expensive, since he lived at Eastbourne and would need to board at Darlington during floorwork. Both were available, so Bev was asked to produce *La Belle Hélène* and Bob was asked to do the autumn show, though this had not yet been chosen.

Meanwhile, the day-to-day business of the Society continued. Barrie Dargue got his 25-year long-service award and Bernard Sanderson got his 40-year one. Sue Hewgill agreed to be Choreographer for *La Belle Hélène*, Sam Herdman was able to report the surplus on *Kiss Me Kate*, and Charlotte Aiken, at the age of sixteen, was to have a chance at being Stage Manager for *Kismet* since Ray Porteus was unable to assist for the show. She was helping Ray and Stephen for the concert and this would be useful experience for her in her chosen career, as she wanted to go to stage school to specialize in backstage work.

The *Kismet* cast worked particularly hard in the knowledge that this would be Joy's last show. John Hurlstone was cast in the role of Hajj which Kenneth Richardson had played so well 26 years earlier, and John Parker was back, after missing two shows, to play the Wazir (Ann was playing one of the Ayahs). Sam was originally cast as Jawan the brigand chief but had to pull out of the show, and the part was taken by Cliff Walker. Omar the poet was John Lloyd, Mike Walker was the Chief of Police and Shirley Dodd was the Widow Yussef. Of the chief dancers Adele Lee was Zubbediyah, Christine Murray was Samaris, and Janet Steel, Jayne Summerbell and Margaret Singer were the Princesses of Ababu. Connie Reeves, Mavis Wilson, Sharon Emmerson and June Aiken were slave girls, and Gary Winn, Tom Kent and David Barkes were beggars. Barrie Dargue played the roles of the Imam of the mosque (who opens the show) and the Bangle Man, while Ian Whitfield indulged in his speciality by managing to play more roles than anyone else: a business man, a policeman, a prosecutor and an informer! Joe Cooper was Hassan-Ben, the two Peters – Sowerby and Sanderson – were dancing, and Cecil Grieveson was in the chorus, clocking up, at the age of 72, his 50th show with the Society. There were new faces, too. Tiffany Edwards came into the Society to play the leading role of Marsinah. She was a pupil of Great Ayton-based Zuilmah Hopkins and was only seventeen, but had a lovely voice which promised even better things to come. She had already played Maria in a production of *West Side Story* at Middlesbrough Little Theatre when only fifteen. Maggie Thorp came, too, and was just right for the part of Lalume, been a professional dancer and singer, on the stage and in cabaret both in clubs and on board ship. She was with Stockton Stage Society and was too late to get into the Darlington society for *Kiss Me Kate*, but she and Doreen Orton, a contralto, came along together for *Kismet*; Doreen took the part of the Ayah to Zubbediyah and suffered agonies in learning the fictitious language for the song she had to sing. Her eyes spoke volumes at rehearsals though of course she mastered the thing in the end. It took a while to get a Caliph but eventually Colin Kerr (who had played Freddy in *My Fair Lady*) agreed to come and take on the role.

Before *Kismet*, though, came the concert: *Farewell to Joy*. John Beagle assembled a wealth of Society talent – 77 members, past and present – to perform a wide variety of material as a tribute to Joy and to express thanks for all her work for the Society. The programme of musical items, drama and dance bears quoting in its entirety because of its great diversity. After an overture played by the orchestra of ten plus Pat McIntyre and Stephen Sild on piano, Janet Robinson and the chorus did *Another Op'nin', Another Show*, followed by *Brush Up Your Shakespeare* sung by Arthur Ellis and Mike Walker. Then the children did *You're Never Fully Dressed Without a Smile* from *Annie*. This was followed by the chorus with *The Girls The Boys Dream*

About from *Robert and Elizabeth*, and then Brian Sheppard played Grieg's *Wedding Day at Troldhaugen* on the piano. There then followed an Ivor Novello selection: Vera and Barrie sang *We'll Gather Lilacs*; Kiran Singh had come back specially from London to appear and she sang *Shanty Town*. Then the chorus sang *Spring in Vienna*. Eunicé Cockburn, who had not been in a show since *King's Rhapsody* in 1982, sang *Some Day My Heart Will Awake* from that show, and that was followed by *Why is There Ever Goodbye?* Doreen Orton then sang *Fly Home, Little Heart*. The *Sabbath Prayer* from *Fiddler on the Roof* came next; then Tiffany sang one of her solos from *West Side Story: There's a Place for Us*, and John Parker sang *She's Too Far Above Me* from *Half a Sixpence*. Connie followed that with *Open a New Window* from *Mame*, and the chorus came next with *Maybe It's Because I'm a Londoner*, which led on to Pauline Curtis and *Wouldn't It be Luvverly* from *My Fair Lady*. John Hurlstone then sang *If Ever I Would Leave You* from *Camelot* and *I've Grown Accustomed to Her Face* from *My Fair Lady*, and the first half concluded with Doreen Orton singing *Rose of England* from Novello's *Crest of a Wave*.

Connie opened the second half with *Before the Parade Passes By* and *Goodbye* from *Hello Dolly!*, and then there was some tap-dancing – dancing, after all, had been Joy's *forte* originally. This was followed by Maggie Thorp singing and dancing the number *Vitality* from Novello's *Gay's the Word*, then Tiffany sang again, this time *Somewhere Over the Rainbow* from *The Wizard of Oz*; next Kiran sang Sondheim's *Send In the Clowns* from *A Little Night Music* before Eileen Young gave her peerless rendering of *Nobody Loves a Fairy When She's Forty*. A Rodgers and Hammerstein selection followed this: the chorus sang *If I Loved You* from *Carousel*, Roula Murray sang *Bali Ha'i* from *South Pacific* and Mavis Wilson followed that with *Honey Bun*. The chorus then went back to *Carousel* for *When You Walk Through a Storm*, followed by Vera with *Hello, Young Lovers* from *The King and I*, then Pauline and David Curtis sang the *Oklahoma!* duet *People Will Say We're in Love*, and Eunicé returned with *Climb Every Mountain* from *The Sound of Music*. Shirley Dodd gave a song/monologue entitled *They Don't Make Them Like That Any More*, which came from a show called *Phil the Fluter* and had originally been performed by Evelyn Laye. This was followed by a sketch by Noël Coward: *Red Peppers*, very well acted by Steve Luck, Kath Robinson, Stan Lloyd and Sam Herdman. The show, which had been interspersed with linking speeches by Bill Jones, was drawing to a close now, and Bill took to the stage as a performer – for the first and last time since *Song of Norway* back in 1970 – to sing Noël Coward's *The Party's Over*. He was then joined by John Parker and they performed a specially-written, apposite version of *Thanks for the Memory* before the chorus sang *Sail Away*. The programme concluded with the chorus singing

We'll Keep a Welcome in the Hillside, followed by *I'll See You Again* from *Bitter Sweet* and *Wish Me Luck as You Wave Me Goodbye* with Maggie singing the solo part.

Joy undoubtedly enjoyed it, and the audience certainly seemed to. The *Darlington & Stockton Times* was there and said, 'The concert was a triumph, not only with the chorus work at which the society habitually excel . . . but with a succession of solo performances that wouldn't have disgraced the West End.'[16] This was certainly music to the Society's ears, but the main aim was that Joy should have the memory to take away with her of so many people wanting to pay tribute to her. The Society had also commissioned a portrait of Joy to hang with the one of Lady Starmer in the boardroom at the theatre. A copy of this was used on the front of the concert programme.

Joy had not finished yet, however. There was still *Kismet* to be put on – her concert had been so early only because that was the only date which the theatre could offer – and she would allow no slacking.

Five weeks before opening night three quarters of the tickets had been sold and there were no seats at all left for the last night. There was a record number of Vice-Presidents and Patrons, too, but the show unfortunately brought in £200 less ticket money than had *Kiss Me Kate*. It was a shame that it did not play to full houses because it was a spectacular show to look at. The costumes were glamorous – John Lloyd received a special 'Academy Award' at the after-show party for having the most striking hat, which was described in the citation as 'The Flying Pumpkin'! Special props had been made by Ernie Mann, George Aiken and Brian Hubbard (a Visual Merchandise Manager at Binns department store and a great asset to the Society), and there were even an Afghan Hound and a Borzoi in the Caliph's procession. The critics enjoyed it, though the *Northern Echo* and the *Darlington Advertiser* both mentioned the fact that two large pieces of scenery toppled over on the first night and threatened to flatten the slave girls who hastily rearranged themselves and carried on. 'John Hurlstone,' said the *Northern Echo*, 'effortlessly holds the strands together with a finely tuned performance.'[17] Tiffany and Colin sang well, and the production was, as expected, strong on dancing. The *Darlington Advertiser* made particular mention of the dancing of Janet, Jayne and Margaret as the Princesses of Ababu, as well as praising the 'fine singing'[18] of Colin and Tiffany and the performances of John Hurlstone and Maggie. The *Darlington & Stockton Times* agreed that the three princesses merited a special word of praise from among a chorus and dancers who 'could not be faulted'[19] and also declared that John Hurlstone was 'excellent as always' and Maggie was perfect as the Wazir's seductive wife with the roving eye. John Parker, as the Wazir, was

Kismet 1988. Colin Kerr, Tiffany Edwards.

described as 'deliciously witty' and Colin and Tiffany 'looked good and sang beautifully'. The reviewers' conclusion was that the large amount of money spent to mount the production was amply justified and urged the public to 'brave the elements' – the weather was appalling that autumn – 'and get along to the ticket office at once'. So Joy could be justly proud of her last show, though it had been a difficult one to do – Joy herself owned that she had forgotten just how difficult it was. The first dress rehearsal had not ended until 1.20 a.m. and there had been illness among the cast. John Hurlstone had had voice problems, Ann Parker had not been well, Adele Lee had hurt her back but had managed to appear each night (though only in her solo spot) and Christine Murray had done her Salamis of Bangalore dance one night, gone off stage and promptly fainted!

Joy left for New Zealand a matter of days after the end of *Kismet*'s run. She was made an Honorary Life Member of the Society and has kept in constant touch. She has been back to England for a few extended stays to see everyone, and has said that she still misses the Society. She runs her own dancing school in Auckland and is still a force to be reckoned with in the world of dance. In 1994 one of her pupils, Meika McHardy, won a scholarship to a prestigious ballet school in America, becoming one of the first New Zealanders to be accepted into the Kirov Academy in Washington DC.

The Society now had to adjust to a new producer, of course, and when Bev Jones began the floorwork rehearsals for *La Belle Hélène* the company was soon very much aware that he had a totally different approach from Joy. Where Joy had always had a complete plan for the show worked out beforehand, Bev had a general idea, looked at the abilities of his cast, and then took it from there. He was full of ideas, had an exceptional gift for comedy and combined an outstanding talent for graphic phraseology with such a friendly nature that few could take offence. His character was as colourful as his language – in short he had the company jumping through hoops. Speed of learning and concentration were of the essence, because Bev had only half the floorwork-time that Joy had had. He was producing shows for amateur societies in Harrogate and York on a regular basis, as well as intermittently for other groups, so his time with the Darlington society was necessarily limited. For the company, used as they were to Joy's more leisurely pace, it was like being descended upon by a whirlwind, but once swept up in it they managed to adjust to the different pace remarkably quickly.

By mid-December the show was almost totally cast. The autumn 1989 show, to be produced by Bob Marlowe, was fixed as Vivian Ellis and Richard Myers's *Mr Cinders*, the Cinderella story in reverse. Bob wrote a long letter to the Committee outlining his plans for auditions, for his rehearsal schedule and for a 'Movement for Non-Movers Workshop', and mentioning his requirement of a Production Assistant and a Dancing Mistress.

When the Annual General Meeting came round in March 1989 Mike Walker, as Chairman, was looking ahead to the two shows. Things would be very different with two new producers and he urged members to show themselves to be flexible and adaptable and to strive all the time to improve their standards. It was a timely reminder, as the Society had been rather like a rudderless ship without its President/Producer. Bev, however, had arrived to inject a lot of enthusiasm just the previous Sunday and the Society was to have a new President. In view of his long, loyal and hardworking service, Sam Herdman was unanimously elected, and a portrait of him was commissioned to hang alongside those of Lady Starmer and Joy Beadell at the theatre.

The subject of the theatre was a matter of great concern by now, for massive refurbishment was planned and it was to close for ten months in 1990, from the end of the pantomime at the beginning of February until the opening of the next pantomime in December. A new box office would be constructed next to the stage door, facing Parkgate, with offices above.

Four houses in Borough Road adjacent to the theatre would be demolished and incorporated into the building, providing space for a new bar
and coffee bar, amongst other offices. Special stalls boxes would be put
in at the back of the auditorium to accomodate wheelchairs, and the
control box would be moved to the centre of the back of the stalls. The
upper circle would be opened up again after its long closure, and, when
reopened, the seating capacity of the theatre would be increased from six
hundred to nine hundred.

This gave the Society much food for thought. The theatre *had* been
closed before, of course, but that was over thirty years earlier and then a
different venue had had to be found for only one show. More sophisticated
audiences, now well-used to lavish television shows, expected more, even
from an amateur company, than in those days. When television entertainment was laid on universally in their own homes, would the public
be as willing to go to two Operatic Society shows at venues (as yet
unknown) which would have considerably less in the way of atmosphere
and facilities than the Civic Theatre? Would they return to Operatic
Society shows when the year was over? This would all have to be mulled
over in the ensuing year, but for now the 1989 shows would have to pull
in a lot of people to supplement the 'cushion' of the Society's investments
in case of problems in 1990. Margaret Cunningham did, however, make
the valid point that when schools were independent (such a scheme was
under discussion at the time) they would need extra funds, and headmas-
ters/headmistresses would be able to hire out their halls for a time long
enough for the run of a show.

After this meeting the chairmanship of the Society passed from Mike
Walker to Greta Sanderson, and Vera Davison and Liz Holton (who had
been so impatient to become just a lowly member of the Society so many
years before) were co-opted onto the Committee.

Just over three weeks before *La Belle Hélène* things were not looking too
good. Although rehearsals were going wonderfully well and the cast, who
had had such fun rehearsing it, all knew that it was going to be an
exceptional offering, the public, perhaps suspicious of the French title,
were not flocking to buy tickets. These had gone up by 15p but such a
small price rise had never made any difference before. There were higher
expenses this time – for one thing radio microphones were being hired
for the principals at a cost of around £40 each (plus £1.50 per battery –
and the batteries did not last very long). There were those who thought
them unnecessary, but it had been agreed to try them out.

La Belle Hélène opened on 3 May. Offenbach's comedy work, fantastic
in the true sense of the word, is intended to be something of an 'over-
the-top' show. Bev took it *right* over the top, knowing that this can be

done successfully only if the singing and acting is first class. He had a winning team. David Curtis primped and preened as the narcissistic Paris and Maggie Thorp was a predatory Helen. Sam Herdman, in his 62nd show for the Society, was in excellent form as her deceived husband, Menelaus. He had played Ajax the last time the show was performed, in 1965, and he, Cliff Walker (as Agamemnon) and Bernard Sanderson (in the chorus) were the only cast members who had been in that previous show – Cliff had played Philocomus and Bernard had played Agamemnon. This time John Lloyd was playing the lecherous old Philocomus to Arthur Ellis's double-dealing Calchas. Zoë Kent and Liz Holton were Leona and Cressida, and Barrie Dargue made up the unholy trio of young rebels as Orestes, wearing a wig reminiscent of 'Bubbles' in the well-known painting by Sir John Millais! Shirley Dodd was playing Nesta, Helen's handmaiden, and the two remaining kings, Ajax and Achilles, were played by Mike Walker and Paul Arnold. The three beautiful goddesses, Juno, Minerva and Venus, were played – with feeling – by Jacqui Carbert, June Aiken and Vera Davison: Jacqui in her curlers when the curtain first rose, busy with her yards-long piece of knitting, June with her fright-wig and cello, and Vera, the very vision of a love-goddess, busy ironing a pair of large pink bloomers and wearing a turban and wrap-around apron, a cigarette hanging from the corner of her mouth. Mercury, complete with winged helmet and Sinclair C5 three-wheeled electric car, was played by John Parkin – a man of many voices – and the cast was completed by a wonderfully comic Cupid – Janet Robinson – who made up in weight for what she lacked in toxophilitic skill and revelled in the role.

The show opened in front of a wonderful audience – some of the cast said it was the best first night they had ever known. The *Northern Echo* called it '. . . a gloriously funny production . . . which displays a rib-tickling sense of the ridiculous. Maggie Thorp's vampish Helen and David Curtis as a preening Noël Coward-like Paris,' the critic went on, 'are both beautifully done, although keeping a straight face can't be easy. The Greeks probably had a word for it,' he concluded, '– I'd call it entertaining . . . A pity that ticket sales are not up to the Society's usual levels. The delighted first-night audience will hopefully spread the word.'[20] He enjoyed all the performances, but, for him, Shirley Dodd's myopic Nesta stole the show. That went for the *Darlington Advertiser*, too, though Janet Robinson, the review said, '. . . must also be applauded for daring to take on the role, among others, as Cupid. Never before has Cupid been such a heavyweight. This production of Offenbach's operetta,' it went on, 'combines just enough tongue-in-cheek humour with the excellent standard of singing and dancing which has come to be expected of the Society.'[21] This review also praised Maggie and David for managing to keep straight faces, and reference was made to John Parkin's mode of transport and also to Sam's exit on a bicycle to do his 'month's penance in Crete'. 'Look out,' the review concluded, 'for the stage hands too.' This was a reference to George Aiken and to Terry Coleman, the theatre's own Stage Manager. Terry appeared on stage to relieve Arthur of one of the props and contrived to deliver a different *ad lib* each night, which brought the house down. Then, in Act Two, comes Helen's beautiful solo *The Moment Now is Drawing Near*, Maggie managed to deliver it flawlessly every time, despite George entering with a yardbrush and unhurriedly sweeping the stage round her, pausing only to lean on his brush and contemplate her steadily and with supreme indifference for a few moments before continuing his sweeping, unmoved by either the glamorous nightdress and negligée or by the superb soprano voice. The audiences did not know whether to laugh or cry, so they did a lot of both. Bill Duff, of the *Darlington & Stockton Times* opened his review with the words 'DOS's *La Belle Hélène* has everything to make a perfect night's entertainment, and that is the key word.'[22] He said that the parts of Helen and Paris were 'incomparably sung', and he loved Shirley's performance and those of Mike and Paul in their duet *Two Mighty Men at Arms*. (The same tune is also known as *The Two Gendarmes* or *The Gendarmes' Duet* – Offenbach stole tunes from himself all the time!) 'Sam Herdman's voice,' continued the review, 'has lost none of its power nor has his acting ability dulled with the passing years.' Sam was certainly in good form and very agile, as anyone else who has tried to dance in frogmen's flippers could testify. The review also praised Zoë, Liz and Barrie ('a priceless Orestes'). There was a special mention for the young dancers who performed a delightful and serious little ballet, choreographed by Sue Hewgill, as a contrast to all the hilarity and irreverence, and also for Stephen Sild's orchestra, which was 'excellent'. Bill Duff thought that the funniest scene was the one on the seashore with the cast in bathing costumes – and yes, among them *were* the men's bathing costumes from *The Gondoliers*! 'This,' concluded the review, 'is a show that should be seen.' Denis Weatherley, the bass singer, well known as a teacher of singing and as an ex-Headmaster, as well as for his recordings of Northern ballads, agreed with him. He went to see the show twice and remarked that it was the best amateur show he had seen.[23] It is certainly true that some members of the public wrote letters of appreciation, and some made contact during the show to order tickets for the next one. Perhaps one of the most touching accolades was one which came by word of mouth. A lady in early middle age was taken to see the show by a friend; she had recently been widowed suddenly and the friend thought that the outing would do her good. She telephoned her friend the following day to say that the show had put her into such a relaxed frame of mind that she had had her first good night's sleep since her husband's death. Several people went to see the show more than once, but of course that was farther into the run when the word had gone round and, in fact, the theatre was only half full on the second night. Ultimately the show lost over £1,600 despite Maggie's husband managing to get sponsorship from three local companies and a bank to pay for the hire of the radio microphones. These were a great success and some were bought by the theatre after this.

The experience of working with Bev had been so rewarding and this first show under his direction had been such a success with those who *did* go to see it that he was asked to direct both shows in 1990. The new version of *The Pirates of Penzance* was tentatively chosen for the spring and a *Songs from the Shows* production for the autumn, since the Committee was still searching for venues and these were shows which could be performed with limited space and fewer facilities.

A difficult summer followed the cheerful spring. Steve Emmerson re-signed from the Committee because Sharon, who had been in several shows, was very ill. There was considerable difficulty in finding a venue for 1990; the Dolphin Centre, Hummersknott School, and Polam Hall School were all discussed but there were difficulties with all of them. Bob Marlowe said that he could not cast *Mr Cinders* with the talent available in the Society, so it was cancelled. He said he *could* cast *The Sound of Music* and it was also good box office, so while the one show was being cancelled the other was being booked. Bill Jones was not having an easy time either, because his brother-in-law had died. He flew out to be with his sister in South Africa, so Sam had to make some of the arrangements for *The Sound of Music*. The rights holders insisted that the Society pay to hire scores and scripts, though several members already had their own from the last time it was performed. Of course, two sets of six children were needed and they had to be advertised for and then auditioned. Everything was very unsettled and Bob Marlowe said he could not cast anyone who would be taking any holiday during floorwork, which was reasonable but not popular.

In July things began to look up a little. Two hundred children turned up to audition for the parts, and Stephen Sild made a speedy and excellent job of making a short-list from these and getting them down to the required twelve. John Lloyd had already received a good many requests for booking forms before they were even printed, and several requests had been made for block bookings. It was incredibly early for bookings to be coming in and he suggested a matinée 'but got no support'![24] It was just as well that the Committee had agreed to buy him a telephone answering machine the previous year because his telephone rang constantly, which was good for the Society but not so good for the nervous system. The calls would start before 8 a.m. and continue until around midnight, weekends included, and as a result the Assistant Ticket Secretary was turning from a comparatively peaceable individual into a shrew!

By 10 September – six and a half weeks before the show opened – 85% of the tickets were sold. Ten days later 95% were sold and the Assistant Ticket Secretary would have been combining plans for a monumental nervous breakdown and a divorce had it not been for the telephone answering machine! The signs were all good: if *The Sound of Music* sold like this, and the Society made a good job of it, it should help to gain support for the 'wilderness year' of 1990. Stephen Sanderson had had the bright idea of asking about using the hall at the College of Technology in Cleveland Avenue as it was not only a reasonable size, but was central, was easy to get to, and had car-parking space in the streets around it.

The show opened on 25 October after an uneasy floorwork period. There were some personality clashes and Bob called the company 'amateurish'. The two dress rehearsals were disastrous, though the show had a very good cast. Tiffany Edwards was back again to play Maria, and Warnock Kerr had got the part of Captain von Trapp. Barrie Dargue was playing Max Detweiler again, and Liz Holton, Tricia Freeman and Cecil Grieveson were the only other people in the cast who had taken part in the show's previous airing in 1975. Vera Davison was playing the elegant Elsa, Baroness Schraeder, and Doreen Orton was the Mother Abbess, with Jacqui Carbert, Connie Reeves and Suzanne Dalton as Sister Berthe, Sister Margaretta and Sister Sophia. Rachel Green, who had originally joined as a dancer for *La Belle Hélène*, got the part of Liesl and Melvyn Dawson played her sweetheart Rolf, while the sinister Franz the butler, and the housekeeper, Frau Schmidt, were played by John Parkin and Shirley Dodd. Baron Elberfeld was played by Dave Smith, who had also come along to be in *La Belle Hélène*, and Betty Cooke ended her performing days with the Society in a named part by playing Baroness Elberfeld. The children were divided into two teams to play alternate nights. In descending order of age, one team consisted of Patrick Freeman, Maria Wallace, James Allison, Sarah Wright, Carey Lea and Gemma Pontone; the other consisted of James Coates, Emma Parker, Nathan Smith, Emma Hardwick, Rachel Boyle and Laura Cave. Charlotte Aiken, at the age of seventeen, was a seasoned Assistant Stage Manager by now, and she needed all her expertise on the night when Tiffany (as Tiffany readily admits) completely forgot the prayers she was supposed to say in the scene where the children become frightened by the storm, and made up ones of her own to fill the time in. Charlotte spent the time vainly searching for the correct cue-words with which to coordinate lightning flashes and thunder rolls!

The audiences loved the show, apart from the fact that the Nazis were received with a giggle or two rather than a sharp intake of breath for there were too few of them to be menacing, as the usual man-shortage prevailed. The press were more reticent. The *Northern Echo* began its review by saying 'One of the great mysteries of our time remains the enormous popularity of this Rodgers and Hammerstein musical,'[25] though the reviewer then said 'It is well cast, nicely played, moves at a fair pace and makes something familiar seem as fresh as new.' Tiffany, he thought, brought 'a welcome youthfulness and pleasant singing voice' to the part of Maria. He thought Warnock was a touch too unbending (though since this is in the nature of the character the criticism was a touch on the harsh side). Doreen, Vera and Barrie had made the most of their roles, and the children had done so, too. He concluded his review by saying that on the distaff side *(sic)* the Nazis were more Keystone Cops than Third Reich. It was the children who stole the show with their professional performances, according to the *Darlington Advertiser*, though Tiffany had taken on her part 'with enthusiasm and confidence'.[26] This reviewer picked out June Aiken from the rest of the cast; June had a cameo role as a tone-deaf concert performer in the concert during which the von Trapp family escape, and was dressed in a Wagnerian Brünnhilde-style costume, with helmet and spear. The spear had been a sore trial to her in every way and she had finally managed to break her toe with it at rehearsal! The reviewer accused Warnock of being 'wooden' but the *Darlington & Stockton Times* reviewer, Jill Neill, referred to the character as being 'stiff and starchy',[27] which was perhaps fairer. She had enjoyed the show: her headline read 'Amateurs tackle one of the greats – with magnificent results' and she attributed 'confidence and professionalism which belied her seventeen years' to Tiffany. She had enjoyed the performances of Doreen, Barrie ('convincingly rogueish') and Vera ('calm and classy') and also those of Shirley and Sam, though she, too, gave the Nazis a trouncing. She also felt that more emotion could have been wrung from the scene in which Rolf was torn as to whether or not to betray the family, not knowing that poor Melvyn had had troubles of his own in an earlier scene, having missed his cue and left Barrie and Vera to improvise small talk until he appeared! All in all, though, she described it as 'a polished, professional performance' but it was obvious from the tenor of all the reviews that there was something missing that none of the critics could quite put a finger on. There were letters and telephone calls of appreciation from the public, however, which showed that the show had been generally well received. In the end there were only six seats unsold over the whole run of *The Sound of Music*, and there were 283 Vice-Presidents and Patrons and 45 block bookings. Yet still it lost money – it was becoming obvious that the enlargement of the theatre was necessary to give a higher income from reasonable ticket prices.

Tiffany left the Society after this production and went to study singing at the Royal College of Music. She received her Performer's Diploma in 1994 but, intent on an operatic career, embarked on a two-year post-graduate course to be followed by two years at opera school. Charlotte Aiken also left. She had been accepted, from among a large number of applicants, by two colleges which specialized in Theatre Studies, and chose to go to the prestigious Rose Bruford College of Speech and Drama in Kent to study Stage Management.

As the year drew to a close the company at least knew where the 1990 shows would take place. Stephen Sanderson's bright idea was to come to fruition and the hall at the College of Technology was to be used. From the Committee's point of view there were a lot of decisions to make: what price, for instance, should the tickets be? What should be paid to the orchestra when Musicians' Union rates did not apply for playing in the College building? What should be done about refreshments and the entertaining of the Chairman's guests? What was certain was that expenses had been so high that there had been a loss of around £3,000 on the two shows in 1989, which was depressing. Even more depressing was the number of deaths which had occurred during the year. No fewer than five obituaries appear at the back of the programme for *The Sound of Music*. There was Sharon Emmerson, only in her early thirties, who had gamely planned to appear in *Kismet* despite her illness. Her husband, Steve, had been a very useful member of the Committee until he had had to resign in order to give more time to looking after the couple's young son. There was also Jimmy Hall whose most recent role had been that of the Heavenly Friend in *Carousel* – he was only middle aged. Jim Fraser Murray also died suddenly that year, and of course he had been thoroughly involved in the Society for most of his life. He had been Chairman twice, as well as being the Regional Representative in NODA for many years. Finally there were the comparatively young husbands of two members: Ian Cunningham, husband of Margaret (née Teasdale), and Colin Singer, husband of Margaret (née Taylor).

There were anxious times ahead and fresh challenges to face now that the theatre was about to close. Although the College of Technology was much more convenient for the public to reach than the school at Hummersknott had been when *No, No, Nanette* had been given in 1957 there was still no guarantee that there would be full houses. Large block bookings, for instance, might well fall off when there were considerably fewer seats available and there was not the full range of theatre facilities. Still, the Society had weathered many problems and it had no intention of letting its standards slip when there was the prospect of attracting even bigger audiences when the theatre reopened. Bev could be trusted to make *The Pirates of Penzance* a lively and novel show, so they now put themselves in his hands and awaited results.

Chapter 11

1990–1994

Early in January 1990 some new men were voice-tested to join the Society for *The Pirates of Penzance*. It was a show for twenty-one men and fifteen women so competition was keen among the ladies. They had to look young, of course, because they all, with the exceptions of Ruth 'the pirate maid of all work' and Queen Victoria, were supposed to be Major General Stanley's daughters. As far as the men's chorus was concerned, Paul Arnold, Joe Cooper, Cecil Grieveson, John Lloyd and Ian Whitfield were Society members already, but they were now joined by Ian Black, Keith Bowran (husband of Chris who had joined the chorus for *Carousel*), Robert Ellis, Stuart Gordon, Richard Grey, Viv Hardwick (father of Emma, who was in *The Sound of Music*), Barry Million, Karl Oldridge, Les Oxley, David Plumpton and Martin Simpson. Rarely has the Society managed to acquire eleven new men all at once, and Barry, David and Les are still with the Society and likely to remain so.

Of the four named 'daughters', Liz Holton was playing Isobel and there were some new members to play the others. Alison Cochlan, originally from Scotland but living at Catterick with her husband, came to play Kate. She had been in Youth Theatre in Scotland and was now singing at the mediaeval banquets at the Redworth Hall Hotel. Claire Williams, who came to play Edith, was a student at Durham University, and Andrea Durham, who played the leading role of Mabel, was a pupil of Carol Andrew, the Darlington singer. Andrea lived in Northallerton and was a member of the operatic society there as well as of the Northallerton Amateur Variety Company. The rest of the 'daughters' consisted of Maxine Allinson (who had joined the Society in time to be in *Fiddler on the Roof*), Elizabeth Cooper, Rhoda Frazer (who came from the Richmond society for this one show), Sarah Mann, Ann Oxley, Kath Robinson, Melanie Short (who had joined for *The Sound of Music*), Carolyn Smiles (who had joined at the same time) and Margaret Webb. One or two of these turned out to be around the same age as their 'father', because that role went to John Parker, but they tripped around 'like young gazelles' (to quote one of Bev's favourite phrases) and the suspension of disbelief was not, in fact, difficult. June Aiken got the part of Ruth and Eileen Young made a comeback as Queen Victoria. Gary Winn was cast in his first 'named' role as the Sergeant of Police (and began to show comic talent to be reckoned with in the process) and Barrie Dargue was Samuel, the Pirate King's Lieutenant. (Came the show and Barrie had to have a parrot on his shoulder. Whatever it was it was certainly not a parrot, nor even an ex-parrot; a stricken budgerigar is probably nearer the mark, but it underwent a process of such serious deterioration during the show that we shall never know for certain what it was!) Two notable names are missing from this cast list: not only did the show lack a hero, as had been the case so many times before, it lacked *both* heroes. There was no Frederick and no Pirate King. This was a major matter for the Committee to mull over in the earliest months of the year, together with how arrangements could be made to make the College hall as theatre-like as possible employing DIY techniques. They had a further reason for trying to be as economical as possible: the theatre was still very much in their minds and they wanted to be able to sponsor the new dress circle coffee bar there.

The set for *Pirates* was being built by George Aiken, Ray Porteus and Stephen Sanderson, using Durham Theatre Company's facilities at the Arts Centre, and it was being painted by Brian Hubbard and Sally Wade. The costumes were being hired from Homburg's. Fred Dawson had volunteered to organize the seat numbering and also to do front-of-house duties, and Bernard Sanderson was House Manager. The College itself offered to provide a bar staffed by students, and Bob Blyth, the College Technician, had also volunteered to help with the staging of the show. Dressing-rooms were a problem, though. There were only two rooms available and they had no running water, but the College hoped to get washbasins installed before the show.

The Committee waited anxiously to see what the public response would be once the booking opened. By the time they assembled for their March meeting John Lloyd reported that there was a steady stream of bookings, but there were still a lot of tickets to sell though the price was the same as for *The Sound of Music*. It was an agonizing time; if the tickets did not go well for a full show, what would be the response to the collection of items which would make up *The Magic of the Musical* in the autumn? There was no option but to wait and see. The anxiety was evident in Greta Sanderson's opening remarks at the Annual General Meeting at the end of March when she owned that her Chairmanship had caused her some sleepless nights. She did have some good news to impart, however: Tom Kent had won the NODA Northern area trophy again for the programme for *La Belle Hélène* and had come second with the one for *The Sound of Music*. He had also won the NODA National trophy for the best poster with the one for *The Sound of Music*. More good news came from Elizabeth

1990 NODA trophies
Greta Sanderson, Tom Kent.

Cooper, who, as part of the Social and Fundraising section of the Committee (though she was shortly to move to Publicity), was able to report that most of the social events were being well supported. The Society was happy, at this meeting, to confer Honorary Life Membership on Shirley Dodd, Sue Robinson and Joan Herdman, Sam's ever-supportive wife, but the predominant mood was uncertainty. Bill Jones pointed out that, once back in the theatre, the Committee would have to choose shows very carefully; the opening one, in particular, would have to be a proven box office success since there would be 3,000 more seats to fill over the ten nights. Ticket prices would be bound to go up, as the theatre costs would have to rise dramatically. Sam wondered whether the Society would be able to afford to do two shows each year, bearing in mind that there was an *overall* reduction in the funds – the first time this had happened since 1974, even though there had been losses on just the actual productions since then. It was hard work making money for charity in this way, but the Society had managed to donate £28,000 since 1946 and it was about to give a donation to the Telethon 90 appeal. Greta had thought her sleepless nights as Chairman were over, but this was not to be. Tom Kent did not wish to be Chairman again. He had quite enough to do already, as he and Judi were involved in the Richmond society as well as with Darlington, so Greta was asked if she would agree to be re-elected. It can only be assumed that she was shell-shocked, because she agreed and went back to the sleepless nights!

Much casting around was done for two male leads for the show, and finally it was discovered that Michael Geddes, who had played Luiz for Darlington in *The Gondoliers* in 1984, was free to play Frederick. He had played the part for the Tyne Theatre Musical Theatre Group, and, what is more, would be able to bring along Frank Lloyd who had played the part of the Pirate King on that occasion. Enormous relief spread through the company, though this was mingled with concern that the pair were unable to turn up for a number of the floorwork rehearsals.

By April there was good news and bad news. The good news was that the Society's membership now stood at 126, showing that it was in a healthy state and that there was plenty of interest. The scenery construction was going very well indeed and its builders were proud of it. Also, Lilian Higginbottom, the Chief Usherette from the Civic Theatre, had been kind enough to offer her services to help front-of-house for the show. The bad news was that there were still 1,600 tickets left to sell, and that there might be problems with the acoustics at the College. There was much discussion in the Committee about the possible use of radio microphones but, as Stephen Sanderson said, there was no sound system at the College and this would be extremely costly. It would have to be discussed with Bev and with Stephen Sild. The other irksome thing concerned one particular member of the public. She had the misfortune to own a telephone number that differed by one digit from that of the Ticket Secretary and her number had been printed in an advertisement in mistake for his. The unfortunate woman was driven to distraction with requests for tickets and information. The Society tried to make amends in some measure by making her a special guest at one of the performances of the show and it is good to be able to record that she enjoyed the experience, the more so because she had been a singer herself, and Gilbert & Sullivan shows were among her favourites.

The cast wondered how the public would take to this updated version of the show, and it was not without its problems. The borrowed antique tricycle, which Gary Winn had been going to ride, was stolen, vandalized, and left in a road near the Arts Centre, so the props staff hastily procured a child's scooter as a substitute, and fitted a flashing blue light to it. At the dress rehearsal two main fuses blew one after the other, so there was no proper lighting for the first act. And to add insult to injury the lights failed again on the first night and the lighting operators struggled for fifteen minutes to cover the entire stage with two spotlights while repairs were taking place. The audience numbered only 200 but they enjoyed the show, and Mark Robinson, who attended for the *Northern Echo*, said of those 200 in his review, '. . . it's doubtful whether any of them will see a better version of the Gilbert and Sullivan am-dram fave-rave. Not only did the production bring out the existing comic elements, it added some excellent ones of its own. The director was blessed with leading characters whose comic timing could not have been better.'[1] Frank Lloyd, Michael Geddes and John Parker received special mention, as they also did in the *Darlington & Stockton Times*, along with June Aiken and Andrea Durham whose solo, *Sorry Her Lot*, the paper chose as one of the highlights of the evening. 'From a dramatic start the performance went from strength to strength,' said the reviewer, having first ventured the opinion that the Society had '. . . taken Gilbert & Sullivan by the throat and dragged them triumphantly into the 1990s.'[2] It was gratifying that the paper also felt that, although the show was brought up to date with inventive pieces of humour (for Bev had put in a good many gags), the essential spirit of Gilbert & Sullivan had not been lost. Like *La Belle Hélène*, a lot of licence can be used if the singers are good enough, and the singing was well done, despite the lack of radio microphones. Eileen Young's cameo performance as Queen Victoria, regal in her black bustled dress and white cap, and complete with a shopping trolley full of crowns for the newly-elevated pirates, was a triumph. At the age of 75 she had lost none of her stage presence or timing.

Though the show looked good from the audience's point of view, things were not easy backstage. Two dressing-rooms are not large enough to accomodate so many people at all, let alone with any degree of comfort. People were getting changed at various levels on the stairs, and Jennifer Hird and Eileen Singh were making tea for the cast at the top! There is little regard for modesty in an operatic society – there is no time for it – but backstage at the College it looked like party time at Raymond's Revue-Bar! It was a happy show, though, and even though that bird on Barrie's shoulder *did* look like something left over from a Monty Python sketch, even though some of the men's tights were of such hues that they looked both indecent *and* incandescent, even though John Parker's hair *was* nearly set on fire by an over-enthusiastic 'daughter', and even though John forgot his words in the patter song (*Modern Major General*) one night and had to cover it up with some very clever *ad libbing* with Stephen Sild, such mishaps only added to the fun, and everyone had a good time.

The *Darlington & Stockton Times* review concluded with the words, 'The talented members of DOS have once again turned in as professional a performance as you are likely to see on the amateur stage' – it was fair comment, according to the audience.

The venture worked out quite well financially. The audiences were naturally much smaller than for a show at the theatre and the number of Vice-Presidents and Patrons was about 60 down on the last time, but overheads were considerably less at the College, so there was a reasonable surplus on the show.

The next thing to think about was *The Magic of the Musical*. This would run for nine nights rather than ten and Bev had arranged a varied programme with chorus snippets from shows, solos from shows and compilations of past and present popular songs. These would be performed by a 36-strong company. The orchestra would consist of only a double bass, a trombone, two trumpets and a percussionist. Bev himself would be Musical Director and would play piano and keyboards (sometimes simultaneously) as well as conducting (no one thought that this was possible until they had actually seen it done!) Auditions consisted of members who wanted to perform solo items going along and doing their 'party pieces' and it looked as though it would be fun for everyone.

Information began to come through at this point about what the theatre costs would be on its reopening. The costs in general were to increase by more than one third, and there would be 1,500 extra tickets to sell over the ten nights of a show. There was, as can be imagined, 'much discussion' as to what the first show should be, but the Committee finally chose *Oklahoma!* since it was a popular box office show with plenty of chorus work. Bev was to produce it and Stephen was to be Musical Director, though there was, as yet, no Choreographer.

Having settled this, the Committee addressed the problem of the accomodation at the College. Someone had the bright idea of hiring a Portakabin for the men to use as a dressing room: it could be easily accomodated in the College car park, close to an entrance. This was done and it eased the situation considerably. Radio microphones of some sort would also be used if a way could be found.

With these matters settled the summer break was taken and the Committee reassembled in mid-September to take stock. For the forthcoming show the Portakabin was hired, and Elsie Campbell and Kath Porteus had arranged to hire, from Homburg's and from the Newton Aycliffe Operatic Society, such costumes as could not be provided or made by Society members or by Kath and Elsie themselves. For *Oklahoma!* the dates had been booked with the theatre, the costumes had been booked, and the provision of scenery had been arranged with Stagesets; in order to improve the agility of the men for the show Pam Tallentire (a local dance teacher who would shortly marry Pete Sowerby) had agreed to hold aerobics classes for them.

By mid-October rehearsals were going well for *The Magic of the Musical* and two-thirds of the tickets had been sold. The theatre's box office staff, then located in a sort of temporary 'burrow' in the Town Hall, had offered to sell tickets, too, and 8% had been allocated to them. Tom Kent's poster for *The Sound of Music* had won that national award from NODA, so the name of the Society was being kept at the forefront of operatic circles.

When the show was performed it was much enjoyed by the public, and though the newspaper critics viewed it with modified rapture they did agree that it had something for everyone. June Hawdon, for the *Darlington Advertiser*, said that it was 'once again a polished and professional performance from the society'[3] though she had not cared for some of the modern 'pop' content. Jill Neill, for the *Darlington & Stockton Times*, felt that, though some of the solos were weak, '. . . most of the two-hour programme was delivered with punch and verve.'[4] Snippets from two shows were

The Magic of the Musical 1990 – 1940s Medley. *See page xii for full list.*

presented: *Sweet Charity* and *Les Miserables*, and there were duets or solos from *Showboat*, *Veronique*, *Aspects of Love*, *The New Moon*, *Rio Rita*, *Carousel*, *Gypsy*, *Brigadoon*, *Gentlemen Prefer Blondes* and *The King and I*. Shirley Dodd performed the Joyce Grenfell classic *Stately as a Galleon* and a whimsical little number called *Me and My Dog*. The cast performed a 1940s medley in Forces uniforms and Liz Holton, Ann Oxley and Zoë Kent gave a very convincing impression of the Andrews Sisters. Maggie Thorp gave a superb performance of a song originally written for a man: *Love Changes Everything* from *Aspects of Love*, and just before the final medley of modern songs there was Eileen Young, with bent wand and drooping drawers, once again lamenting the fact that *Nobody Loves a Fairy When She's Forty*. She got the biggest round of applause every time. Apart from a number of the cast getting sore throats towards the end of the run, the only hiccup was that Arthur Ellis got held up in Liverpool with his work and was still there just one and a half hours before curtain-up. Fortunately he arrived in time to make his appearance just before the interval, but it certainly got the cast's adrenalin flowing!

The year's experiences were good for the Society in two ways. First, there was a surplus on both shows meaning that donations could be distributed as usual. Second, the reminder was there that some other amateur societies had to give their shows under difficult conditions all the time, though, let it be said, the staff and students at the College could not have been more helpful.

Immediately after the show, all the members' thoughts turned towards the newly-refurbished theatre, now almost complete, and towards *Oklahoma!* The ticket prices were fixed first. Theatre publicity material would henceforth be sent out very early and the Committee would have to be ready with the details. There was 'much discussion' about prices. The budgeting for shows had moved into a different league with the refurbishment, for there was such a large number of seats to sell. Eventually the general price was set at £5.50, with the upper circle at £5 and £1 extra on all the tickets for the final night. For the first night and the Monday all seats would be £4.50 and there would be a reduction for OAPs on the first Thursday and for children on the first Friday. The most ominous prospect, for the Ticket Secretary, was that the box office was now computerized. By the end of the year the theatre was open again and his worst fears were realized. Unless one has seen around 5,000 tickets as long computer print-outs, and has actually had to contemplate tearing them into 'singles', one can have no conception of how daunting it is! (Fortunately, once the scale of the operation became apparent to some of the other committee members, they volunteered to share this thankless task between them.) The tickets for the upper circle were only printed as needed, and the theatre was given a quota of seats to sell, but the arrangements meant that a great deal of goodwill and cooperation was needed from the box office staff, and happily this was, and is, readily forthcoming.

The year ended on an optimistic note, with the whole Society looking forward to getting back into the theatre again (wherein they now had another 'mole' in the person of Stephen Sanderson who had recently taken up the post of Chief Electrician there) and preparing for the auditions in January.

January found Sam gloomily contemplating his budgets. In addition to all the other cost increases, Musicians' Union rates had gone up and the insurance premium had increased. There was no option but to increase the ticket prices, which had been agreed so recently, by yet another 50p, apart from the upper circle. The programme price went up to £1.

At least by February the autumn show had been fixed as *Annie*, which would be having its first airing by the Society, and *Oklahoma!* – which had caused some concern over casting – had a full complement of players, plus a Choreographer: Sue Hewgill, who found the job infinitely more to her taste than being a goatherd in *White Horse Inn!* Sam's gloom, however, had deepened with the news that the overtime rates for the Arts Centre staff (payable for Sundays, the Society's main floorwork day) had increased.

The *Oklahoma!* cast were getting down to business and, as was the norm, there were faces old and new. Sue Robinson, of course, was playing Aunt

Eller for the third time, and Andrea Durham and Alison Cochlan stayed with the Society to play Laurey and Ado Annie respectively. Their opposite numbers were played by newcomers. Wayne Shellard, an ambulanceman from Middlesbrough and a member of Stockton Stage, Middlesbrough Operatic, and Teesside Operatic Societies, was playing Curly. Wayne is a young man with much musical talent as an instrumentalist and musical director, as well as being a singer. (As his fair hair is naturally straight he opted to have it permed in the interests of verisimilitude, though he was very glad when the perm grew out!) Philip Mezzo, a self-confessed operatic nomad who had appeared with many North-East operatic societies over a number of years, came to play Will Parker. Sam, having had to relinquish the part of Andrew Carnes in the 1976 production, was now able to play it at last; Gary Winn, whose ability to play comedy roles well was becoming increasingly apparent, was Ali Hakim; and Arthur Ellis was playing Jud Fry again. Ian Whitfield as Slim, and John Lloyd as Cord Elam the sheriff were joined by another new member, David Wiseman, as Ike Skidmore; Melanie Short emerged from the chorus to play Gertie Cummings and perfected a laugh (Gertie's trademark in the piece) which had all the delicacy and sweetness of a rusty nail being scraped over a galvanized bucket. The Dream Ballet this time was danced by Christine Murray as Laurey, with Steve Luck as Curly and Robert Rowell (the fiddler from *Fiddler on the Roof*) as Jud. There were also several new dancers, the men being particularly important in this area because of the dance which the men do in the *Kansas City* number with Will Parker. Barry Million, Stuart Gordon and Martin Simpson, now established members, plus Martin Roberts, Phil Motley and Graeme Hall, who had all just come into the Society, had to tap-dance, along with Steve, Robert, and Pete Sowerby, for this number, and some of them had never so much as donned a pair of tap shoes before they began rehearsing for the show. There were other little problems to be sorted out, too. Firearms were, of course, used in the show and they are a complication in themselves. A responsible person in the Society has to have a firearms licence, guns cannot be sent by rail or road but must be collected and returned by an individual, special insurance has to be taken out, and the police must be informed. (Rules grow tighter with every year that passes. If, for instance, there is to be a naked flame on stage, of whatever kind – candles, perhaps, or a cigarette lighter – the theatre must be notified in writing and there must be special insurance.) As luck would have it, Howard Keel, star of a number of Hollywood film musicals among other things, was giving a concert on the Sunday during the show so there was notification that the ground-floor dressing-rooms would have to be cleared on the Saturday night so that he and his supporting cast could get in.

(Now and then confessions have to be made, and it is confession-time now. The Assistant Ticket Secretary was badgered by callers trying to book seats for the Howard Keel concert – this is not unusual, as people have tried to book through the Operatic Society's Ticket Secretary every-thing from Chris Bonington* lectures, through the Russian ballet, to the pantomime – and her patience was wearing thin. When, eventually, a caller said that she had heard that Howard Keel was appearing as Curly in the Operatic Society's show and enquired as to whether this was true, the temptation was too great. The Assistant Ticket Secretary replied that he had auditioned but did not get the part . . .)

Tickets for the show were selling well as early as mid-February, even without Howard Keel, and the show was receiving plenty of publicity apart from the usual banner, stickers and posters. The Arts Centre held an Open Day on 2 March and the Society's rehearsal was thrown open so that the public could spectate; also, shortly before the show opened, BBC2's *Newsnight* filmed part of a rehearsal for a television programme featuring Darlington. Also, eager to improve themselves as much as possible for their return to the Civic Theatre, some of the cast attended a workshop (paid for by the Kenneth Richardson Trust) by the singer Ann Linstrum.

By the time the Annual General Meeting was held at the beginning of April Sam had cheered up – even despite the fact that the change in the rate of VAT to 17½% would have the effect of increasing the VAT content of the ticket prices. The good news was that, as well as the Society being able to give donations of well over £3,000 during the year, there was some money left over to go into the General Fund to increase the Society's 'cushion' against future loss. The Annual General Meeting was a cheerful affair overall. First of all, the roll of Honorary Life Members was increased to fifteen with the addition of Lilah Hudson who had been Joy's dancing-school pianist and a member of the Society in its various forms since 1932. (The Committee was later very glad that this honour had been conferred on Lilah, for she died only fifteen months afterwards.) Everyone had worked hard to keep the Society well to the fore while the theatre was out of commission, money had been made in the process, and all were looking forward to going back into the theatre with all its new facilities, which now included the luxury of radio microphones. These would be very useful to the principals – even more so now that there was an extra tier of seats which their voices must reach. The cast members were enjoying rehearsals. The tickets were selling well and there were only

* The mountaineer.

Oklahoma! 1991. *Left to right:* Arthur Ellis, Andrea Durham, Wayne Shellard, Alison Cockburn, Phil Mezzo, Gary Winn, Sue Robinson.

restricted viewing seats and upper circle left for most nights. There had been a number of highly successful social events and the Ladies' Committee had purchased a new tea boiler, so God was obviously in His Heaven and all was right with the world (though George Todd felt that the Society was not keeping itself as closely involved with NODA as he would have liked and this ought to be remedied). Tom Kent had even had the forethought to put an advertisement in the *Oklahoma!* programme, advising that children would be required for the production of Strouse and Charnin's *Annie* and giving notice that there would be a full advertisement in the press about it.

The total audience for the show, in the end, amounted to 7,900 – around 90% capacity – and they appeared to be vastly entertained by it, not least by the fact that on the final night Phil Mezzo nearly fell into the orchestra pit while trying to gather up the 'money' which was dropped on the stage, that as John Lloyd uttered the words 'Better get him [Jud] over to the doctor's place' the sound of a wailing ambulance outside filled the theatre, and that Sam's moustache made an escape-bid. The *Northern Echo* critic pointed out that the audience would know all the songs, which would enhance the show for them; she gave full marks to Alison and Phil and to Gary and Arthur, but described the rendering of Andrea and Wayne's characters as 'averagely played',[5] which was a little upsetting to Andrea though not to Wayne, who promptly joked her out of her hurt feelings – Laurey, after all, is a difficult character to play because she is so 'sweet' that the part does not give the leading lady very much chance for character-acting. For this critic the chorus numbers were 'the triumph of this vibrant production'. Jill Neill, of the *Darlington & Stockton Times*, enjoyed being able to 'sit back and enjoy a few hours of old-fashioned escapism' [6] and for her the time flew during the production. She gave great credit to Sue Hewgill for the dance routines, especially for the Dream Ballet, and, while remarking especially on the performances of Alison ('hilarious'), Wayne ('our hero') and Arthur ('superb'), said that in their acting and singing the twelve principals acquitted themselves admirably; their accents were also convincing. Even Elsie Campbell got a mention for having such a careful eye on the costumes, and Stephen Sild's orchestra gave 'fine performances' of all the musical numbers. She concluded by wondering how the autumn production would be able to live up to the same standard. The company wondered that, too.

The answer was supplied when autumn came: assemble a good cast, train them all rigorously and then allow them to enjoy themselves. That training began, as always, the Thursday following the final night of the current show and continued through the summer with a break in August.

Meanwhile the Committee was taking stock again and planning for the future now that the first show in the new-look theatre was over. It soon became clear that *Oklahoma!* had been a financial success. Moreover, the number of Vice-Presidents and Patrons had rocketed from 205 for *The Magic of the Musical* to 313. So, though the royalties to be paid for *Annie* were high (15%), it was decided that not only would the general ticket prices stay the same but the upper circle would be reduced by £1 as an experiment to try to sell more seats up there, and the seats for the proposed matinée on the first Saturday would be only £3. (The exception to the Society's normal matinée-phobia is usually when a show has a number of children in it, for obvious reasons.) Productions for 1992 and 1993 were also being considered with more confidence now that the portents seemed favourable, but there was 'lengthy discussion' before repeats of *Half a Sixpence* and *The Merry Widow* were chosen for 1992. For spring 1993 –

perhaps the success of *Oklahoma!* had made the Committee bold – the decision came down in favour of *Sweet Charity*, but fingers may well have been crossed in view of its track record in Darlington – or lack of it.

The auditioning of little girls for *Annie* loomed large. Bev and Stephen were Producer and Musical Director, and Bev decided that he would be happy to have twelve children in it, rather than the six specified in the script, and to run two teams of children to do alternate performances. They would all have to be good at singing, dancing and acting and have good personalities. He would also have two Annies, one to go with each team. 'Elizabeth Cooper,' announced the minutes, grandly, 'will arrange the necessary publicity for the audition.'[7] Elizabeth Cooper did so, and she did it, as usual, in style. On Friday 14 June, at 6.30 p.m. she must have wondered what she had unleashed, for, in a queue which meandered round the corridors of the Arts Centre, there were little girls as far as the eye could see: 457 of them! Pat McIntyre (who was at the piano) and Stephen Sild broke out into light perspiration, but they auditioned them all and actually managed, that same night, to form a short-list of 57. All those who auditioned were given bars of chocolate, solicited by Elizabeth from Candy Corner, and Liz Holton – lucky girl – had the task of writing to each of the 57 informing them that the final auditions would take place on 14 July, the same day as the adult auditions.

By the time the next committee meeting came round the two teams had been finalized, together with the two Annies: Rebecca Iles and Rachel Humphrey, though the search was on to find a suitable dog to play the essential role of Sandy. By mid-September, after two lots of auditions, most of the adults were also cast and the tickets were selling well. With a tiny gleam of malice John Lloyd reported that the matinée was proving very popular – Elizabeth Cooper's publicity was bearing fruit. Two weeks before opening night the floorwork was going well and a dog had been found: Chiff-Chaff, a golden retriever. Barrie Dargue was playing Daddy Warbucks with Maggie Thorp as his secretary, Grace Farrell, and the three 'baddies' were June Aiken as the gin-fragrant Miss Hannigan, Steve Luck as her brother Rooster, and Kath Robinson as his vacuous girlfriend Lily. David Wiseman was Bert Healey, the radio presenter, with Stuart Gordon and Barry Million as his sidekicks Fred McCracken and Jimmy Johnson. Ann Oxley, Julia McLean and Nicola Curry were the Boylan Sisters (a trio sharing close harmony and, apparently, a single brain cell) on the radio show. Greta Sanderson managed to be in this show – her 50th – having at last handed over the Chairmanship to Bill Jones after the last Annual General Meeting. After her two-year stint as Chairman she probably felt quite at home playing a servant! John Lloyd was playing President Franklin D. Roosevelt (and bore an uncanny resemblance to the man himself, once in costume, make-up and a wheelchair) with Ian Whitfield, Joe Cooper, Sam Herdman, Tom Kent and Graeme Hall as Senators. The ticket requests were still coming in apace and the Committee cautiously admitted that it looked as though the show would do well.

After two horrendous technical/dress rehearsals the show opened to a most receptive audience, and though the representatives of the press numbered only two, at least they were an appreciative two. Extra support was received from an unexpected quarter, namely the Education Minister and MP for Darlington, Michael Fallon, in his *View from Westminster* column in the *Darlington Advertiser*. 'Each year,' he said, 'our Operatic Society do us proud with two musicals . . . I've seen at least one each year since *The Music Man* back in 1983 and the productions are so professional that it's hard to remember that they're all done by volunteers.'⁸ The two critics were equally impressed. The first of the reviews appeared on the first Saturday. '*Annie* triumph for amateurs'⁹ read the headline, and the review was full of praise for Rebecca Iles who had played the title role on opening night. 'The youngsters,' said the column, 'appear as completely natural players and integrated well with the experienced principals and the talented chorus.' June ('sumptuously vulgar and cruel'), Barrie ('played convincingly') and Steve and Kath ('masterly') were chosen for particular praise and the critic enjoyed hearing, among all the American accents, 'the delicious English voice and song of Maggie Thorp'. John Lloyd received his one and only review in the press: 'Many familiar names do well,' it said, 'but it was a surprise to see the society's devoted ticket secretary John Lloyd blossom forth as Franklin D. Roosevelt.' A star was born – albeit briefly! The review in the *Darlington Advertiser* was headed '*Annie* supershow'¹⁰ and went on to say that the Society's 'illustrious history of providing superlative entertainment to the people of Darlington and its surrounding towns and villages proved itself once more with this ambitious production of *Annie* (though in fact some people come from further still to see the shows; they regularly come from Cumbria, all over Yorkshire, and from London, and one couple have started to come from Dumfries. He is a NODA representative but they are kind enough to say that they do not come for that reason but because they enjoy the Darlington society's shows). The critic felt that Rebecca '. . . handled the role [of Annie] with great maturity.' The same characters were chosen for particular praise as were singled out by the *Darlington & Stockton Times*. The supporting cast got a mention and also 'the efficient backroom boys and girls who did such slick changes' – which was pleasing, because usually when they do their job efficiently, they are not even noticed. The only real problem in the show was the dog. It was fine at

Stephen Sild and auditioners for *Annie*, 1991.

rehearsals but once in the theatre it did not like the lights and it did not like the noise of the orchestra. It managed six nights but was clearly very unhappy and it was deemed wiser not to prolong the unhappiness. John and Ann Parker offered *their* golden retriever, but poor Toby, not having rehearsed, nor got used to the company, nor having had any experience of the theatre, experienced total stagefright and was replaced the following night by Debbie, who was borrowed by Frances Sanderson from her mother. Debbie was bewildered and gave the impression that she was not too taken with the acting business, but she was an equable animal and completed the run of the show.

Annie sold 700 more tickets than *Oklahoma!* (many of these being accounted for, to John Lloyd's glee, by the matinée), and Tom Kent won the NODA trophies for both the poster and the souvenir programme.

Much encouraged by *Annie*'s success the Society launched into rehearsals for *Half a Sixpence* and the Committee determined to have a new banner made to hang across Skinnergate, larger than the previous one which had been so damage-prone. Costs were still rising steadily; the theatre contract showed that rates had been increased by 25% and box office commission to 20% (the refurbishment and modernization had cost dear). Although the surplus from the shows gave enough for £2,000 to be donated to charity it was decided that ticket prices would have to go up by 50p for *Half a Sixpence*. This would allow some cushioning for *The Merry Widow*, for which the costume bill would be particularly high in view of the lavish outfits required. (In fact the costumes already cost as much as £19.50 each even for *Half a Sixpence*, and that was at a reduced rate.)

To ensure a high-quality show even the chorus members were auditioned for *Half a Sixpence* and by mid-February it was cast, with only three exceptions: Chitterlow, Young Walsingham and Helen Walsingham. A month later they, too, had been found. Barrie Dargue would play Chitterlow, a young newcomer called Kevin Allenby had been deemed suitable for Young Walsingham, and Nadine Bell, a seventeen-year-old pupil from Polam Hall School, was cast as Helen. Wayne Shellard had come back to play Arthur Kipps, and Melanie Short, who had progressed by leaps and bounds since her début as the shrill Gertie in *Oklahoma!*, was playing Ann Pornick. Steve Luck, who had played the gloomy Buggins nearly fourteen years previously, was playing Ann's brother, Sid. The other two apprentices were played by Nick Myers (who would shortly go to drama school) and Graeme Hall. The shop girls were Elizabeth Cooper, Kath Robinson (for the second time around), Christine Murray and Nicola Whitfield. Ian Whitfield was Mr Shalford the shop-owner with John Lloyd as his floorwalker, Carshot. June Aiken had cleaned up her act after playing the gin-sodden Miss Hannigan and was being very aristocratic as

Half a Sixpence 1992. *Left to right*: Melanie Short, Wayne Shellard,
Kath Robinson, Graeme Hall, Christine Murray, Nick Myers,
Nicola Whitfield, Steve Luck, Elizabeth Cooper, Ian Whitfield.

Mrs Walsingham. So everything was going smoothly when the Annual
General Meeting was held at the end of March. Bill Jones had to give
reports as both Chairman and Secretary and he expressed the feelings of
all when he said that it was good to be back 'home' in the theatre. The
price of progress was high, however, and he pointed out that the standing
charges had increased by 133% in the last three years, so it was imperative
that the members should make every effort to sell tickets and to fulfil the
general aims of the Society which were to educate and entertain the public
while supporting charities – donations to which now amounted to £35,000
since the war. He said kind things about the Ticket Secretaries (whose
workload had, in fact, quadrupled in the last year) and about the backstage
crew. He also made special mention of Sam Herdman's two-monthly
newsletter. This had been going for about eight years and had proved to
be a valuable vehicle for informing all the members of what was going
on in all departments. The Fund-Raising Committee and the Ladies'
Committee were still providing staunch backing and the Society's healthy
state was due, in no small part, to these people. Elsie Campbell and Peggy
Todd were made Honorary Life Members.

When the Committee next met, rehearsals for *Half a Sixpence* were
proceeding with enthusiasm and one of the chorus, Martin Roberts, was

so taken with stage work by now that he was hoping to attend the Arts International Drama School near York.*

Two weeks before the show opened, about three-quarters of the tickets had been sold, though as usual the upper circle was very slow to sell, in spite of the reduced price of the tickets, principally because it was a long climb to get there.

Just before the show Melanie developed chickenpox, but there was no such luxury as an understudy and she would not have missed a performance in any case. She put on thicker make-up over her spots and proceeded undeterred. During the show Wayne suffered from multiple lacerations inflicted by Tricia Freeman's cat, Thomas, who was playing the important role of Edwin the shop cat, and who felt that he should register a protest when he was plucked in an unseemly fashion from his comfortable resting place under the 'shop counter' each night. A cat, especially a star cat, needs his rest. Justine Denham, one of the dancers, was rushed to hospital four days before the show with a throat haemhorrage, and Kate Wall, who was only fourteen, made an heroic effort and learned the songs and the choreography in time to take her place. So it was not an easy start, even though Tommy Steele, the original West End star of the show, had sent a good luck photograph and a message – perhaps he should have stuck to the more usual theatrical good wish: 'Break a leg'!

The reviews were lukewarm about the show itself but enthusiastic about the performers. One wonders what went wrong in the translation of the H. G. Wells story, regarded as a classic, into the musical, which follows the original storyline quite closely, when critics fourteen years apart say similar things about the show. Frances Griss, in the *Darlington Advertiser*, more or less echoed the sentiments of the *Evening Despatch* critic who wrote about the show in 1978. 'DOS,' she said, 'battled against a thin storyline to produce an ultimately enjoyable show . . .'[11] Wayne, for her, had been outstanding, and Melanie ('bubbly') and Nadine ('prim') had supported him well. Barrie had also put in a 'delightfully over-the-top performance', but despite strong performances she felt that the show had been a bad choice. She gave honourable mention to the scenery and costumes but her overall reaction was summed up in her headline: '*Half a Sixpence* gets halfway there'. The *Darlington & Stockton Times* liked the same characters but in addition picked out Steve Luck and also Ann Oxley. Ann's was a tiny role, as Gwendolin the cheeky parlourmaid, and she managed to convey scorn and insubordination to perfection without having to utter a word – for the *Darlington & Stockton Times* 'the show was very nearly stolen'[12]

---

* He did so, and in 1993 won the Student of the Year Award.

by Ann. The experience of playing a leading role well and playing it in a prestigious theatre gave Melanie such a taste for the theatrical life that she gave up her job in a bank and followed Martin Roberts's example by going to the same theatre school, though during *Half a Sixpence* she was much amused when one young fan's primary interest in meeting her was to inspect the remains of her chickenpox!*

It transpired that 1,500 fewer seats were sold for *Half a Sixpence* than for *Annie* (though, of course, there was no matinée) and 800 fewer than for *Oklahoma!* Only about 10% of the upper circle was sold. There was considerable discussion. The Committee knew that prices would have to go up by 50p again for *The Merry Widow* but the upper circle was obviously an ongoing problem. They considered prices between £3 and £5, and finally decided to make two moves. They would charge £3.50 and shift the problem in the box office's direction by giving them the whole of the offending area to sell! It was at least worth trying as an experiment for one show.

Shows containing children seemed to succeed better than any others, reflected the Committee when thinking about productions for the following year. *Sweet Charity*, of course, was already booked for spring 1993 (though there was a problem with scenery and costumes just as there had been on the other three occasions on which they had tried to stage it) but perhaps a show containing boys could be done in the autumn. Bearing in mind the results of the survey that had been done in 1987, what else could it be but *Oliver!*?

The auditions for *The Merry Widow* were held just over a month after the run of *Half a Sixpence* and it was more or less cast, as far as principals were concerned, with the notable exception of Camille. Pauline and David Curtis were both in this show and both were taking leads – as Anna and Danilo. Maggie Thorp was Valencienne and Doug Clayton, who was from Barnard Castle (though he was a member of Darlington's Pilgrim Players and regarded himself as much more of an actor than a singer), was her husband, Baron Zeta. Sam, who had played Kromov the attaché last time around, was playing Njegus, the Baron's factotum. This time Les Oxley was playing Kromov, with Margaret Webb as Olga, his flirtatious wife. Pritsch and Bogdanovitsch, the other attachés, were John Parkin and Ian Whitfield. The two diplomats, St Brioche and Cascada were Graeme Hall (rapidly getting into his stride as an actor) and David

---

* Melanie graduated in 1994 and, after working as a performer at Alton Towers and as First Assistant Director and Lighting Director on a new television series (*The Sharpe End*), took a job as a receptionist at Pineapple Studios in London and began the round of auditions for acting work.

The Merry Widow 1992
Left to right: Pauline Curtis, David Curtis, Philip Tsaras, Maggie Thorp.

Wiseman. The two Embassy guests, Sylvia and the predatory Praskovia, were Kath Robinson and Rachel McGovern (who had been in the chorus since she joined the Society with her friend Julia McLean for *Kismet* in 1988). The Grisettes were Jayne Summerbell, Christine Murray, Eileen Miller, Tricia Freeman, June Aiken, and finally Liz Holton, who was in the show despite the sudden death of her father, Gordon, for, having been Stage Director for so many shows, he of all people would not have wished her to drop out.

All the show now lacked was a Camille, the six or eight dancers required by Sue Hewgill (who was Choreographer), and a chandelier, and all these were obtained during the summer: Philip Tsaras (though the Society members still thought of him as Philip Murray) had agreed to play

Camille, staying with Roula, his mother, while he was in Darlington, Sue had recruited some dancers from Great Ayton, and Ray Porteus was constructing a chandelier.

It was at the August committee meeting that Bill Jones dropped his bombshell. He was going to resign. He had had a difficult year: his sister (the one whose husband had died suddenly) was running her own business in South Africa and had two sons to care for, and Bill was going to join her there. He would be a tremendous loss. He had been in the Society for 40 years, and had been Secretary for eighteen of those years. His work had been largely unsung, for it all went on in the background of Society affairs, but he would be sorely missed now. He had resigned in good time so that he would be able to help whoever took over from him, and ease his successor into the job as gently as possible. Greta Sanderson was asked to take on the secretaryship and accepted. There was talk of spreading the duties if necessary, but in fact Greta managed to do it all herself, with Liz Holton, who had been Assistant Secretary before, to help her when necessary.

Four weeks before *The Merry Widow* the new banner was triumphantly hoisted in Skinnergate and the bookings were coming in – but still they did not come in for the upper circle, though the stalls and dress circle were nearly full two and a half weeks before the show. In the end, 79% of the tickets were sold, the least (though not by a great amount) to be sold since the Society had gone back into the theatre. Perhaps the reviews had something to do with this, perhaps not, but the fact remains that the critics condemned the storyline, the most charitable review being the one in the *Darlington & Stockton Times*, which described it as 'the story of people in love behaving in a maddening and soppy manner'[13] while admitting that it was '. . . full of froth and fun and just the sort of show to banish thoughts of the recession and the unseasonably rotten weather.' The reviewer found no fault with the cast: rather she praised David and Pauline's 'extreme professionalism', Maggie's 'superb voice' and Philip's 'seemingly effortless tenor performance' as well as Doug's 'lovable' Baron Zeta. The men's 'Tiller Girl' routine in *Women, Women, Women* also appealed to her. She found the first act tedious – though she said that this was the fault of the show, not the cast – and the review published in the *Darlington Advertiser* on 5 November agreed with this, also making a feature of the fact that the 'summerhouse' fell down and had to be repaired there and then by backstage staff while the cast continued with the action. The *Northern Echo*, conspicuous by its absence from the previous two shows, referred to *The Merry Widow* as '. . . a slim story . . . a poor excuse for lots of lilting melodies, glittering costumes and energetic dancing. All of which Bev Jones' colourful, tuneful production has in abundance.'[14] David and

Pauline were described as 'effective', as were Maggie and Philip. 'The team of high-kicking, knicker-showing Grisettes,' said the critic, 'display an enthusiasm above and beyond the call of duty.' Whatever the press thought about it, many people took the trouble to write letters of congratulation to the Society about it. Consequently, members wondered if *Sweet Charity*, the antithesis of *The Merry Widow*, would be a hit with the press and not with the public! The curious thing was that the number of Vice-Presidents and Patrons was increasing dramatically. For *Annie* there had been 308 and for *Half a Sixpence* 331. For *The Merry Widow* there were 362, so it was no use thinking that the slightly older generation, who were more likely to want to become Vice-Presidents and Patrons, were too biased towards the sort of soap opera drama which abounded on television to want to attend a more classical show. It was a mystery.

At the end of this show the Society said its official farewell to Bill Jones, presenting him with a watch and a painting as mementoes of the company and his many friends within it. He was, however, present for the first night of *Sweet Charity*, which helped to make it a very happy occasion. The show was actually going ahead at last after its rough passage in the Society's history, and the ticket prices had been kept the same as for *The Merry Widow*, thanks to the advantageous arrangements made by Bill with the rights holders. Only the upper circle seats would have the slightly higher price of £5, since the experimental lowering of the charge had made no appreciable difference to their occupancy. Though not many were sold, there are some people who like to sit up there – for one thing, the sound carries well from the stage, and for another there is a great deal more leg room.

1993 arrived. The year was new, and so were many other things for the Society. Ruth Eastwood became the Director of the Civic Theatre (when Brian Goddard moved on to be Director of the Wolverhampton Grand Theatre) and at the same time was made Director of the Arts Centre – the first time that a woman had held such a dual post in the North. Wayne Shellard, who was to play the leading role of Oscar, was taking the singing rehearsals, for Stephen Sild was ill, and the pianist problem had reared its head again, too. Pat McIntyre had had an accident and was unable to attend rehearsals, and Gavin Bailey, a new accompanist introduced to the Society by Stephen, was unable to come to help out Brian Sheppard as he had no transport because he normally came with Stephen. So Brian played for as many rehearsals as he could and stand-ins were arranged wherever possible. Even Andrew Christer, better known as an organist, played for one of the dancing rehearsals! There was a new choreographer, too. Sue Hewgill had too many commitments at this time to work on the show, so she had recommended Edward Lynch of Leeds.

He was a founder-member of the Phoenix Dance Company, he had appeared on television as well as teaching in many schools and colleges throughout Yorkshire, and he is very dynamic. *Sweet Charity* was his first venture into musicals and there is no doubt that he drew the very best out of the Darlington society, assisted by his colleague Donald Edwards. The girl who played the title role was also new to the Society and had been brought along by Wayne. Her name was Mandy Brown and she was everything that Charity should be: lively, cheerful, a very good singer and dancer and an excellent actress. The Society considered itself exceptionally lucky to get her. Another new girl, Amanda Blane, who had joined the company for *The Merry Widow*, was playing Ursula, the spoiled girl-friend of the film star Vittorio Vidal. Barrie Dargue was originally cast as Vittorio but had to drop out into a smaller role, so the Committee asked Bill Witcomb from Stockton Stage Society to take on the part, which he did. Steve Luck, who had been cast as Daddy Brubeck, also dropped out (he was working at York, of course) so Arthur Ellis combined the role with that of Herman the Fan-Dango Ballroom owner, and had Barry Million (the Society's star ticket-seller!) and Graeme Hall (who had come second in the ticket-sales stakes along with Greta) as his assistants. So with all these comings and goings the show was still not all plain sailing. Jayne Summerbell and Liz Holton were cast as Hélène and Nickie, Charity's particular friends, and the other dance-hall hostesses were Rachel Green (who had played Liesl in *The Sound of Music*), Eileen Miller and Gillian Smith (who had both joined for *Half a Sixpence*), Judi Kent, Nicola Whitfield (as Rosie, the 'new girl'), and June Aiken, at her most formidable – and that word can be pronounced and understood in either the English *or* the French way – as the 'old girl'!

Margaret Webb, Ian Whitfield and Graeme Hall were elected to the Committee at the Annual General Meeting so they joined with the rest in exercising their minds over the requirements for *Oliver!* The Society would have to advertise for boys, just as it had for girls for *Annie*, though they hoped that the response would not be *quite* so overwhelming. In the mean time there was excellent news already as far as the costumes were concerned. A new firm – Northern Costume Hire – had opened at Skipton, which was not only close to home but offered costumes for only £11.50 each – about half the usual rate. Elsie Campbell and Kath Porteus (who had just joined Elsie as Joint Wardrobe Mistress – *Sweet Charity* was Elsie's 45th show with the Society and Wardrobe is a lot of work) went to have a look at what was on offer and were impressed. There was no such luck with scenery. The set from Fredericks was considerably cheaper than the one from Stagesets (which was, admittedly, new) but it was too small for the stage – it was the 'swings and roundabouts' syndrome. The

Committee also had to consider future shows; for 1994, and especially for 1995 which would be the Golden Jubilee year of the re-formed society. Shows such as *Most Happy Fella, Carmen, High Society, Blitz, Showboat,* another *Magic of the Musicals* selection, and *Die Fledermaus* were suggested. The last was the hoped-for choice for autumn 1995, which would mark the actual anniversary, but unfortunately the D'Oyly Carte company, who had added it to their repertoire since they had begun to diversify from Gilbert & Sullivan works, were touring the country with it and would present it in Darlington in autumn 1994, so the idea had to be abandoned. The deliberations continued on and off throughout the summer, during which *Gigi, La Vie Parisienne,* Sammy Fain's *Calamity Jane,* and Cole Porter's *Anything Goes* entered the frame. Finally they chose *Gigi* for spring 1994, followed by *Anything Goes* in the autumn, and *Calamity Jane* and *La Vie Parisienne* in 1995.

Sweet Charity, however, was the show of the moment and this time no more hitches occurred to stop it being staged – except that poor Mandy developed a throat problem after the first night, causing horrible forebodings that the show might still be jinxed. She was slightly croaky on the second night and there was no understudy, of course, but Vera Davison was ready with an answer though she had just had an operation on her nose. She volunteered to be ready to stand in if Mandy's voice went completely, just to sing the part while Mandy did the acting. Vera's nose began bleeding copiously again, but she still stood in readiness in the wings with a vocal score in one hand and a wad of tissues in the other! Fortunately Mandy's voice had only suffered a slight strain and all was well.

All the cast enjoyed doing the show, including Bill Witcomb, whose appearance on stage was limited and who longed to be in the *Rhythm of Life* number. He seized his opportunity one night when one of the chorus members had to be away for a funeral; Bill appropriated the absentee's hippy costume and joined in the number with great alacrity, tossing his wig and flaunting his flared trousers and beads. The rest of the cast were quite startled since they were supposed to be one short and no one at first recognized this manic creature gyrating alongside them. Consequently, once realization dawned, they waxed hysterical as they came off stage, but Bill had had his little fling and was content! They had nearly choked to death in any case at the beginning of that scene, when the stage staff had been a little too free with the synthetic smoke, used to simulate the fog created by the 'reefers' which the participants were supposed to be smoking, but it went down well with the audience. What is more, the 'fickle finger of fate' always seems to point to some poor victim in every show and this time it was pointing firmly at Judi Kent. The dance-hall hostess costumes were much abbreviated – very short and very tight –

Sweet Charity 1993 – Chorus. *See page xii for full list.*

and plastered with sequins and beads, and the girls had a quick-change in the dark at the side of the stage. Judi wriggled into her dress, pulled it straight and felt down the side where it was split up to the thigh, only to discover, to her horror, that she had it on back to front. However, since it was supposed to plunge in *all* directions, she got away with it and was lulled into a sense of security – but not for long. Her wig was a work of art: a splendid creation, composed of beautifully coiffed chestnut-red hair, and it was so impressive that when it came off during the dancing in *I Always Cry at Weddings*, where the girls were pulled, rock 'n' roll style, through the men's legs, the audience could not help but notice. Poor Judi rushed off stage, leaving her partner, Barry Million, to execute a *pas seul*, while the wig lay like some small, dead, russet animal until it was retrieved. A *real* animal in the show caused much amusement, too. This was Jasper, Tricia Freeman's black labrador. He is a remarkably stoical dog and took his stage appearance in his stride, but he made his mark in the production in his one short scene near the beginning of the show when Charity is pushed into the park lake and the passing public gather round. Brian Bean and Andrea Hall had been 'picnicking' on a park bench and Brian still had a sandwich in his hand as he joined the crowd. Jasper, who was standing nearby with Tricia, was quick to spot the sandwich and he reached up and gently abstracted it. Needless to say, this piece of 'business' was kept in in future and Jasper was happy to oblige.

Sweet Charity 1993
Clockwise from left: Liz Holton, Eileen Miller, Rachel Green, June Aiken, Judi
Kent, Gillian Smith, Arthur Ellis, with Mandy Shellard and Jayne
Summerbell.

Sweet Charity was a tremendous success. The cast enjoyed it, the audiences enjoyed it (there was only one complaint, from someone who did not care for the show's content), and the press enjoyed it. Everyone agreed that Mandy had given a superlative performance. 'Dynamic,'[15] said the

Darlington & Stockton Times, and 'very reminiscent of Shirley McLaine',[16] said the *Northern Echo*. The *Darlington Advertiser* concurred, saying that Mandy 'may have made a good understudy to Shirley McLaine'.[17] They all agreed that Wayne had been an excellent leading man. The *Darlington Advertiser* credited him with playing the part of Oscar 'with great wit and feeling', the *Northern Echo* said he was 'a perfect match' for Mandy (he was, too – they were married in 1994!) and the *Darlington & Stockton Times* commented particularly on his 'polished and mellow singing voice'. Arthur and Bill and the dance-hall girls all came in for their fair share of praise, as did Edward Lynch for his expert choreography, and overall it was only the precise words used by the three papers which differed. 'A breathtaking performance' was the view of the *Darlington Advertiser*, 'DOS took a dive into the unknown . . . and came up smiling. So did the audience,' said the *Darlington & Stockton Times*. '*Sweet Charity* must surely go down as one of the society's most entertaining shows, living up to their reputation of always turning out a polished performance,' said the *Northern Echo*. The excellence of Mandy's performance was minuted at the committee meeting which followed the show and a number of letters arrived, congratulating the company and especially Mandy. And even though the number of Vice-Presidents and Patrons was down from *The Merry Widow*, more block bookings were made so there was a comfortable surplus from which to distribute the customary donations.

Now, though, it was time to to look towards *Oliver!* Bev and Stephen were Producer and Musical Director as usual, and Irene Hand (née Skippon) was asked to be Choreographer. Graeme Hall promoted the show on local radio and sent information to fifty local schools in the search for suitable boys. Then the Committee waited to see how many would turn up to audition. They had to be between the ages of eight and fourteen, with unbroken voices, and under five feet tall. 108 arrived to the first audition, which, it has to be said, was something of a relief after the avalanche of young hopefuls for *Annie*. These were reduced to a short-list of 31 (including Elizabeth and Joe Cooper's boys, Adam and Nicholas, and Rachel McGovern's little boy, Peter) who would return for the main auditions on the afternoon of 19 June. (It would make this show 'full house' for the Coopers, since both boys were accepted and Elizabeth and Joe were both in it, too.) That day was a very full one, as the auditions for the adults were also taking place. Seventy auditions were heard and from these a cast was chosen. Eighteen boys were picked to take part in the show, plus two pairs to play Oliver and the Artful Dodger on alternate nights. The two who were not in the leading parts each night would join in with the rest of Fagin's gang. There was some upset over casting the part of Fagin, though. One member, who would be away, sent a video to be watched as an audition and was most upset that this was not even viewed, but the usual practice was to choose from those actually present if possible, then to consider others not present but wishing to audition, and finally, if necessary, to ask people from outside the Society to audition. As it happened Ken Horsley, whose last show with the Society had been *The Music Man*, had applied to audition and was a splendid Fagin, so the Committee looked no further. Zoë Kent, who had just recovered from throat surgery, was taking her first leading role as Nancy, and Arthur Ellis was playing Bill Sikes again. Barrie Dargue was appearing as Mr Sowerberry once more and this time Kath Robinson was playing his wife. Widow Corney and Mr Bumble were Connie Reeves and George Browne, who had been a newcomer for *Sweet Charity* in which he had won everyone's hearts as the totally disgusting and scrofulous proprietor of the sleazy café where Charity and Oscar meet. Bet, Nancy's friend, was played by Samantha Currie, who had also been new to the Society for *Sweet Charity*, while Noah and Charlotte were played by Andy Myers and Angela Smallman, both of whom had joined very recently. Shirley Dodd and Doug Clayton were playing Mrs Bedwin and Dr Grimwig, but Mr

Oliver! 1993
Arthur Ellis and Sam.

Brownlow remained uncast until Sam was persuaded to play the part. The two Olivers were Kieran Nokes and Paul Taylor and the two Artful Dodgers were Adam Savage and Paul Frost. All that was needed now was an English Bull Terrier to play the part of Bullseye, so Elizabeth Cooper began contacting dog training groups in the hope of finding one suitable.

There was no doubt that *Oliver!* was going to sell well. In their first week on sale, 3,000 tickets were sold. This was a particularly welcome start for there were an extra 900 to be sold because of the matinée, planned for the first Saturday. One person even rang to try to book seats for the *Sunday* evening. The theatre did have tickets for the Sunday, but it was a one-night stand by Chris Bonington and since he is not noted for singing and dancing the patron might have suffered keen disappointment!

By mid-September a dog had been found – and what a dog he was! He was an eighteen-month-old white English Bull Terrier with a black patch round his eye, just as in the original story. He had a majestic name: Aricon Angus the Archer – Sam to his friends. Thus the cast list was complete and intensive rehearsal could begin. It was chaotic at times. Those who had been in the last production of *Oliver!* had forgotten what little boys in large numbers could be like! Eight noble souls volunteered to supervise them, including two of the boys' mothers. One of them, Liz Tyreman, mother of Ben, stayed with the Society and was elected to the Ladies' Committee in 1994, and Ben's father, Joe, also came along and became one of the regular backstage workers. Allan Andrews, father of Robert, joined the chorus too.

The tickets continued to sell like hot cakes. Two weeks before opening night 7,500 of the available 9,900 had gone; by opening night only 91 were left unsold (in the upper circle) – not bad considering that there are 152 seats in the theatre which are classed as restricted viewing! The numbers of Vice-Presidents and Patrons had risen to 376 and the 50 blocks that had booked last time had all returned. It is noteworthy that after this show the Committee agreed that a private telephone line should be provided for the Ticket Secretaries and their original one kept purely for Society business, for it was rumoured that one of them had been overheard enquiring as to the availability of a whisky and tranquillizer cocktail which could be taken continuously and intravenously . . .

Oliver! went very well, although there was the usual problem which occurs when firearms are used: the period flintlock gun which Barry Million fired to kill Arthur did not go off on the first night. The company indulged in discussion as to alternative ways for Arthur to die ('Oh dear, I think I may be having a heart attack' was rejected out of hand) and it was finally agreed that Joe Cooper should stab him if necessary. Of course the gun then worked on the second night when Joe was ready with his knife, and Arthur was seen to be well and truly killed by both methods. After that a gun was fired off stage and produced a satisfactorily loud report – though no-one warned Zoë, who was lying dead on stage, so the shot evinced very belated death-throes.

It would be nice to say that all the reviews were raves, but sadly the *Northern Echo* did not attend the show and the *Darlington Advertiser*, amid compliments, insinuated that the audience was composed of the partici-pants' families! Ken Horsley's Fagin, however, for this reviewer, 'lifted the whole production'.[18] Zoë's Nancy was not far behind, but the two leading children's singing voices were 'sometimes inaudible' and the other boys looked too clean. Nonetheless, concluded the review, it was 'the best of the recent DOS productions I have seen!' The *Darlington & Stockton Times* took a different view. For this critic the boys stole the show, particularly the two leads, and the role of Fagin was handled by Ken 'like a professional'.[19] Zoë was 'ideal' in the part of Nancy. Arthur was complimented for his characterization, and George and Connie were also commended, as were Barrie, Shirley and Doug. The headline to the review was 'Rush now for more of this sparkling *Oliver!* – and Sam'. Sam was everyone's darling as soon as he appeared. He stayed in the crew-room backstage until he was needed, and in a very short time he knew what the cues were for his appearances. Only once was he left in a state of indecision: in the normal way, Arthur would come down a flight of steps into the 'tavern' with him, and after a few preliminaries would hand Sam's lead to one of the others on stage, who would have in his pocket a supply of goodies with canine appeal. On the night in question one of the boys gave Sam a piece of Mars Bar just before his entrance, leaving him with divided loyalties. However, Arthur prevailed. Sam was a star – and, of course, he was word-perfect. So were the boys, though their stagecraft left something to be desired from time to time at rehearsals! Most notable was the incident at the dress rehearsal when the lights went up on Fagin's den and the boys were lying on their sacks, spread around the floor. The atmospheric music came to an end and then there was an awkward silence. To put it politely, Bev enquired as to the whereabouts of the boy who should have been there to speak the next lines. Back came a nonchalant little voice from the stage: 'Oh, he's gone to the toilet.' Bev's reaction is best not recorded here verbatim, but it consisted of advice, which, if taken and acted upon, would be an instant solution to the problem!

There were many letters of congratulation from people who had attended the show. One person had brought a guest who was staying with her; he was an American theatre director who said that it was the best amateur performance he had seen in England – though, to be fair, no one knows how many amateur shows he *had* actually seen in England! However, these things, together with the facts that the Society was able to give substantial donations (including £1,000 to a new Day Centre in Darlington) and that everyone had enjoyed being in the show, made the hard work well worthwhile for the members. The annual after-autumn-show firework party at Frances and Stephen Sanderson's was an especially cheerful one.

It was back to work immediately, however, not only for *Gigi* but also for *Anything Goes*. Liz Holton and Jayne Summerbell were choreographers for the latter, and they instituted tap-dance classes for it to run concurrently with singing rehearsals for *Gigi*, so that everyone would have the opportunity to learn to tap. This made life even busier, with two rehearsal nights each week instead of one, and there were still social activities going on, though not so many as there had been the previous year. The Society was still planning to sing Christmas carols, as usual, in Binns store.

The Society did not lack occupation in the new year. There was to be a singing/acting workshop, paid for by the Kenneth Richardson Trust, given by Theresia von Sertima and Caroline Noh, and a number of the members took part, as extras, in the second series of the television programme *Harry*, starring Michael Elphick as a Darlington-based journalist. Society members were used because they were all used to acting and knew each other well so that they were convincing as a crowd socializing.

In mid-January 1994 auditions were held for *Gigi*. Bev, as usual, was producing and Stephen was Musical Director. Irene Hand, helped by her daughter Joanne, was the Choreographer, and Samantha Currie, who had played Bet in *Oliver!*, was to play the title role. She had played the title role in *Annie* while at Sedgefield Community College (where the Producer was Eunicé Cockburn) and had been in shows with the Youth Theatres in Darlington and Stockton. Barrie Dargue was playing Honoré, Shirley Dodd, who had played Aunt Alicia in the Society's last production of the show, was playing Mamita in this one, while Maggie Thorp took the part of Aunt Alicia. Liz Holton was Liane D'Exelmans, Gary Winn was Manuel (the effete valet), Graeme Hall was the Telephone Installer, and the two lawyers, Du Fresne and Duclos, were Sam Herdman and Ian Whitfield. A heavyweight was needed to play Charles, Aunt Alicia's servant, for in this production the character was to own a dog – and Bev wanted a St Bernard. The Society was lucky enough to get a beautiful St Bernard whose kennel name was Mountside Movie Star but who was known as Hannah. She had recently won the title of Champion St Bernard at Crufts and was a stoical, benevolent animal. Pound for pound, George Browne was just about her equal, though, as Tom Kent wrote in the programme notes: 'We hope Hannah enjoys her appearance on stage. We don't suppose anyone will stop her if she decides to leave!!' There was much rejoicing in the company because the Blain family had returned to the North from Devon, and all four of them were involved in the show. Avril was in the chorus, Steve was handling the sound, and their two daughters, Romana and Selina, were the 'little girls' mentioned in Honoré's song, *Thank Heaven for Little Girls*, along with Frances and Stephen Sanderson's two daughters, Helen and Jennifer, and Charlotte Westgarth, whose mother Caroline was helping as a supervisor to the children. As had been the case so many times before, the show lacked a leading man – the Committee had learned that, contrary to supposition, it made sense

Gigi 1994
Left to right: Rory Mulvihill, Samantha Currie, Maggie Thorp, Barrie Dargue.

to choose a show and worry about getting a leading man later, as long as the other parts could be cast! David Curtis had been a possibility, but was committed to appearing in an opera at Durham, so the Committee began the search for a Gaston.

When the time of the Annual General Meeting came round the tickets for *Gigi* were going reasonably well, though not so quickly as they had for *Oliver!*, for the upper circle was looking bare. However, the show at least had a Gaston. He was Rory Mulvihill, who had been acting since he was twelve years old. He lived in York, worked as a solicitor in Leeds, and was in Bev's 'home' society, York Light Opera Group. The Darlington society knew him, having seen him in productions with that company, and welcomed him warmly.

The committee meeting which followed the Annual General Meeting was an extra-special one, for it was then that John Lloyd handed over the Chairman's chain of office to Elizabeth Cooper, who was to be the Society's third lady Chairman. It was the first time the ladies had hit double top, as it were, for Liz Holton was now Vice-Chairman. So Elizabeth presided over her first show in April 1994, and, once her nerves were under control, enjoyed the experience, though in some ways she found it more tiring than being in a show.

Gigi was generally well-received and several letters of congratulation were sent by the public, though it has to be said that one very critical one also arrived. The newspaper reviews were very good without being ecstatic. The *Darlington Advertiser* thought Samantha was 'handicapped by not having a really good song',[20] the *Northern Echo* said that the dancers looked 'a little cramped'[21] (they were), and the *Darlington & Stockton Times* said 'The storyline is weak'[22] – a sad reflection on Colette, the French author who wrote the original book. This said, they seemed to enjoy the performances not only of the principals but of the cast as a whole. The *Darlington Advertiser* picked out 'the male chorus members cavorting in Victorian swimming costumes' as a highlight (yes – those *Gondoliers* bathing suits were back!) and Gary Winn's camp performance as Manuel. The *Northern Echo*, along with plaudits for the other leading actors, singled out Shirley Dodd's 'vast professionalism' as Mamita – and also Gary Winn. 'All in all,' concluded the *Northern Echo* review, 'this is good, old-fashioned entertainment.' The *Darlington & Stockton Times* gave a slightly broader view, saying that the Society ' . . . again staked its claim as one of the top amateur companies in the area with a performance full of gaiety and charm.' Rory enjoyed himself so much that he declined to accept the travelling expenses which were due to him – how that would have gladdened the hearts of the Committee in those early years! – and asked that the Committee consider him for future roles. Hannah enjoyed herself too – a letter was received from her owner telling the Committee so – and she had behaved perfectly, apart from rounding off her two weeks of performances by giving herself a good shake on stage on the final night and showering the assembled company with two jowls' worth of saliva – a move which brought the show to a halt while everyone, including the audience, composed themselves!

81% of the tickets were sold for *Gigi* – not as many as for *Oliver!*, of course, but sufficient to provide a surplus – and the numbers of Vice-Presidents, Patrons, and visiting organizations was staying more or less constant by now, showing sustained support for the Society. This was probably partly because the seat prices for these amateur shows were running at about one-third of those for professional productions. To manage this, the Committee was still making great efforts to keep expenses down: to reduce the bill for props for *Gigi* one of Greta and Bernard's rooms had been virtually stripped bare of furniture and curtains!

In the mean time assiduous tap-dance practice was taking place ready for *Anything Goes*, with varying degrees of proficiency being reached. Auditions were held and there was keen competition among the ladies to get into the show. This was one of its drawbacks: parts for ladies were very limited in number and so much depended on the standard of tap-dancing which had been attained. Sadly, the auditions left some ladies, who had worked hard, very disappointed. Avril Blain got the part of Hope, the *ingénue*, with Gary Winn as her 'intended' – Sir Evelyn, a chinless wonder of an English aristocrat – and with June Aiken as Mrs Wadsworth T. Harcourt, her mother. Billy Crocker, the hero, was Warnock Kerr, back again after a long absence. Bonnie, the birdbrain of the piece, was Kath Robinson, and Moonface Martin (or 'Public Enemy Number Thirteen' as he prefers to be known in the show) was Arthur Ellis. Doug Clayton was playing the part of Billy's irascible and myopic boss, Elisha J. Whitney. There was considerable difficulty this time in getting a leading lady who had a strong enough voice to play Reno Sweeney the ex-evangelist night-club owner – the part that made Ethel Merman a Broadway star. Eventually Bev Jones had a brainwave and introduced Dawn Oostdijck (née O'Connor), from Middlesbrough, as a candidate. She was a good tap-dancer and a very good singer, having worked in cabaret on cruise liners, she was easy to get along with and she had worked with Bev before. The company had found its Reno. Her four 'Angels' were played by Elizabeth Cooper (Purity), Liz Holton (Chastity), Jayne Summerbell (Charity) and Mandy Shellard (Virtue – 'the easy kind'!). Sam Herdman was appearing in his 70th show for the Society as Bishop Henry T. Dodson (a missionary and the victim of mistaken identity) with David Plumpton and Graeme Hall as his two Chinese 'converts', Ling and Ching.

The run-up to *Anything Goes* was anything but easy. Stephen Sild was to be Musical Director again but suffered a lengthy and debilitating illness which prevented him from attending many rehearsals. In the end he had to withdraw from the production and Bev agreed to be Musical Director as well as Producer. It was fortunate for the Society that Gavin Bailey now had his own transport rather than relying on Stephen to bring him, so he was able to share the accompanying with Brian Sheppard.

By late September 5,000 of the tickets had been sold, the tap-dancing was going well and the cast were enjoying rehearsals. Morale had been boosted by the fact that there was a reasonable surplus in the production account from *Gigi* and some money had been saved on props for the current show by Dawn Oostdijck's husband Govert. A master-carpenter, who was working on a set for *42nd Street* at Middlesbrough at the time, he made a machine-gun (out of a single piece of wood) and a violin case for Arthur Ellis to carry, with a special interior to hold it. He also showed entirely unexpected talent in the cabaret at the customary after-show party when he joined Arthur, Joe Cooper, Gary Winn and Graeme Hall as 'Reno and her four fallen Angels' in a hilarious take-off of Dawn and the girls, rendering an arrangement of *Take Me Back to Manhattan*, retitled for the occasion *Take Me Back to Newcastle*. Gary was particularly convincing as Elizabeth Cooper. She had not been in *Gigi* and had forgotten how short-sighted she was without her glasses, so in *Take Me Back to Manhattan* (and fortunately only at the technical rehearsal!) Liz Holton had had to seize her by the seat of her trouser-suit costume (they were back to back at the start of the number in the show) and haul her into position under the pool of spotlight. Gary and Joe naturally capitalized on this event. (Elizabeth also forgot, when she came to make her last-night-of-the-show speech from the stage, that although she had her notes in her hand she *still* did not have her glasses on . . . Still, undaunted, she soldiered on and improvized splendidly!)

Anything Goes opened at the end of October and reactions to it were anxiously awaited since it was new to the Society and also to many of the audience. There was considerable variation in opinions ranging from 'it was well done but not my favourite show' to 'the best show I've seen the Society do'. There is no doubt that the cast found it fun, though it was quite difficult to make the timing slick enough – the lines have to follow almost on top of each other to give it the necessary punch. Ian Whitfield had to take particular care. In his role as the Purser on board the *SS American* he had to make nineteen entrances, most of which were key ones as his appearance was the cue for other characters to speak their lines. In a quick-fire show such as this one, of course – wordy and full of 'one-liners' which make it difficult to pick up cues – there were plenty of potential crises, though the cast managed to avoid most of them. As the action and timing improves, however, it can become harder rather than easier to keep out of trouble. For the first time ever, both June and Arthur missed entrances. June was the first to do this, having gone to the wrong side of the stage. One of her lines mentioned cocktails so the two unfor- tunates who awaited her on stage began light (but desperate) chit-chat about cocktails until June appeared. Thereafter if anyone was late on stage the 'cocktail' chat began – Avril became adept at it. Arthur's missed entrance nearly induced apoplexy in Kath as they were to back onto the stage from opposite sides and collide. When Kath entered, all she encoun- tered was space. Alone in all this space she began to hiss 'Moonie . . . Moonie!' looking desperately into the wings. Since Arthur was in the crew-room backstage, thinking he had plenty of time, he gave the matter no thought until he heard George Aiken bellowing over the backstage tannoy 'Moon on stage! Moon on stage!' It was an unfortunate turn of phrase – Arthur was not sure whether it was a summons or an instruction! Kath was almost gibbering by the time he appeared. Although the gist of the question she hissed at him as he arrived in the wings was 'Where have you been?' the precise words meant that it was just as well that the volume of her radio-microphone was not turned up!

Steve Blain, who was responsible for sound, had a hideous moment which was apparent to *everyone*. In the evening of the middle Sunday Val Doonican had given a one-night show and consequently the computerized sound-schedule for *Anything Goes* had been disturbed. The following night, when Arthur shouted 'Man overboard!' and Joe Cooper (as a drunk) rushed off and supposedly jumped into the sea, instead of a resounding splash there came a resounding gunshot. Steve had to endure a good many gibes about 'hard water' and other comments of a similar nature . . . the sequence of sounds was in perfect order thereafter.

Sadly for the Society it seemed that the press had now largely lost interest in its productions. Only one of the six complimentary seats was taken but its occupant, Jill Neill, enjoyed the show and wrote reviews for both the *Northern Echo* and the *Darlington & Stockton Times*. She considered *Anything Goes* to be 'first-class entertainment'[23] and gave favourable mentions to Avril and Warnock, to Arthur and the four Angels, to Dawn ('more than a touch of Bette Midler'), and especially to Gary Winn whose portrayal of the lisping, upper-class Sir Evelyn stole the show as far as she was concerned. She loved the costumes, the scenery, the choreography and the special effects (though she felt that the lighting was sometimes too subdued) and summed up her review in the *Northern Echo* with the words, 'Cole Porter's genius and the Society's talent combine to offer a real treat to music lovers.'[24]

Once *Anything Goes* was over the company had to concentrate on both shows for jubilee year. When the Society had last given *La Vie Parisienne*, in the spring of 1969, Joy Beadell and Frank Murray had felt that there was so much work to be done on such a big production that singing rehearsals should take place alongside those for *Camelot* in order to get as much polish as possible on the music. Similarly, in 1995, singing rehearsals would start in March while those for *Calamity Jane* had, of course, begun on the Thursday immediately following the close of *Anything Goes*. Sadly, Stephen Sild was still ill but Wayne Shellard had agreed to act as Chorus Master until Bev Jones, who had been booked to produce both the jubilee year shows, was able to take over as Musical Director.

There was some consternation over the ticket prices for the show. They had already been set to rise by 50p when Greta received notification from the theatre that the hire-charge was going up, but after discussion the idea of an even greater rise was abandoned – the Committee wanted to avoid excessive charges and to make sure that the public felt that they were still getting value for money – for they *were* getting value for money. For example, in 1945 the cost of the best seats was six shillings; for *Calamity Jane* fifty years later the general price was set at £8.50. Since the average wage has increased by a factor of about fifty that six shillings would be equivalent to about £15 today.

The portents for 1995 were looking promising as 1994 drew to a close. The Society had managed to distribute over £3,000 to various charities over the year, and not least among the good omens was the fact that seven young members were welcomed into the company following the auditions at the end of the year. Karen Hursey, Jacqui Drysdale, Julie Williams, Michelle Collings, Paul Phillips (who had been one of Fagin's boys in *Oliver!* and had subsequently brought his father, David, along) and Peter Norris auditioned, and Emma Hardwick, who had been one of the children in *Annie* in 1991, who was now over sixteen and therefore eligible to become a full member.

So, 50 years on from its re-formation, the Society is still going strong, still maintaining a good reputation and, what is more, still attracting young people – surely a sign of its good health; moreover the theatre which it struggled to save from demolition all those years ago is still one of the most successful provincial theatres in the country and is as much loved by the professionals who perform there as by the amateurs.

It seems fitting that the story (so far!) of this company of enthusiastic amateurs should end on a particularly happy note. The loyalty of someone who so longed to be a member of the Society when she was much too young to join, who went along to the shows in the lowly position of 'call boy' just to be a part of it all, and who has gone on to take major roles and to choreograph for *Anything Goes* and *Calamity Jane*, is about to be rewarded. For Liz Holton, in 1995 the Golden Jubilee year, is to be Chairman, at last, of Darlington Operatic Society!

Postscript

As this book went to press malevolent fate struck the Society yet again when, almost unbelievably, plans for the big jubilee show planned for autumn 1995 went awry once more. The D'Oyly Carte company announced in March that one of the shows they would present at Darlington Civic Theatre in October would be – yes – *La Vie Parisienne*! After a hasty re-think on the part of the Committee, therefore, the lavish *Waltzes from Vienna*, the story of Johann Strauss and his son, was chosen instead – and everyone crossed their fingers.

Appendix 1

Joseph (Jos.) Hall was born on 16 December 1883 and was a clerk at a local firm, Pease and Partners. He was very interested in acting and was a keen member of Darlington Medley Dramatic Club and also of the Darlington branch of the British Empire Shakespeare Society. He had aspirations to enter the professional theatre – among his papers is a letter from F. R. Benson of The New Theatre Royal at Middlesbrough, dated 29 October 1902, giving him advice. There is also a note by Jos. Hall himself, in the magazine *The Actor Illustrated* for July 1905, saying that amateur dramatic clubs give the best training for entry into a professional career.

He was still an amateur, however, in 1916, still with the Darlington branch of The British Empire Shakespeare Society and also with Mrs Paget Steavenson's party of friends who performed plays in aid of charity. So, sadly, his ambition was never realized. He did, however, put together the book of press cuttings and programmes mentioned in the text, entitled *The Memoirs of Jos. Hall.*

The kindness of Mrs Marjorie Hall in offering the loan of Jos. Hall's book is most gratefully acknowledged, for without it the information about that part of the history of Darlington Operatic Society would have been woefully scarce.

Appendix 2

Darlington Operatic Society Organization 24 June 1929

The Chairman should:
§ preside at meetings.
§ not be hedged with hard and fast rules.
§ have the full confidence of the committee.
§ act on his own initiative with the support of the committee.
§ act as general supervisor.

The Treasurer should:
§ look after the Society's financial well-being.
§ keep a close watch on finance and keep an accurate record.
§ report at committee meetings on financial position. Cheques to be signed by him and one other (Chairman, Secretary, or Financial Secretary).

Financial Secretary is the accountant of the Society and should:
§ look after ledgers, bank book, cheque book.
§ look after subscriptions, entertainment tax, ticket money and box office returns.
§ Patrons Secretary should control and record all matters with regard to patrons.

General Secretary is the general dogsbody and should:
§ link with the Producer and Musical Director.
§ record the membership at rehearsals.
§ record those present at committee meetings.
§ keep a petty cash account with £5 for running expenses.

Producer and Musical Director to be responsible with the committee for actual stage presentation.

The Committee should exercise a keen and active interest and co-operate in any way to give a successful production, both artistically and economically.

General:
- § Each official conducts his own correspondence and produces same at committee meetings; he can authorize small amounts of expenditure up to £1.
- § Committee meetings are held monthly from September to February and as necessary.
- § Five members constitute a quorum.

Committee meetings now take place all the year round but the duties are very much the same today. The offices of Treasurer, Financial Secretary and Patrons Secretary, however, have been amalgamated and then divided between the Treasurer, the Assistant Treasurer and the Ticket Secretary. Also the £5 rule no longer applies for the Secretary and the rigid restriction on expenditure by individual committee members has been lifted!

Cast Lists Since 1945

Note: Where principals were also in the chorus they may be named in both lists.

1945 MERRIE ENGLAND

PRINCIPALS: Audrey Walker, William T Burrell, W F Harris, James Mathieson, Robert F Leeman, Robert H Theakston, Dennis Ward, Rita Hamilton, Jack Lyall, Chas R Clifford, W Roy Heylings, Beryl Preston, Nancy Bertram, Don Fraser, Wilf Robinson, F R M Eddy, Minerva Davison, Olive Gill, Stephen Wood, Donald Elliott, Peter Thompson, Wynsome Thwaites.

CHORUS NOT LISTED

1946 KATINKA

PRINCIPALS: Eileen Young, William T Burrell, Alan Hanson, Don Fraser, Nancy Bertram, Minerva Davison, Fred Thompson, Stephen Wood, James Mathieson, George Goodyear, Rita Hamilton, Doris L Thompson, Walter F Harris, Wynsome Thwaites.

CHORUS: Mesdames Angus, Binner, Dunn, Hardaker, Howes, Scott, Soulsby, Stephenson, Thompson, Misses Berry, Boyd, Gill, Goldsborough, Hughes, Taylor, Walker, Williams, Messrs Birkett, Clarke, Cummings, Eddy, Gaskin, Leeman, Langford, Reed, Theakston, Webster, Ward, Whitfield, Wood.

CHOIR BOYS: Masters Gaylor, Hedworth, Soulsby, Redpath, Thompson, Simmons, Wych.

DANCERS: Mesdames Bramwell, English, Hardy, Misses Birkett, Edwards, Farrage, Halstead, Herdman, Hetherington, Hull, Lockey, Lowes, Pirt, Robinson, Thwaites, Wright.

1947 GOOD NIGHT VIENNA

PRINCIPALS: Molly Bramwell, Audrey Walker, Doris L Thompson, George Goodyear, Don Fraser, Eric Thompson, Nancy Bertram, Fred Thompson, Alan Hanson, Alice Howes, Walter Harris, Dorothy Turner, Vera Dickinson, Evelyn Berry.

CHORUS ETC. NOT LISTED.

1947 THE DUCHESS OF DANTZIC

PRINCIPALS: Irene Ross, Vivienne Farrage, Don Fraser, Alan Hanson, Eric Thompson, Ellis Breeze, E Binner, John Reed, Doris Thompson, Alice Howes, Betty Steele, Nancy Bertram, Master G Wild, Master P Thompson, Walter Harris, Ken Richardson.

CHORUS: Mesdames Binner, Donkin, Dodd, Johnson, Sherwood, Hardaker, Howatson, Hardy, English, Stephenson, Willans, Dickinson, Dunn, Thompson, Misses Alderson, Turner, Shirren, G Murray, Berry, Stockdale, Garthwaite, Moran, Lowes, M Taylor, Dixon, Simpson, Neasham, Wright, Thwaites, Walker, Dent, D Taylor, Young, Maddison, Allison, Welford, Messrs Appleby, Taylor, A Robinson, Clark, Eddy, Boddy, W Robinson, Leeman, Grieveson, Willans, Smith, Knight, Sadler.

1948 THE NEW MOON

PRINCIPALS: Joy Beadell, J May, Alan Hanson, Kenneth Richardson, F Boddy, H Harris, John Reed, Don Fraser, W Burrell, Paul Leeming, Nancy Bertram, E Binner, J Mathieson, J Willans, Doris Leslie, George Goodyear, Vera Dickinson.

CHORUS: Mesdames I Binner, I Dodd, M Hardaker, G Howatson, A Howes, M Johnson,

E Sherwood, G Thompson, Misses M Alderson, E Berry, N Dixon, G Garthwaite, M Hughes, D Leslie, S Lowes, G Maddison, I Moran, G Neasham, D Robinson, M Taylor, P Welford, P Wright, E Young, Messrs G Allport, E Appleby, P Biott, F Blackburn, E Breeze, W A Clark, W Clark, J Eddy, C Grieveson, D Grogan, J Hocklin, C Knight, H Knight, R Leeming, C Main, J Mathieson, R Mathieson, S Mitchell, F Murray, V Roberts, W Robinson, W Sinclair, W Stockdale.

DANCERS, Mesdames M Anderson, A English, E Hardy, Misses H Dent, V Farrage, M Johnson, G Murray, D Pinkney, C Shirren, V Simpson, I Stockdale, E Steele, W Thwaites, A Walker

1948 ROSE MARIE

PRINCIPALS: Doris Leslie, Vivienne Farrage, Doris Thompson, Joy Bishop, George Goodyear, Don Fraser, William Burrell, Kenneth Richardson, Bernard J Clark, John Reed, Jim Mathieson.

CHORUS: Mesdames M Hardaker, C Murray, I Dodd, E Goodyear, V Dickinson, A Howes, G Thompson, G Howatson, M Johnson, L Sinclair, Misses J Maddison, E Berry, M Taylor, N Bertram, E Young, S Lowes, D Robinson, I Moran, E Neasham, M Hughes, J Alderson, E Allison, N Dixon, W Thwaites, P Wright, Messrs F Murray, E Appleby, S Mitchell, C Cowley, F Boddy, R Leeman, T Sanderson, W Dodshon, W Sinclair, S Main, E Breeze, G Wild, W Harris, E Hicklin, R W Nunn, W Robinson, F R M Eddy, C Knight, J Stockdale, A Clark, A Biott.

DANCERS: Mesdames E Hardy, A English, Misses G Murray, C Smirren, H Dent, D Pinkney, H Johnson, H Brown, E Pyle, V Simpson.

1949 THE LISBON STORY

PRINCIPALS: Kenneth Richardson, Doris Leslie, Philip Greenwood, Nancy Bertram, Eileen Young, George Cummings, Mark H Kay, George W Llewellyn, Wilf Robinson, F R M Eddy, Bernard Sanderson, Vivienne Farrage, Donald Fraser, Doreen Robinson, Joy Beadell, Cecil Grieveson, Walter Harris, Bernard J Clark, James Mathieson, David Ormerod, Greta Murray.

CHORUS: B Dunn, V Dickinson, I Dodd, P Donkin, E Goodyear, M Hardaker, G Howatson, A Howes, Misses J Anderson, J Angus, E Berry, E Glover, M Hughes, S Lowes, I Moran, E Neasham, M Taylor, D Turner, P Wright, Messrs F Boddy, A Clark, W T Grainger, E Hicklin, C Knight, S Layfield, R Leeman, S Mitchell, W Sinclair, E Smith, I Stockdale, G Wild, J S Whitfield, Dennis Ward.

CORPS DE BALLET: Mesdames L Boddy, A English, E Hardy, Misses M Bell, H Brown, E Davie, H Dent, M Johnson, A Layfield, G Murray, E Oliver, V Simpson.

1950 THE DESERT SONG

PRINCIPALS: Kenneth Smith, Cecil Grieveson, Philipa Donkin, John Reed, Philip Greenwood, Doris Leslie, Mark H Kay, George Goodyear, Eileen Young, Gwen Howatson, William Burrell, Vera Dickinson, Bernard Sanderson, James Mathieson, George Cummings, Edward Scott.

CHORUS: Mesdames I Dodd, M Hardaker, A Howes, M Johnson, G Sinclair, M Chapman, G Thompson, Misses E Berry, M Hughes, S Lowes, I Moran, E Neasham, M Taylor, D Turner, P Wright, M Stevenson, I Thompson, Messrs F Boddy, W T Grainger, E Hicklin, C Knight, S Layfield, R Leeman, S Mitchell, W Sinclair, I Stockdale, J S Whitfield, G Llewellyn, F R M Eddy, K Richardson, C Wake, S Plews, R H F Evans, A Robinson, A Haffner.

DANCERS: Mesdames L Boddy, A English, E Hardy, Misses H Brown, E Davie, H Dent, M Johnson, A Layfield, G Murray, E Oliver, D Pinkney, N Bertram, D Robinson, A Crudass.

1950 WILD VIOLETS

PRINCIPALS: Robert White, Vera Dickinson, Shirley Dodd, Alwyn Robinson, George Goodyear, Kenneth Richardson, Kenneth Smith, Teresa Howell, Elsie Chapman, Vivienne Farrage, Greta Murray, Mary Johnson, Alan Hanson, Nancy Bertram, George Cummings, Fred Eddy.

CHORUS Mesdames I Dodd, B Dunn, E Goodyear, M Hardaker, M Hart, J Lucas, C Murray, G Thompson, Misses E Berry, S Dodd, B Hopps, M Hughes, E Neasham, E Raine-Howes,

M Stevenson, M Taylor, C Thompson, K Turner, P Wright, E Young, Messrs F Boddy, W A Clark, C Cowley, G Cummings, F E Eddy, W Grainger, P Greenwood, A Haffner, C Knight, S Layfield, R Leeman, J Mathieson, S Mitchell, S Plews, B Richardson, A Robinson, W Robinson, B Sanderson, E Scott, W Sinclair, I Stockdale.

DANCERS: Mesdames L Boddy, A English, E Hardy, Misses P Batchelor, H Brown, A Crudass, E Davey, M Johnson, N Lillie, E Oliver, D Pinkney, V Simpson.

1951 THE VAGABOND KING

PRINCIPALS: Kenneth Smith, James Mathieson, Teresa Howell, Connie Murray, Vera Dickinson, Doris Leslie, Fred Thompson, Philip Greenwood, Kenneth Richardson, Alan Hanson, Nancy Bertram, Don Fraser, William Burrell, Cecil Grieveson, Barbara Hopps, George Goodyear, Raymond Burgin, Don Fraser, Ada English, Joy Beadell, F R M Eddy, S Layfield

CHORUS: Misses R Barnes, E Berry, S Brown, S Conway, V Farrage, G Gregg, S Hanson, D Hildreth, M Hughes, B Siddle, M Stevenson, M Taylor, C Thompson, K Turner, P Hooley-Wright, E Young, Mesdames E Chapman, V Dickinson, I Dodd, A English, E Hardy, M Hardaker, E Hart, A Howes, G Howatson, M Hudson, C Murray, G Thompson, S N Warde, Messrs J Bell, F R M Eddy, W Grainger, A Haffner, F Howes, D Innis, C Knight, S Layfield, J Louth, S Mitchell, J Fraser Murray, F C Murray, J Pearson, K Newton, S Plews, F S Porritt, B Richardson, W Robinson, B Sanderson, E Scott, F Stockdale, J H Willans.

DANCERS: Lorrie Boddy, Hilda Brown, Anne Crudass, Margaret Johnson, Norma Lillie, Greta Murray, Eileen Oliver, Delia Pinkney.

1952 THE STUDENT PRINCE

PRINCIPALS: S Mitchell, C Akers, F S Porritt, S Layfield, Fred Howes, Kenneth Richardson, George Goodyear, F R M Eddy, Cecil Grieveson, Doris Leslie, Joy Beadell, Albert Haffner, W A Clarke, Syd Plews, Philip Greenwood, George Cummings, Bernard Sanderson, Vera Dickinson, Barbara Hopps, Ken Smith, Doreen Hildreth, Peter Dearden, Fred Boddy.

CHORUS: Mesdames L Boddy, I Dodd, A English, M Hardaker, E Hardy, E Hart, L Hudson, C Murray, S M Warde, Misses R Barnes, E Berry, N Bertram, H Brown, S Brown, S Conway, H Dent, V Farrage, S Hanson, P Hooley-Wright, G Howatson, T Howell, M Hughes, N Lillie, M Linfoot, G Murray, E Oliver, D Pinkney, M Stevenson, M Taylor, I C Thompson, K E Turner, H Whitman, E Wilson, E Young, Messrs C Akers, R Baker, F Boddy, J M Brown, W T Grainger, N Jowett, C Knight, S Layfield, J Mathieson, S Mitchell, K Newton, J B Peart, B Richardson, I Stockdale, J S Whitfield

DANCERS: Nancy Bertram, Lorrie Boddy, Hilda Brown, Hilda Dent, Ada English, Norma Lillie, Greta Murray, Delia Pinkney, Eileen Oliver.

THE MIKADO

PRINCIPALS: Don Fraser, Ronald Brown, Kenneth Richardson, H R Herdman, Fred Howes, Hilda Whitman, Vivienne Farrage, Ena Hart, Teresa Howell, Peter Thompson.

CHORUS: Mesdames R Barnes, E Berry, N Bertram, L Boddy, H Brown, S Brown, H Dent, V Dickinson, I Dodd, A English, M Hardaker, E Hardy, M Hughes, D Leslie, N Lillie, C Murray, C Thompson, A Howes, M Chilton, D Caygill, J Gregg, M Johnson, D Lucas, E Neasham, A Moore, D Pinkney, M Taylor, D Taylor, G Thompson, I Skippon, J Smith, G Sanderson, K Turner, W Thwaites, P Hooley-Wright, E Young, Messrs R Baker, J Brown, W A Clarke, G Cummings, F E Eddy, D S Fox, W Grainger, P Greenwood, W Hodgson, T W Jones, C Knight, G W Llewellyn, J Mathieson, S Mitchell, K Newton, J Peart, F Porritt, F Robson, B Sanderson, K Smith, I Stockdale, E W Scott, E Scott, W Smith.

1953 MAGYAR MELODY

PRINCIPALS: Vera Dickinson, Frank Robson, F E Eddy, J E Sinclair, Alan Hanson, Ken Smith, Hilda Whitman, K Fraser, Constance Murray, Kenneth Richardson, H R Herdman,

John Pitkeathley, Barbara Hopps, Doreen Hildreth, Sheila Conway, Dorothy Caygill, Evelyn Berry, W Grainger, Michael Lucas, Ken Bodden, Ena Hart.

CHORUS: Mesdames M Chilton, I Dodd, S Hanson, M Hardaker, D Lucas, M Stephenson, P Hooley-Wright, K Turner, M Taylor, A Moore, I C Thompson, E Young, Messrs F Boddy, C Cowley, D Dawes, S Mitchell, T W Jones, J B Peart, E W Scott, J E Sinclair, I Stockdale, K Wheadon.

DANCERS: Mesdames L Boddy, H Brown, H Dent, R Barnes, V Farrage, D Halliwell, A Hudson, E Hardy, A English, N Lillie, M Leeming, I Oliver, Messrs R Baker, J E Brown, W Cobban, C Knight, G Llewellyn, K Newton, A Haffner, J Sinclair.

THE GONDOLIERS

PRINCIPALS: Kenneth Richardson, Ken Fraser, H R Herdman, George Llewellyn, Robert White, Michael Lucas, T W Jones, Bernard Sanderson, K M Bodden, Alice Howes, Hilda Whitman, Nancy Bertram, Barbara Hopps, Vivienne Farrage, Dorothy Caygill, Jean Campbell, Constance Murray.

CHORUS: Mesdames E Berry, L Boddy, H Brown, S Brown, H Dent, E Hart, N Little, E Hart, V Dickinson, I Dodd, S Dodd, A English, S Hanson, M Hardaker, E Hardy, C Thompson, M Chilton, J Gregg, D Lucas, D Neasham, A Moore, M Taylor, D Taylor, I Skippon, K Turner, P Hooley-Wright, E Young, J Young, D Hildreth, L Hudson, R Hoban, Messrs J Brown, D Dawes, F Porritt, W Cobban, G Cummings, C Grieveson, B Jones, K Wheadon, W A Clark, H May, J Peart, K Newton, B Sanderson, I Stockdale, F Boddy, D Fraser, G Dyson.

1954 CINDERELLA

PRINCIPALS: Meg Leeming, Vera Dickinson, Eileen Young, Robert White, Vivienne Farrage, Shirley Dodd, Nancy Bertram, Fred Thompson, Sid Plews, Cecil Grieveson, Carl Knight, Fred Boddy, Bernard Sanderson, Joy Beadell.

CHORUS: Pam Hooley-Wright, Jean Campbell, Doris Leslie, Shirley Hanson, Dorothy Caygill, Kay Turner, Margaret Stevenson, Marjorie Conway, Ena Hart, Rene Thompson, Sheila Conway, John Brown, Kenneth Richardson, Denis Dawes, Syd Mitchell, Ivan Stockdale, Kenneth Newton, Don Fraser.

DANCERS: Greta Murray, Julia Thornton, Moyra Robson, Irene Skippon, Delia Pinkney, Lorrie Boddy, Chris Marshall, Freda Thompson, Joan Bunn, Ann Thompson, Ada English, Emily Hardy, Hilda Brown, Judith Hodgson

THE DANCING YEARS

PRINCIPALS: Ken Leeming, Meg Leeming, Kenneth Richardson, Vera Dickinson, Robert White, Thomas Jones, Hilda Whitman, Ken Bodden, Marjorie Willans, Ken Smith, Kathleen Pipe, Sam Herdman, Frank Porritt, Jean Campbell, Clive Storey, William Clark, Albert Haffner, Harold Brown, Evelyn Berry.

CHORUS: Judith Barker, Lorrie Boddy, Dorothy Caygill, Sheila Conway, Shirley Dodd, Shirley Hanson, Ena Hart, Alice Howes, Audrey Leighton, Inga Lister, Nessie Milroy, Hazel Skelton, Margaret Stevenson, Elaine Varley, Elizabeth Wiseman, Fred Boddy, John Brown, Cyril Cowley, Dennis Dawes, Robert Kirton, George Llewellyn, Joseph Peart, Frank Porritt, Reginald Rowe, Raymond Simmons, Ivan Stockdale, Douglas Walker.

DANCERS: Rosemary Bentley, Joan Bunn, Ada English, Vivienne Farrage, Emily Hardy, Mavis Hudson, Delia Morris, Greta Sanderson, Joyce Shipman, Freda Thompson, Norma Willey, Albert Gill, Neville Gill, Robert Kirton, Ken Newton.

1955 ALADDIN

PRINCIPALS: Shirley Hanson, Sheila Conway, Robert White, Carl Knight, Eileen Young, Vera Dickinson, Meg Leeming, W A Clark, H R Herdman, Vivienne Farrage, Barbara Pilkington, Robert Kirton, Joy Beadell, Colin Worth.

CHORUS: Evelyn Berry, Lorrie Boddy, Hilda Brown, Jean Campbell, Marjorie Chilton, Dorothy Caygill, Shirley Dodd, Inga Lister, Nessie Milroy, Kathleen Pipe, Joyce Shipman,

Margaret Stevenson, Elaine Varley, Bessie Wiseman, Fred Boddy, W H Foster, Albert Gill, Thomas Jones, Ken Newton, R Pinkney, Kenneth Richardson, Reg Rowe, Bernard Sanderson, Ivan Stockdale, Ray Simmons, John B Snaith.

DANCERS: Joan Bunn, Ada English, Emily Hardy, Pauline Hardy, Mavis Hudson, Sheila McLaughlin, Jean Morris, Moira Robson, Irene Skippon, Freda Thompson, Ann Thompson, Norma Willey.

THE QUAKER GIRL

PRINCIPALS: Donald Clayton, Marjorie Willans, Dennis Dawes, W Arthur Clark, Kathleen Pipe, Vera Dickinson, Audrey Hartley, Hilda Whitman, Kenneth Richardson, Robert White, Joyce Shipman, Shirley Hanson, Sam Herdman, Joy Beadell, Arnold Grieve, Kenneth Bodden.

CHORUS: Mary Bell, Evelyn Berry, Lorrie Boddy, Jean Campbell, Marjorie Chilton, Pauline Coates, Ada English, Margaret Hardaker, Emily Hardy, Ena Hart, Inga Lister, Nessie Milroy, Audrey Moore, Connie Murray, Barbara Peacock, Barbara Pilkington, Kathleen Pipe, Pat Scott, Sylvia Simmons, Margaret Taylor, June Thomas, Freda Thompson, Elaine Varley, Eileen Young, Kenneth Bodden, Fred Boddy, Graham Cox, Dennis Dawes, Cecil Grieveson, Albert Haffner, Thomas Jones, Ken Newton, Joseph Peart, Gordon Pinder, Bernard Sanderson, Ivan Stockdale.

DANCERS: Joan Bunn, Pauline Hardy, Suzanne Pottage, Adela Iveson, Moyra Robson, Irene Skippon, Ann Thompson, Julia Thornton.

1956 PERCHANCE TO DREAM

PRINCIPALS: Sam Herdman, William Foster, Robert White, Donald Clayton, Lorrie Boddy, Una Strong, Hilda Whitman, Graham Cox, Kenneth Richardson, Shirley Dodd, Greta Sanderson, William Jones, Fred Boddy, Kathleeen Pipe, Nessie Milroy, Pauline Hardy, Joan Bunn, Maureen Milburn, Ann Thompson, Julia Thornton, Moyra Robson, Marie Jowett, Ken Newton.

CHORUS: Mary Bell, Evelyn Berry, Jean Campbell, Marjorie Chilton, Pat Coates, Emily Hardy, Ena Hart, Audrey Hartley, Evelyn Hodgson, Inga Lister, Nessie Milroy, Barbara Peacock, Barbara Pilkington, Margaret Taylor, Patricia Scott, Pat Smith, Margaret Stevenson, Ruth Thurgood, Veronica Tringham, Elaine Varley, John Brown, Gordon Clarke, Sam Goldberg, Cecil Grieveson, Albert Haffner, Michael Hiley, Peter Hoyle, Carl Knight, Peter McQuillan, Ken Newton, Gordon Pinder, Ivan Stockdale, David Toase, Keith Wheadon

THE DUBARRY

PRINCIPALS: Joyce Shipman, Nessie Milroy, Veronica Tringham, Jean Campbell, Eileen Young, Connie Murray, Robert White, Gordon Pinder, John Brown, Kenneth Richardson, Donald Clayton, Audrey Hartley, George Goodyear, Lorrie Boddy, Kenneth Bodden, Arthur Clarke, Shirley Dodd, Sam Herdman, Beryl Gregg, William Jones, Dennis Dawes, Cecil Grieveson.

CHORUS: Lillian Chilton, Marjorie Chilton, Patricia Coates, Mary Hall, Evelyn Hodgson, Inga Lister, Mary O'Brien, Barbara Peacock, Kathleen Pipe, Yvonne Simpson, Pat Smith, Margaret Taylor, Ruth Thurgood, Elaine Varley, Leslie Allen, Fred Boddy, Peter Henderson, Carl Knight, Peter McQuillan, Joseph Peart, Frank Porritt, Bernard Sanderson, Ray Simmons, Ivan Stockdale, Keith Wheadon.

DANCERS: June Brooks, Joan Bunn, Josephine Dobson, Mavis Hudson, Adela Iveson, Marie Jowett, Maureen Milburn, Susanne Pottage, Moyra Robson, Carol Routh, Ann Thompson, Margaret Thompson, Hazel Thynne, Norma Willey.

1957 NO, NO, NANETTE

PRINCIPALS: Eileen Young, Shirley Dodd, John Brown, Elizabeth Bartram, Mavis Hudson, Raymond Simmons, Kenneth Richardson, Lorrie Boddy, Veronica Tringham, Vera Dickinson.

CHORUS: M Lockey, B Gregg, E Varley, M Hall, P Smith, B Peacock, L Chilton, E Hodgson,

D Bilton, Messrs F Boddy, G Pinder, L Allen, W Jones, P Henderson, K Newton, I Stockdale, P McQuillan

DANCERS: H Thynne, J Bunn, J Dobson, M Jowett, A Thompson.

1958 WHITE HORSE INN

PRINCIPALS: Ena Hart, Ian Robertshaw, John Sinclair, Kenneth Richardson, Vera Dickinson, Sam Herdman, Evelyn Hodgson, Terry Frame, John Brown, William Foster, Greta Sanderson, Sidney Plews, Evelyn Berry, Eileen Young, Eric Roberts, Dennis Quinn, Sonny Carlin, Ken McLoughin, Alan Oatey, Robert White

CHORUS: Elizabeth Bartram, Shirley Dodd, Audrey Dunn, Eva Hart, Mary Newton, Josephine Dobson, Anna Saunders, Susan Swift, Ada English, Emily Hardy, Vikki Tringham, Joan Geeves, Ann Wheadon, Maureen Sutton, Margaret Taylor, Lorrie Boddy, Margaret Hardaker, Carol Swift, Brenda Thompson, Marjorie Willans, Gladys Wooley, Lilian Chilton, Valerie Chew, Dorothy Hutchinson, Doreen Hildreth, Kathleen Pipe, Lesley Dunn, Peter Henderson, Bill Jones, Gordon Pinder, Raymond Simmons, Carl Knight, Dennis Dawes, Tony Trees, David Symons, Bertram Dunn, Peter McQuillan, Cecil Grieveson, Keith Wheadon, Ivan Stockdale, John Sinclair, Quintin Oswell, Reginald Hamer.

DANCERS: Pauline Hardy, Hazel Thynne, Joan Burn, Josephine Dobson, Maureen Milburn, Ann Towers, Margaret Thompson, Julia Thornton.

OKLAHOMA!

PRINCIPALS: Susan Swift, Terry Frame, Joan Geeves, Len McCabe, Robert King, Bill Jones, Sam Herdman, Carol Swift, Kenneth Richardson, Doreen Hildreth, Ann Thompson, Denis Quinn, Ted I Dacres, Brenda Halliwell, Josephine Dobson.

CHORUS: Margaret Anderson, Dorothy Allison, Elizabeth Bartram, Evelyn Berry, Margaret Bowser, Lillian Chilton, Margaret Connor, Christine De Roerk, Audrey Dunn, Jean Herdman, Anne Henderson, Doreen Harper, Ena Hart, E Johnson, Doreen Kearton, Margaret Manuel, Barbara Peacock, Anna Saunders, Jacqueline Smith, Faith Taylor, Vikki Tringham, Brenda Thompson, Ruth Thurgood, Ann Wheadon, John Bean, John Cole, Thomas Coates, Donald Clayton, Stan Crook, Bertram Dunn, Peter Hamer, Peter Henderson, Peter McQuillan, Kenneth Newton, Henry Shepperd, Ray Simmons, Ivan Stockdale, Brian Thorpe, Horace Wilson.

DANCERS: Joy Beadell, Pauline Hardy, Julia Thornton, Irene Skippon, Hazel Thynne, Maureen Milburn, Josephine Dobson, Brenda Hampton, Brenda Halliwell, Ann Towers, Fay Wilson, Ann Thompson.

1959 DICK WHITTINGTON

PRINCIPALS: Keith Wheadon, Adela Iveson, Eileen Young, Vera Dickinson, Arthur Messenger, Susan Swift, Brenda Thompson, Denis Quinn, Vicky Tringham, Meg Leeming, Anne Henderson, Carol Swift, Glennis Beresford, Len McCabe.

CHORUS NOT LISTED.

THE MERRY WIDOW

PRINCIPALS: June Williams, William Foster, Kenneth Richardson, Joan Geeves, Raymond Simmons, Kenneth Bodden, Sam Herdman, George Goodyear, Bill Jones, Glennis Beresford, Leonard McCabe, Tony Trees, Audrey Dunn, Marjorie Willans.

GRISETTES: Doreen Kearton, Carol Swift, Jean Herdman, Vikki Tringham, Anne Wheadon, Margaret Anderson.

CHORUS: Dorothy Allison, Elizabeth Bartram, Evelyn Berry, Margaret Bowser, Vera Boyd, Lilian Chilton, Valerie Chew, Barbara Gent, Anne Henderson, Doreen Hildreth, Elizabeth Johnson, Vira Longstaff, Margaret Manuel, Connie Murray, Vera Lowes, Anna Saunders, Susan Swift, Margaret Taylor, Maureen Thompson, Eileen Young, John Cole, Thomas Coates, Wade Cobban, Arthur Gladwin, Peter Hamer, Peter Henderson, Peter McQuillan, Alan Oatey, Denis Quinn, Roland Wigington.

SHOW BOAT

PRINCIPALS: Robert White, Raymond Simmons, Kenneth Bodden, Elizabeth Johnson, Susan Swift, Kenneth Richardson, Carol Swift, Brian Thorpe, Horace Wilson, June Williams, George Goodyear, Bill Jones, Joan Geeves, Sam Herdman, Wade Cobban, Denis Quinn, Terence Sullivan, Eileen Young, Faith Taylor, David Todd, Vikki Tringham.

CHORUS: Glennis Beresford, Margaret Bowser, Stella Davies, Doreen Kearton, Meg Leeming, Vira Longstaff, Brenda Thompson, Dorothy Tomlinson, Ann Wheadon, Elizabeth Bartram, Evelyn Berry, Valerie Chew, Lilian Chilton, Ada English, Emily Hardy, Ann Henderson, Jean Herdman, Doreen Hildreth, Molly Jaques, Margaret Manuel, Joyce Plows, Mary Robertshaw, Anna Saunders, Jean Stanley, Faith Taylor, Maureen Taylor, John Brown, Arthur Gladwin, Peter McQuillan, Tony Trees, Roland Wigington, Horace Wilson, Brian Wragg, Cecil Grieveson, Peter Hamer, Peter Henderson, A Hodgson, Herbert Kidd, Len McCabe, Geoffrey Plews.

DANCERS: Dawn Allison, Jacqueline Bailey, Brenda Hampton, Margaret Jobling, Maureen Milburn, Hazel Thynne.

1960 JACK AND THE BEANSTALK

PRINCIPALS: Meg Leeming, Greta Sanderson, Susan Swift, Carol Swift, Adela Iveson, Anne Henderson, Eileen Young, Denis Quinn, Herbert Burgin, Ray Simmons, Cecil Grieveson, Horace Wilson, Ivan Stockdale, David Todd.

CHORUS: Elizabeth Bartram, Maureen Taylor, Molly Jaques, Doreen Kearton, Ann Wheadon, Valerie Chew, Mary Robertshaw, Glennis Beresford, Lilian Chilton, Mavis Dauber, Betty Gargett, Beryl Gregg, Audrey Dunn, Kenneth Richardson, Peter Hamer, Wade Cobban, John Pickles, Terry Sullivan, Tony Trees, John Bean, Bert Dunn, Peter Henderson.

DANCERS: Fay Wilson, Hazel Thynne, Ann Towers, Pauline Hardy, Maureen Milburn, Ann Thompson, Irene Skippon, Margaret Johnson, Toni Leeming, Dawn Allinson

CHILDREN: Elizabeth Horsley, Heather Gray, Denise Johnson, Angela Francis, Elizabeth Holiday, Fiona Bishop, Lynn Cooper, Angela Jackson, Brenda Fuller, Susanne Murray, Pamela Kelsey, Kathleen Durrant, Carol Hindmarch, Susan Wormald, Avril Edwards, Jane Hope, Ruth Hirst, Lesley Dobson, Patricia Sandwick, Lorna Jackson.

THE KING AND I

PRINCIPALS: Wade Cobban, John Murray, Una Strong, John Brown, Kenneth Bodden, Kenneth Richardson, David Todd, Raymond Simmons, Dorothy Matthew, Molly Jaques, Michael Airey, George Goodyear, Pixie Routh.

ROYAL PRINCESSES & PRINCES: Christine Eglinton, Ann Gilderslieve, Margaret Murray, Michelle Newell, Diana Stockdale, Jacqueline Batey, Gillian Brown, Janice Moss, Christine Simmons, Jean Wilson, Philip Murray, Peter Sanderson, Stephen Sanderson, Ivan Stockdale, Michael Young, Keith Brown, Barry Grieveson, Howard Wilson, Peter Wilson, David Wormald.

DANCERS & CHORUS: Dawn Allinson, Joan Aylett, Pauline Hardy, Anne Henderson, Rita Hudson, Maureen Milburn, Irene Skippon, Ann Thompson, Fay Wilson, John Brown, Cecil Grieveson, Peter Henderson, Bill Jones, James Lillie, Ray Simmons, Ivan Stockdale, Terry Sullivan, Glennis Beresford, Valerie Chew, Lilian Chilton, Audrey Dunn, Jean Herdman, Doreen Kearton, Vira Longstaff, Anna Saunders, Susan Swift, Ann Wheadon, Elizabeth Bartram, Roula Murray, Barbara Peacock, Maureen Taylor, Fred Boddy, Bert Dunn, Peter Hamer, Peter McQuillan, Brian Wragg, Ian Robertshaw.

BRIGADOON

PRINCIPALS: George Goodyear, Tony Trees, Wade Cobban, Bernard Sanderson, Peter McQuillan, Adela Iveson, Denis Quinn, Brian Thorpe, Peter Henderson, Anna Saunders, Sam Herdman, Molly Jaques, Fay Wilson, Robert Witcher, Kenneth Bodden, Irene Skippon, Ann Thompson, David Clark, David Todd, Betty Gargett.

CHORUS: Glennis Beresford, Valerie Chew, Yvonne Dale, Audrey Dunn, Betty Gargett, Ena Hart, Jean Herdman, Doreen Kearton, Vira Longstaff, Margaret Manuel, Dorothy Matthew, Barbara Peacock, Zylpha Pletts, Mary Robertshaw, Margaret Seager, Susan Swift, Maureen Taylor, Brenda Thompson, Carol Thorpe, Vikki Tringham, Ann Wheadon, Eileen Young, Louis Barnett, Bill Bishop, John Brown, Bert Dunn, Peter Hamer, Kenneth Richardson, Ian Robertshaw, Peter Robertshaw, Ivan Stockdale, Terry Sullivan, Horace Wilson.

DANCERS: Dawn Allinson, Olive Farley, Ann Henderson, Rita Hudson, Diana Jameson, Irene Skippon, Ann Thompson, Anne Towers.

1961 AURORA

PRINCIPALS: Eileen Young, Kenneth Richardson, Bernard Sanderson, Lily Henderson, Anna Saunders, Brian Thorpe, Sam Herdman, Glennis Beresford, Vikki Tringham, Ray Simmons, Colin Musgrave, Kenneth Bodden.

CHORUS: Valerie Chew, Yvonne Dale, Marian Davies, Audrey Dunn, Christine Ellwood, Ann Henderson, Muriel Jones, Doreen Kearton, Pat Leader, Eveline Lee, Pat Rourke, Susan Swift, Maureen Taylor, Brenda Thompson, George Angel, Louis Barnett, Billy Bishop, Bert Bunn, Peter Hamer, Peter Henderson, Ian Robertshaw, Peter Robertshaw, Tony Trees, Roland Wigington.

DANCERS: Dawn Allison, Olive Farley, Adela Iveson, Diana Jameson, Elizabeth Kirk, Elizabeth Murray, Irene Skippon, Diana Snow, Ann Thompson, Fay Wilson.

CHILDREN'S TROUPES: Lesley Dobson, Elizabeth Holiday, Jane Hope, Lorna Jackson, Susan Mann, Janice Moss, Susanne Murray, Christine Nicholson, Lynn Cooper, Kathleen Durrant, Anne Gilderslieve, Christine Graham, Elizabeth Horsley, Pamela Kelsey, Denise Johnson, Patricia Sandwick.

SOUTH PACIFIC

PRINCIPALS: Fiona Bishop, Phillip Murray, Kenneth Layton, Meg Leeming, George Goodyear, Roula Murray, Eileen Young, Peter Henderson, Cecil Grieveson, Horace Wilson, Wade Cobban, Ray Simmons, Kenneth Bodden, Roy Tatman, Harry Featherstone, Bert Dunn, Louis Barnett, Roland Wigington, David Todd, Denis Quinn, Keith Wilkinson, Ian Robertshaw, Peter Robertshaw, Brenda Thompson, Dorothy Matthew, Glennis Beresford, Ann Wheadon, Susan Swift, Betty Gargett, Margaret Bowser, Muriel Jones, Carol Thorpe, Jackie Rae, Audrey Dunn, Irene Skippon, Brian Wragg, Christopher Clark.

CHORUS: Valerie Chew, Yvonne Dale, Diana Jameson, Doreen Kearton, Pat Leader, Toni Leeming, Valerie Lister, Pat Rourke, Maureen Taylor, Ann Thompson, Ann Towers.

1961 CAROUSEL

PRINCIPALS: Glennis Beresford, Anna Saunders, Susan Swift, Raymond Simmons, Horace Wilson, Roy Tatman, Peter Hamer, Phillip Murray, Muriel Lees, Denis Quinn, Sam Herdman, Irene Skippon, Christopher Clarke, Carol Thorpe, Ian Robertshaw, David Todd, Kenneth Richardson, George Goodyear, Wade Cobban, Ann Thompson, Peter Henderson, Harry Featherstone, Brian Thorpe.

CHORUS: Audrey Bowen, Valerie Chew, Yvonne Dale, Marian Davies, Audrey Dunn, Molly Jaques, Muriel Jones, Doreen Kearton, Pat Leader, Sally Mountain, Mary Newton, Jackie Rae, Pat Rourke, Dorothy Tatman, Vikki Tringham, Dorothy Walker, Ann Henderson, Louis Barnett, Eoin Bishop, Christopher Clarke, Bert Dunn, Peter Henderson, Kenneth Layton, Kenneth Richardson, Ian Robertshaw, Peter Robertshaw, Roland Wigington, Horace Wilson.

DANCERS: Dawn Allinson, Olive Farley, Diana Jameson, Pauline Keogh, Irene Skippon, Diana Snow, Pamela Steele, Ann Thompson, Ann Towers.

CHILDREN: Jean Barton, Lynn Cooper, Brenda Fuller, Elizabeth Holiday, Jane Hope, Diana Stockdale, Fiona Bishop, Denise Johnson, Susan Mann, Margaret Murray, Susanne Murray, Susan Willey.

1962 KISMET

PRINCIPALS: Denis Quinn, Muriel Jones, Ray Simmons, Brian Thorpe, Bertram Dunn, David Todd, Peter Henderson, Harry Featherstone, Kenneth Layton, Wade Cobban, Kenneth Richardson, Vikki Tringham, Billy Bishop, Eoin Bishop, Rita Hudson, Bernard Sanderson, Roy Tatman, Glennis Beresford, Adela Iveson, Irene Skippon, Ann Thompson, Roula Murray, Jackie Rae, Susan Swift, Carol Thorpe, Muriel Jones, Pauline Keogh, Audrey Dunn, Clifford Walker.

CHORUS: Audrey Bowen, Margaret Bowser, Valerie Chew, Jacqueline Connor, Yvonne Dale, Marie Delamotte, Ann Gough, Ann Henderson, Doreen Hildreth, Molly Jaques, Pat Leaser, Betty MacFall, Vanessa Meak, Irene Mounter, Sally Mountain, Pat Rourke, Sylvia Spence, Dorothy Tatman, Dorothy Walker, Ann Wood, Sandy Curr, John Murray, Keith Wilkinson.

DANCERS: Dawn Allinson, Ann Appleton, Elizabeth Denham, Diana Jameson, Pamela Steele, Pixie Routh.

CHILDREN: Fiona Bishop, Diana Stockdale, Susan Willey, Phillip Murray, Peter Sanderson, Stephen Sanderson.

THE BELLE OF NEW YORK

PRINCIPALS: Sam Herdman, Brian Thorpe, Bertram Dunn, Kenneth Bodden, Raymond Simmons, Denis Quinn, Clifford Walker, Wade Cobban, Harry Featherstone, David Todd, Cecil Grieveson, Dorothy Matthew, Glennis Beresford, Lorrie Boddy, Greta Sanderson, Yvonne Dale, Muriel Jones, Kenneth Layton, Bernard Sanderson.

CHORUS: Audrey Bowen, Margaret Bowser, Audrey Dunn, Betty MacFall, Ann Henderson, Doreen Hildreth, Irene Mounter, Pat Paterson, Enid Robinson, Christine Sedgewick, Sylvia Spence, Susan Swift, Dorothy Tatman, Audrey Temple, Carol Thorpe, Dorothy Walker, Ann Wood, Eileen Young, Sandy Curr, Cecil Grieveson, Peter Hamer, Peter Henderson, Bert Horner, Kenneth Robinson, Roy Tatman, Roland Wigington.

DANCERS: Elizabeth Denham, Diana Jameson, Pauline Keogh, Pixie Routh, Pamela Steele, Margaret Sidebottom, Ann Thompson, Ena Waiter, Bert Horner.

1963 THE PIRATES OF PENZANCE & TRIAL BY JURY

PIRATES PRINCIPALS: Kenneth Bodden, Sam Herdman, Clifford Walker, Brian Thorpe, Roland Wigington, Dorothy Matthew, Anne McKenna, Adela Iveson, Pam Gannan, Lorrie Boddy.

TRIAL PRINCIPALS: Roland Wigington, Vikki Tringham, Gordon MacFall, Denis Quinn, Sam Herdman, Robert King, Edward Sinnott, Anne McKenna.

CHORUS: Sheila Adams, Margaret Bowser, Yvonne Dale, Marie Delamotte, Audrey Dunn, Ann Henderson, Molly Jaques, Muriel Jones, Pat Leader, Betty MacFall, Irene Mounter, Mary Robertshaw, Enid Robinson, Vera Spoors, Susan Swift, June Todd, Dorothy Walker, Anne Whitfield, Audrey Wigington, Gordon Clarke, Neil Doran, Bertram Dunn, John Edwards, Robert Gilmour, Sam Goldberg, Ray Graham, Robert King, Robert Kirtley, Paul Newman, David Parkin, John Plowman, Tim Rawle, Kenneth Robinson, Dennis Wigington, David Todd, Jeffrey Wragg, Keith Wilkinson.

THE MAID OF THE MOUNTAINS

PRINCIPALS: Brian Thorpe, Raymond Simmons, Clifford Walker, Bertram Dunn, Denis Quinn, Bill Jones, Molly Jaques, Sam Herdman, Adela Iveson, Susan Swift, Kenneth Richardson, Wade Cobban, Sam Goldberg, Harry Featherstone, Dorothy Walker, Roland Wigington.

CHORUS: Joan Blenkey, Yvonne Dale, Audrey Dunn, Joyce Elliott, Christine Ellwood, Doreen Elsworth, Beryl Gregg, Ann Henderson, Jean Herdman, Muriel Jones, Pat Leader, Betty MacFall, Dorothy Matthew, Roula Murray, Pat Paterson, Enid Robinson, Alice Sedgewick, Shirley Spence, Vera Spoors, Dorothy Tatman, Carol Thorpe, June Todd, Audrey Wigington, Sandra Wilkins, Tony Cambell, Gordon Clarke, John Edwards, Robert Gilmour, Cecil Grieveson, Robert Kirtley, Kenneth Layton, Gordon MacFall,

David Parkin, Tim Rawle, Kenneth Robinson, Jeffrey Rudderforth, Edward Sinnott, Roy Tatman, David Todd, Brian Wragg, Jeffrey Wragg, Trevor Crocker.

DANCERS: Elizabeth Denham, Pamela Hewitson, Diana Jameson, Pauline Keogh, Christine Marshall, Elizabeth Murray, Greta Sanderson, Julia Thornton.

1964 THE MUSIC MAN

PRINCIPALS: Bertram Dunn, Robert Gilmour, Sam Goldberg, Robert Kirtley, Peter Paterson, Kenneth Richardson, Jeffrey Rudderforth, David Todd, Clifford Walker, Brian Thorpe, Raymond Simmons, Kenneth Bodden, Jeffrey Wragg, Roland Wigington, Horace Wilson, Bernard Sanderson, Sam Herdman, Harry Featherstone, Joyce Elliott, Lorrie Boddy, Fiona Bishop, Phillip Murray, Susan Swift, Julia Thornton, Ann Thompson, Muriel Jones, Eileen Young, Jean Herdman, Allene James, Wade Cobban.

CHORUS: Margaret Bowser, Eunicé Cockburn, Hazel Duffy, Audrey Dunn, Rosemary Green, Doreen Hildreth, Pat Higgins, Molly Jaques, Margaret Nicholson, Pat Paterson, Jackie Rae, Joan Reynolds, Enid Robinson, Pat Rourke, Alice Sedgewick, Shirley Spence, Vera Spoors, Dorothy Tatman, Carol Thorpe, June Todd, Dorothy Walker, Audrey Wigington, Sandra Wilkins, John Alderson, Kenneth Bell, Gordon Clarke, Tony Di Duca, David Parkin, Peter Paterson, Denis Quinn, Kenneth Richardson, Kenneth Robinson, Roy Tatman.

CHILDREN: Peter Sanderson, Stephen Sanderson, Michael Walker.

DANCERS: Elizabeth Denham, Pamela Hewitson, Jennifer Hildon, Diana Jameson, Pauline Keogh, Margaret Sidebottom, Ann Thompson, Una Warriner, Judith Wilcox, Eoin Bishop, Peter Henderson, Kenneth Layton, John Plowman.

THE GIPSY BARON

PRINCIPALS: Denis Quinn, Kenneth Richardson, David Todd, Margaret Nicholson, June Todd, Dorothy Walker, Sam Herdman, Lorrie Boddy, Joyce Elliott, Eunicé Cockburn, Kenneth Richardson, Frederick Sinden, Jeffrey Wragg, Clifford Walker.

CHORUS: Margaret Bowser, Audrey Dunn, Doreen Elsworth, Maureen Gamble, Beryl Gregg, Ann Henderson, Doreen Hildreth, Muriel Jones, Betty Parry, Marianne Pearson, Joan Reynolds, Enid Robinson, Alice Sedgewick, Enid Spencer, Vera Spoors, Susan Swift, Dorothy Tatman, Susan Watson, Audrey Wigington, Sandra Wilkins, Gordon Clarke, Wade Cobban, Tony Di Duca, Bertram Dunn, Harry Featherstone, Sam Goldberg, Cecil Grieveson, Peter Henderson, Kenneth Layton, David Parkin, Peter Paterson, Tim Rawle, Roy Tatman, Brian Wragg.

DANCERS: Fiona Bishop, Barbara Brown, Elizabeth Denham, Pamela Hewitson, Jennifer Hildon, Elizabeth Holliday, Elizabeth Horsley, Diana Jameson, Denise Johnson, Ann Thompson, Una Warriner.

1965 LA BELLE HÉLÈNE

PRINCIPALS: Eunicé Cockburn, Joyce Elliott, Enid Spencer, Maureen Gamble, Phillip Logan, Kenneth Bodden, Kenneth Richardson, Clifford Walker, Bernard Sanderson, Sam Herdman, Roland Wigington, Jean Herdman, Margaret Bowser, Lorrie Boddy, Dorothy Walker, Sam Goldberg.

CHORUS: Maureen Dawson, Audrey Dunn, Julie Ellis, Allene James, Muriel Jones, Valerie Lister, Carol Lockwood, Diane Lockwood, Roula Murray, Marianne Pearson, Jacqueline Ramsey, Joan Reynolds, Alice Sedgewick, Shirley Spence, Susan Swift, Audrey Wigington, Sandra Wilson, Eileen Young, John Alderson, Gordon Clarke, Wade Cobban, Bertram Dunn, Robert Kirtley, Denis Quinn, Roy Tatman, David Todd, Jeffrey Wragg.

DANCERS: Fiona Bishop, Barbara Brown, Elizabeth Denham, Pamela Hewitson, Jennifer Hildon, Elizabeth Holliday, Elizabeth Horsley, Denise Johnson, Pauline Keogh, Greta Sanderson, Ann Thompson, Julia Thornton, Peter Henderson, George Sharratt.

KING'S RHAPSODY

PRINCIPALS: Greta Sanderson, Fiona Bishop, Wade Cobban, Lorrie Boddy, Joyce Elliott,

Kenneth Bodden, Colin Hauxwell, Shirley Dodd, Sam Herdman, Kenneth Richardson, Roula Murray, Susan Swift, Eileen Young, Ray Graham, Gordon Clarke, George Sharratt, Pauline Keogh, Barbara Brown, Pamela Hewitson, Peter Henderson, Marie le Mare, Phillip Murray, Melvyn Gray.

CHORUS: Margaret Bowser, Doris Burt, Maureen Dawson, Audrey Dunn, Julie Ellis, Doreen Elsworth, Maureen Gamble, Ann Henderson, Joyce Jinks, Jo Jones, Muriel Jones, Marianne Pearson, Jacqueline Ramsey, Enid Robinson, Alice Sedgewick, Jean Shaw, Carolyn Smailes, Dorothy Tatman, Christine Taylor, Dorothy Walker, Joyce Ward, Audrey Wigington, Sandra Wilkins, Eileen Young, Fred Boddy, Kenneth Layton, Joe Lee, Denis Quinn, Bernard Sanderson, Howard Swanston, Horace Wilson, Jeffrey Wragg.

DANCERS: Fiona Bishop, Barbara Brown, Elizabeth Denham, Pamela Hewitson, Elizabeth Holliday, Elizabeth Horsley, Pamela Kelsey, Pauline Keogh, Susan Mann, Christine Marshall, Pixie Routh, Greta Sanderson, Wade Cobban, Bertram Dunn, Peter Henderson, Phillip Murray, George Robson, George Sharratt, Raymond Simmons, Roy Tatman.

1966 ANNIE GET YOUR GUN

PRINCIPALS: Kerry James, Peter Sanderson, Kenneth Richardson, Roy Tatman, Denis Quinn, Audrey Dunn, Greta Sanderson, Roland Wigington, Allene James, Michael Walker, Susan Willey, Judith Dunn, Lynn Robson, Sam Herdman, Joyce Jinks, Eileen Young, Alice Sedgewick, David Todd, Denis Quinn, Ray Layton, Pauline Keogh, Horace Wilson, Clifford Walker, Gordon Clarke, George Sharratt, Marie le Mare.

CHORUS: Maureen Bainbridge, Lorrie Boddy, Doris Hart, Margaret Bowser, Eunicé Cockburn, Nancy Greenwood, Ann Henderson, Jean Herdman, Muriel Jones, Marion MacDonald, Roula Murray, Mary Newton, Marianne Pearson, Jacqueline Ramsey, Joan Reynolds, Joan Shaw, Elaine Stephenson, Susan Swift, Dorothy Tatman, Christine Taylor, Dorothy Walker, Joyce Ward, Audrey Wigington, Fred Boddy, David Carter, Ron Cherry, Bertram Dunn, Sam Goldberg, Bert Hassall, Ray Layton, Denis Lochtie, Kenneth Robinson, Roy Tatman, David Todd, John Wood.

DANCERS: Louise Atkinson, Elizabeth Denham, Pamela Hewitson, Jane Hope, Pamela Kelsey, Pauline Keogh, Susan Mann, Pixie Routh, Julia Thornton, Paddy Wagstaff, Ray Barnett, Maurice Cook, John Kindleysides, Philip Murray, George Sharratt, Michael Stephenson, Brian Whitehead.

DIE FLEDERMAUS

PRINCIPALS: Shirley Dodd, Ray Sollett, Eunicé Cockburn, Sam Herdman, Denis Quinn, Clifford Walker, Raymond Simmons, Greta Sanderson, Kenneth Richardson, Denis Lochtie, Marion MacDonald.

CHORUS: Ann Bennett, Lorrie Boddy, Margaret Bowser, Doris Burt, Charlotte Cook, Nancy Greenwood, Ann Henderson, Muriel Jones, Marie le Mare, Roula Murray, Marianne Pearson, Enid Robinson, Susan Robinson, Alice Sedgewick, Joan Shaw, Christine Taylor, Dorothy Walker, Sylvia Wall, Joyce Ward, Fred Boddy, David Carter, Gordon Clarke, Wade Cobban, Maurice Cook, Sam Goldberg, Cecil Grieveson, Colin Johnson, Brian Leckenby, Gordon MacFall, Kenneth Robinson, Bernard Sanderson, Howard Swainston, Roy Tatman, David Todd, John Wood, Brian Wragg.

CORPS DE BALLET: George Sharratt, Louise Atkinson, Fiona Bishop, Elizabeth Horsley, Pamela Hewitson, Pauline Keogh, John Kindleysides, Philip Murray, Jane Hope, Susan Mann, Christine Marshall, Lynn Robson.

1967 ORPHEUS IN THE UNDERWORLD

PRINCIPALS: Eunicé Cockburn, Shirley Dodd, Dorothy Walker, Anne Bennett, Adela Iveson, Lorrie Boddy, Denis Quinn, William H Foster, Sam Herdman, Bernard Sanderson, Kenneth Robinson, George Sharratt, Gordon Clarke, Roland Wigington, Denis Lochtie.

CHORUS: Enid Allison, Margaret Bowser, Doris Burt, Audrey Dunn, Nancy Greenwood,

Ann Henderson, Lorna Jackson, Muriel Jones, Marion MacDonald, Marie le Mare, Mollie Moor, Marianne Pearson, Joan Reynolds, Susan Robinson, Joan Shaw, Dorothy Tatman, Christine Taylor, Audrey Wigington, Fred Boddy, David Carter, Wade Cobban, Bertram Dunn, Sam Goldberg, Bert Hassall, Peter Henderson, Colin Johnson, Brian Leckenby, Gordon MacFall, Peter Pring, Richard Roberts, Howard Swainston, Roy Tatman, David Todd, Ray Todd, Denis Wigington, Horace Wilson, John Wood.

CORPS DE BALLET: Louise Atkinson, Jacqueline Batey, Fiona Bishop, Pamela Stephenson, Pamela Hewitson, Elizabeth Horsley, Pauline Keogh, Susan Mann, Pat Porteus, Lynn Robson, Greta Sanderson, George Hathaway, Philip Murray, Michael Stephenson, Brian Whitehead.

GIPSY LOVE

PRINCIPALS: Sam Herdman, Eunicé Cockburn, Marie le Mare, Shirley Dodd, Nancy Greenwood, Dorothy Matthew, Constance Overend, David Carter, Clifford Walker, Raymond Simmons, Peter Henderson, Horace Wilson, Denis Quinn.

CHORUS: Enid Allison, Rita Bellwood, Lorrie Boddy, Margaret Bowser, Doris Burt, Ann Henderson, Adela Iveson, Lorna Jackson, Muriel Jones, Marion MacDonald, Mollie Moor, Lorrayne Orr, Ann Palmer, Marianne Pearson, Joan Reynolds, Enid Robinson, Joan Shaw, Dorothy Tatman, Christine Taylor, Jackie Taylor, Margaret Teasdale, Dorothy Walker, Audrey Wigington, Fred Boddy, Wade Cobban, Gordon Clarke, William Foster, Sam Goldberg, Cecil Grieveson, Bert Hassall, Brian Leckenby, Denis Lochtie, John Porritt, Peter Pring, Denis Quinn, Kenneth Richardson, David Todd, John Wood.

DANCERS: Jacqueline Batey, Fiona Bishop, Pamela Hewitson, Jane Hope, Elizabeth Horsley, Kathleen Hunt, Susan Mann, Patricia Porteus, Lynn Robson, Greta Sanderson, Maurice Cook, Philip Murray, George Sharratt.

1968 BLESS THE BRIDE

PRINCIPALS: Dorothy Walker, Clifford Walker, Bert Hassall, Adela Iveson, Bill Jones, Rita Bellwood, Marie le Mare, Pat Durkin, Dorothy Matthew, Greta Sanderson, Gordon Toft, Eunicé Cockburn, Sam Herdman, Shirley Dodd, Kenneth Bodden, Eileen Young, Lorrie Boddy, Frederick Bynoe, Roy Tatman, David Todd, Kenneth Bodden, Jeff Wragg, Denis Quinn, John Porritt.

CHORUS: Enid Allison, Margaret Bowser, Lynn Dennis, Audrey Dunn, Nancy Greenwood, Margaret Haire, Ann Henderson, Muriel Jones, Marion MacDonald, Mollie Moor, Constance Overend, Ann Palmer, Joan Reynolds, Enid Robinson, Susan Robinson, Joan Shaw, Dorothy Tatman, Margaret Teasdale, Audrey Wigington, Fred Boddy, Gordon Clarke, Bertram Dunn, Bill Foster, Brian Leckenby, Gordon MacFall, Kenneth Richardson, Roy Tatman, David Todd, Dennis Wigington, Horace Wilson, John Wood, Jeffrey Wragg.

DANCERS: Louise Atkinson, Jacqueline Batey, Pamela Hewitson, Jane Hope, Kathleen Hunt, Pauline Keogh, Patricia Porteus, Norma Willey, Anthony Armstrong, Wade Cobban, Maurice Cook, Russell Dunn.

MY FAIR LADY

PRINCIPALS: Margaret Teasdale, Eunicé Cockburn, Jeff Wragg, Kenneth Bodden, Bertram Dunn, Kenneth Richardson, Bert Hassall, Brian Leckenby, John Wood, Horace Wilson, Clifford Walker, Denis Lochtie, David Todd, Brian Wragg, Sam Herdman, Raymond Simmons, Alan Round, Eileen Young, Audrey Dunn, Denis Quinn, Shirley Dodd, Roy Tatman, Gordon Clarke, Kennneth Layton, Dennis Wigington, Doris Burt, Peter Pring, Rita Bellwood, Bill Jones, Fred Boddy, Julie Stevens, David Carter, Margaret Bowser.

CHORUS: Enid Allison, Lorrie Boddy, Pat Durkin, Nancy Greenwood, Ann Henderson, Adela Iveson, Muriel Jones, Marie le Mare, Marion MacDonald, Mollie Moor, Joan Reynolds, Enid Robinson, Greta Sanderson, Joan Shaw, Margaret Teasdale, Barbara Toft, Dorothy Walker, Audrey Wigington, Ann Wood, David Carter, Ray Simmons, Roy Tatman, David Todd.

DANCERS: Jacqueline Batey, Judith Dunn, Hilary Greenwood, Jane Hope, Kathleen Hunt,

Susan Mann, Pauline McMain, Patricia Porteus, Norma Willey, Wade Cobban, Philip Murray, John Stephenson, Ian Stevenson.

1969 LA VIE PARISIENNE

PRINCIPALS: Eunicé Cockburn, Margaret Umpleby, Pat Durkin, Marie le Mare, Greta Sanderson, Dorothy Walker, Raymond Simmons, Jeff Wragg, Denis Quinn, Sam Herdman, Kenneth Richardson, Denis Lochtie, Clifford Walker, William Foster, Wade Cobban, Dennis Wigington.

CHORUS: Enid Allison, Lorrie Boddy, Margaret Bowser, Pauline Brown, Lynn Dennis, Shirley Dodd, Nancy Greenwood, Ann Henderson, Norma Hurren, Muriel Jones, Roberta Lochtie, Marion MacDonald, Mollie Moor, Ann Palmer, Marianne Pearson, Joan Reynolds, Enid Robinson, Joan Shaw, Elaine Stephenson, Margaret Teasdale, Dorothy Wakefield, Audrey Wigington, Ann Wood, Fred Boddy, David Carter, Gordon Clarke, Brian Leckenby, Les Parker, Peter Pring, Dennis Williams, Brian Wragg.

DANCERS: Jacqueline Batey, Judith Dunn, Hilary Greenwood, Kathleen Hunt, Pauline McMain, Tricia Porteus, Sally Robson, Margaret Taylor, Janet Thompson, Norma Willey, Susan Willey, Sandra Williamson, Russell Dunn, Philip Murray, Alistair Reeves.

CAMELOT

PRINCIPALS: Clifford Walker, Peter Pring, Jeff Wragg, David Todd, Denis Quinn, Kenneth Richardson, Eunicé Cockburn, Nancy Greenwood, Dorothy Walker, Pat Durkin, John Hurlstone, Dennis Williams, Sam Herdman, Philip Murray, Muriel Jones, Michael Walker.

CHORUS: Lorrie Boddy, Margaret Bowser, Pauline Brown, Lynn Dennis, Shirley Dodd, Audrey Dunn, Marianne Pearson, Joan Reynolds, Joan Shaw, Elaine Stephenson, Margaret Teasdale, Dorothy Wakefield, Ann Wood, David Carter, Gordon Clarke, Bertram Dunn, William Foster, Cecil Grieveson, Tom Kent, Brian Leckenby, Les Parker, Kenneth Robinson, Raymond Simmons.

DANCERS: Jacqueline Batey, Alison Binks, Lesley Charlton, Judith Dunn, Hilary Greenwood, Kathleen Hunt, Susan Mann, Sally Robson, Greta Sanderson, Margaret Taylor, Norma Willey, Susan Wishlade, Russell Dunn, Philip Murray.

1970 SONG OF NORWAY

PRINCIPALS: David Carter, Alison Walker, Rosamund How, Michael Walker, Peter Sanderson, Zoë Herdman, Carol Willey, Judith Todd, Katherine Leckenby, Pat Durkin, Raymond Simmons Sam Herdman, Bernard Sanderson, Mollie Moor, Susan Mann, Denis Quinn, Kenneth Bodden, Eunicé Cockburn, David Todd, Jeff Wragg, Muriel Jones, Joan Shaw, Dorothy Walker, Ann Wood, Enid Allison, Shirley Dodd, William Foster, Kenneth Richardson, Greta Sanderson, Norma Willey, Bill Jones, Denis Lochtie, Kathleen Hunt.

CHORUS: Carol Barr, Lynn Dennis, Nancy Greenwood, Ann Henderson, Ann Palmer, Linda Pennie, Joan Reynolds, Enid Robinson, Christine Taylor, Audrey Wigington, David S Carter, Gordon Clarke, Tom Handy, Brian Leckenby, Denis Quinn, David Todd, Clifford Walker, Horace Wilson.

DANCERS: Jacqueline Batey, Alison Binks, Lesley Charlton, Jennifer Dorrington, Hilary Greenwood, Kathleen Hunt, Susan Mann, Tricia Porteus, Sally Robson, Greta Sanderson, Margaret Taylor, Norma Willey, Susan Willey, Susan Wishlade, Russell Dunn, Philip Murray.

MERRIE ENGLAND

PRINCIPALS: Pat Durkin, Tom Handy, Bert Hassall, Kenneth Robinson, Gordon Clarke, Sam Herdman, Clifford Walker, Marie le Mare, John Hurlstone, Wade Cobban, Jeff Wragg, Kenneth Richardson, Trevor Harder, Eunicé Cockburn, Kenneth Bodden, Nancy Chilver.

CHORUS: Sheila Adams, Margaret Bowser, Linda Cox, Shirley Dodd, Audrey Dunn, Nancy Greenwood, Muriel Jones, Molly Moor, Ann Palmer, Joan Reynolds, Enid Robinson, Joan Shaw, Olwyn Studd, Margaret Teasdale, Dorothy Walker, Audrey Wigington, Ann Wood,

David Carter, Bertram Dunn, Cecil Grieveson, Tom Kent, Brian Leckenby, Denis Quinn, Roy Tatman, David Todd, Paul Urdi, Horace Wilson, Brian Wragg.

DANCERS: Ann Appleton, Jacqueline Batey, Lesley Charlton, Jennifer Dorrington, Judith Dunn, Kathleen Hunt, Susan Mann, Susan Murray, Sally Robson, Greta Sanderson, Margaret Taylor, Norma Willey, Susan Willey, Susan Wishlade.

1971 THE GRAND DUCHESS

PRINCIPALS: Eunicé Cockburn, Trevor Harder, Sam Herdman, Kenneth Richardson, John Kindleysides, Marie le Mare, Ann Wood, Muriel Jones, Dorothy Walker, Clifford Walker, George Dixon, Pat Durkin, Roy Tatman, Jeff Wragg, David Todd, Horace Wilson, Denis Lochtie.

CHORUS: Sheila Adams, Elizabeth Cleverley, Linda Cox, Audrey Dunn, Nancy Greenwood, Mollie Moor, Marianne Pearson, Joan Reynolds, Joan Shaw, Olwyn Studd, Margaret Teasdale, Audrey Wigington, Alan Adams, David Carter, Gordon Clarke, Bertram Dunn, Gordon MacFall, John Parker, Paul Urdi, Peter Wishlade, Brian Wragg.

DANCERS: Jacqueline Batey, Lesley Charlton, Judith Dunn, Patricia Freeman, Kathleen Hunt, Susan Mann, Susan Murray, Sally Robson, Margaret Taylor, Norma Willey, Susan Willey, Susan Wishlade.

KISS ME KATE

PRINCIPALS: John Hurlstone, Kenneth Richardson, Marie le Mare, Wade Cobban, Eunicé Cockburn, Eileen Young, Alan Round, John Lavalle, Sam Herdman, John Parker, Bertram Dunn, Kenneth Bodden, Jimmy Hall, Jeff Wragg, Cecil Grieveson, Roy Tatman, Gordon Clarke, John Kindleysides.

CHORUS: Enid Allison, Ann Appleton, Margaret Bowser, Chris Coates, Lynn Dennis, Shirley Dodd, Audrey Dunn, Nancy Greenwood, Trudy Holmes, Joan Johnson, Muriel Jones, Sheila Lee, Betty MacFall, Ann Palmer, Patricia Port, Joan Reynolds, Barbara Riding, Enid Robinson, Susan Robinson, Greta Sanderson, Joan Shaw, Margaret Teasdale, Dorothy Walker, Audrey Wigington, Ann Wood, Alan Adams, David Carter, Tom Kent, Raymond Simmons, Paul Urdi.

DANCERS: Jacqueline Batey, Alison Binks, Lesley Charlton, Judith Dunn, Tricia Freeman, Hilary Greenwood, Kathleen Hunt, Susan Mann, Sally Robson, Margaret Taylor, Norma Willey, Susan Wishlade, Peter Kane, Tom Kent, Peter Wishlade.

1972 HELLO DOLLY!

PRINCIPALS: Eunicé Cockburn, Muriel Jones, Denis Lochtie, Sam Herdman, Fiona Bishop, Raymond Simmons, John Parker, Marie le Mare, Susan Wishlade, Shirley Dodd, Clifford Walker, Phllip Bethell, Kenneth Robinson.

CHORUS: Sheila Adams, Christine Coates, Linda Cox, Pam Davies, Nancy Greenwood, Margaret Hall, Betty MacFall, Ann Palmer, Patricia Port, Joan Reynolds, Barbara Riding, Enid Robinson, Joan Shaw, Margaret Teasdale, Dorothy Walker, Audrey Wigington, Ann Wood, Alan Adams, David Appleton, Gordon Clarke, Peter Cutchie, George Dixon, Tom Handy, Kenneth Richardson, Roy Tatman, David Todd, Paul Urdi, Horace Wilson, Peter Wishlade, Jeff Wragg.

DANCERS: Ann Appleton, Jacqueline Batey, Alison Binks, Lesley Charlton, Judith Dunn, Tricia Freeman, Kathleen Hunt, June Park, Greta Sanderson, Norma Willey

FIDDLER ON THE ROOF

PRINCIPALS: Stephen Henley, Eunicé Cockburn, Kathleen Robinson, Susan Wishlade, Fiona Bishop, Carol Willey, Judith Todd, Shirley Dodd, Raymond Simmons, Jeff Wragg, Sam Herdman, George Dixon, Jimmy Hall, Barry Dargue, Clifford Walker, Horace Wilson, Susan Robinson, Muriel Jones, Kenneth Richardson, John Parker, Audrey Dunn, Peter Sanderson, Stephen Wragg, Peter Cutchie.

CHORUS: Enid Allinson, Ann Appleton, Alison Binks, Lesley Charlton, Christine Coates,

Linda Cox, Pam Davies, Judith Dunn, Elizabeth Ellis, Joan Gotts, Hilary Greenwood, Nancy Greenwood, Margaret Hall, Maureen King, Betty MacFall, Susan Mann, Mary Newton, Ann Palmer, Joan Park, Joyce Plowman, Pat Port, Joan Reynolds, Barbara King, Joan Shaw, Margaret Taylor, Margaret Teasdale, Dorothy Walker, Audrey Watson, Audrey Wigington, Norma Willey, Susan Willey, Ann Wood, Alan Adams, Peter Cutchie, Bertram Dunn, Peter Hydes, Tom Kent, Denis Lochtie, Ernest Mann, Peter Oxley, John Plowman, Bernard Sanderson, John Simpson, Roy Tatman, David Todd, Peter Wishlade, Brian Wragg.

1973 ROBERT AND ELIZABETH

PRINCIPALS: Toni Di Duca, Frank Hagan, Peter Exlee, Clifford Walker, Alan Adams, Brian Leckenby, Kenneth Richardson, Barry Dargue, Stephen Henley, Shirley Dodd, Greta Sanderson, Raymond Simmons, Jeff Wragg, Peter Cutchie, David Todd, Peter Hydes, John Parker, Fiona Bishop, Geoff Heeley, Ray Danby, Roy Tatman, Dorothy Walker, Eunicé Cockburn, Ann Appleton, Keith Tate, Susan Wishlade, Kathleen Robinson.

CHORUS: Joan Adams, Sheila Adams, Christine Coates, Rowena Cutchie, Pam Davies, Nancy Greenwood, Judi Kent, Maureen King, Betty MacFall, Joan Reynolds, Enid Robinson, Joan Shaw, Margaret Teasdale, Audrey Watson, Audrey Wigington, Ann Wood.

DANCERS: Lesley Charlton, Jacqueline Eyles, Hilary Greenwood, June Park, Sally Robson, Norma Willey.

THE MERRY WIDOW

PRINCIPALS: Eunicé Cockburn, John Hurlstone, Kenneth Richardson, Carol Biggin, Jeff Wragg, John Parker, Denis Lochtie, Sam Herdman, Peter Cutchie, Greta Sanderson, Peter Hydes, Jimmy Hall, Sheila Adams, Susan Robinson.

GRISETTES: Ann Wood, Norma Willey, Ann Appleton, Hilary Greenwood, Kathleen Hunt, Susan Wishlade.

CHORUS: Joan Adams, Christine Coates, Rowena Cutchie, Pamela Davies, Shirley Dodd, Judith Gotts, Nancy Greenwood, Elizabeth Jackson, Judi Kent, Maureen King, Betty MacFall, Christine Marshall, Joan Shaw, Dorothy Walker, Audrey Watson.

DANCERS: Ann Appleton, Fiona Bishop, Lesley Charlton, Tricia Freeman, Hilary Greenwood, Elizabeth Holton, Julie Hugall, June Park, Jane Robinson, Kathleen Robinson, Margaret Taylor, Norma Willey, Susan Willey, Susan Wishlade.

1974 GUYS AND DOLLS

PRINCIPALS: Jeff Wragg, Ray Simmons, Tom Kent, Christine Swales, Clifford Walker, John Parker, Roy Tatman, Ray Danby, Kenneth Richardson, Susan Wishlade, John Hacking, John Parker, Hilary Greenwood, Dorothy Walker, Eileen Young, Barry Dargue, Sam Herdman, Geoff Heeley.

CHORUS AND DANCERS: Joan Adams, Christine Coates, Eunicé Cockburn, Pam Davies, Shirley Dodd, Jacqueline Eyles, Tricia Freeman, Hilary Greenwood, Nancy Greenwood, Elizabeth Holton, Judi Kent, Betty MacFall, June Park, Joan Reynolds, Jane Robinson, Kathleen Robinson, Joan Shaw, Margaret Taylor, Audrey Watson, Audrey Wigington, Ann Wood, Florence Woods, Alan Adams, Jimmy Hall, John Plowman, Kenneth Richardson, Paul Urdi, Peter Wishlade, Mike Williams.

BITTER SWEET

PRINCIPALS: Eunicé Cockburn, John Larsen, Shirley Dodd, Ann Parker, John Parker, Clifford Walker, Edna Ford, Sam Herdman, Margaret Todd, Peter Cutchie, Jeff Wragg, Kenneth Robinson, Bernard Sanderson, Roy Tatman, Alan Adams, Tom Kent, Enid Allinson, Dorothy Walker, Hilary Greenwood, Judith Gott, Elizabeth Jackson, Christine Hacking, Susan Wishlade, Elizabeth Helliwell, Sheila Adams, Greta Sanderson, Roger Millard, Kenneth Richardson, Kenneth Bodden, Susan Williams, Tricia Freeman, Betty MacFall, Judith Bond, Peter Hydes, Barry Dargue, Norman Wright.

CHORUS: Christine Coates, Pam Davies, Jacqueline Eyles, Nancy Greenwood, Elizabeth Holton,

Judi Kent, June Park, Joan Reynolds, Elizabeth Robinson, Jane Robinson, Joan Shaw, Margaret Taylor, Margaret Teasdale, Audrey Wigington, Susan Williams, Ann Wood, Ian Cunningham, Arthur Duncan, Cecil Grieveson, Alfred Jackson, Terry Laverick, Alfred Robinson, Peter Rudd, Brian Sheppard, Mike Williams, Norman Wright.

1975 THE SOUND OF MUSIC

PRINCIPALS: Carol Biggin, Muriel Jones, Dorothy Walker, Mollie Moor, Greta Sanderson, Kenneth Richardson, Clifford Walker, Eileen Young, Hilary Greenwood, Nigel Walker, Kim Matthews, John Murray, Ruth Connelly, Ruth Hauxwell, Fiona Holiday, Mark Robinson, Jill Foggin, Andrew Pyke, Joanna Davison, Helen Heaton, Christine Richardson, Brian Carr, Enid Allison, June Aiken, Barry Dargue, Roger Millard, Alfred Robinson, Betty MacFall, Bernard Sanderson.

CHORUS: Christine Coates, Shirley Dodd, Tricia Freeman, Nancy Greenwood, Elizabeth Holton, Elizabeth Jackson, June Park, Joan Reynolds, Kathleen Robinson, Margaret Taylor, Margaret Teasdale, Marie Terry, Audrey Wigington, Susan Williams, Ann Wood, Alan Adams, Ian Cunningham, Arthur Duncan, Fred Farley, Cecil Grieveson, Tom Kent, Alf Robinson, Peter Rudd, Ian Whitfield, Mike Williams, Norman Wright.

THE DESERT SONG

PRINCIPALS: Colin Raine, Horace Wilson, Shirley Dodd, John Parker, Arthur Ellis, Eunicé Cockburn, Clifford Walker, John Hacking, Susan Wishlade, June Aiken, Kathleen Robinson, Sam Herdman, Margaret Lowther, Tom Kent, Jeff Wragg, Peter Hydes, Ian Cunningham.

CHORUS: Avril Blain, Christine Coates, Pamela Davies, Vivien Good, Nancy Greenwood, Margaret Harsley, Rikki Hughes, Kathryn Mason, Joan Shaw, Margaret Teasdale, Dorothy Walker, Florence Woods, Steve Blain, Bob Calvert, Gordon Clarke, Malcolm Donnelly, Cecil Grieveson, Tom Handy, Edward Liddle, Christopher Noble, Kenneth Richardson, Alf Robinson, Ian Whitfield.

DANCERS: Betty Cooke, Hilary Greenwood, Elizabeth Holton, Elizabeth Jackson, Glynis Johnson, Judi Kent, June Park, Jane Robinson, Alison Walker, Norma Willey, Susan Williams, Ann Wood.

1976 OLIVER!

PRINCIPALS: Simon Treadgold (Understudy John Murray), Sam Herdman, Susan Robinson, Barry Dargue, Muriel Jones, Avril Blain, Steve Blain, Andrew Wallace (Understudy Stephen Harrison), Ray Danby, Judi Bond, Sue Wishlade, Clifford Walker, Arthur Ellis, Dorothy Walker, Ted Liddle, Rikki Hughes, June Aiken, Tom Kent, Ian Whitfield.

BOYS: Simon Appleyard, Richard Bainbridge, Steven Campbell, Gordon Cook, Anthony Cox, Philip Davison, Adrian Dove, Kevin Franks, Stephen Harrison, Hugh Jackson, Graeme Johnson, Rikki Lorenti, Kevin Mooney, John Murray, Richard Parsons, Andrew Pyke, Mark Robinson, Nigel Walker.

CHORUS: Ann Bainbridge, Hazel Brayshaw, Bob Calvert, Christine Coates, Maurice Cook, Linda Egginton, Vivienne Good, Margaret Harsley, Liz Jackson, Steve Luck, Betty MacFall, Jackie Vaughan, Dorothy Walker, Florence Woods.

DANCERS: S Blain, Betty Cooke, Liz Holton, Glynis Johnson, Judi Kent, T Kent, S Luck, June Park, Kath Robinson, Alison Walker, I Whitfield, Sue Wishlade.

OKLAHOMA!

PRINCIPALS: Susan Robinson, Graham Saunders, Hilary Hydes, Barrie Dargue, Peter Hydes, John Parker, Arthur Ellis, June Aiken, Kenneth Richardson, Sue Wishlade, John Hacking, Tom Kent.

CHORUS: Fiona Allen, Enid Allison, Avril Blain, Steve Blain, Hazel Brayshaw, Bob Calvert, Christine Coates, Ian Cunningham, Peter Cutchie, Ian Dodds, Graham Dove, Linda Egginton, Nancy Greenwood, Margaret Harsley, Geoff Heeley, Katy Mascal, Michelle Miller,

Kevin Mooney, Carol Newton, Margaret Nicholls, Chris Noble, Joan Reynolds, Alf Robinson, Enid Robinson, Joan Shaw, Margaret Teasdale, Jackie Vaughan, Dorothy Walker, Mike Walker, Ian Whitfield, Audrey Wigington, Ann Wood, Florence Woods.

DANCERS: Christine Coates, Betty Cooke, Peter Cutchie, Barry Dargue, Graham Dove, Tricia Freeman, Liz Holton, Peter Hydes, Liz Jackson, Glynis Johnson, Judi Kent, Tom Kent, Steve Luck, Kevin Mooney, June Park, Kathleen Robinson, Margaret Singer, Alison Walker, Mike Walker, Ian Whitfield, Mike Williams, Susan Williams, Sue Wishlade, Ann Wood.

1977 THE BOY FRIEND

PRINCIPALS: Shirley Dodd, Hilary Hydes, June Aiken, Sue Wishlade, Judi Kent, Avril Blain, Alan Davison, Steve Luck, Peter Cutchie, Eunicé Cockburn, Craig Gaddas, Arthur Ellis, David Lynch, Kenneth Richardson, Ian Whitfield, Tom Kent, George Sharratt, Joy Beadell, Betty Cooke, Tricia Freeman, Liz Holton, Ronnie Egginton.

THE STUDENT PRINCE

PRINCIPALS: David Todd, John Lloyd, Ken Robinson, Cecil Grieveson, John Hacking, Alf Robinson, Keith Tate, John Larsen, Sam Herdman, June Aiken, Philip Bethell, John Parker, Tom Kent, Arthur Ellis, Jeff Wragg, Ian Whitfield, Eunicé Cockburn, Greta Sanderson, Sue Wishlade, Alan Davison, Dorothy Walker.

CHORUS: Fiona Allen, Avril Blain, Chris Coates, Linda Egginton, Margaret Harsley, Ann Phillips, Joan Reynolds, Vivienne Robson, Linda Roots, Florence Woods, Ann Wood, Guy Allen, Nigel Copestake, Ian Dods, Graham Dove, Ron Egginton, Alf Jackson, Kevin Mooney, Chris Noble, Keith Phillips, Peter Sanderson, Keith Sleightholme, Lindesay Steel, Mike Walker.

DANCERS: Christine Coates, Betty Cooke, Janet Cooke, Tricia Freeman, Elizabeth Holton, Glynis Johnson, Sian Kirkwood, June Park, Janet Scruby, Margaret Singer, Judith Todd, Kathleen Robinson.

1978 GIGI

PRINCIPALS: Stan Lloyd, Arthur Ellis, Debbie Traice, Richard Boucher, Sue Wishlade, Kath Robinson, Susan Robinson, Shirley Dodd, Geoff Heeley, Steve Luck, Kenneth Richardson, Sam Herdman, Clifford Walker, June Aiken, Jackie Vaughan, Alan Davison, Ian Whitfield.

CHORUS: Fiona Allen, Avril Blain, Christine Coates, Rowena Cutchie, Linda Egginton, Christine Hacking, Margaret Harsley, Ingrid Jansson, Muriel Jones, Joan Kirkwood, Joan Reynolds, Greta Sanderson, Linda Roots, Vivienne Robson, Dorothy Walker, Audrey Wigington, Florence Woods, Noel Bennet, Tom Handy, Chris Noble, Alf Robinson, John Lloyd, Peter Sanderson, Lindesay Steel.

DANCERS: Christine Coates, Betty Cooke, Janet Cooke, Liz Holton, Glynis Johnson, Judi Kent, Sian Kirkwood, Tricia Freeman, June Park, Ann Parker, Janet Scruby, Margaret Singer, Judith Todd.

HALF A SIXPENCE

PRINCIPALS: John Parker, Peter Hydes, Steve Luck, Warnock Kerr, Sue Wishlade, June Aiken, Kath Robinson, Avril Blain, Stan Lloyd, Sam Herdman, Greta Sanderson, Muriel Jones, Hilary Hydes, Sue Williamson, Guy Allen, Kenneth Richardson, Judi Kent, Lynne Kerr, Chris Noble, Steve Blain, John Hacking, Lindesay Steel, Linda Roots.

CHORUS: Ann Bainbridge, Maggie Barnes, Christine Coates, Elizabeth Connagh, Linda Egginton, Audrey French, Margaret Harsley, Rebecca Hauxwell, Joan Kirkwood, Kim Keeler, Connie Reeves, Joan Reynolds, Susan Robinson, Vivienne Robson, Lisa Rossitter, Linda Roots, Jackie Vaughan, Dorothy Walker, Ann Wood, Graham Dove, John Hacking, Tom Handy, Tom Kent, John Lloyd, Chris Noble, Alf Robinson, Peter Sanderson, Lindesay Steel, Michael Walker, Ian Whitfield.

DANCERS: Christine Coates, Betty Cooke, Janet Cooke, Tricia Freeman, Susan Hewgill, Elizabeth Holton, Judi Kent, Sian Kirkwood, Glynis Johnson, June Park, Janet Scruby, Judith Todd.

1979 SALAD DAYS

PRINCIPALS: Peter Topping, Avril Blain, Stuart Parsons, Shirley Dodd, June Aiken, Connie Reeves, Sue Wishlade, Stan Lloyd, Barrie Dargue, Warnock Kerr, Ian Corner, Mike Walker, Steve Luck.

CHORUS: Chris Coates, Tricia Freeman, Sue Hewgill, Kath Robinson, Peter Sanderson.

WHITE HORSE INN

PRINCIPALS: Connie Reeves, Garry Reeves, Toni Di Duca, Sue Hewgill, Kenneth Richardson, Alf Robinson, John Hurlstone, Eunicé Cockburn, Bob Jarratt, Lindesay Steel, Chrissie Coates, Sam Herdman, Anna-Maria Wilson, Barrie Dargue, Philip Bethell, Lynne Kerr, Ian Whitfield, Linda Roots, Ann Wood.

CHORUS: Fiona Allen, Maggie Barnes, Christine Coates, Elizabeth Connagh, Linda Egginton, Christine Hacking, Margaret Harsley, Vivienne Jackson, Anne Johnson, Kim Keeler, Dawn Kidd, Joan Kirkwood, Jean Manners, Victoria Taylor, Dorothy Walker, Heather Wane, Graham Dove, John Hacking, Tom Kent, John Lloyd, Christopher Noble, John Parker, Peter Sanderson, Mike Walker, Jeff Wragg.

DANCERS: Chrissie Coates, Betty Cooke, Janet Cooke, Susanne Davison, Tricia Freeman, Liz Holton, Pauline Hurley, Glynis Johnson, Judi Kent, June Park, Kath Robinson, Janet Scruby, Judith Todd.

1980 THE DANCING YEARS

PRINCIPALS: Jeff Wragg, Kath Robinson, Steve Luck, Susan Robinson, Judi Kent, Sue Hewgill, Lynne Kerr, Christopher Noble, Warnock Kerr, Eunicé Cockburn, Kenneth Richardson, Margaret Lowther, June Aiken, Peter Sanderson, Graham Saunders, Garry Reeves, Sam Herdman, Ian Whitfield, Victoria Taylor, Jonathan Kent, Connie Reeves.

CHORUS: Fiona Allen, Maggie Barnes, Avril Blain, Vivienne Cordial, Margaret Cunningham, Linda Egginton, Liz Huddleston, Kim Keeler, Dawn Kidd, Joan Kirkwood, Eileen Oliver, Greta Sanderson, Dorothy Walker, Heather Wane, Margaret Webb, Barrie Dargue, Cecil Grieveson, John Lally, John Lloyd, Neil McDonald, Kevin Mooney.

DANCERS: Chrissie Coates, Betty Cooke, Janet Cooke, Susanne Davison, Tricia Freeman, Rachel Harrison, Ruth Hauxwell, Pauline Hurley, Glynis Johnson, Sian Kirkwood, June Park, Warnock Kerr, Neil McDonald, Kevin Mooney, Christopher Noble, Peter Sanderson, Ian Whitfield.

CAMELOT

PRINCIPALS: Clifford Walker, Ian Whitfield, Christopher Noble, Keith Tate, Kenneth Richardson Warnock Kerr, Connie Reeves, Dorothy Walker, Susan Ledger, John Larsen, Tom Kent, Sam Herdman, Steve Luck, Muriel Jones, Garry Reeves, June Park, Barrie Dargue.

CHORUS: June Aiken, Fiona Allen, Maggie Barnes, Alwyn Bartlett, Betty Cooke, Shirley Dodd, Liz Huddlestone, Kim Keeler, Lynne Kerr, Linda Roots, Teresa Sansbury-Straughan, Heather Wane, Mavis Wilson, Guy Allen, Cecil Grieveson, John Lloyd, Peter Sanderson, Lindesay Steel, Mike Walker.

DANCERS: Chrissie Coates, Janet Cooke, Tricia Freeman, Rachel Harrison, Ruth Hauxwell, Susan Hewgill, Kath Robinson, Janet Steel, Neil McDonald, Peter Sanderson, Lindesay Steel, Mike Walker.

HERALDS: Judi Kent, Eileen Oliver.

1981 THE MIKADO

PRINCIPALS: John Hurlstone, Keith Tate, Kenneth Richardson, Sam Herdman, Ian Kirkbride, Susan Ledger, Connie Reeves, Mavis Wilson, Nancy Chilver.

CHORUS: June Aiken, Maggie Barnes, Alwyn Bartlett, Felicity Burt, Margaret Cunningham, Linda Egginton, Audrey French, Liz Huddlestone, Kim Keeler, Dawn Kidd, Joan Kirkwood,

Eileen Oliver, Susan Robinson, Linda Roots, Greta Sanderson, Tina Spence, Dorothy Walker, Heather Wane, Margaret Webb, Barrie Dargue, Tony Di Duca, Cecil Grieveson, John Lloyd, Steve Luck, Neil McDonald, Christopher Noble, Bernard Sanderson, Peter Sanderson, Mike Walker, Ian Whitfield, Jeff Wragg.

DANCERS: Chrissie Coates, Betty Cooke, Janet Cooke, Susanne Davison, Tricia Freeman, Rachel Harrison, Pauline Hurley, Kath Robinson, Glynis Wilkinson, Steve Luck, Neil McDonald, Peter Sanderson, Mike Walker.

BRIGADOON

PRINCIPALS: Barrie Dargue, Ian Kirkbride, Clifford Walker, Steve Luck, John Parker, Ian Whitfield, Sam Herdman, Susan Ledger, Kath Robinson, June Aiken Christopher Noble, Sue Hewgill, Kenneth Richardson, Keith Tate, John Lloyd, Mavis Wilson.

BAGPIPES: Arthur Middleton or Tony Middleton.

DANCERS: Chrissie Coates, Betty Cooke, Janet Cooke, Tricia Freeman, Ruth Hauxwell, Pauline Hurley, Carmen Munnerley, June Park, Janet Steel, Glynis Wilkinson, David Barkes, Ian Corner, Neil McDonald, Peter Sanderson, Mike Walker, Ian Whitfield.

CHORUS: Maggie Barnes, Avril Blain, Felicity Burt, Shirley Dodd, Linda Egginton, Gillian Egglestone, Audrey French, Liz Huddlestone, Muriel Jones, Kim Keeler, Judi Kent, Joan Kirkwood, Eileen Oliver, Joan Reynolds, Susan Robinson, Greta Sanderson, Tina Spence, Dorothy Walker, Margaret Webb, Mavis Wilson, David Barkes, Ian Corner, Cecil Grieveson, Eric Munnerley, Colin Thornton.

1982 GODSPELL

Caroline Burton, Rosemarie Dodd, Sarah Goddard, Steve Luck, Kath Robinson, Jill Rowcroft, Geoffrey Stevens, Chris Thorns, Mike Walker, David Beaverstock, Janet Cooke, Kim Keeler, Jonathan Keighley.

KING'S RHAPSODY

PRINCIPALS: Christine Murray, Sue Hewgill, Guy Allen, Nancy Chilver, Eunicé Cockburn, Clifford Walker, Richard Boucher, Mike Walker, Shirley Dodd, Sam Herdman, Steve Luck, Mavis Wilson, Greta Sanderson, Cecil Grieveson, John Lloyd, John Hurlstone, Ian Whitfield, Bernard Sanderson, David Barkes, Mark Lawrence, Janet Cooke, Kath Robinson, Linda Roots, Simon Cutchie.

DANCERS: Betty Cooke, Janet Cooke, Susanne Davison, Sue Hewgill, Pauline Hurley, Christine Murray, June Park, Margaret Singer, Janet Steel, Glynis Wilkinson, Guy Allen, David Barkes, Richard Boucher, Mark Lawrence, Ian Whitfield.

CHORUS: June Aiken, Avril Blain, Felicity Burt, Margaret Cunningham, Linda Egginton, Liz Huddlestone, Joan Kirkwood, Susan Ledger, Connie Reeves, Dorothy Shotton, Tina Spence, Dorothy Walker, Heather Wane, Margaret Webb, Nora Wheeler, Jeff Wragg.

1983 MAME

PRINCIPALS: Melvyn Dawson, Kath Robinson, Shirley Dodd, Connie Reeves, Ian Whitfield, Ian Kirkbride, Mike Walker, Cecil Grieveson, Peter Sanderson, Colin Thornton, John Lloyd, June Aiken, Steve Luck, Ken Horsley, John Hacking, Joan Kirkwood, Susan Robinson, Eileen Young, Steve Blain, Christopher Noble, Sam Herdman, Mavis Wilson, Avril Blain, Paul Dodds.

DANCERS: Betty Cooke, Janet Cooke, Susanne Davison, Tricia Freeman, Pauline Hurley, Christine Murray, Janet Steel, Glynis Wilkinson, Cecil Grieveson, Steve Luck, Christopher Noble, Peter Sanderson, Colin Thornton, Ian Whitfield.

CHORUS: Avril Blain, Felicity Burt, Linda Egginton, Audrey French, Judi Kent, Kim Keeler, Catherine Noble, Irene Pinkney, Joan Reynolds, Tina Spence, Deborah Stephens, Dorothy Walker, Margaret Webb, Nora Wheeler, Karen Winter, Tom Kent, Ian Kirkbride, John Parker, Bernard Sanderson, Lindesay Steel, Colin Thornton, David Todd, Jeff Wragg.

THE MUSIC MAN

PRINCIPALS: Guy Allen, David Barkes, Tom Kent, John Lloyd, Peter Sanderson, Mike Walker, Sam Herdman, Cecil Grieveson, Ken Horsley, John Parker, John Hacking, John Hurlstone, Andrew Taylor, Bernard Sanderson, Ian Kirkbride, Steve Luck, Connie Reeves, Joan Kirkwood, Brigitte Freeman, Paul Dodds, Susan Robinson, Christine Murray, Janet Steel, Dorothy Walker, Shirley Dodd, June Aiken, Eileen Young, Ian Whitfield.

CHILDREN: Joy Hewgill, Zoë Kent, Emma Parker, Helen Wilson, Melvyn Dawson, Patrick Freeman, Martin Ledger.

DANCERS: Betty Cooke, Janet Cooke, Tricia Freeman, Elizabeth Holton, Pauline Hurley, Fay Nutting, Kath Robinson, Glynis Wilkinson, Jennifer Wood, David Barkes, Richard Boucher, Adrian O'Hickey, Anthony Kelly, Peter Sanderson, Mark Swainston, Mike Walker.

CHORUS: Fiona Allen, Florence Bolton, Felicity Burt, Margaret Cunningham, Linda Egginton, Audrey French, Debbie Longstaff, Judi Kent, Kim Oldham, Lindsay Ramsey, Joan Reynolds, Enid Robinson, Linda Roots, Tina Spence, Deborah Stephens, Margaret Webb, Nora Wheeler, Karen Winter, Jimmy Hall.

1984 THE GONDOLIERS

PRINCIPALS: Stan Lloyd, Michael Geddes, John Hurlstone, David Beall, David Curtis, Barrie Dargue, John Hacking, Sam Herdman, Nancy Chilver, Gillian Marshall, Susan Kirkbride, Connie Reeves, Pauline Curtis, Jacqueline Wright, Sharon Priestley, June Aiken.

DANCERS: Betty Cooke, Tricia Freeman, Liz Holton, Pauline Hurley, Christine Murray, Fay Nutting, Kath Robinson, Margaret Singer, Glynis Wilkinson, Jennifer Wood, Richard Boucher, Jimmy Hall, Mike Walker, Ian Whitfield.

CHORUS: Linda Egginton, Anne Johnson, Judi Kent, Joan Kirkwood, Claire Lavin, Kim Oldham, Christine Pearson, Ruth Pinsey, Sharon Priestley, Sandra Rutt, Tina Spence, Dorothy Walker, Margaret Webb, Nora Wheeler, Mavis Wilson, Richard Boucher, Fred Gibbon, Cecil Grieveson, Jimmy Hall, Peter Henderson, John Lloyd, Mike Walker, Ian Whitfield.

MY FAIR LADY

PRINCIPALS: Joan Kirkwood, Pauline Curtis, Colin Kerr, Stan Lloyd, John Hurlstone, John Hacking, Sam Herdman, Ian Whitfield, Martin Swainston, Anthony Kelly, Jimmy Hall, John Parker, Mike Walker, Ian Kirkbride, Greta Sanderson, June Aiken, Shirley Dodd, David Barkes, John Lloyd, Kim Oldham, Bernard Sanderson, Judi Kent, Heather Wane, Barrie Dargue, Mavis Wilson, Ann Parker, Avril Blain, Florence Bolton, Joan Reynolds, Linda Roots, Susan Robinson, Dorothy Walker.

DANCERS: Pamela Carter, Betty Cooke, Tricia Freeman, Liz Holton, Pauline Hurley, Fay Nutting, Kath Robinson, Janet Watson, Glynis Wilkinson, Jennifer Wood, Richard Boucher, Jimmy Hall, Mike Walker, Ian Whitfield.

CHORUS: Lynn Coulson, Margaret Cunningham, Linda Egginton, Audrey French, Claire Lavin, Christine Pearson, Ruth Pinsey, Enid Robinson, Tina Spence, Margaret Webb, Nora Wheeler, Richard Boucher, Cecil Grieveson, Jimmy Hall.

1985 HELLO DOLLY!

PRINCIPALS: Connie Reeves, June Aiken, Steve Luck, Sam Herdman, Tricia Freeman, Barrie Dargue, John Parker, Christine Swales, Avril Blain, Shirley Dodd, Clifford Walker, Keith Tate, Kath Robinson.

DANCERS: Pamela Carter, Betty Cooke, Liz Holton, Fay Nutting, Kath Robinson, Janet Watson, Glynis Wilkinson, Jennifer Wood.

CHORUS: Florence Bolton, Lyn Coulson, Shirley Dodd, Christine Flatman, Anne Johnson, Judi Kent, Joan Kirkwood, Kim Oldham, Ann Parker, Christine Pearson, Ruth Pinsey, Linda Roots, Sandra Rutt, Kiran Singh, Tina Spence, Debbie Stephens, Margaret Webb,

Nora Wheeler, Mavis Wilson, Suzanne Winskill, Karen Winter, David Curtis, Cecil Grieveson, John Hacking, Jimmy Hall, Anthony Kelly, John Lloyd, Mike Walker, Ian Whitfield.

SOUTH PACIFIC

PRINCIPALS: Nicola Whitfield, Patrick Freeman, Mike Taylor, Mavis Wilson, John Hurlstone, Roula Murray, Betty Cooke, Richard Boucher, Adrian Fawlk, Keith Craney, John Parker, Barrie Dargue, John Hacking, John Lloyd, Mike Walker, Jimmy Hall, Tom Kent, Stephen Emmerson, David Barkes, Ian Whitfield, Cecil Grieveson, Jillson Lawrence, Allan Carver, Ray Simmons, Margaret Webb, Vera Davison, Ann Parker, Lyn Coulson, Christine Flatman, Katie Sharp, Avril Blain, Linda Dawson, Kim Oldham, Judi Kent, Fay Nutting, Steve Luck, Melvyn Dawson.

NUNS, NATIVES AND NURSES: Maxine Allinson, Linda Egginton, Julie Gamble, Ann Oxley, Christine Pearson, Linda Roots, Sandra Rutt, Suzanne Winskill.

ENSIGN DANCERS: Pamela Carter, Liz Holton, Tricia Freeman, Margaret Singer, Janet Steel, Jayne Tweddle, Janet Watson, Glynis Wilkinson, Jennifer Wood.

MARINE CORPORALS: Jonathan Curren, Nigel Hayler, Christopher Lepingwell, Jonathan Parkin.

1986 ANNIE GET YOUR GUN

PRINCIPALS: Patrick Freeman, John Parker, Ian Whitfield, Tom Kent, Greta Sanderson, Avril Blain, Jonathan Curren, Mark Ellis, Kiran Singh, Helen Wilson, Emma Parker, Nicola Whitfield, Indra Singh, Sam Herdman, Joan Kirkwood, Janet Robinson, Tina Spence, Bernard Sanderson, Steve Emmerson, Jillson Lawrence, Mike Walker, Liz Holton, Clifford Walker, Keith Craney, Richard Boucher, John Lloyd, Judi Kent, Katie Sharp, Maxine Allinson.

DANCERS: Andrea Hobson, Janet Hodgson, Liz Holton, Tricia Freeman, Michele Marshman, Pamela Walker, Jennifer Wood, David Barkes, Richard Boucher, Darren Dargue, Robert Rowell, Peter Sowerby, Michael Stephenson.

CHORUS: Alison Aisbitt, Elizabeth Cooper, Lyn Coulson, Linda Dawson, Sharon Emmerson, Judi Kent, Joan Kirkwood, Victoria Lester, Kim Oldham, Ann Oxley, Vanessa Redhead, Janet Robinson, Linda Roots, Katie Sharp, Tina Spence, Yvonne Stoddart, Margaret Webb, Mavis Wilson, David Barkes, Joe Cooper, Barrie Dargue, Darren Dargue, Steve Emmerson, Cecil Grieveson, Robert Lamb, Robert Rowell, Pete Sowerby, Michael Stephenson.

CAROUSEL

PRINCIPALS: Mavis Wilson, Vera Davison, June Aiken, Arthur Ellis, Jimmy Hall, Ian Whitfield, Sam Herdman, Kath Robinson, Connie Reeves, Janet Watson, Barrie Dargue, Steve Blain, Jayne Summerbell, Doreen Steel, Mike Walker, Pete Sowerby, Steve Emmerson, Keith Craney, Nicola Whitfield, Richard Boucher, Melvyn Dawson, John Lloyd.

DANCERS: Andrea Hobson, Janet Hodgson, Liz Holton, Tricia Freeman, Michele Marshman, Fay Nutting, Margaret Singer, Janet Steel, Jayne Summerbell, Pamela Walker, Janet Watson, Glynis Wilkinson, Jennifer Wood, David Barkes, Richard Boucher, Jonathan Curren, Darren Dargue, Pete Sowerby, Mike Walker, Ian Whitfield.

CHORUS: Alison Aisbitt, Maxine Allinson, Chris Bowran, Florence Bolton, Betty Cooke, Elizabeth Cooper, Linda Dawson, Sharon Emmerson, Sharon Hodgson, Victoria Lester, Ann Oxley, Vanessa Redhead, Janet Robinson, Linda Roots, Doreen Steel, Yvonne Stoddart, Margaret Webb, Amanda Wilcox, David Barkes, Jonathan Curren, Darren Dargue, Steve Emmerson, Cecil Grieveson, Robert Lamb.

1987 GUYS AND DOLLS

PRINCIPALS: John Parker, Mike Walker, Jillson Lawrence, Avril Blain, Bernard Sanderson, Margaret Webb, Richard Boucher, Joe Cooper, Keith Craney, Barrie Dargue, Kath Robinson, Michael Stephenson, John Lloyd, Judi Kent, Susan Robinson, Ian Whitfield, Cecil Grieveson, Sam Herdman, Jimmy Hall.

HOT BOX AND DANCER DOLLS: Fay Carter, Sharon Emmerson, Tricia Freeman, Andrea Hobson, Liz Holton, Judi Kent, Jayne Summerbell, Pamela Walker, Janet Watson, Glynis Wilkinson.

CHORUS GUYS AND DOLLS: Susan Adams, Alison Aisbitt, Mark Auton, Lawrence Bowker, Chris Bowran, Jacqui Carbert, Betty Cooke, Lyn Coulson, Steve Emmerson, Gregory Newman, Ann Oxley, Ann Parker, Vanessa Redhead, Janet Robinson, Pete Sowerby, Doreen Steel, Dorothy Walker, Gary Winn.

FIDDLER ON THE ROOF

PRINCIPALS: Bev Jones, Connie Reeves, Christine Murray, Pamela Walker, Zoë Kent, Nicola Reeves, Emma Parker, Shirley Dodd, Peter Sowerby, David Curtis, Sam Herdman, Michael Mitton, Tom Kent, Gary Winn, Ian Whitfield, Joe Cooper, Susan Robinson, Mavis Wilson, Clifford Walker, Melvyn Dawson, Doreen Steel, Robert Rowell, Barrie Dargue, John Lloyd, Richard Boucher, Patrick Freeman, Kristen Hird.

VILLAGERS: June Aiken, Alison Aisbitt, Maxine Allinson, David Barkes, Steve Berriman, David Birkett, Avril Blain, Florence Bolton, Lawrence Bowker, Chris Bowran, Jacqui Carbert, Fay Carter, Betty Cooke, Lyn Coulson, Margaret Cunningham, Vera Davidson, Linda Dawson, Sharon Emmerson, Tricia Freeman, Cecil Grieveson, Liz Holton, Renate Hutchings, Adele Lee, Victoria Lester, Sarah Mann, Ann Oxley, Ann Parker, Vanessa Redhead, Janet Robinson, Kath Robinson, Margaret Singer, David Smith, Sarah Smith, Janet Steel, Jayne Summerbell, Mike Walker, Margaret Webb, Jennifer Wood.

1988 KISS ME KATE

PRINCIPALS: John Hurlstone, Clifford Walker, Liz Holton, Steve Emmerson, Vera Davison, Janet Robinson, Barrie Dargue, Michael Stephenson, Arthur Ellis, Mike Walker, Ian Whitfield, Sam Herdman, Kim Oldham, Lyn Coulson, John Lloyd, David Barkes, Steve Berriman, Pete Sowerby, Michael Mitton.

DANCERS: Fay Carter, Tricia Freeman, Christine Murray, Kath Robinson, Margaret Singer, Sarah Smith, Janet Steel, Jayne Summerbell, Pamela Walker, Janet Watson, Nicola Whitfield, Jennifer Wood, David Barkes, Peter Sowerby, Ian Whitfield.

CHORUS: June Aiken, Alison Aisbitt, Maxine Allinson, Florence Bolton, Jacqui Carbert, Sarah Mann, Elizabeth Cooper, Betty Cooke, Linda Dawson, Shirley Dodd, Sharon Emmerson, Laura Meecham, Ann Oxley, Vanessa Redhead, Deborah Stephens, Margaret Webb, David Barkes, Steve Berriman, Cecil Grieveson, Michael Mitton.

KISMET

PRINCIPALS: Barrie Dargue, Gary Winn, Tom Kent, David Barkes, Pete Sowerby, Peter Sanderson, John Lloyd, John Hurlstone, Tiffany Edwards, Ian Whitfield, Joe Cooper, Clifford Walker, Liz Holton, Barrie Dargue, Mike Walker, John Parker, Maggie Thorp, Cecil Grieveson, Steve Berriman, Margaret Singer, Janet Steel, Jayne Summerbell, Colin Kerr, June Aiken, Judi Kent, Connie Reeves, Mavis Wilson, Adele Lee, Doreen Orton, Christine Murray, Ann Parker, Shirley Dodd.

DANCERS: Fay Carter, Tricia Freeman, Liz Holton, Zoë Kent, Adele Lee, Christine Murray, Pamela Walker, Jennifer Wood, Nicola Whitfield, Peter Sanderson, Pete Sowerby.

CHORUS: Alison Aisbitt, Maxine Allinson, Jacqui Carbert, Betty Cooke, Linda Dawson, Sarah Mann, Rachel McGovern, Julia McLean, Ann Oxley, Alison Schofield, Paul Arnold, Cecil Grieveson, Gary Winn.

1989 LA BELLE HÉLÈNE

PRINCIPALS: Maggie Thorp, Shirley Dodd, Zoë Kent, Liz Holton, David Curtis, Sam Herdman, Arthur Ellis, John Lloyd, Clifford Walker, Mike Walker, Paul Arnold, Barrie Dargue, Jacqui Carbert, June Aiken, Vera Davison, John Parkin, Janet Robinson.

DANCERS: Karen Brown, Rachel Green, Pippa Hague, Jennie Hynd, Claire Park, Rachel Swan, Nicola Whitfield.

CHORUS: Maxine Allinson, Chris Bowran, Betty Cooke, Suzanne Dalton, Linda Dawson, Rachel McGovern, Julia McLean, Ann Oxley, Alison Schofield, Margaret Webb, David Barkes, Bernard Sanderson, Michael Mitton, Dave Smith, Steve Berriman.

THE SOUND OF MUSIC

PRINCIPALS: Tiffany Edwards, Jacqui Carbert, Connie Reeves, Doreen Orton, Suzanne Dalton, Warnock Kerr, John Parkin, Shirley Dodd, Rachel Green, Melvyn Dawson, Vera Davison, Barrie Dargue, Tom Kent, Dave Smith, Betty Cooke, Julia McLean, Sam Herdman, June Aiken, John Lloyd.

CHILDREN TEAM 1: Patrick Freeman, Maria Wallace, James Allison, Sarah Wright, Carey Lea, Gemma Pontone.

TEAM 2: Jamie Coates, Emma Parker, Nathan Smith, Emma Hardwick, Rachel Boyle, Laura Cave.

CHORUS: Alison Aisbitt, Chris Bowran, Linda Dawson, Tricia Freeman, Liz Holton, Zoë Kent, Rachel McGovern, Ann Oxley, Janet Robinson, Joanne Mitton, Carolyn Smiles, Melanie Short, Alison Schofield, Helen Thornton, Nicola Whitfield, Gina Williams, Jeremy Buckton, Richard Gray, Cecil Grieveson, David Plumpton.

1990 THE PIRATES OF PENZANCE

PRINCIPALS: Frank Lloyd, Barrie Dargue, Michael Geddes, June Aiken, Andrea Durham, Claire Williams, Alison Cochlan, Liz Holton, John Parker, Gary Winn, Eileen Young.

DAUGHTERS: Maxine Allinson, Elizabeth Cooper, Rhoda Frazer, Sarah Mann, Ann Oxley, Kath Robinson, Melanie Short, Carolyn Smiles, Margaret Webb.

PIRATES AND POLICEMEN: Paul Arnold, Ian Black, Keith Bowran, Joe Cooper, Robert Ellis, Stuart Gordon, Rich Grey, Cecil Grieveson, Viv Hardwick, John Lloyd, Barry Million, Karl Oldridge, Les Oxley, David Plumpton, Martin Simpson, Ian Whitfield.

THE MAGIC OF THE MUSICAL

COMPANY: June Aiken, Alison Aisbitt, Chris Bowran, Alison Cochlan, Vera Davison, Suzanne Dalton, Shirley Dodd, Linda Egginton, Tricia Freeman, Janice Gray, Liz Holton, Zoë Kent, Doreen Orton, Ann Oxley, Melanie Short, Joan Smart, Carolyn Smiles, Helen Thornton, Maggie Thorp, Sheila Truby, Geraldine Watson, Jo Whitbread, Joe Cooper, Barrie Dargue, Arthur Ellis, Winston Francis, Stuart Gordon, Paul Hewgill, Viv Hardwick, Jack Higgins, John Lloyd, Barry Million, Martin Simpson, Pete Sowerby, Ian Whitfield.

1991 OKLAHOMA!

PRINCIPALS: Susan Robinson, Wayne Shellard, Andrea Durham, David Wiseman, Ian Whitfield, Philip Mezzo, Arthur Ellis, Alison Cochlan, Gary Winn, Melanie Short, Sam Herdman, John Lloyd.

DREAM BALLET: Christine Murray, Steve Luck, Robert Rowell.

DANCERS: Katamya Bradshaw, Natasha Dearle, Christine Murray, Claire Park, Janet Ray, Gillian Smith, Jayne Summerbell, Alison Towns, Nicola Whitfield, Stuart Gordon, Graeme Hall, Steve Luck, Philip Motley, Barry Million, Martin Roberts, Robert Rowell, Martin Simpson, Pete Sowerby.

CHORUS: June Aiken, Chris Bowran, Nicola Curry, Suzanne Dalton, Vera Davison, Linda Egginton, Tricia Freeman, Liz Holton, Zoë Kent, Rachel McGovern, Julia McLean, Sarah Mann, Catherine Mitford, Ann Oxley, Janet Robinson, Kath Robinson, Joan Smart, Carolyn Smiles, Maggie Thorp, Helen Thornton, Margaret Webb, Jo Whitbread, Brian Bean, Barrie Dargue, Andrew Hawkes, Jack Higgins, Ray Hughes, Les Oxley, John Parkin, Dave Smith, Barry Wilson.

ANNIE

PRINCIPALS: June Aiken, Stuart Gordon, Ian Whitfield, Dave Smith, Barry Million, Shirley Dodd, Maggie Thorp, Gary Winn, Vera Davison, Greta Sanderson, Liz Holton,

Tricia Freeman, Barrie Dargue, Steve Luck, Kath Robinson, David Wiseman, Ann Oxley, Nicola Curry, Julia McLean, John Parker, John Lloyd, Joe Cooper, Sam Herdman, Tom Kent, Graeme Hall, Les Oxley, Brian Bean.

CHILDREN: Red Team: Stacey Walker, Rachel Boyle, Ailsa Todd, Stephanie Fanner, Joanne Carey, Catherine Lamb, Laura Cave, Clare-Louise Hall, Rachel Coad, Christine Rutherford, Andrea Jones, Chantal Loiseau, **Rebecca Iles**. Blue Team: Heather Walton, Andrea Ross, Leandra Ashton, Samantha Waine, Melanie Park, Sarah Middleton, Caroline Hague, Stephanie Greenhow, Katy Purvis, Hayley Blades, Claire Hardy, Emma Burn, **Rachel Humphrey**.

CHORUS: Alison Aisbitt, Jayne Brett, Janice Gray, Julie McKeown, Julia McLean, Ann Oxley, Andrea Roberts, Christine Roberts, Janet Robinson, Carolyn Smiles, Ruth Stahl, Shelia Truby, Karen Wright, Cecil Grieveson, Graeme Hall, David Plumpton, Martin Roberts, Barry Wilson.

1992 HALF A SIXPENCE

PRINCIPALS: Wayne Shellard, Steve Luck, Nick Myers, Graeme Hall, Elizabeth Cooper, Kath Robinson, Christine Murray, Nicola Whitfield, Ian Whitfield, John Lloyd, Shirley Dodd, June Aiken, Melanie Short, Nadine Bell, Kevin Allenby, Barrie Dargue, Carolyn Smiles, Linda Dawson, Sarah Mann, Martin Roberts, Brian Bean, Ann Oxley.

DANCERS: Elsebeth Danielson, Justine Denham, Janet Ray, Miranda Richardson, Gillian Smith, Stuart Gordon, Philip Motley, Martin Roberts, Robert Rowell, Martin Simpson, Pete Sowerby.

CHORUS: Chris Bowran, Jayne Brett, Linda Egginton, Tricia Freeman, Charlotte Geldard, Rachel Green, Liz Holton, Sarah Mann, Julia McLean, Eileen Miller, Ann Oxley, Andrea Roberts, Helen Thornton, Margaret Webb, Joe Cooper, Stuart Gordon, Barrie Million, Philip Motley, David Plumpton, Martin Roberts, Robert Rowell, Martin Simpson, Pete Sowerby.

THE MERRY WIDOW

PRINCIPALS: Pauline Curtis, David Curtis, Doug Clayton, Maggie Thorp, Philip Tsaras, Sam Herdman, Graeme Hall, David Wiseman, Les Oxley, Margaret Webb, Ian Whitfield, John Parkin, Kath Robinson, Rachel McGovern, June Aiken, Tricia Freeman, Liz Holton, Eileen Miller, Christine Murray, Jayne Summerbell.

DANCERS: Nina Crookall, Rachel Jukes, Christine Murray, Jayne Summerbell, Katrina Thompson, Natalie Wright.

CHORUS: Alison Aisbitt, Amanda Blane, Jayne Brett, Margaret Cunningham, Vera Davison, Linda Egginton, Charlotte Geldard, Rachel Green, Stephanie Glenn, Andrea Hall, Maggie Iles, Julia McLean, Catherine Mitford, Angela Paterson, Andrea Roberts, Brian Bean, Arthur Ellis, Cecil Grieveson, Brian Jackson, John Lloyd, Barry Million, David Plumpton, Terry Riney, Barry Wilson.

1993 SWEET CHARITY

PRINCIPALS: Mandy Brown, Barry Million, Jayne Summerbell, Liz Holton, June Aiken, Rachel Green, Judi Kent, Gillian Smith, Eileen Miller, Arthur Ellis, Barrie Dargue, Amanda Blane, Bill Witcomb, Sam Herdman, Carolyn Smiles, Wayne Shellard, Graeme Hall, Nicola Whitfield.

NEW YORKERS: Sam Currie, Linda Dawson, Linda Egginton, Heather Franklin, Tricia Freeman, Suzanne Gray, Andrea Hall, Caroline Lillystone, Julia McLean, Christine Murray, Nikki Payne, Janet Ray, Miranda Richardson, Carolyn Smiles, Janet Steel, Kate Wall, Karen Wright, Jai Abu Bakar, Brian Bean, George Brown, Bob Curtis, Joseph Di Duca, Stuart Gordon, John Lloyd, David Plumpton, Pete Sowerby.

OLIVER!

PRINCIPALS: **Kieran Nokes**, **Paul Taylor**, George Brown, Connie Reeves, Barrie Dargue, Kath Robinson, Angela Smallman, Andy Myers, **Adam Savage**, **Paul Frost**, Ken Horsley,

Zoë Kent, Samantha Currie, Christopher Moran, Sam Herdman, Arthur Ellis, Shirley Dodd, Douglas Clayton, June Aiken, Vera Davison.

WORKHOUSE BOYS AND FAGIN'S GANG: Robert Andrews, Christopher Bolam, Daniel Burton, Glen Cochrane, Adam Cooper, Nicholas Cooper, Charles Jeffrey, David Laheney, Anthony Little, Peter McGovern, Chris Moran, Paul Phillips, Russell Storey, Neil Thompson, Ben Tyreman, Dale Williamson, Matthew Wright.

DANCERS: Rachel Boyle, Leandra Dodsworth, Tricia Freeman, Emma Hardwick, Christine Murray, Janet Steel, Jayne Summerbell, Nicola Whitfield.

CHORUS: Alison Aisbitt, Judith Collinson, Elizabeth Cooper, Liz Holton, Karen Johnson, Julie Kitson, Rachel McGovern, Julia McLean, Eileen Miller, Catherine Mitford, Ann Oxley, Nikki Payne, Joan Smart, Maggie Thorp, Karen Wright, Margaret Webb, Allan Andrews, Joe Cooper, Cecil Grieveson, Graeme Hall, Robert Lamb, Barry Million, David Plumpton, Ian Whitfield, Barry Wilson, Gary Winn, David Wiseman, Mark Zeltins.

1994 GIGI

PRINCIPALS: Barrie Dargue, Rory Mulvihill, Liz Holton, Samantha Currie, Shirley Dodd, Maggie Thorp, George Browne, Graeme Hall, Gary Winn, Sam Herdman, Ian Whitfield.

CHILDREN: Romana Blain, Selina Blain, Helen Sanderson, Jennifer Sanderson, Charlotte Westgarth.

DANCERS: Rachel Boyle, Leandra Dodsworth, Tricia Freeman, Emma Hardwick, Christine Murray, Miranda Richardson, Jayne Summerbell, Nicola Whitfield.

CHORUS: Alison Aisbitt, Avril Blain, Judith Collinson, Fiona Elcoat, Rebecca Hall, Alison Hulford, Karen Johnson, Zoë Kent, Rachel McGovern, Catherine Mitford, Alison Park, Nikki Payne, Carolyn Smiles, Margaret Webb, Angela Wilcox, Julie Winn, Brian Bean, Cecil Grieveson, John Lloyd, Barry Million, Andy Myers, David Plumpton, David Vollans.

ANYTHING GOES

PRINCIPALS: Doug Clayton, David Phillips, George Browne, Joe Cooper, Gary Winn, June Aiken, Avril Blain, Sam Herdman, Dawn Oostdijck, Warnock Kerr, Arthur Ellis, Graeme Hall, David Plumpton, Ian Whitfield, Kath Robinson, John Lloyd, Liz Holton, Elizabeth Cooper, Mandy Shellard, Jayne Summerbell.

CHORUS: Debbie Barrigan, Jayne Brett, Samatha Currie, Sally Dixon, Linda Egginton, Fiona Elcoat, Tricia Freeman, Alison Hulford, Zoë Kent, Julia McLean, Catherine Mitford, Allison Park, Nikki Payne, Nicola Whitfield, George Browne, Cecil Grieveson, Graeme Hall, John Lloyd, Andy Myers, David Phillips, David Plumpton, David Vollans, Ian Whitfield.

References

Chapter 1

1   *The Northern Echo* 20:09:1912
2   *Darlington & Stockton Times* 7:02:1914
3   *The North Star* 8:12:1920
4   *Darlington & Stockton Times* 11:12:1920
5   *Northern Despatch* 2:12:1921
6   *Northern Despatch* 6:12:1921
7   *The North Star* 6:12:1921
8   *The Northern Echo* 6:12:1921
9   *Darlington & Stockton Times* 12:12:1925
10 *The Northern Echo* 7:12:1926
11 *Darlington & Stockton Times* 30:09:1933
12 *Darlington & Stockton Times* 28:10:1933
13 *Darlington & Stockton Times* 10:03:1934
14 *Darlington & Stockton Times* 16:06:1934
15 *Northern Despatch* 5:03:1937
16 Sheridan Morley, *Spread a Little Happiness*, Thames and Hudson, 1987, page 32
17 *Darlington & Stockton Times* 4:12:1937

Chapter 2

1   *Darlington & Stockton Times* 5:05:1945
2   *Darlington & Stockton Times* 3:11:1945
3   *The Northern Echo* 30:04:1946
4   *Darlington & Stockton Times* 4:05:1946
5   *Northern Despatch* 30:04:1946
6   Minutes of Darlington Operatic Society 12:10:1947
7   *The Northern Echo* 25:11:1947
8   *Darlington & Stockton Times* 29:11:1947
9   *Northern Despatch* 25:11:1947
10 *Darlington & Stockton Times* 8:05:1948
11 *The Northern Echo* 4:05:1948
12 *Northern Despatch* 4:05:1948
13 *The Chicago Tribune* 21:08:1939
14 *The Northern Echo* 23:11:1948
15 *Darlington & Stockton Times* 27:11:1948

16 *Northern Despatch* 23:11:1948
17 *The Northern Echo* 8:11:1949
18 *Northern Despatch* 8:11:1949
19 Sheridan Morley, *Spread a Little Happiness* page 104

Chapter 3

1   *Darlington & Stockton Times* 29:04:1950
2   *Darlington & Stockton Times* 18:11:1950
3   *The Northern Echo* 14:11:1950
4   *Darlington & Stockton Times* 14:04:1951
5   *Darlington & Stockton Times* 17:11:1951
6   *The Northern Echo* 29:04:1952
7   *Northern Despatch* 29:04:1952
8   *The Northern Echo* 29:04:1952
9   Minutes 30:10:1952
10 *Darlington & Stockton Times* 15:11:1952
11 *The Northern Echo* 11:11:1952
12 *Darlington & Stockton Times* 15:11:1952
13 *Northern Despatch* 11:11:1952
14 *The Northern Echo* 11:11:1952
15 *Darlington & Stockton Times* 15:11:1952
16 *Darlington & Stockton Times* 14:11:1953
17 *Northern Despatch* 10:11:1953
18 Minutes 14:11:1953
19 Minutes 16:12:1953
20 *Darlington & Stockton Times* 13:02:1954
21 Minutes 21:07:1954
22 *The Northern Echo* 23:11:1954
23 *Darlington & Stockton Times* 27:11:1954

Chapter 4

1   *Darlington & Stockton Times* 26:02:1955
2   *Northern Despatch* 22:02:1955
3   *Darlington & Stockton Times* 12:11:1955
4   *Northern Despatch* 8:11:1955
5   *The Northern Echo* 8:11:1955
6   *The Northern Echo* 24:04:1956
7   *Northern Despatch* 24:04 1956
8   *Darlington & Stockton Times* 28:04:1956
9   Minutes 17:05:1956
10 *The Northern Echo* 13:11:1956
11 *Darlington & Stockton Times* 17:11:1956
12 *Darlington & Stockton Times*C1 26:10:1957
13 *The Northern Echo* 22:10:1957
14 *Northern Despatch* 22:10:1957
15 *The Northern Echo* 29:04:1958

16 *Darlington & Stockton Times* 3:05:1958
17 *Northern Despatch* 29:04:1958
18 *Darlington & Stockton Times* 29:11:1958
19 *The Northern Echo* 25:11:1958
20 *Northern Despatch* 25:11:1958
21 *Darlington & Stockton Times* 24:01:1959
22 *The Northern Echo* 20:01:1959
23 *Northern Despatch* 20:01:1959
24 *Darlington & Stockton Times* 25:04:1959

Chapter 5

1 *Northern Despatch* 12:01:1960
2 *The Northern Echo* 3:05:1960
3 *Darlington & Stockton Times* 7:05:1960
4 *Northern Despatch* 3:05:1960
5 Steve Luck, *Nine Hundred for the Nineties,* A History of Darlington Civic Theatre, Parkgate Press, 1990
6 *Darlington & Stockton Times* 12:11:1960
7 *Northern Despatch* 10:01:1961
8 *Darlington & Stockton Times* 14:01:1961
9 *Northern Despatch* 2:05:1961
10 *The Northern Echo* 31:10:1961
11 *Darlington & Stockton Times* 4:11:1961
12 *Northern Despatch* 31:10:1961
13 *Northern Despatch* 1:05:1962
14 *Darlington & Stockton Times* 5:05:1962
15 *The Northern Echo* 1:05:1962
16 *Northern Despatch* 26:03:1963
17 *Darlington & Stockton Times* 30:03:1963
18 *Northern Despatch* 29:10:1963
19 *Darlington & Stockton Times* 2:11:1963
20 *The Northern Echo* 29:10:1963
21 *Northern Despatch* 5:05:1964
22 *Northern Despatch* 27:10:1964
23 *Darlington & Stockton Times* 31:10:1964
24 *The Northern Echo* 27:10:1964

Chapter 6

1 *Darlington & Stockton Times* 8:05:1965
2 *Northern Despatch* 4:05:1965
3 *Darlington & Stockton Times* 7:05:1966
4 *Northern Despatch* 3:05:1966
5 *Northern Despatch* 25:10:1966
6 *The Northern Echo* 2:05:1967
7 *The Northern Echo* 24:10:1967
8 *The Northern Echo* 30:04:1968

9   *Northern Despatch* 30:04:1968
10   *The Northern Echo* 29:10:1968
11   *Darlington & Stockton Times* 2:11:1968
12   *Northern Despatch* 29:10:1968
13   *Northern Despatch* 6:05:1969
14   *The Northern Echo* 28:10:1969
15   *Darlington & Stockton Times* 1:11:1969

Chapter 7

1   *The Northern Echo* 8:05:1970
2   *Darlington & Stockton Times* 9:05:1970
3   *Darlington & Stockton Times* 31:10:1970
4   *Evening Despatch* 30:10:1970
5   *Darlington & Stockton Times* 8:05:1971
6   *The Northern Echo* 7:05:1971
7   *The Northern Echo* 29:10:1971
8   *Darlington & Stockton Times* 13:05:1972
9   *The Northern Echo* 9:05:1972
10   *Evening Despatch* 9:05:1972
11   Sheridan Morley, *Spread a Little Happiness*, page 161
12   Ditto page 163
13   *Darlington & Stockton Times* 4:11:1972
14   *The Northern Echo* 4:05:1973
15   *Darlington & Stockton Times* 5:05:1973
16   *Darlington & Stockton Times* 3:11:1973
17   *The Northern Echo* 3:11:1974
18   *Evening Despatch* 3:11:1974
19   *The Northern Echo* 31:10:1974

Chapter 8

1   *Darlington & Stockton Times* 3:05:1975
2   *Evening Despatch* 1:05:1975
3   Minutes 19:11:1975
4   Minutes 17:12:1975
5   Minutes 18:02:1976
6   *The Northern Echo* 29:04:1976
7   *Darlington & Stockton Times* 1:05:1976
8   *Evening Despatch* 28:10:1976
9   *The Northern Echo* 28:10:1976
10   *Darlington & Stockton Times* 30:10:1976
11   Minutes 16:02:1977
12   *The Northern Echo* 28:04:1977
13   *Evening Despatch* 28:04:1977
14   *Darlington & Stockton Times* 30:04:1977
15   Draft copy for *Darlington & Stockton Times* 5:11:1977
16   *The Northern Echo* 27:04:1978

17 *Evening Despatch* 27:04:1978
18 *Darlington & Stockton Times* 29:04:1978
19 Radio Cleveland broadcast by Jan Verrall 27:04:1978
20 *The Northern Echo* 27:10:1978
21 *Darlington & Stockton Times* 28:10:1978
22 *Evening Despatch* 27:10:1978
23 *Evening Despatch* 25:10:1979
24 *Darlington & Stockton Times* 27:10:1979

Chapter 9

1   Minutes 16:10:1980
2   *The Northern Echo* 23:10:1980
3   *Darlington & Stockton Times* 25:10:1980
4   *Evening Despatch* 23:10:1980
5   *The Northern Echo* 28:04:1981
6   *Evening Despatch* 28:04:1981
7   *Darlington & Stockton Times* 2:05:1981
8   *Evening Despatch* 28:10:1981
9   *The Northern Echo* 29:10:1981
10 *Darlington & Stockton Times* 31:10:81
11 *Evening Despatch* 22:02:1982
12 *The Northern Echo* 20:04:1982
13 *Evening Despatch* 20:04:1982
14 *Darlington & Stockton Times* 24:04:1982
15 *Darlington & Stockton Times* 30:10:1982
16 Darlington & Stockton Times 30:04:1983
17 *Evening Despatch* 26:04 1983
18 *The Northern Echo* 25:10:1983
19 *The Northern Echo* 27:10:1983
20 *Darlington & Stockton Times* 29:10:1983
21 *The Northern Echo* 15:05:1984
22 *Evening Despatch* 15:05:1984
23 *Darlington & Stockton Times* 19:05:1984
24 *Evening Despatch* 25:10:1984
25 *The Northern Echo* 25:10:1984
26 *Darlington & Stockton Times* 27:10:1984

Chapter 10

1   *The Northern Echo* 30:04:1985
2   *Darlington & Stockton Times* 4:05:1985
3   *Evening Despatch* 24:10:1985
4   *The Northern Echo* 24:10:1985
5   *Darlington & Stockton Times* 26:10:1985
6   *The Northern Echo* 1:05:1986
7   *Darlington & Stockton Times* 3:05:1986
8   *The Northern Echo* 23:10:1986

9 *Darlington & Stockton Times* 25:10:1986
10 *The Northern Echo* 1:05:1987
11 *Darlington & Stockton Times* 2:05:1987
12 *The Northern Echo* 30:10:1987
13 *Darlington & Stockton Times* 31:10:1987
14 *The Northern Echo* 28:04:1988
15 *Darlington & Stockton Times* 30:04:1988
16 *Darlington & Stockton Times* 15:09:1988
17 *The Northern Echo* 27:10:1988
18 *Darlington Advertiser* 3:11:1988
19 *Darlington & Stockton Times* 29:10:1988
20 *The Northern Echo* 4:05:1989
21 *Darlington Advertiser* 10:05:1989
22 *Darlington & Stockton Times* 6:05:1989
23 Author's diary 10:05:1989
24 Minutes 19:07:1989
25 *The Northern Echo* 26:10:1989
26 *Darlington Advertiser* 2:11:1989
27 *Darlington & Stockton Times* 28:10:1989

Chapter 11

1 *The Northern Echo* 26:04:1990
2 *Darlington & Stockton Times* 28:04:1990
3 *Darlington Advertiser* 8:11:1990
4 *Darlington & Stockton Times* 3:11:1990
5 *The Northern Echo* 26:04:1991
6 *Darlington & Stockton Times* 27:04:1991
7 Minutes 15:05:1991
8 *Darlington Advertiser* 7:11:1991
9 *Darlington & Stockton Times* 2:11:1991
10 *Darlington Advertiser* 7:11:1991
11 *Darlington Advertiser* 7:05:1992
12 *Darlington & Stockton Times* 2:05:1992
13 *Darlington & Stockton Times* 31:10:1992
14 *The Northern Echo* 30:10:1992
15 *Darlington & Stockton Times* 1:05:1993
16 *The Northern Echo* 30:04:1993
17 *Darlington Advertiser* 6:05:1993
18 *Darlington Advertiser* 4:11:1993
19 *Darlington & Stockton Times* 30:10:1993
20 *Darlington Advertiser* 5:05:1994
21 *The Northern Echo* 29:04:1994
22 *Darlington & Stockton Times* 30:04:1994
23 *Darlington & Stockton Times* 29:10:1994
24 *The Northern Echo* 31:10:1994

Index

NB Maiden or former surnames are given in brackets. In the case of Christian names, shortened versions are given if these are always used. If, however, the full Christian name has been used in some cast lists the more usual abbreviation is given in brackets.

Porteus, Claire 125, 257
Porteus, Judith 257
Porteus, Kath 125, 237, 257, 262, 291, 308
Porteus, Ray 125, 165, 191, 227, 256, 257, 258, 261, 272, 287, 306
Porteus, Ray (Senior) 125, 235, 257
Porteus, Sarah 125, 257
Priestley, Sharon 240
Pursey (Martin), Sylvia 128
Purvis, Christine 180, 198, 205, 210, 212, 240
Putnam, Sir Thomas 6

Quinn, Denis 87, 88, 98, 99, 105, 111, 119, 120, 121, 122, 124, 125, 135, 137, 138, 242

Raine, Colin 177
Raine, Parkin 143, 185, 191
Raven, Sir Vincent L. 6
Reed, John 19, 26, 30, 35–6, 41, 52, 106, 174, 183, 186, 212–13
Reeves, Connie 199, 201, 203, 206, 210, 213, 214, 215, 216, 218, 231, 233–4, 236, 238, 240, 247, 248–9, 256, 258, 266, 267–8, 273, 274, 282, 313, 315
Reeves, Garry 206, 210, 213
Reeves, Nicola 256, 266
Renshaw, Mr 15
Reynolds, Joan 109–10, 144
Richardson, Kenneth 19, 30, 32, 35, 38, 44, 49, 51, 52, 53, 54–5, 60, 65, 66, 67, 71, 76, 78, 80, 85, 88, 90, 92, 94, 101, 106, 108, 111, 112, 116, 117, 120, 121, 131, 132, 136, 137, 138, 142, 143, 144, 147, 148, 150, 157, 161, 162, 163, 169, 172, 173, 183, 188, 189, 199, 201, 202, 206, 210, 213, 216, 218, 221, 223, 226, 230, 231, 248, 250, 273, 295, 316
Riding, Barbara 141, 149–50

Ridley, Arthur 19, 31, 34, 42, 45, 49, 52
Roberts, Eric 75
Roberts, Graham 15
Roberts, Martin 294, 302–3, 304
Robinson, Alf 172, 186
Robinson, Alwyn 44
Robinson, Doreen 38, 39
Robinson, Janet 270, 273, 279
Robinson, Julie 134
Robinson (Hunt), Kathleen (Kath) 125, 126, 136, 141, 142, 148, 152, 154, 157, 163, 174, 177, 191, 194, 197, 199, 203, 207–8, 210, 223, 228, 231, 233, 234, 240–1, 256, 257, 260, 264, 274, 286, 298, 299, 301, 305, 313, 319, 320–1
Robinson, Kenneth (Ken) 99, 106, 122, 124, 155, 164, 165, 172, 178, 187, 198
Robinson, Phil 154, 191, 257
Robinson, Sally 191, 257
Robinson (Swift), Susan (Sue) 78, 80, 84, 85, 86, 94, 99, 108, 110, 119, 122, 134, 157, 181, 182, 183, 188, 194, 197, 231, 232, 237, 238, 260, 266, 288, 293–4
Robson, Frank 53
Robson, J. R. 130
Robson, Sally 136
Roots, Linda 186, 200
Ropner, Colonel Sir Leonard, MP 49
Ross, Charles 64, 67
Ross, Irene 30
Rossiter, Lisa 201
Round, Alan 131–2, 150
Rowcroft, Jill 228
Rowell, Jack 110, 132, 160
Rowell, Robert 266, 294
Royce, Edward Jun 77–8, 82
Rutter, Clare 35

Sadler, Councillor S. A. 7
Sampson, Richard 32, 43–4, 63,